每天看一点

《越狱》

轻松学地道口语

丛书主编　文　英

本书主编　孙　喆

参　编　刘　美　卓张凤　王小玉　詹慧文　崔明元

　　　　惠思源　吴　琼　郭　鸿　宋令梅　刘新芝

　　　　裴俊玲　杨学梅　范琳琳

PRISONBREAK

机械工业出版社
CHINA MACHINE PRESS

《越狱》（*Prison Break*）是由温特沃斯·米勒和多米尼克·珀塞尔等人主演的一部悬疑电视剧，讲述了一个关于拯救的故事。主人公迈克尔为了营救他被人陷害入狱的哥哥林肯，计划越狱并成功逃脱，在逃亡生涯中再次入狱，最后收集证据以求脱罪。

　　在美剧迷的眼里，《越狱》不止是一部情节错综复杂、跌宕起伏的好剧，更是一个时代的标志。可以说，很多中国观众都是从《越狱》开始了解和关注美剧的，美剧的风潮随着获奖无数的《越狱》开始在中国盛行。

　　剧中有大量的俚语以及工程学词汇，非常值得看一看，学一学！

图书在版编目（CIP）数据

每天看一点《越狱》轻松学地道口语 / 孙喆主编.
—北京：机械工业出版社，2017.12
（每天看一点英美剧轻松学地道口语 / 文英主编）
ISBN 978-7-111-58798-9

Ⅰ. ①每… Ⅱ. ①孙… Ⅲ. ①英语—口语—美国—自学参考资料
Ⅳ. ① H319.9

中国版本图书馆 CIP 数据核字（2017）第 320237 号

机械工业出版社(北京市百万庄大街 22 号　邮政编码 100037)
策划编辑：张若男　　责任编辑：张若男
版式设计：吴凯贤　　责任印制：张　博
三河市宏达印刷有限公司印刷
2018 年 1 月第 1 版第 1 次印刷
169mm × 239mm · 19.25 印张 · 341 千字
标准书号：ISBN 978-7-111-58798-9
定价：42.80 元

凡购本书，如有缺页、倒页、脱页，由本社发行部调换
电话服务　　　　　　　　　网络服务
服务咨询热线：010-88361066　机工官网：www.cmpbook.com
读者购书热线：010-68326294　机工官博：weibo.com/cmp1952
　　　　　　　010-88379203　金 书 网：www.golden-book.com
封面无防伪标均为盗版　　教育服务网：www.cmpedu.com

前　言

老师常说，学英语得听新闻。那是因为要应试。而要练地道口语，自然是要看剧。所谓艺术来源于生活，英美剧中的情节多与我们的生活息息相关，所说的台词也都是我们在与人交流时真正需要用到的口语。因此，在欣赏英美剧的同时，我们就为自己营造了一个自然的、毫不做作的口语学习环境。

在跌宕起伏的情节当中，我们可以追随那些富有感染力的人物，同时也能体会或幽默诙谐、或富有哲理的精彩语言。基于此种考量，我们为英美剧爱好者、英语美语学习者打造了这套轻松、愉快同时又紧凑、活泼的英美剧欣赏及口语学习系列丛书。

我们的**"每天看一点英美剧轻松学地道口语"**丛书具有以下几大特点：

● 选材新颖，题材广泛

经过在英语美语学习者和英美剧爱好者之中进行广泛的调查，我们力求选取最受欢迎、最受推崇的剧集，涉猎多种主题和题材，不论是生活、爱情、科学、魔幻，只有你喜欢的，才会成为你学习的动力，引发学习兴趣。我们还将继续聆听剧迷们的声音，选取更多的剧集，为你量身打造最适合你的图书。

● 单剧成册，量身打造学习重点

每部剧的特点不同，欣赏、学习的侧重点也就不同，如果在一本书中同时包含多部剧集，看似丰富多彩，实则重点散漫，不适合学习。所以我们用单剧成册的方法，针对每一部剧，用心分析、编写该部剧集最适合学习的内容，以求能充分达到学以致用的目的。

● 精心打造各个板块，学习、欣赏两不误

每部剧选取最为经典的 120 ～ 150 个片段，"时间—地点—人物—事件"一应俱全，帮助你充分回味剧集内容；"精彩亮点"分析剧集片段中的经典——或为爆笑段子，或为哲理名句，或为真情流露……帮你解答心中的疑惑、说出你心中的声音；"知识点拨"帮助读者理解独具特色的表达方法、积累专业名词及了解特殊的文化概念；最后还有"词汇加油站"，生词、难词全在这里。单词虽小，也是英语学习中的重要"地基"，一砖一瓦，都不能忽视。

精彩的英美剧千千万万，经典的剧情层出不穷，我们将打造最适合大家的精彩剧集王国，不断推出新剧、好剧。好戏连连，敬请期待吧！

Michael Scofield

Wentworth Miller（温特沃斯·米勒）**饰演**

国籍：美国
出生地：英国牛津郡
职业：演员、编剧
毕业院校：普林斯顿大学
生日：1972 年 6 月 2 日
星座：双子座
血型：O 型
身高：185 cm
代表作品：《越狱》《生化危机Ⅳ：来生》
主要成就：2006 年金球奖电视剧类最佳男演员提名
眼睛颜色：左眼淡褐色，右眼淡绿色

温特沃斯·米勒 1972 年 6 月 2 日出生于英国牛津郡奇平诺顿，在他的父亲完成了在英国的学业之后，他们一家回到了纽约。温特沃斯在布鲁克林度过了他的少年时代，那时他的父亲就教育他"做每一件事都要做到最好，不能半途而废"。米勒于 1990 年毕业于纽约一所名牌中学 Midwood High School，之后温特沃斯进入了普林斯顿大学，并获得了英语文学学士学位。1995 年初他开始在洛杉矶的一家小型电视制作公司任职，此后转入演艺界。

演艺经历

2005 年因在电视剧《越狱》中饰演迈克尔·斯科菲尔德而为观众所熟知，2006 年被提名为金球奖电视剧类最佳男演员。2010 年出演电影《生化危机Ⅳ：来生》；2014 年，出演《闪电侠》并饰演冰冻队长。

Lincoln Burrows

Dominic Purcell（多米尼克·珀塞尔）饰演

国籍： 美国

职业： 演员

毕业院校： 西澳大利亚表演学院

生日： 1970 年 2 月 17 日

星座： 水瓶座

身高： 185 cm

代表作品： 《越狱》《碟中谍 II》《刀锋战士 III》《闪
电侠》《撕裂的末日》

主要成就： 澳大利亚电影协会最佳男演员奖

　　多米尼克·珀塞尔 1970 年在英国出生，两岁的时候随挪威籍父亲与爱尔兰籍母亲搬到澳大利亚。儿时的梦想是当一名园林设计师，高中时中途退学，与几位朋友一起做田园设计工作，偶尔上上网。但看完电影《野战排》后，他决定要当一名演员，并开始尝试演戏，在澳大利亚出演过电视剧并大受好评。他最终考取澳大利亚西澳表演艺术学院，与 Hugh Jackman 和 Frances O'Connor 成为同学。

演艺经历

　　1998 年，刚毕业的珀塞尔主演了澳洲的一部电视剧 *RAW FM*，开始了他的表演生涯。2002 年，出演动作电视剧 *John Doe*，在剧中饰演 John Doe 一角。2005 年，因出演美剧《越狱》中林肯·布鲁斯一角而受到广泛关注。2007 年，凭借影片《越狱》获得澳大利亚电影协会最佳男演员奖。2014 年，加盟电视剧《闪电侠》，饰演 Mick Rory（Heat Wave）。2015 年，加入 CW 电视网秋季新剧《闪电侠》与温特沃斯·米勒再度合作出演反派漫画人物"热浪"。

Alexander Mahone

William Fichtner（威廉·菲德内尔）**饰演**

国籍：德国

出生地：纽约长岛

职业：演员

毕业院校：玛丽沃尔高中（Maryvale High School）

生日：1956 年 11 月 27 日

星座：射手座

身高：187 cm

代表作品：《完美风暴》《黑鹰坠落》《越狱》《撞车》
《狂暴飞车》

主要成就：演员工会奖《撞车》
影评协会演技奖提名《黑鹰坠落》
土星奖提名《入侵》

威廉·菲德内尔大学学的是法律专业。不过毕业后，他的兴趣却转向了表演。

演艺经历

　　1988 年，他参加连续剧 *As the World Turns* 的演出，从此进入影视界。1997 年，菲德内尔获得机会出演电影《超时空接触》，和他演对手戏的是朱迪·福斯特。同年，他出现在凯文·斯佩西的影片《白色鳄鱼》中，饰演一名神经质的杀手；次年，他又在布鲁斯·威利斯主演的电影《世界末日》里，演一名冷酷而较真的宇航员；2000 年，菲德内尔和乔治·克鲁尼一起合作，在《完美风暴》中饰演出海的渔夫；2001 年，他在《黑鹰坠落》里饰演一位在绝境中仍全力尽职的军官；2007 年，在大热美剧《越狱》的第二季中，谁都不能忽视 FBI 马霍的存在，尽管不是男一号，但他的精湛表演，足以让我们心生敬意。

T-Bag

Robert Knepper（罗伯特·克耐普）饰演

国籍：美国
出生地：俄亥俄州弗里蒙特
居住地：加州洛杉矶
职业：演员
生日：1959 年 7 月 8 日
星座：巨蟹座
身高：177 cm
代表作品：《越狱》《饥饿游戏Ⅲ：嘲笑鸟》
　　　　　　《非常人贩Ⅲ》《超能英雄第四季》
主要成就：2007 年青少年选择奖最佳电视剧反派提名

　　罗伯特·克耐普的父亲唐纳德·克耐普是一名兽医，母亲帕特·德克在当地一个社区剧院的道具室工作（2003 年过世）。由于母亲是社区剧院的工作者，克耐普从小就对舞台剧拥有浓厚的兴趣，少年时的他就经常在小区和高中校园内表演戏剧。1977 年，克耐普高中毕业后，考入西北大学学习戏剧，同时在芝加哥出演电影和电视剧；临近毕业时，他退学前往纽约发展。克耐普与托里·海劳尔德于 2005 年结婚，婚后育有一子，2010 年两人离异；2013 年 7 月 8 日，他与纳丁·卡莉结婚。

演艺经历

　　1986 年，克耐普参演剧情片《顽皮老爸》，片中饰演配角 Steve Larwin；同年客串律政剧《力争上游》第四季及罪案剧《洛城法网》第一季。1987 年，首次以主演身份加盟剧情片《仲夏夜魔法》。2005 年，主演的罪案剧《越狱》首播，46 岁的克耐普凭借剧中争议性角色 T-bag 为观众所熟知，并被美国《纽约时报》评选为该剧最受欢迎的角色；随后他继续参演了该剧的第二、三、四季以及相关的电视电影和宣传短片。此后，克耐普连续获得多部电影的演出机会，包括：《晚安，好运》《火线对峙》《地球停转之日》等。2016 年，参演动作片《终极标靶Ⅱ》、历史剧《双峰》《越狱》重启版（预计 2017 年 3 月播出）；7 月，现身圣迭戈漫展，为《越狱》重启版登台宣传；10 月，参演由汤姆·克鲁斯主演的动作片《侠探杰克Ⅱ：永不回头》，克耐普饰演反派人物哈克尼斯将军。

Fernando Sucre

Amaury Nolasco（阿马里·诺拉斯克）**饰演**

出生地：波多黎各
职业：演员
毕业院校：波多黎各大学
生日：1970 年
身高：179 cm
代表作品：《越狱》《速度与激情》

　　阿马里·诺拉斯克毕业于波多黎各大学，是全日制的生物学专业的学生。起初他想当一名医生，但是有位导演找到了他并让他拍摄了一部商业电视剧。在有了几次演艺经验后，诺拉斯克来到了纽约，在一间英美戏剧艺术学校接受培训。这位年轻的演员在莎士比亚类型的戏剧方面得到了良好的训练，他注重方言技巧、人物性格以及舞台风格。

演艺经历

　　阿马里·诺拉斯克在环球电影出品的《速度与激情Ⅱ》中第一次担当配角，饰演 Orange Julius，他在开场的那个飙车镜头中的演技令人难忘。随后与伯尼·麦克联合主演了《三千大佬》并在《板凳队员》中与罗伯·施奈德和大卫·斯派德演对手戏。他还完成了一部迈克尔·贝执导的由热门动画片《变形金刚》改编的真人电影，但给观众留下深刻印象的要算是他在电视剧《越狱》和电影《越狱特别篇：最后一越》中的精彩演出了，他在剧中扮演了菲尔南多·苏克雷这个角色。

Sara Tancredi

Sarah Wayne Callies(莎拉·韦恩·卡利斯)**饰演**

国籍: 美国
出生地: 伊利诺伊州
职业: 演员
毕业院校: 达特茅斯学院
生日: 1977 年 6 月 1 日
星座: 双子座
代表作品: 《圣境预言书》《越狱》《不惧风暴》

　　在美剧《越狱》中出演女一号莎拉的演员莎拉·韦恩·卡利斯出生于伊利诺伊州的 La Grange 农庄,她的父母都是大学教授。一岁的时候随家人搬到了夏威夷的首府檀香山。莎拉毕业于贵族私立学校,1999 年从达特茅斯学院毕业,学习女权主义方面课题,在本色化神学方面获得高级研究基金,之后她因为爱好艺术从而进入了丹佛国家戏剧音乐学院学习,并在那里得到了美术研究生学位。毕业之后卡利斯到了纽约,并开始了幕前的演艺工作。

　　毕业后,卡利斯在《至尊皇后》里面曾和 Oliver Platt 演过对手戏,她还在电视剧《法律与秩序:SVU》《警网擒凶》和《数字追凶》中客串过,卡利斯演得最好的角色当数电视短剧《泰山》里的简。

Brad Bellick

Wade Williams（韦德·威廉姆斯）**饰演**

国籍：美国
出生地：俄克拉何马州
职业：演员
生日：1961 年 12 月 24 日
星座：摩羯座
身高：180 cm
主要作品：《越狱》《匪帮传奇》《犯罪心理》

　　韦德和他的三个兄弟姐妹在俄克拉何马州的塔尔萨长大。高中毕业之后他本打算在塔尔萨大学学习医学，不过在他报名学习声乐课之后，他毅然地改变了他的人生规划。开始学习戏剧并取得了戏剧专业的学士学位，之后师从威廉·埃斯珀，获得了表演方向的硕士学位。

演艺经历

　　毕业后，韦德·威廉姆斯在纽约莎士比亚节中找到了工作。他第一次演出是和摩根·弗里曼、崔茜·尤玛在中央公园的 Delicort 剧院表演 The Taming of the Shrew，之后和丹泽尔·华盛顿合作表演了《理查德三世》。威廉姆斯不断地在百老汇和非百老汇表演，并在全美巡回表演如 Guys and Dolls，Les Miserables，Kiss of the Spiderwoman 和 Ragtime and Showboat 等作品。韦德·威廉姆斯还在美剧《越狱》中扮演狱警布拉德·贝里克一角，他在电视、电影和戏剧方面十分多产。在大银幕上，韦德在 2000 年福克斯拍摄的电影 Flicka 中是与玛丽亚·贝罗、艾莉森·洛曼并肩的明星，他还出现在 Jarhead，Collateral，Ali 和 Erin Brockovich 等影片中。他参与的电视演出包括 Over There，Six Feet Under，24，NYPD Blue，CSI 以及 The Bernie Mac Show。

Don Self

Michael Rapaport（迈克尔·拉帕波特）饰演

国籍： 美国
出生地： 纽约
职业： 演员、编剧、导演
生日： 1970 年 3 月 20 日
星座： 双鱼座
血型： A 型
身高： 193 cm
代表作品： 《老友记》《家庭战争》《愚人善事》

迈克尔·拉帕波特是一个地道的纽约人，他是广播电视节目项目经理的儿子，本应在高中毕业后搬到洛杉矶尝试单人喜剧表演，但他从未忘记或放弃自己的"根"，这一点可体现在他的作品中。

演艺经历　　拉帕波特曾出演过多部观众所熟知的热门电视剧，最早曾在《老友记》中饰演过剧中女主角菲比的男朋友，之后曾出演过情景喜剧《家庭战争》中的搞笑老爸。之后，迈克尔·拉帕波特一直在 NBC 的情景喜剧《愚人善事》中客串出演一个监狱中的犯人，也是非常搞笑的角色。

Contents | 目录

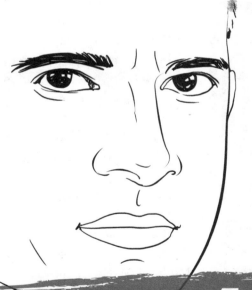

Prison Break

Season 1 福克斯河监狱

Scene 1 为救哥哥，弟弟冒险入狱

时间： 第 1 集 00:00:00—00:02:35
地点： 文身馆，银行
人物： 迈克尔，希德，银行职员
事件： 迈克尔文身后持枪抢劫银行。

精彩亮点

1
　　迈克尔·斯科菲尔德找文身师希德做刺青，今天他完成了最后一幅刺青。看到迈克尔全身的刺青不禁令人不寒而栗，那么，他做刺青到底有何目的呢？

2
　　希德的话道出了观众的心声：迈克尔在短短几个月内做这么多刺青到底用意何在？本剧一开头，就吸引了观众的好奇心。

3
　　从迈克尔的话中我们不难看出，他在与时间赛跑，所剩时间不多了。到底发生了什么事让他如此不安？

4
　　就在迈克尔完成最后一幅刺青的转天，他持枪抢劫了一家银行。而且看这样子他好像故意想让自己被捕入狱。这在常人看来简直是疯狂之举，一场激动人心的越狱之旅即将拉开大幕。

Sid: That's it.① Can I just, you know, look at it for a minute?☺1

Michael: You're an artist, Sid.

Sid: You're telling me you're just gonna walk out of here② and I'm never going to see it again?

Michael: There's a good chance of③ that, yes.

Sid: Most guys, you know, for the first one, they start with④ something small. "Mom", girlfriend's initials, something like that. Not you. You get a full set of sleeves, all in a couple of months⑤.☺2 Takes guys a few years to get the ink you got.

Michael: I don't have a few years.☺3 Wish to hell⑥ I did. The vault. Open it.☺4

Clerk: We can't. The branch manager's not here.

Michael: Where is he?

Clerk: It's lunchtime. He's at White Castle⑦.

Michael: White Castle?

Clerk: It's a fast food restaurant. They serve those little square burgers.

Michael: I know what it is. I'm not playing games. Open it.

Clerk: Sir, you have a half a million dollars cash in your bag. Don't you think it would be better…?

译文

希　　德：完成了。能不能让我再欣赏会儿？

迈 克 尔：你是个艺术家，希德。

希　　德：你是说你就这么走了，然后我就再也看不到这个杰作了？

迈 克 尔：很有可能是这样。

希　　德：你知道，大多数人最初开始文身时都会先文一些小的东西，比如"妈妈"、女朋友名字的缩写什么的，但你不是这样。你在几个月的时间里就做了一整套。别人得花好几年工夫呢！

迈 克 尔：我可没那么多的时间，我恨不得马上都文好！（地点切换至银行）把保险柜打开！

银行职员：我们做不到，分行长不在这里。

迈 克 尔：他在哪里？

银行职员：现在是午饭时间，他在白色城堡。

迈 克 尔：白色城堡？

银行职员：那是个快餐店，他们供应那些方形的小汉堡。

迈 克 尔：这个我知道。我没在跟你玩，把保险柜打开！（向空中连开两枪）

银行职员：先生，你袋子里已经有 50 万美元的现金，你是不是可以再重新考虑一下……（警笛响起）

知识点拨

1. That's it. 表示"完了，就这样，没有别的了"。例：That's it? Can I do the story? 就这些吗？我能做这个节目吗？

2. be gonna = be going to，口语常见用法，注意前面要有系动词 be，后面跟动词原形。例：I'm gonna sleep. 我要睡觉了。

3. a good chance 在此处指很大的可能性。例：If you were farther inland, you'd have had a good chance of finding a bug that was black with red spots. 如果你走进更远的内陆，你更有可能找到黑色红斑的瓢虫。

4. start with 表示"以……开始"。例：We all start with preconceived notions of what we want from life. 我们开始时都对自己想从生活中得到什么抱有一些预想。

5. a couple of 既可以指两个也可以指几个，要结合具体语境。在文中表示"几个"。例：I'm still in the air force, though I'll be demobbed in a couple of months. 我还在空军部队服役，不过几个月之后我就要复员了。

6. wish to hell 表示"极想，从心里盼望"。例：Wish to hell I did. 我真希望自己能做到。

7. White Castle 即"白色城堡"，美国第一家汉堡快餐连锁店。于 1921 年创办于堪萨斯州威奇托市，这家汉堡连锁店距今已有 90 多年的历史，它见证了美式快餐文化的发展历程，如今依然备受欢迎。

词汇加油站

initial [ɪˈnɪʃl] *n.* 首字母

ink [iŋk] *n.* 墨水

branch [bræntʃ] *n.* 分支

cash [kæʃ] *n.* 现金

sleeve [sliːv] *n.* 袖套

vault [vɔːlt] *n.* 保险库

castle [ˈkæsl] *n.* 城堡

million [ˈmɪljən] *n.* 百万

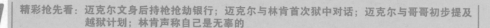

时间： 第 1 集 00:10:56—00:12:18
地点： 监狱中
人物： 迈克尔，林肯，苏克雷
事件： 迈克尔初识苏克雷，迈克尔与林肯首次狱中对话。

 精彩亮点

1

苏克雷是迈克尔的狱友，很快两个人便成了朋友。迈克尔一进来就向他打听林肯的情况，这让苏克雷不由得感到奇怪。

2

迈克尔并没有向苏克雷隐瞒事实，直接道出林肯就是他的哥哥，观众此时恍然大悟：迈克尔故意让自己入狱肯定与他的哥哥有关，他的哥哥到底被判了什么罪呢？

3

从林肯的话中我们得知他被判了死刑，而且处决期很快就到了，狱中的林肯此时已陷入了极度绝望中。

4

迈克尔此时无法确定哥哥是否杀了人，但林肯向他发誓自己绝没有杀人，这也是贯穿全剧的一个关键线索：林肯到底有没有杀人？他被指控杀了谁呢？林肯的一席话让观众察觉到此案件并不简单。

Michael: John Abruzzi?

Sucre: John Abruzzi. **Why you wanna① see Burrows so bad anyhow?**☺₁

Michael: **Because he's my brother.**☺₂

Lincoln: They denied the motion.

Michael: Then do it again.

Lincoln: I can't. That's it②. May 11. That's the date, man. That's the date they, uh… you know… execute me.☺₃

Michael: I know.

Lincoln: I didn't kill that man, Michael.

Michael: The evidence says you did.

Lincoln: **I don't care what the evidence says. I didn't kill him.**☺₄

Michael: Swear to me③.

Lincoln: I swear to you, Michael.

Michael: But how did they get it wrong④ then?

Lincoln: The courts, the appeals…Don't know. Don't know. I keep thinking, looking back on⑤ it is, uh… I was set up⑥. And, whoever it was that set me up wants me in the ground⑦ as quickly as possible.

译文

迈克尔： 约翰·阿布兹吗?

苏克雷： 是的，是约翰·阿布兹。为什么你这么着急想见布鲁斯?

迈克尔： 因为他是我哥哥。

林 肯： 他们驳回了上诉。

迈克尔： 那就接着上诉。

林 肯： 我没办法这样做，就是这样。因为5月11日就是……那天……你知道的，处决我的日子。

迈克尔： 我知道。

林 肯： 我没杀那个人，迈克尔。

迈克尔： 可证据表明人是你杀的。

林 肯： 我不管证据如何，反正我就是没杀人。

迈克尔： 向我发誓。

林 肯： 我向你发誓，迈克尔。

迈克尔： 可是为什么他们会弄错?

林 肯： 可能是法庭，或是上诉……我也不清楚，不清楚。现在仔细回想起来，我是被陷害的。不管是谁想陷害我，都恨不得我赶快入土。

知识点拨

1. wanna 是一个非正式的口语化的词。表示"想要，有意愿的"，和 want to 的用法相同。例：I just wanna make sure we're comparing the products apples to apples. 我只是想确保我们谈论的产品是具有可比性的。

2. 此处的 that's it 表示"反感或失望"，意为"够了，行了，得了，好了，算了"。例：That's it. Haven't you said enough? 好了，你还没说够吗?

3. swear to sb. 表示"向某人郑重承诺；向某人发誓"。例：I swear to God, I'll kill you right there. 我发誓，我将在那儿杀了你。此外，swear to sth. 表示"断言……"。

4. get sth. wrong=get wrong sth. 表示"提供错误情况，对……了解有误"。例：But remember, get it wrong, and he's gonna kill you. 但记住，一旦说错了什么，他就会杀了你。

5. look back on 表示"回忆"。例：I can look back on things with a clear conscience. I did everything I could. 我可以问心无愧地回首过去，我已经尽力了。

6. be set up = get tricked 表示"被陷害，中圈套"。例：He said that the man in red set him up. 他表示那个红衣服的男子陷害了他。

7. put sb. in the ground 表示"把某人给杀死、把某人给弄死"。例：I would've put him in the ground. 我肯定打得他满地找牙。

词汇加油站

anyhow ['enɪhaʊ] *adv.* 不管怎样

motion ['moʊʃn] *n.* 动机

evidence ['evɪdəns] *n.* 证据

court [kɔːrt] *n.* 法院

deny [dɪ'naɪ] *vt.* 拒绝承认

execute ['eksɪkjuːt] *vt.* 处死

swear [swer] *v.* 发誓

appeal [ə'piːl] *n.* 上诉

片段三

时间： 第 2 集 00:05:13—00:05:55
地点： 监狱中
人物： 迈克尔，林肯
事件： 迈克尔与哥哥初步提及越狱计划。

精彩亮点

1
　　迈克尔的到来令林肯对自己的未来又燃起了希望，他知道距离执行死刑的日子越来越近了，于是急迫地想知道弟弟有没有什么好计划。

2
　　迈克尔了解到医务室是安保力量最薄弱的地方，可以自由进出，于是进入医务室就是当务之急。他向林肯提了一种叫作朋纳克的药物，这种药物可以抑制胰岛素吸收，从而让迈克尔患上高血糖，就可以顺利进入医务室了。

3
　　此时的林肯还不了解迈克尔计划的全部内容，由于隔着玻璃板，迈克尔也不方便向林肯透露太多细节。更重要的是，迈克尔此时的计划尚不成熟。

4
　　林肯怀疑弟弟的计划，认为仅凭几片药片就能救自己是不可能的事。但事实上，这几片药正是后面迈克尔打通医务室地道的关键。兄弟俩的越狱计划正式启动。

Lincoln: What the hell[①] were you thinking, Michael? How are we doing it? ☺1

Michael: The infirmary.

Lincoln: Infirmary?

Michael: It's the weakest link in the security chain. As long as I get that PUGNAc[②], I'll get all the access I need.

Lincoln: What the hell's a PUGNAc?

Michael: It lowers my insulin levels to the point that I'm hyperglycemic. As long as the good doctor thinks I'm diabetic, I'll have plenty of[③] time in there to do what I need to do. ☺2

Lincoln: Which is?

Michael: A little work. A little prep for your arrival. That's the idea, anyway. ☺3

Lincoln: The idea?

Michael: There's a little hitch in getting the PUGNAc, that's all[④]. They don't exactly stock it at the commissary.

Lincoln: You're telling me this whole thing's riding on[⑤] a bunch of[⑥] pills.

Michael: Someone's working on it[⑦] as we speak. ☺4

6

译文

林　肯： 你到底是怎么想的，迈克尔？我们该怎样做？

迈克尔： 医务室。

林　肯： 医务室？

迈克尔： 医务室是安保力量最薄弱的地方。只要我能搞到朋纳克，就能进出所有我想进出的地方。

林　肯： 朋纳克是什么？

迈克尔： 它可以将我体内的胰岛素含量降到一定程度，让我患上高血糖。只要那位好医生认为我是糖尿病人，我就有足够的时间在那里做我想做的事。

林　肯： 什么事？

迈克尔： 做一点儿工作，为你所做的准备。总而言之，这就是我的计划。

林　肯： 计划？

迈克尔： 搞到朋纳克是有点儿困难，但仅此而已。他们在监狱的杂货店可不存这个。

林　肯： 你是说这个计划的成功与否完全取决于这几片药？

迈克尔： 说话这会儿就有人忙着搞这个药了。

知识点拨

1. what the hell 可用以加强语气或咒骂，表示"究竟，到底"。例：What the hell do I want with an emotional retard? 和一个感情用事的傻瓜在一起，我究竟是图什么？

2. Pugnac 即"朋纳克"，一种药物，全名为 N-乙酰抑制剂，一种阻止胰岛素吸收的药剂，非处方药。

3. plenty of 表示"大量的，充裕的"，用来修饰可数名词和不可数名词，用法同 a lot of / lots of，片中用来修饰不可数名词 time。

4. That's all. 表示"仅此而已"，通常置于句尾。例：I can boot up from a floppy disk, but that's all. 我可以用一张软盘来启动，但其他的就无能为力了。也可用于结束演讲或发言等，表示"（我要说的）就是这些"。

5. ride on 在片中表示"取决于……，依靠……"，相当于 rely on / depend on。

6. a bunch of 可表示"一群，一束，一堆……"，较常见的是 a bunch of flowers "一束花"，文中表示"一堆……"。

7. work on 在片中表示"从事于……，致力于……"。 例：He promised to get to work on the state's massive deficit. 他承诺着手解决国家庞大的财政赤字问题。

 词汇加油站

infirmary [ɪnˈfɜːrməri] *n.* 医务室　　　　security [səˈkjʊrəti] *n.* 安全工作，保护措施

insulin [ˈɪnsəlɪn] *n.* 胰岛素

hyperglycemic [ˌhaɪpəˈglaɪˈsiːmɪk] *adj.* 血糖过多的

diabetic [ˌdaɪəˈbetɪk] *n.* 糖尿病患者　　　hitch [hɪtʃ] *n.* 暂时的困难

commissary [ˈkɑːmɪseri] *n.* （监狱）杂货商店　bunch [bʌntʃ] *n.* 捆，扎

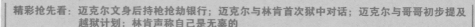

片段四

时间： 第2集 00:24:43—00:26:03
地点： 监狱中
人物： 林肯，多诺万
事件： 多诺万劝林肯收手，林肯声称自己是无辜的。

精彩亮点

多诺万是林肯的前女友，但因为林肯此前嗜赌成性，令她失望至极，于是离开了林肯。在迈克尔持枪抢劫一案中，作为律师的多诺万极力为迈克尔辩护，在她看来迈克尔入狱都是因为林肯。

1

多诺万在录像带中亲眼见到林肯杀了人，但林肯坚称自己绝没有杀人，他承认自己吸了毒，但神志清醒，事实真相到底怎样呢？

2

尽管林肯极力辩解，但多诺万仍坚持认为林肯杀了人，于是林肯厉声说自己是被陷害的。说完，他便开始回忆当天晚上的情景。

3

从林肯的回忆中，我们不难发现他还没有扣动扳机，车里的人就已经死了。而车里的人正是女总统卡罗琳的弟弟特伦斯，这也是林肯被判死刑的原因。

4

Donovan: I think it's time① you quit the charade, don't you? ☺₁

Lincoln: What?

Donovan: It's starting to ruin people's lives. Michael's in here because he thinks you're innocent.

Lincoln: He told you?

Donovan: He hasn't told me anything, but I know, Lincoln. I know what he's planning. Call him off②. If you love him, call him off. I saw the tape.

Lincoln: What's on the tape's not how it went down③.

Donovan: I know what I saw.

Lincoln: I know what I saw. I was there, remember? I got high④ that night. I had to. It was the only way I could go through with it. I never pulled the trigger. They guy was already dead. ☺₂

Donovan: Yeah, I know. You've told me a thousand...

Lincoln: Then listen! I was set up! ☺₃ I went that night to clear a debt⑤. Crab Simmons was on my ass⑥ for the 90 grand I owed him. He told me the mark was some scumbag drug dealer and if I took it, we'd be clean. I never pulled the trigger. All I know is that somebody wanted me in the same garage as Terrence Steadman that night. ☺₄

译文

多诺万：我想该停止这场猜谜游戏了吧？

林　肯：你说什么？

多诺万：你正在毁掉别人的生活，迈克尔进监狱就是因为他认为你是无辜的。

林　肯：是他告诉你的？

多诺万：林肯，他什么都没跟我说，但是我知道，我知道他的计划，让他放弃吧。如果你还爱他，就让他停止行动。我看过录像带了。

林　肯：录像带里的内容不是真的。

多诺万：我很清楚自己看到了什么。

林　肯：我也清楚我看到了什么。我当时在那儿，记得吗？那天晚上我吸了毒，但我必须这么做，这是我唯一可以完成任务的办法。我绝对没有扣动扳机，那个人早就死了。

多诺万：是的，我知道，你已经跟我说过无数次了……

林　肯：那么听着！我是被陷害的！那天晚上我是去还债的，我欠了科莱博·西蒙斯 9 万美金。他告诉我说是个什么卑鄙的毒贩子，如果我能干掉他，我们就两清了。我绝对没有扣动扳机，我知道的是那天晚上有人想让我跟特伦斯·斯特德曼待在同一个车库里。

知识点拨

1. It's time 意为"该是……的时候了"，常见用法为：1）It's time for + n. "该是（干）……的时候了。" 2）It's time + (for sb.) to do sth. 表示"该是（某人）干……的时候了。" 3）It's time + that clause，that 可省略，从句中的谓语动词或者用动词的过去式（be 用 were）；或者用 should+ 动词原形（should 不能省略），表示"现在某人该做某事了"。

2. call off 表示"取消；点名；转移（某人的注意力等）"。例：Greenpeace refused to call off the event. 绿色和平组织拒绝取消这一活动。

3. go down 意思很多，现归纳如下：1）下去；2）下降，减少，失去价值；3）下沉，落下；4）记下；5）被打倒；被推翻；6）消退，瘪了；7）被接受，被赞许；8）被咽下。例：How did his lecture go down with the students? 他的课学生反应如何？

4. get high 表示"过瘾；吸毒"。例：If you don't feel like getting high, that's cool with me. 如果你还不过瘾，我也无所谓。

5. clear a debt 表示"还清债"。例：A large loan payment to clear a debt. 要付清债务需要支付一笔巨额贷款。

6. A is on B's ass 表示"A 指责批评 B"。

词汇加油站

charade [ʃəˈreɪd] *n.* 看手势猜字谜游戏

innocent [ˈɪnəsnt] *adj.* 无辜的

trigger [ˈtrɪɡər] *n.* （枪）扳机

scumbag [ˈskʌmbæɡ] *n.* 讨厌的人

ruin [ˈruːɪn] *vt.* 毁灭

tape [teɪp] *n.* 带子

debt [det] *n.* 债务

garage [ɡəˈrɑːʒ] *n.* 车库

Scene 2 背后文身惹人疑

时间： 第 3 集 00:03:55—00:04:58

地点： 监狱外草坪上

人物： 迈克尔，林肯

事件： 迈克尔欲将计划告诉苏克雷，林肯强烈反对。

 精彩亮点

曾任芝加哥暴徒首领的阿布鲁兹是当前福克斯河监狱中最声名狼藉的罪犯，他掌控着监狱。由于他人脉广，迈克尔想跟他合作，保证在越狱当晚搭乘飞机离开。 **1**

迈克尔知道要想完成越狱计划，必须找一个合作伙伴，这样在以后执行计划时可以有所照应。迈克尔是否心中已有人选呢？ **2**

迈克尔看中了苏克雷，虽然林肯对这个人表示深度怀疑，但迈克尔深知不管他有怎样的过去，都必须选择他，因为他是迈克尔的室友，今后自己干什么都离不开他的视线。 **3**

林肯还是不希望迈克尔将他们的计划告诉其他人，多一个人知道就多一分危险，但是，迈克尔深知实施越狱计划，牢房里的一举一动都受到苏克雷的制约，将计划告诉他是无奈之举但也是必然之举。 **4**

Michael: We get him on board①, there's gonna be a midnight flight waiting for us the night we get outside those walls.☺1

Lincoln: You're willing to risk the entire escape on a guy you don't even know?

Michael: Preparation can only take you so far. After that, you gotta take a few leaps of faith②.

Lincoln: Abruzzi's a huge leap of faith, Michael.

Michael: I'm not talking about Abruzzi. There's someone else who holds the key to③ this entire thing. With him, it either works or it doesn't. Problem is, I couldn't know who that was until I got in here.☺2

Lincoln: Sucre? You can't be serious④. The guy's a thief, Michael; he can't be trusted.

Michael: Gonna have to trust him, because he's my cell mate.☺3

Lincoln: How well⑤ do you know him? About as well as a man can in a week. You tell him, he tells everyone, we're done⑥. You know that, right?

Michael: We don't get him on board, there's not going to be any digging in that cell, and if there's no digging in that cell… then there's no escape.☺4

译文

迈克尔： 如果让他跟我们合作，就可以保证我们在午夜起飞，离开这四面高墙。

林　肯： 你愿意把整个逃亡的成败压在你还不了解的这个人身上？

迈克尔： 谋事在人，成事在天。

林　肯： 迈克尔，我不相信阿布鲁兹这个人可以依赖。

迈克尔： 我说的不仅仅是阿布鲁兹，还有一个人是整个逃亡计划的关键人物，他可以决定最后的成败。问题是，不到那一步我还不能确定这个人是谁。

林　肯： 苏克雷？你开玩笑吧？他是个贼，迈克尔，你不能信任他。

迈克尔： 必须相信他，因为他是我的牢友。

林　肯： 你对他了解多少？你不过认识他一周而已。如果你告诉他，就等于告诉所有人，那样的话，我们就完了，你明白吗？

迈克尔： 他不加入的话，我没法在牢房采取任何行动，如果这样的话，我们的逃亡只不过是一场梦罢了。

知识点拨

1. get sb. on board 表示"让某人加入"，on board 多用于职场英语，表示"入职报到"。例：Welcome on board. 意为"欢迎您的加入"。

2. a leap of faith 运用了比喻的修辞手法（metaphor），直译是"以绝大的信念跳入（峡谷）"，表示"放手一搏"。例：I took a leap of faith when I bought the shares of Apple, but it worked out all right. 我买了苹果公司的股票赌了一把，但看来我没有做错。

3. hold the key to... 表示"抓住关键；支配……"，此处 to 为介词。例：Germany holds the key to resolving the crisis. 德国掌握着解决危机的关键。

4. You can't be serious. 表示"你不是认真的"。例：You can't be serious. You want to apply to become an airline pilot? 你在开玩笑吧，你想应征做飞行员？

5. how well 表"程度"，可译为"多好，多么"。例：How well does this thesis stand up to close examination? 这个命题经得起推敲吗？

6. We're done. 表示"我们完蛋了，我们完了"。例：We need his help or we're done for, dead and gone, lost. 我们需要他的帮助，否则我们就完蛋了，倒霉了，彻底从人间蒸发了。

 词汇加油站

leap [li:p] *n.* 飞跃
thief [θi:f] *n.* 小偷
dig [dɪg] *v.* 挖掘

faith [feɪθ] *n.* 信任
cell [sel] *n.* 小牢房
escape [ɪ'skeɪp] *n.* 逃走

时间： 第 3 集 00:09:36—00:10:28

地点： 监狱中

人物： 迈克尔，维罗妮卡

事件： 维罗妮卡约见利蒂西娅寻找林肯枪杀案的重要线索。

片段二

精彩亮点

1

通过连日来的调查，维罗妮卡也发现林肯杀人案并不那么简单。她想劝迈克尔放弃越狱计划，但迈克尔知道如果深入调查，寻找真相，只会加速林肯的死期，而且维罗妮卡也会遭遇危险。

2

维罗妮卡提到的利蒂西娅是科莱博·西蒙斯的女朋友，她联系维罗妮卡并希望见面和她细谈，电话中利蒂西娅说："我们在公共场所见面，这样他们就不能找到我们。"那么，"他们"到底是谁呢？

3

维罗妮卡的这一信息至关重要，如果能让利蒂西娅成功举证，至少能延缓林肯的死刑期。那么，维罗妮卡能否成功见到利蒂西娅呢？

4

迈克尔深知维罗妮卡此行极度危险，因为如果真如她所说存在刺杀副总统兄弟的幕后黑手，那么凡是与此相关的证人都是"他们"要铲除的目标。

Michael: A year ago, I was doing exactly what you're doing. Trying to find out the truth. It's a bottomless pit, Veronica. **They designed it that way, so that, by the time ① you got to the bottom of it, Lincoln would be dead.** ☺₁

Veronica: Why didn't you tell me you were doing this?

Michael: Once the day was set, once that final appeal had been rejected, he had 60 days to live. Figured I could play their game and watch him die in the process, or I could take matters into my own hands.

Veronica: You don't have to do that. **Leticia knows something.** ☺₂ If I can get it out of her ②, maybe we can reopen Lincoln's case ③.

Michael: What'd she tell you?

Veronica: She said that somebody else was behind ④ the killing of the Vice President's brother. ☺₃ She took off ⑤ before I could get anything out of her. She's holed up ⑥ in the Elysian Fields Projects. I'm going to go see her this afternoon.

Michael: Place is dangerous. You should take someone with you.

Veronica: Who?

Michael: Fiancé would be a good place to start. ☺₄

译文

迈克尔： 一年前我做的和你一样，试图找出真相。维罗妮卡，这是个无底洞。他们都设计好了，所以一旦你试图找寻真相，林肯会被杀。

维罗妮卡： 为什么你没有告诉我你一直在查这件事？

迈克尔： 一旦日子定下来，最终上诉被驳回，他只剩下 60 天的时间能活了。我不想被他们玩弄，看着他死而无动于衷，我宁可自己采取行动。

维罗妮卡： 你不必这样做的。利蒂西娅知道一些事儿，我要看看能不能让她说出来，这样一来，我们或许能重开林肯的案子。

迈克尔： 她跟你说什么了？

维罗妮卡： 她说有人是刺杀副总统兄弟的幕后黑手，在她说出来以前她就走了。她是伊甸园计划的一分子，今天下午我就要去见她。

迈克尔： 那地方很危险，你应该找个人陪你去。

维罗妮卡： 找谁？

迈克尔： 你的未婚夫就不错。

知识点拨

1. by the time 表示"到……为止"时，一般要求主句用过去完成时；表示"当……的时候"如果只是说过去某个时候的状况，则用过去时而不用完成时。

2. get out of 表示"摆脱，逃避"。例：How did we get into this recession, and what can we do to get out of it? 我们是怎样陷入这次经济衰退的，又该做些什么才能从中摆脱呢？

3. reopen a case 表示"翻案"。例：A judge later agreed to suspend her deportation order and reopen her asylum case. 法官随后同意延缓执行对她的放逐指令，决定为她的政治避难一案翻案。

4. behind 一词用法很多，在这里提及几个与 behind 搭配的短语：fall / drop behind "落在后面"；leave sth. behind "（某人）走后留下（掉下）某物"；stay / remain behind "留下，在别人后面留下"。

5. take off 表示"起飞，脱掉；（使）离开，突然成功"等，在片中指"离开"。例：He took off at once and headed back to the motel. 他立刻离开，回到汽车旅馆。

6. hole up 表示"龟缩，躲藏起来，离群索居"。例：Do you mind if I hole up with you for a while? 你是否介意我和你一起躲藏起来待一会儿？

词汇加油站

exactly [ɪg'zæktli] *adv.* 确切地
pit [pɪt] *n.* 井
reject [rɪ'dʒekt] *vt.* 拒绝
Fiancé [ˌfiːɑ:n'seɪ] *n.* 未婚夫

bottomless ['bɑ:təmləs] *adj.* 无底的
appeal [ə'pi:l] *n.* 上诉
Elysian [ɪ'li:ʒən] *adj.* 乐园的

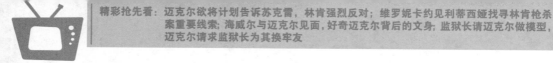

时间： 第4集 00:04:30—00:05:43
地点： 迈克尔所在牢房
人物： 迈克尔，海威尔，医生
事件： 海威尔与迈克尔见面，好奇迈克尔背后文身。

精彩亮点

在进监狱之前，海威尔只是一位在数学方面有突出表现的博士候选人，但在他进行紧张的研究期间，开始表现出明显的精神病症状。不久以后的一天，他来到父母的卧室，挥舞着滑膛枪，杀死了熟睡中的父母。刚一见面，海威尔便对迈克尔背后的文身表现出了极大的兴趣。 **1**

海威尔被送进了福克斯河监狱的精神病区，在四年大剂量的药物治疗和严密监视之后，他的病情有了很大进展。从他说话的语气中不难看出，他并不认为自己有精神病。 **2**

迈克尔十分谨慎，在这里不能轻信任何一个人说的话，海威尔看到了自己的文身，并且起了疑心，这让迈克尔想尽快结束和他的对话，以免给自己带来麻烦。 **3**

海威尔并没有放弃请求迈克尔给他看背后的文身，甚至请迈克尔给他看完整的文身，但迈克尔断然拒绝，此时的迈克尔并不知道，就是海威尔看的这一眼成为他们越狱的关键。 **4**

Haywire: Your tattoos.

Michael: What about① them?

Haywire: What are they of? What are they? Like, some kind of a… ☺₁

Michael: They're just tattoos.

Doctor: It's candy time, Haywire.

Haywire: They think I have schizoaffective disorder② with bipolar tendencies. ☺₂

Doctor: Think you got it?

Haywire: Whatever③. I take the pills, keep the quacks off④ my back. Bye, now. Get out of the way⑤.

Michael: You know, maybe they give you those things for a reason⑥. ☺₃

Haywire: Yeah. To keep me dull. To keep me in their invisible freakin' handcuffs. Seriously, though, those tattoos, they're beautiful. You mind if I, you know, look at the whole thing?

Michael: I do, actually. ☺₄

Haywire: Why?

译文

海威尔：你的文身。

迈克尔：这些文身有什么问题吗？

海威尔：你文的是什么呀？什么图案？像是一种……

迈克尔：只是一般文身而已。

医　生：该吃药了，海威尔。

海威尔：他们觉得我精神紊乱，有分裂症。

医　生：你自己觉得有吗？

海威尔：随便吧。我吃了药，这帮白痴就不来烦我了。再见，让开。

迈克尔：你知道，他们给你吃药总归是有理由的。

海威尔：是的，为了让我像白痴，这样一来，可以无形地囚禁我。说实话，那些文身真是太漂亮了，你介意让我……完整地看一下吗？

迈克尔：非常介意。

海威尔：为什么？

知识点拨

1. what about 表示"怎么样，以为如何（提出建议或用以引出话题）"。例：What about my copier? Can you get it going again? 我的复印机怎么样了？你能把它修好吗？

2. schizoaffective disorder 分裂情感性精神病，在遗传学上是介于精神分裂症和双相情感性精神病之间的一种病。

3. "whatever"是一个带有忍耐意味的表达，在语气加重时，它常被说成"WHAT'-ehv-errr"。whatever 可在结束争论时使用，或者可用来表示"漠不关心"。

4. keep off 用法很多，可表示"（使）不接近；禁食；（雨、雪等）没有下；避开某一话题"等。片中指"（使）不接近"。例：The afflicted person should keep off solid foods and drink plenty of fluids. 病人不应吃固体食物而要多喝流质食物。

5. get out of the way 表示"躲开，让开，避开"。例：Look out! A truck's coming! Get out of the way. 车来了，快闪开！

6. for a reason 表示"有原因"。例：You started doing this thing for a reason. 你开始做这件事肯定是有原因的。

 词汇加油站

candy ['kændi] *n.* 糖果

schizoaffective [skizoʊ'fektiv] *adj.* [医] 情感性分裂的

disorder [dɪs'ɔːrdər] *n.* 混乱

pill [pil] *n.* 药丸

invisible [ɪn'vɪzəbl] *adj.* 看不见的

bipolar [,baɪ'poʊlər] *adj.* 双极的

quack [kwæk] *n.* <英> 江湖医生

handcuff ['hændkʌf] *n.* 用手铐铐住（某人）

时间： 第 4 集 00:08:13—00:09:26
地点： 监狱长办公室
人物： 迈克尔，监狱长波普
事件： 监狱长请迈克尔做模型，迈克尔请求监狱长为其换牢友。

 精彩亮点

监狱长出现，这也是他与迈克尔首次深度接触，他让迈克尔帮他做个泰姬陵的模型以取悦他的妻子。在这里要提一点，迈克尔是个出色的建筑师，获得了土木工程硕士学位，所以，做一个模型对他而言就是小菜一碟。**1**

迈克尔很聪明，他帮助监狱长制作泰姬陵模型以博取他的好感。难道仅仅是这样吗？迈克尔是否还有其他计划呢？**2**

监狱长听了迈克尔的一席话知道泰姬陵不好做，作为对迈克尔的报答，他主动提出要给迈克尔一笔钱，或让迈克尔提其他要求。贝里克长官之前给迈克尔更换了牢友，就是那个精神病患者海威尔，他一直对迈克尔背后的文身感兴趣，这样下去，迈克尔的越狱计划很容易泄露，所以当务之急就是把苏克雷换回来，监狱长能答应他的请求吗？**3**

海威尔是个出了名的"疯子"，所以监狱长认为讨厌他是正常的，但想要换牢友还是要和贝里克谈，他无权干预此事。迈克尔暗示他"贝里克觉得我们是好搭档"，想要让监狱长答应他的请求，那么，最终迈克尔成功了吗？**4**

Pope: It's really coming together①, isn't it? ☺₁

Michael: Yep.

Pope: You think it will be done in time?

Michael: Well, I figure, we still have the interior alcoves and pilasters to do, which is no small task. But, yes, I think so. ☺₂

Pope: Listen, I have to say, I... I really appreciate all the effort that you put into② this. I wish there was some way I could, you know, pay you or something.

Michael: There is one thing you could do for me. My cellmate. ☺₃

Pope: Ah, the inimitable Charles Patoshick. Haywire?

Michael: Then you know.

Pope: Hold it right there③. Officer Bellick is in charge of④ cell transfers. You're gonna have to talk to him about that.

Michael: I tried, but he seems to think we're a good match⑤. ☺₄

Pope: Unfortunately, unless there's some evidence of violence or sexual predation between cellmates, those kinds of requests fall on deaf ears⑥ around here. Prison system's a little too crowded for requests based on personality. It's not exactly Sandals out there.

译文

波 普：看上去快完工了，是吧？

迈克尔：是的。

波 普：你觉得能及时完工吗？

迈克尔：嗯，我想，我们还有内壁和支柱要处理，这可是不小的工程。但我想还是能赶上时间的。

波 普：听着，我必须得说，我……我真的很感谢你为此付出的一切。你知道的，我真希望我能有办法回报你什么，比如给你工钱或是什么。

迈克尔：有件事你倒是能帮我，帮我换一下牢友。

波 普：啊，就是那个不睡觉的疯子？海威尔？

迈克尔：你知道他？

波 普：你还是忍忍吧。贝里克长官负责分配囚犯，这个你得跟他谈。

迈克尔：我试过，但他看起来觉得我们是好搭档。

波 普：很遗憾，除非有囚室暴力迹象或是性侵犯，一般我们对这种要求都置之不理。监狱里可没人有空来管基于性格不合提出的请求，这里可不是桑道斯度假村。

知识点拨

1. come together 可以表示"聚会；相见；汇集"。例：Companies will come together because of the sheer costs involved in globalising their businesses. 由于业务全球化的成本太高，公司将进行合并。

2. put effort into 表示"对某事付出很大力气"。例：Dad wants me to put more effort into my school work. 我爸希望我多花些心力在课业上。

3. 如果两个人辩论，吵架，抬杠，你要别人"打住"，可以说："Hold it right there."

4. be in charge of 在片中表示"负责"。例：People in the green will be sent to be in charge of the project. 年轻力壮的人会被派去负责这项工程。

5. a good match 可以指"棋逢对手"或"十分般配"，片中取后一个意思。例：They are both very vital people and a good match. 他俩都很有活力，十分般配。

6. fall on deaf ears 表示"未受到重视，未被理睬，不被听取"。例：His speech is full of common sense and logic, yet it will fall on deaf ears. 他的演讲富有常识性和逻辑性，但不会有人听的。

 词汇加油站

figure ['fɪɡjər] *vt.* 估计
alcove ['ælkoʊv] *n.* 凹室
inimitable [ɪ'nɪmɪtəbl] *adj.* 不可仿效的
violence ['vaɪələns] *n.* 暴力

interior [ɪn'tɪriər] *adj.* 内部的
pilaster [pɪ'læstər] *n.* 壁柱
transfer ['trænsfɜːr] *n.* 转移，调动
predation [prɪ'deɪʃn] *n.* 掠夺行为

Scene 3 挖掘工作受阻

时间： 第5集 00:05:56—00:07:09
地点： 牢房
人物： 迈克尔，监狱长波普
事件： 迈克尔要被转移，监狱长别无他法。

精彩亮点

1 从监狱长的话中，我们知道他恼怒于迈克尔对他隐瞒了进监狱的真正目的。监狱长突然间态度大变，这到底是为什么呢？

2 监狱长说要将迈克尔转移到一个小城市去，这无疑破坏了整个越狱计划。无奈之下，迈克尔坦白地告诉监狱长，自己进监狱是为了哥哥。

3 面对监狱长的质问，迈克尔没有否认，只求监狱长能让他留下来，迈克尔的这番苦心能否打动监狱长呢？

4 监狱长见迈克尔态度如此诚恳，也坦白地说不是自己要转移他，而是他得罪了上面的人，再一次印证了林肯枪杀案没有那么简单。事实上，正是女总统的助手黑尔和克勒曼用一份机密文件"说服"监狱长转移迈克尔的。

Pope: Why do I get the feeling that there's more to you than meets the eye①, Scofield? Anything you want to tell me? Some other reason you're in here, besides holding up② a bank? You're being transferred.☺1

Michael: What?

Pope: We're moving you over to Statesville.

Michael: You can't do that.

Pope: Yes, I can. I'm the boss here. This is my house.

Michael: Three weeks.

Pope: What for③?

Michael: Lincoln Lincoln... he's being executed in three weeks.☺2

Pope: Well, I'm aware of that. What's that to you?

Michael: He's my brother. When I knew I was being sent to prison, my attorney petitioned the D.O.C.④

Pope: So you could be near him.

Michael: That's right. Don't take that away from me. Not until it's over.☺3

Pope: I'm not the one behind the transfer. You're up against⑤ much bigger fish⑥ than me.☺4

译文

波　普： 为什么我觉得你有事瞒着我呢，斯科菲尔德？你有没有什么想跟我说的？除了抢银行，你进监狱还有什么其他原因吧？你要被转走了。

迈克尔： 什么？

波　普： 我们要把你送到斯泰茨维尔去。

迈克尔： 你不能这么做。

波　普： 不，我能。我是这儿的长官，这是我的地盘。

迈克尔： 三周。

波　普： 那怎么了？

迈克尔： 林肯，林肯……他三周后就会被处死。

波　普： 哦，这个我知道。那和你有什么关系？

迈克尔： 他是我哥哥。当我知道我要被送进监狱时，我的律师就向监狱总局提出了申请。

波　普： 这样你就能接近他。

迈克尔： 是的。在一切都结束以前别把我转走。

波　普： 不是我要把你转走的，你遇上了比我更大的麻烦。

知识点拨

1. 如果说某事或人 more to something than meets the eye，意思就是此事或人并不像起初看到的那样简单。

2. hold up 有多个意思，可以表示"举起、支撑；耽搁；持械抢劫"。片中表示"持械抢劫"。例：A thief ran off with hundreds of pounds yesterday after holding up a petrol station. 一名窃贼昨天持械抢劫了一家加油站后带着数百英镑逃跑了。

3. what for 一般情况下可以与 why 互换。例：Why did you go there?=What did you go there for?

4. D.O.C. 的全称是 Department of Correction（监狱总局），位于美国俄勒冈州，自1987 年由州立法机关设立，并被授权掌管12 个州的监狱。

5. be up against 表示"面临，面对"。例：When I entered the competition I did not know I'd be up against the club champion. 当我参加比赛时，我不知道我会与俱乐部冠军竞赛。

6. 我们一起来看一看"大人物"的英文表达有：big cheese, big shot, big gun, big wheel, big enchilada, big fish。此 外，somebody 和 something 也都可以表示"（大）人物"。

词汇加油站

transfer [trænsˈfɜːr] *vt.* 使转移
execute [ˈeksɪkjuːt] *vt.* 处死
attorney [əˈtɜːrni] *n.* 律师

boss [bɔːs] *n.* 上司
prison [ˈprɪzn] *n.* 监狱
petition [pəˈtɪʃn] *v.* 请求，申请

时间： 第 5 集 00:19:05—00:20:04
地点： 技工工作室
片段二
人物： 维罗妮卡，技工，尼克
事件： 技工从录像带中发现了重大问题，录像带成为为林肯翻案的重要证物。

精彩亮点

为了搜集证据，还原事件真相，维罗妮卡和同事尼克一道将记录林肯枪杀女总统的弟弟的录像带拿到技工面前。不愧是专业人士，技工一眼就发现了其中的玄机。

1

技工的话再次印证了陷害林肯的人背景深不可测，使得整个案件越来越扑朔迷离，也暗示想为林肯翻案更是难上加难。

2

技工从专业角度为维罗妮卡和尼克深层剖析这卷录像带的"秘密"。虽然从视觉上看的确是林肯杀了女总统的弟弟，但声音的轨迹是撒不了谎的，这可谓是一个重大发现。

3

维罗妮卡和尼克给技工拿的是复制后的录像带，而维罗妮卡想让技工出庭作证，技工的条件是必须要拿到原始的录像带。维罗妮卡和尼克能否拿到呢？

4

Mechanic: This is a top-dollar job. Do you know who did it? ☺1

Nike: No, do you?

Mechanic: People who do this kind of work are ghosts, man. The guy behind the guy behind the guy…You know what I mean? ☺2

Veronica: You see anything? Definitive cuts? Any place that proves the tape might've been doctored①?

Mechanic: The thing's clean. No footprints. I mean, usually, you peel a video back② a couple of layers and anything bogus comes off③. You know, now you see it, now you don't. But not this one. It's laced. Ingrained. ☺3

Nike: You see something?

Mechanic: No. The problem with your eyes is that they play tricks on④ you. Now, but your ears... ears don't lie. Look. Here's the audio track⑤ from the tape. Sound pretty true, right?

Nike: Yeah.

Mechanic: But noise is a lie. See, it doesn't just die like that. Stripped down⑥, those levels should be dancing. I mean, a room that size would give you a… a… blam, blam, blam, blam. You know? Like, one off each wall, split second after the other. On yours, the reverb's bouncing at the same time. ☺4

20

译文

技　工： 这个活儿做起来可得花不少钱。你知道是谁做的吗？

尼　克： 不知道，你知道吗？

技　工： 伙计，做这种工作的人都是幽灵一般存在的。那家伙背后的背后的人……你明白我的意思吗？

维罗妮卡： 你发现什么了？精确的剪切？有能证明这带子可能被修改过的地方吗？

技　工： 做得很干净，没有留下任何痕迹。我的意思是，通常你将录像分成几层后，就会出现伪造的痕迹。现在你看见了，什么都看不到，所以这盘带子不是这样，它被处理过，而且隐藏得很深。

尼　克： 你看出什么了？

技　工： 不，问题是你的眼睛欺骗了你，但你的耳朵……耳朵是不会说谎的。看，这是从录像带里提取出来的声音。听起来很像真的，是不是？

尼　克： 是的。

技　工： 不过声音是假的。看，声音不是像这样消失的。逐渐消失，这些线条应该是跳跃的。我的意思在那种大小的房间里应该是……一种……砰，砰，砰，砰的声音。你知道吗？就像声波是一个接一个依次从每个墙上消失的一样。但你们的录像带里，回声是同时响起的。

知识点拨

1. doctor 做及物动词，可以表示"修理，装配；假造；修改，修饰"。例：They doctored the prints to make her look as awful as possible. 他们修改了照片，尽可能地丑化她的容貌。

2. peel back 表示"剥离；背面卷页；剥落卷页"。例：I do intend to encourage you to peel back the layers of any technology to make sure it's right for you. 我的目的是鼓励您对任何技术进行详细地分析，确保它是正确的选择。

3. come off 可以表示"成功；举行；表现；能被去掉（或除去）"，片中取"能被除去"之意。例：The handle has come off. 把儿脱了。

4. play tricks on sb. 表示"捉弄某人"，与它类似的一个表达是 play jokes on sb. 意思是"嘲笑，戏弄某人"。从程度上看，play tricks on sb. 程度更深。

5. audio track 表示"音频磁迹，伴音声迹"。例：To keep the audio track of his recording clear, the diver turned off all the alarms on his dive computer. 为了保持录音清晰，这个潜水者关掉了他潜水计算机上的所有警报。

6. strip down 表示"拆开，剥下来，脱掉"，片中表示"拆开"。例：I've decided to strip down my motorbike and rebuild it. 我决定拆掉摩托车重新安装。

词汇加油站

top-dollar [tɑːpˈdɑːlər] *n.* （北美，非正式）很高的价钱

ghost [ɡoʊst] *n.* 鬼

footprint [ˈfʊtprɪnt] *n.* 脚印

lace [leɪs] *vt.* 使编织（或交织、缠绕）在一起

strip [strɪp] *vt.* 剥除

reverb [ˈrɪːvɜːrb] *n.* <口> 反响

definitive [dɪˈfɪnətɪv] *adj.* 精确的

bogus [ˈboʊɡəs] *adj.* 伪造的

ingrained [ɪnˈɡreɪnd] *adj.* 根深蒂固的

split [splɪt] *vt.* 分开

时间： 第6集 00:07:06—00:08:07
地点： 迈克尔牢房
人物： 迈克尔，苏克雷
事件： 迈克尔挖掘工作遇阻碍，苏克雷提议"戒严"。

片段三

精彩亮点

1
迈克尔在挖掘时遇到了一道坚实的水泥墙。虽然他能挖开它，但是监狱里一天之内要有多次查房，这就严重阻碍了他的越狱进程。

2
苏克雷认为既然迈克尔有办法挖开那堵墙又何必心急，在狱中的时间多得是。但是，迈克尔的哥哥执行死刑的日子越来越近了，如果再拖延下去，哥哥就要没了。迈克尔怎能把时间耽误在挖水泥墙上呢？

3
苏克雷欲言又止，说明他肯定知道能避免点名的方法，但这个方法是什么呢？为什么苏克雷不想告诉迈克尔呢？

4
迈克尔提及苏克雷的女友迫使苏克雷说出了这个办法：禁闭，但问题是如何能被禁闭呢？苏克雷提议让迈克尔到监狱的电源控制室把电断掉，这样一来，没有了空调，这些囚犯们势必会惹事。戒严自然水到渠成。

Michael: I can't <u>get through</u>[1] the wall, Sucre.

Sucre: What do you mean; you can't get through the wall?

Michael: I know how to do it. I just don't have the time to do it. ☺1

Sucre: We're <u>locked up</u>[2]. All we got is time.

Michael: You don't understand. ☺2 I planned this break on a schedule. Constantly coming up here for count won't let me do what I need to do to get through that wall. If I'm not back <u>on schedule</u>[3], which means we're through that wall <u>by the end of the day manana</u>, we're not getting out of <u>here</u>[4].

Sucre: Look, there are three things <u>for certain</u>[5] in life-death, taxes and count. Only way to stop count is…

Michael: What?

Sucre: Never mind[6]. **It's a bad idea.** ☺3

Michael: Worse than the idea of losing Maricruz?

Sucre: A lockdown. We get Gen Pop locked down for a day; you'll have all the time you need.

Michael: And no count?

Sucre: Bulls don't even come by[7]. **Only one problem.** ☺4

译文

迈克尔： 苏克雷，我无法打通那道墙。

苏克雷： 什么意思？你无法打通那道墙？

迈克尔： 虽然我知道该怎么做，但就是没有足够的时间。

苏克雷： 我们被关在这儿，可有的是时间。

迈克尔： 你不明白，这次越狱计划本来很周密，但这里不断地要点名，我根本没时间打通那道墙。我要是不能按照计划行事，就意味着我们永远也别想穿过那道墙了，这样我们就出不去了。

苏克雷： 你看，人生中有三件事是无法逃避的——死亡、交税还有点名。想要避免点名的唯一方法就是……

迈克尔： 什么？

苏克雷： 算了，这不是个好主意。

迈克尔： 比失去玛丽克鲁兹还糟糕？

苏克雷： 一级禁闭。我们得想法搞出一天禁闭来，这样你就有充足的时间来做你想做的了。

迈克尔： 不用点名？

苏克雷： 谁也不会来打扰。唯一的问题在于……

知识点拨

1. get through 表示"穿过；完成；读完；用完"，片中表示"穿过"。例：The window was far too small for him to get through. 窗户对他来说实在太小，他钻不过去。

2. lock up 表示"将……锁住/关押；关禁闭"。例：Mr. Milner persuaded the federal prosecutors not to lock up his client. 米尔纳先生说服联邦检察官不把他的当事人关起来。

3. on schedule 表示"如期，按计划；正点"。例：The goods arrived on schedule. 货物已如期运到。

4. by the end of 加过去时间，用于过去完成时；by the end of 加将来时间，用于将来完成时。

5. for certain 这个短语表示"无疑地，确定地"，也可以用 for sure 代替。例：The Prime Minister is heading for certain defeat if he forces a vote. 总理要是强行进行投票的话，那么他必败无疑。

6. never mind 的主要意思有：1）用来安慰某人，意为"别着急；不要紧"2）用来谢绝别人的提供，意为"不用啦；别费事啦"3）用来回答道歉，意为"没关系；没什么"4）用来否定某一想法或提议，意为"算了"。片中取第四个意思。

7. come by 这个短语可以表示"得到；经过，从旁边走过"，片中表示"经过"。例：Did you come by the nearest road? 你是由最近的路来的吗？

 词汇加油站

lock [lɑːk] *vt.* 卡住

constantly ['kɑːnstəntli] *adv.* 不断地

count [kaʊnt] *n.* 数数

lockdown ['lɑːkdaʊn] *n.* <美>（对囚犯的）一级禁闭

gen [dʒen] *n.* 情报，消息

schedule ['skedʒuːl] *n.* 计划；日程安排

manana [mæn'jɑːnə] *adv.* 不久以后

bull [bʊl] *n.* 力大如牛的人

23

时间： 第 6 集 00:20:57—00:22:20

地点： 监狱中

人物： 林肯，尼克，维罗妮卡，贝里克，帝博格

事件： 贝里克侮辱帝博格，尼克欲前往华盛顿找寻线索。

精彩亮点

1
贝里克是监狱负责人，为人凶狠，他嘲讽帝博格的身世，也让我们了解了帝博格性格扭曲的根本原因——家庭背景。

2
尼克称自己是林肯的辩护律师，这让维罗妮卡极为不满，她不信任尼克，对他处处提防。而在此处，林肯提到的那通电话是案发当晚有人匿名给警局打的电话。

3
的确，仅凭这一通电话无法做为法律依据，维罗妮卡提醒林肯，检控方已指出林肯的犯罪证据，这远比那通电话来得直接。

4
尼克这句话也是说给维罗妮卡听的，如果找到打这通电话的人，揭露出他这通电话是假的，的确可作为一个重要依据。他希望林肯和维罗妮卡信任他，自己才能竭尽所能。

Bellick: You know, T-Bag, you really let me down[1], and that's hard to do, because I don't expect much…from the inbred child of a retard. That's right, T-Bag. **I read your psych records…about how your daddy raped his mongoloid sister, and then nine months later, little T-Bag pops out**[2]. ☺1

T-Bag: I'm going to kill you!

Bellick: It's hotter than hell. They'll wear themselves out[3] eventually.

Lincoln: The call was a fake. What about a stay of execution or… ☺2

Nike: No, no, it's legally insufficient.

Lincoln: What the hell does that…mean?

Veronica: It means the prosecution could point out the evidence from your criminal trial[4]. Okay? **The blood, the video, the gun. A questionable phone call is not going to stack up**[5] **to that.** ☺3

Lincoln: But it's something, right?

Nike: Absolutely. We got an area code[6], and my contact is going to track that number to someplace more specific-a building, a neighborhood, a block to the person who made this phone call.

Lincoln: What happens next?

Nike: We need to catch the next flight to D.C. **That is, of course, if you trust me now.** ☺4

译文

贝里克：你知道吗，帝博格？你真的很令我失望，我实在不想说你。因为我对天生智障的人没抱多大期望。是的，帝博格，我看了你的心理档案……我知道你父亲强奸了他那白痴的姐姐，然后九个月后，小帝博格就出生了！

帝博格：我要杀了你！

贝里克：这里真是比地狱还热，用不了多久他们就会吃不消的。

林　肯：那通电话是假的，是不是能凭此申请缓刑或者……？

尼　克：不行，不行，法律依据还不充足。

林　肯：这到底是……什么意思？

维罗妮卡：这表示检控方指出了你的犯罪证据。知道吗？血迹、录像带还有枪，那通可疑的电话并不能否定那些证据。

林　肯：但那能说明些问题，对吗？

尼　克：当然。我们知道了电话区号，然后我的朋友能根据这个区号追踪到更加确切的位置，比如：一幢楼、一个街区或是某个单元，直到找到这个打电话的人。

林　肯：那么接下来要干什么？

尼　克：我们需要赶上下一班去华盛顿的飞机。当然，前提是你们现在得信任我。

知识点拨

1. let sb. down 表示"让某人失望"。例：Our parents work hard to support us so as to make us a knowledgeable person! We should not let them down! 父母为了让我们成为有用之才努力工作支持我们，我们不要让他们失望！

2. pop out 表示"突然出来，跳出来"。例：The rabbit pops out as soon as we open the hutch. 我们一打开兔箱，兔子就突然跑了出来。

3. wear sb. out 表示"使某人筋疲力尽"。例：The past few days had really worn him out. 过去的几天真把他给累坏了。

4. criminal trial 表示"刑事审判"。例：Evidence in a criminal trial concerns the intent, motive, means, and opportunity to commit a crime. 刑事审判中的证据关系到犯罪的目的、动机、方法和机会等。

5. stack up 可以表示"加起来；把……堆在……；与……比较；处于某种状态"。例：The British will be out to see how they stack up to the competition. 英国人将全力以赴，一较高低。

6. area code 表示"电话地区号"。

词汇加油站

inbred [ˌinˈbred] *adj.* 天生的

fake [feɪk] *n.* 诈骗

code [koʊd] *n.* 代码

retard [ˈriːtɑːrd] *n.* 迟钝的人，弱智

stack [stæk] *vt.* (使)放成整齐的一叠

block [blɑːk] *n.* 街区

Scene 4 越狱计划现重重阻碍

时间： 第 7 集 00:24:11—00:25:19
地点： 监狱管道
人物： 迈克尔，莎拉，黑人囚犯
事件： 迈克尔营救莎拉，迈克尔莎拉感情升温。

精彩亮点

为了制造出戒严，监狱里断了电，没有空调使得囚犯们开始闹事。报告说有几个 A 翼的囚犯中暑了，身为医生的莎拉出于责任心最终还是选择进入了 A 翼，但里面早已乱作一团，莎拉也身陷危险之中。**1**

迈克尔冒着生命危险从天花板爬进来救莎拉，虽然他也想要利用莎拉，但不难看出，除此之外，迈克尔也在与莎拉的交往中逐渐爱上了她。**2**

看到迈克尔对这里的布局了如指掌，莎拉不免起了疑心。幸好迈克尔急中生智，以刚进来劳改时在这里清除发霉的管道表面为由应付了过去。**3**

通往来访室的门卡是迈克尔他们成功越狱的重要保障，从这段对话中我们可以看出莎拉和迈克尔两个人现在互有好感，最终莎拉能否帮助迈克尔他们成功越狱呢？让我们拭目以待！**4**

Sarah: Why are you here? ☺1

Michael: What do you mean?

Sarah: Crawling around ① in the ceiling, risking your life ② .

Michael: You needed help, and, uh…I came to find you. ☺2

Sarah: How did you know where to go? ☺3

Michael: When everything went off ③ in A-Wing, the cops left the station and I saw you on the monitor. One of my first assignments on PI ④ , we were up here, cleaning out ⑤ toxic mold. Took days, so, I'm kind of familiar with ⑥ the layout.

Sarah: I hope you wore a mask.

Michael: Excuse me?

Sarah: To prevent inhalation. Mold can be really dangerous.

Michael: Yeah. I wore a mask.

Black Prisoner: Get up. Get up there.

Michael: The door to the visitation room, did you ever use it?

Sarah: Um… not usually, but my access card should work. ☺4

译文

莎　　拉：你为什么会在这儿？

迈 克 尔：你什么意思？

莎　　拉：你冒着生命危险从天花板上爬过来……

迈 克 尔：因为你需要帮助，然后，嗯……所以我来救你。

莎　　拉：你怎么知道该怎么走？

迈 克 尔：A 翼失控时，狱警都走了。我从监视器上看到了你。我刚进来劳改时，最初就在这里清除发霉的管道表面。花了好多天，所以我对这里的布局很熟悉。

莎　　拉：我希望你当时戴着面罩。

迈 克 尔：你说什么？

莎　　拉：可以防止中毒。霉菌有时候确实很致命。

迈 克 尔：的确，我戴面罩了。

黑人囚犯：上去，到上面去。

迈 克 尔：通往来访室的门你打开过吗？

莎　　拉：嗯……不常去，但是我的门卡应该能用。

知识点拨

1. crawl around 表示"爬行"。例：These lizards thrive in warm, humid areas where they crawl around in search of insects to eat. 这些壁虎在温暖潮湿的地方繁殖很快，它们到处爬着找小虫吃。

2. risk one's life 表示"拼死，豁命"。

3. go off 可以表示"进行；爆炸；突然大作；停止运转"。片中表示"停止运转"。例：As the water came in the windows, all the lights went off. 随着水从窗子漫进来，灯全部熄灭了。

4. PI 在这里是 Prison Industries 的缩写，表示"监狱工厂"。

5. clean out 表示"扫除，清除，打扫干净"，是将某物扫除掉，将其扔掉，从而达到干净的效果。注意其与 clean up 的区别，后者表示"打扫干净；整理好"，是对某物进行整理和打扫，使其变得更加干净。

6. be familiar with 一般是指"某人熟悉某人、某物"。注意其与 be familiar to 的区别，后者指"某物、某事为某人熟悉"。

 词汇加油站

crawl [krɔːl] *vi.* 缓慢行进
monitor ['mɑːnɪtər] *n.* 显示屏
mold [moʊld] *n.* 模子
inhalation [ˌɪnhə'leɪʃn] *n.* 吸入

ceiling ['siːlɪŋ] *n.* 天花板
toxic ['tɑːksɪk] *adj.* 有毒的；中毒的
layout ['leɪaʊt] *n.* 布局
visitation [ˌvɪzɪ'teɪʃn] *n.* 访问

时间： 第 8 集 00:01:11—00:02:27
地点： 监狱草场
人物： 迈克尔，约翰，苏克雷
事件： 迈克尔与众人商量越狱路线。

片段二

 精彩亮点

1
这一段是迈克尔的独白，他的哥哥还有 17 天就要受电椅刑罚，时间紧迫，而迈克尔他们的越狱计划也在有条不紊地实施着。

2
迈克尔在监狱的操场上指着关押着他们的牢房对苏克雷说着他们的越狱途径，他将这里的一切比作美国的各个城市，也可以看出他们对于自由的向往。

3
选择在晚上实施越狱计划当然是为了掩人耳目。晚上戒备相对较松，方便众人行动。截至目前，已确定加入越狱计划的人有：迈克尔、林肯、约翰、苏克雷及帝博格。

4
对迈克尔的计划，约翰表示了担忧：他们可以通过墙洞潜入医院，但是林肯被单独关押在死囚区，他又该如何与他们越狱呢？

Michael: 17 days from now they **strap** my **brother to an electric** chair…Send **50,000 volts** coursing through his **body for a crime he didn't commit** [①] . I'm here to make sure that doesn't happen. I've been in Fox River nearly three weeks now. In that time, I've managed to get out the back of my cell and into the old **steam** pipes that **run through** [②] the prison.☺₁ Those pipes are our way out. Think of this place like a map of the U.S. **Our cell over there, that's New York City. The infirmary, our exit, that's California. The pipes beneath** [③] **our feet that connect to the…**☺₂

Sucre: Route 66 [④] .

Michael: Route 66. Our ticket out of here.

John: I assume we're doing this at night.☺₃

Michael: That's right.

John: **We're locked up, fish, and your boy is in solitary.**☺₄ How are we just gonna fly out of our cages and right into your cell, right into New York City?

Michael: You're not. You're gonna meet me half way, in Saint Louis. Route 66 runs directly beneath that building. It's the only building sitting on top of those tunnels.

知识点拨

译文

迈克尔： 17 天后他们就要送我哥哥上电椅，因为一个莫须有的罪名就要让 5 万伏的电流通过他的身体，我来这里的目的就是为了阻止这一切发生。我在福克斯河监狱快三周了，这段时间里，我已经可以成功地从我的狱室后面出来，并进入到可以通遍全监狱的旧蒸汽管道，这些管道就是我们的出路。想象这里就是美国地图，我们的牢房就是纽约，我们的出口医务室就是加利福尼亚。而我们脚下的管道通往……

苏克雷： 66 号公路。

迈克尔： 66 号公路，我们从这里逃出去。

约　翰： 我猜我们是晚上行动吧。

迈克尔： 没错。

约　翰： 我们被关押着，束手无策，而你的哥哥被单独监禁。我们怎样才能从牢里飞出去进入你的牢房呢？又怎样进入纽约呢？

迈克尔： 你不用到我的狱室，我们中途在圣路易斯会合，66 号公路就从那个建筑物下面穿过，那是唯一一个建在管道上面的建筑。

1. commit a crime 表示"犯罪"。例：Offense of helping and encouraging someone to commit a crime. 协助和鼓励他人犯罪的犯法行为。

2. run through 可表示"贯穿，跑着穿过……；（使）在……流过；匆匆查阅"。片中表示"贯穿"。例：The globalization has been run through the whole history of modern times and the development of nationality. 全球化构成了现代历史的线索，同时也贯穿了民族主义的发展。

3. beneath 指"紧挨……之下"，其反义词是 on。与其意思相近的词有 below 和 under。其中 below 指"位置低于某物"或"在某物下方"，但不一定在正下方，所指范围较宽。under 为普通用词，与 over 相对，指在某物的正下方，含"垂直在下"的意思。

4. 美国六十六号公路（Route 66），被美国人亲切地唤作"母亲之路"。呈对角线的 66 号公路，从伊利诺伊州芝加哥一路横贯到加州圣塔蒙尼卡。

词汇加油站

strap [stræp] *v.* 用带捆扎

volt [voʊlt] *n.* 伏特

infirmary [ɪnˈfɜːrməri] *n.* 医务室；医院

solitary [ˈsɑːləteri] *adj.* 单个的

electric [ɪˈlektrɪk] *adj.* 带电的

steam [stiːm] *n.* 蒸汽

beneath [bɪˈniːθ] *prep.* 在……的下方

tunnel [ˈtʌnl] *n.* 隧道

时间： 第 8 集 00:06:37—00:07:56
地点： 监狱草场
人物： 迈克尔，约翰，帝博格
事件： 迈克尔等人商量计划，帝博格遭孤立。

片段三

精彩亮点

1
约翰说的放火的地方是哪里呢？事实上，是警卫室。迈克尔计划派一个人去警卫室放火，当警卫们都去清理火场时，借机挖开位于警卫室下方的排水沟。

2
在迈克尔和约翰他们商量计划时，阴险狡诈的帝博格听到了他们的谈话。之前，苏克雷和约翰等人都表达了对帝博格的不满与不信任，想将帝博格排除在越狱计划之外，他们的计划能否成功呢？

3
很明显，约翰是在敷衍帝博格。他们已想好对策等待合适时机干掉帝博格，因此，现在的计划内容让帝博格知道得越少越好。

4
帝博格怎么会看不出迈克尔他们对自己的看法？但他反过来威胁约翰等人，虽然我有把柄在你们手里（杀死了鲍勃），但要死大家一起死，如果你们不带上我，你们想越狱门儿都没有！

John: Fire. ☺₁

Michael: What?

John: Fire. We <u>burn the place down</u> ① .

Michael: How's that gonna help us?

John: A few years ago, the chapel burned down and the D.O.C. realized they had some toxic issues—you know, asbestos, <u>lead paint</u> ② , you <u>name it</u> ③ . They couldn't find a contractor, so they put the inmates on the job. We spent like five, six hours in there <u>at a time</u> ④ . **But the good news is no guards came around almost at all.** ☺₂

Michael: Can you get us in there?

T-Bag: I've been doing a little, uh…thinking. I'm gonna need a PI card, aren't I? I mean that's where this whole thing is happening, isn't it?

John: It's on its way.

T-Bag: **You're slow-walking me, aren't you?** ☺₃

John: Why would I do such a thing?

T-Bag: You think Bellick's gonna pop me for what happened to that stinking C.O. Bob. Maybe you'll take a little walk and tell him for yourself, right? Then, I'll <u>get out of your hair</u> ⑤ <u>for good</u> ⑥ . Well, I got news for you. **If I go down for killing Bob, believe me, I'm gonna take a little walk of my own. Tell them about that hole you got behind your toilet.** ☺₄

译文

约　翰：火。

迈克尔：什么？

约　翰：火，我们用火烧掉那个地方。

迈克尔：那样做对我们有什么帮助？

约　翰：几年前，小教堂被烧毁，监狱总局意识到有有毒材料燃烧——你知道的，像石棉，导火线，凡是你能说得出的。他们找不到承包商来清理，就让犯人来做，我们一次要在那里待上五六个小时，但好消息是几乎没有看守巡逻。

迈克尔：你能让我们进去吗？

帝博格：我最近一直想。我需要一张 PI 卡，不是吗？我的意思是那里就是所有计划开始发生的地方吧？

约　翰：很快就给你。

帝博格：你在敷衍我吧？

约　翰：我为什么要这样做？

帝博格：你认为贝里克会因为我杀了可恶鲍勃而枪毙我。你可能会偷偷跑去告诉他，是吧？然后，我就永远消失了。不过我要告诉你，如果我杀鲍勃的事被抖出来，相信我，我不会就此罢休的，我会把你水箱后面的洞告诉他们。

知识点拨

1. burn down 表示"焚毁，（火）减弱，（使）烧毁"。例：Six months after Bud died, the house burned down. 巴德死后6个月，这座房子被烧毁。

2. lead paint 表示"铅涂料"。例：You grew up around a lot of lead paint, didn't you? 你是在周围满是铅涂料的地方长大的，不是吗？

3. name it 可表示"讲出来或不一而足"，片中取"不一而足"之意。例：Pickled cucumbers, jam, pickled berries, tomatoes; you name it, they've got it. 酸黄瓜、果酱、腌浆果、西红柿，凡是你说得出的，他们都有。

4. at a time 表示"依次，逐一，每次"。例：You can attack this problem from many angles, but let's take one thing at a time. 这个问题可以从多个角度解决，不过，还是让我们逐个分析吧。

5. get out of your hair 表示"就不打扰你了"。例：I know you have a lot on your plate but this can get done and out of your hair in one day. 我知道你有很多事要忙，但这事儿一天内就可搞定，我就不会来烦你了。

6. for good 表示"永远"，等于 forever。例：When John graduated from school, he decided that he was done with study for good and all. 约翰从学校毕业时，决定永远不再和学习打交道了。

词汇加油站

chapel ['tʃæpl] *n.* 小教堂

asbestos [æs'bestəs] *n.* 石棉

inmate ['ɪnmeɪt] *n.* （监狱里的）犯人

stinking ['stɪŋkɪŋ] *adj.* 非常讨厌的

toxic ['tɑːksɪk] *adj.* 有毒的

contractor [kən'træktər] *n.* 承包人

guard [gɑːrd] *n.* 警卫

hole [hoʊl] *n.* 洞

时间： 第9集 00:07:10—00:09:18
地点： 监狱，尼克家
人物： 迈克尔，林肯，尼克，维罗妮卡
事件： 迈克尔因新人自杀感到愧疚，林肯担心儿子安全。

精彩亮点

1　监狱里来了个新人，迈克尔为眼看这个新人在自己眼前自杀而无能为力深感愧疚，于是便向哥哥倾诉。

2　哥哥林肯的态度却与迈克尔相反。他认为眼下最关键的是要完成越狱计划，因此，他根本没有将这个新人的生死放在眼中。

3　迈克尔从小由母亲带大，母亲给予他的影响十分深刻。那么关于迈克尔的父亲，我们之后还会提及。母亲从小教育迈克尔要在他人有困难时伸以援手，但迈克尔却因为惧怕这样做会引起更大的风波而漠然处之，为此他怀有负罪感。

4　林肯的儿子身负双重谋杀的罪名而出逃，林肯又被他人告知，自己和儿子只能活一个。他深感不安，想马上出狱找儿子，这也是他为何催促迈克尔实施越狱计划的重要原因。

Michael: I could have told the pope. He could've transferred the kid to ad seg①. Then he will be in safe. ☺₁
Lincoln: Go easy②, Michael. You didn't even know him. ☺₂
Michael: That makes it okay? I turned my back on him③ because I didn't want to make waves④. It was just… easier…to look the other way…keep the plan safe.
Lincoln: And you did.
Michael: But at what price? That's not how she raised us. ☺₃ A man's down, you give him your hand. She would roll over⑤ in her grave if she knew what I'd become.
Lincoln: No, she wouldn't. You've given me your hand, Michael. My son's out there with a bull's eye on his back. Do whatever you got to do to get us out of here, please. ☺₄
Nike: What are you doing?
Veronica: I was just looking for some coffee.
Nike: Yeah, there isn't any. They belonged to my father, if you were wondering.
Veronica: How long they been in there?
Nike: I don't know, five years. You know, Veronica, we have been through a lot, and, uh, I'm freaking out⑥ here as much as you are. But you get this look in your eyes sometimes like… like I'm the bad guy.

译文

迈克尔： 我本可以告诉狱长的。这样一来，他就会被送到隔离区，也就安全了。

林　肯： 算了，迈克尔，你都不认识他。

迈克尔： 这样就能心安理得吗？我因为怕惹麻烦而没去帮他。因为更容易……所以……就无视这些事情，只为了确保计划万无一失。

林　肯： 你做到了。

迈克尔： 但我们付出了什么代价呢？妈妈可不是这样教我们的。他人有困难，我们就要伸出援手。如果她知道我成了这样的人，在坟墓里也难以安眠。

林　肯： 不，不会的。迈克尔，你向我伸出了援手。我的儿子在外面危在旦夕，求求你，无论如何也要让我们离开这里。

尼　克： 你在干什么？

维罗妮卡： 我只是想找点儿咖啡喝。

尼　克： 是的，没有咖啡了。那些（枪）是我父亲的，如果你想知道的话。

维罗妮卡： 它们在这放了多久了？

尼　克： 我不知道，五年吧。你知道吗，维罗妮卡？我们在一起经历了那么多事，而且，我跟你一样也心烦意乱，但你看我的眼神有时候就像……就像我是坏人。

知识点拨

1. seg 指"隔离关押（或监禁）室"。

2. go easy 可以指"小心地用，小心地对待或讨论（某事），少量地使用（某物）"，在片中表示"算了，别放在心上"。

3. turn one's back on someone 从字面上看，这是把自己的背对着某人。可是，实际上这是指"根本不理会某人"，或"不肯给那个有困难的人任何帮助"。

4. 我们用 make waves 来形容"某人或事对外产生了影响，引起轰动，甚至制造风波"。此外，与 wave 相关的另一个短语 wave goodbye to sth. 的意思是"向某事或某物挥手告别"，形容接受得不到某物的事实。

5. roll over 表示"从（边上）滚下，（使）翻滚"。例：Most competition cars will only roll over if they hit an obstacle. 大多数赛车只有在撞上障碍物时才会翻车。

6. freak out 表示"（因吸毒等而）产生幻觉，（使）极度兴奋，行为反常"。例：We are going to freak out if you don't show up! 你再不出现我们就要发疯了！

词汇加油站

transfer [træns'fɜːr] *vt.* 使转移

grave [greɪv] *n.* 坟墓

belong [bɪ'lɔːŋ] *vi.* 属于

freak [friːk] *vi.* （像吸过毒似的）行为反常

wave [weɪv] *n.* 汹涌的行动（或思想）态势

bull [bʊl] *n.* 力大如牛的人

wonder ['wʌndər] *vt.* 想弄明白

Scene 5 特伦斯谋杀案惊现疑点

片段一

时间： 第 9 集 00:24:47—00:25:32

地点： 露天咖啡馆

人物： 维罗妮卡，斯蒂德曼夫人，尼克

事件： 尼克、维罗妮卡与斯蒂德曼夫人谈话。

精彩亮点

1 尼克决定调查"蜂王"——"死去的"特伦斯的妻子，他打听到每天中午在列克星敦有集会，而特伦斯的妻子也肯定会在那里享用午餐。于是，他与维罗妮卡便前来与特伦斯的妻子对话。

2 作为上层社会人士，特伦斯的妻子自然懂得圈中的生存法则。她不愿意听维罗妮卡他们的长篇大论，也不在意一个平民的死活。但在维罗妮卡的请求下，她还是坚持听完了他们的话。

3 特伦斯位高权重，想让他下台或是想取他性命的人大有人在，正如特伦斯的妻子所言，关于谋杀他的动机要多少有多少。此外，还有什么依据让特伦斯的妻子说出这样的话呢？

4 公司总裁被指控诈骗罪，而且是上亿美元，若用这笔钱去杀人绰绰有余。因此，如果不是听到警方证实是林肯杀了人，特伦斯的妻子会怀疑在座的每一个人。

Nike: Ma'am, that is not why we're here.☺₁ Actually, may we sit down① ? We were hoping you could help us with② one of our more public cases— the Lincoln Burrows case.

Veronica: As you know, he's making unfounded claims that he's innocent. That others had motive to murder your husband.

Mrs. Steadman: I really don't have time for a long conversation.☺₂

Veronica: Mrs. Steadman, it doesn't have to be a long conversation.

Mrs. Steadman: If we talked about who had motive to kill Terrence, we'd be here all day.

Veronica: I'm sorry?☺₃

Mrs. Steadman: Look around. Half the people in this place were shareholders in his company. Every one of them sat at my husband's memorial, and every one of them was thinking the same thing. "Thank God③ he's gone."

Nike: Why would they think that?

Mrs. Steadman: Money. As soon as④ rumors of the indictment started, you should have seen them run for⑤ the exits.

Veronica: I wasn't aware of any indictment.

Mrs. Steadman: It never came down⑥. He died before it could.☺₄

译文

尼　　克：夫人，我们不是为此事而来。事实上，我们可以坐下说吗？我们希望您能就众多案件中的一件帮帮我们——就是林肯·布鲁斯一案。

维罗妮卡：正如您所知，他因那些伪造的证据被起诉，但他是无辜的。是那些有杀人动机的人谋杀了您丈夫。

斯蒂德曼夫人：我真的没有时间听你们长篇大论。

维罗妮卡：斯蒂德曼夫人，我们不会耽误您太久的。

斯蒂德曼夫人：如果我们要谈谁有谋杀特伦斯的动机，我们可以在这里待上一整天。

维罗妮卡：您这话是什么意思？

斯蒂德曼夫人：看看周围，这个地方有一半人都是他公司的股东。他们每个人都参加了我丈夫的追悼会，但每个人都想着同一件事："谢天谢地他终于死了"。

尼　　克：他们为什么会这样想？

斯蒂德曼夫人：因为钱。指控的流言一传开，你就会看到他们都躲得远远的。

维罗妮卡：我没听过指控的事。

斯蒂德曼夫人：这件事从没被证实过，还没等开始他就死了。

知识点拨

1. sit down 表示"坐下"。例：Have you both sat down and worked out a budget together? 你们有没有同心协力制订出一份预算呢？

2. help sb. with sth., help sb. do sth., help sb. to do sth. 这三个句型都有"帮助某人做某事"的意思。其中 help sb. do sth. 是 help sb. to do sth. 的简略形式，它们可互相使用。而在 help sb. with sth. 中 with 是介词，其后接名词或代词。

3. thank God 表示"谢天谢地（用以表示松了一口气或宽慰）"。例：I was wrong, thank God. 原来我错了，感谢上帝。

4. as soon as 表示"一……就……；一经；不久后，一会儿"。既可以引导时间状语从句，表过去，又可以表示将来。as soon as 引导时间状语从句当主句用一般过去时时，从句中用一般过去时或过去完成时。

5. run for 这个词组可以表示"竞选或赶紧去请、匆匆去取"。片中表示"赶紧去……"。例：Bob was forced to leave the car at the roadside and run for help. 鲍勃被迫把车停在路边，然后跑去求助了。

6. come down 表示"（价格、温度、比率等）下降；着陆；崩塌；决定并宣布（支持或反对）"。片中取最后一个意思。例：When you come down to it, however, the basic problems of life have not changed. 然而，归根结底，生活中一些基本的问题还是没有变。

词汇加油站

unfounded [ʌnˈfaʊndɪd] *adj.* 无事实根据的

motive [ˈmoʊtɪv] *n.* 动机

shareholder [ˈʃerhoʊldər] *n.* 股东

rumor [ˈruːmər] *n.* 传闻

innocent [ˈɪnəsnt] *adj.* 清白的

murder [ˈmɜːrdər] *vt.* 凶杀

memorial [məˈmɔːriəl] *n.* 纪念仪式

indictment [ɪnˈdaɪtmənt] *n.* 起诉书

时间： 第 10 集 00:14:19—00:15:19
地点： 医务室
片段二
人物： 迈克尔，莎拉
事件： 莎拉生日迈克尔送祝福。

精彩亮点

桌上的一束鲜花引起了迈克尔的注意，他问莎拉是不是有了追求者。虽然语气上显得很幽默，但我们也不难听出迈克尔有些吃醋。**1**

原来今天是莎拉的生日，而且这束花是她父亲送给她的。迈克尔不禁放下心来，但他看得出来，莎拉好像在自己生日这天并不是很高兴。这是为什么呢？**2**

莎拉一脸严肃地告诉迈克尔，以前父亲因为工作原因一共才陪她过了 6 次生日，且每次生日都会送她一些花作为补偿。迈克尔不禁感到一些伤感，他想安慰莎拉，但又不知道说些什么。**3**

莎拉已经习惯了在自己生日这天父亲不能陪伴。她外表坚强，也不想让迈克尔同情自己，但迈克尔最后还是真诚地对莎拉说了句"生日快乐"。迈克尔和莎拉的心也在一点点靠近。**4**

Michael: Nice flowers.

Sarah: Right.

Michael: Do we have an admirer? ☺₁

Sarah: They're from my father.

Michael: Ah... what's the occasion?

Sarah: It's my birthday.

Michael: Today? Happy birthday.

Sarah: Thank you.

Michael: Okay. **Nothing. Birthdays are not usually a sore subject, that's all.** ① ☺₂ Unless the celebrant is feeling her age ②, which I don't see how you could be.

Sarah: I'm 29 years old, Michael. I'm not feeling my age. **It's just that out of those 29 birthdays, my father has actually managed to see** ③ **me on precisely… six of them.** ☺₃ So… I get flowers instead. Flowers that end up ④ dead and in the trash a week later. That sounded bitter, huh?

Michael: Kind of ⑤.

Sarah: It's not that big a deal ⑥. **You are all set. I will see you tomorrow.** ☺₄

译文

迈克尔： 很漂亮的花。

莎 拉： 是的。

迈克尔： 你有追求者吗？

莎 拉： 这些是我父亲送的。

迈克尔： 哦……为什么送的？

莎 拉： 我的生日。

迈克尔： 今天吗？生日快乐。

莎 拉： 谢谢。

迈克尔： 是的，没什么，生日通常不是什么痛苦的话题是吧？除非庆祝者想到她的年龄，但这一点我在你身上看不出。

莎 拉： 迈克尔，我 29 岁了，但我没有觉得自己变老。不过是 29 个生日罢了，实际上，我爸爸只陪我过了 6 个生日，因此，就送了我一些花儿做补偿。花儿最后都会枯死的，一个礼拜后就会被丢到垃圾桶里。听起来很伤感是吗？

迈克尔： 有点儿。

莎 拉： 没什么大不了的。好了，明天见。

知识点拨

1. That's all. 表示"仅此而已"。例：I can boot up from a floppy disk, but that's all. 我可以用一张软盘来启动，但其他的就无能为力了。

2. feel one's age 表示"觉得自己老了"。例：A: I feel my age. B: Oh, no. You look fresh, and time has stood still with you. A：我觉得我老了。B：没有，你的精神很好，时光在你身上驻足了。

3. manage to do 表示"设法做成某事"。例：I didn't manage to do it before you had explained how. 你解释了如何干之后，我才设法完成了那件工作。

4. end up 表示"（以……）结束，最终成为，最后处于"。例：If you don't know what you want, you might end up getting something you don't want. 如果你不知道自己想要什么，到头来你可能得非所愿。

5. kind of 表示"稍微，有点儿，有几分"。例：Have you been able to have any kind of contact? 你联系上了吗？

6. 这是一个感叹句，that 修饰 big，起强调作用。

词汇加油站

admirer [əd'maɪərər] *n.* （女子的）爱慕者

sore [sɔːr] *adj.* 使人伤心的

celebrant ['selɪbrənt] *n.* 参加聚会（或庆典）的人

precisely [prɪ'saɪsli] *adv.* 恰好地

bitter ['bɪtər] *adj.* 苦的

occasion [ə'keɪʒn] *n.* 场合

trash [træʃ] *n.* 垃圾

时间： 第10集 00:20:29—00:21:13

地点： 尼克家

人物： 尼克，维罗妮卡

事件： 尼克与维罗妮卡分析特伦斯公司钱款的去向，从中发现疑点。

精彩亮点

1 特伦斯被谋杀后，按理说应该马上公开控告他的诉讼文件，但现在也一直没有公开，这件事就这么不了了之了吗？还是背后另有隐情？

2 在上次谈话中，特伦斯的妻子提到了一件很重要的事就是易科菲尔德公司会因特伦斯的死亡而损失上亿美元，这可不是一笔小数目，如果能找到这笔钱款的去向或许就可以揭开林肯谋杀案的秘密。

3 维罗妮卡发现至少有5亿美元的联邦贷款都用于研发可替代燃料，但奇怪的是，公司不仅没有因此获利，而且也没有研发出任何东西，这不免让人生疑，那么这笔巨款到底用在何处了呢？

4 就在维罗妮卡他们一筹莫展时，新闻报道称副总统卡罗琳日前宣布将会角逐总统选举，且副总统背后有有史以来最大的竞选资本支持，从而使她成为最有可能当选的候选人。这不禁让维罗妮卡和尼克眼前一亮：那笔巨款的最终流向正是副总统卡罗琳。

Nike: Ecofield's SEC filings?

Veronica: Terrence Steadman was murdered, so the information from his indictment wouldn't be made public[1], right? ☺1

Nike: Sure, but since it never saw the light of day[2], we have no way of knowing[3] what they were trying to cover up[4].

Veronica: Steadman's wife said there were hundreds of millions of dollars at stake[5] if her husband went down, so I figure we follow the money, and see where it takes us. ☺2

Nike: $109 million. $212 million…

Veronica: Over half a billion dollars that I have found so far in federal grants to Ecofield for alternative fuel research. ☺3

Nike: That is a hell of[6] a lot of money.

Veronica: But for what? Not only did the company never make a profit. As far as I could tell, they never made anything. No fuel cells, no patents, no findings nothing.

Nike: So EcoField was a sham, it was a cover?

Veronica: Question is, for what? ☺4

译文

尼　　克： 易科菲尔德公司的 SEC 档案？

维罗妮卡： 特伦斯·斯蒂德曼被谋杀了，那么应该公开控告他的诉讼文件才对，是不是？

尼　　克： 当然，但是直至现在还没有被公开，我们无法知道他们到底想掩盖什么。

维罗妮卡： 斯蒂德曼的妻子说如果她的丈夫垮了，公司会损失上亿美元，所以我觉得我们应该沿着钱的线索去找，看看会找到什么。

尼　　克： 1.09 亿美元，2.12 亿美元……

维罗妮卡： 我目前为止发现超过 5 亿美元的联邦政府拨款用于易科菲尔德公司的可替代燃料研发。

尼　　克： 这可真是一笔可观的数目。

维罗妮卡： 但用来干什么了？公司不仅没创造利润，而且据我所知，他们没研发出任何东西。没有燃料电池，没有专利，也没有新发现，什么都没有。

尼　　克： 因此易科菲尔德公司是假的，只是个掩饰罢了？

维罗妮卡： 问题在于，为了什么？

知识点拨

1. make public 表示"发布判决书，披露，公之于众"。

2. see the light of day 表示"诞生，出世"；（书籍）问世"。例：Museum basements are stacked full of objects which never see the light of day. 博物馆的地下室里堆满了永远不会重见天日的物件。

3. have no way of doing sth. 表示"没办法做某事"。例：I have no way of finding out whether they are competent. 我无法弄清他们是否有能力。

4. cover up 表示"掩盖；掩饰；盖起来；裹住"。例：He suspects there's a conspiracy to cover up the crime. 他怀疑有人密谋掩盖犯罪事实。

5. at stake 表示"危如累卵，危险"。例：The life of the sick man is at stake. 病人的性命危在旦夕。

6. a hell of 表示"极恶劣的；使人受不了的"。例：The manager took a hell of a lot of money out of the club. 主教练从俱乐部拿到了很多钱。

词汇加油站

filing [ˈfaɪlɪŋ] *n.* 文件归档

alternative [ɔːlˈtɜːrnətɪv] *adj.* 替代的

patent [ˈpætnt] *n.* 专利

cover [ˈkʌvər] *n.* 掩护

federal [ˈfedərəl] *adj.* 联邦（制）的

hell [hel] *n.* 训斥

sham [ʃæm] *n.* 套

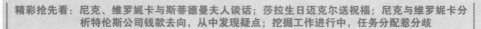

时间： 第 11 集 00:04:38—00:05:33

地点： 监狱

片段四

人物： 约翰，富兰克林，帝博格，林肯

事件： 挖掘工作进行中，任务分配惹分歧。

 精彩亮点

1. 挖掘工作仍在继续，帝博格却成心想找黑人富兰克林的麻烦。他称："这房间太暗了，我没法挖！"实际上是在暗讽富兰克林是黑人，不想与他一起工作。

2. 富兰克林也不甘示弱，他和帝博格两个人本来就不和，这下更是激起了彼此的仇恨。眼看两个人就要大打出手，林肯马上出来制止。

3. 帝博格不满约翰不用干活，实际上，早在一开始我们就知道福克斯河监狱是以约翰为老大的，他自然要做管理员的工作。

4. 富兰克林这番话意在表明如果不注意看好帝博格，很有可能会生出什么事端，到时他就会罢工，将他们的越狱计划透露出来。

John: Okay. Let's rotate. Finally. Sergeant sodomy, you're up[1] next.

Franklin: Yo. Come on[2].

T-Bag: **I don't know about you all, but, uh…this room is getting a little too dark for me to dig.** ☺1

Franklin: Are you telling me that there's a hole in Fox River that you don't want to get into?

T-Bag: What?

Lincoln: **Hey, no one gets hurt.** ☺2

Franklin: You know, I got a question: How come[3] fusilli over here is not grabbing a shovel?

John: I'm handling arrangements on the outside.

Franklin: Really? So what is that transpo? Paper?

John: Exactly. **That makes me manager.** ☺3

Franklin: And that makes us just labor.

John: Now you're getting it.

Franklin: You know, management better keep a close eye on[4] the conditions up in here. **Or the labor is liable to[5] go on strike[6]. You feel me?** ☺4

译文

约　　翰：好了，让我们轮流干吧。终于好了，流氓中士，你是下一个。

富兰克林：喂，快点儿过来。

帝　博　格：我不太认识你，不过，呃……这房间太暗了，我没办法挖呀！

富兰克林：你是想告诉我福克斯河监狱里的那个洞你不想进了？

帝　博　格：什么？

林　　肯：嘿，大家别乱来。

富兰克林：我有个问题要问一下：为什么你这个"长毛怪"不用干活？

约　　翰：我负责处理外面的安排工作。

富兰克林：真的吗？人员配制？文书工作？

约　　翰：没错。我是管理人员。

富兰克林：而我们是劳工。

约　　翰：你现在才明白。

富兰克林：你知道吗？管理员最好多注意点儿这里的环境。否则，工人会罢工的。你懂我的意思了吗？

知识点拨

1. be up 一般与 to 连用，即 be up to。be up to 有两个意思：一是指"某人有能力完成某项任务"或是"接受某项挑战"。也可以指"某人的空闲时间"。

2. come on 表示"快点；开始；前进；开始工作"。例：—Have you said all this to the police? —Aw, come on! 你是不是把这些都告诉警方了？呀，怎么会呢！

3. how come 表示"为什么，怎么会……（那样）"。例："How come we never know what's going on?" he groused. "为什么我们对正在发生的事情总是一无所知？"他抱怨说。

4. keep a close eye on 表示"照看，留心瞧着；注意"。例：But I suggest we keep a close eye on him at all times. 但我建议我们还是密切注意他的一举一动。

5. be liable to do 表示"有……倾向的"。例：Companies must comply from January 1, 2008, and may be liable to fines or deregistration if they do not satisfy the requirements. 从 2008 年 1 月 1 日开始，各企业必须遵守这一规定，如果不能满足要求，也许会遭到罚款或取消注册资格的处分。

6. on strike 表示"罢工中"。

词汇加油站

rotate ['routeɪt] vt. 使轮流

fusilli [fju:'sɪli] n. 螺旋面

shovel ['ʃʌvl] n. 铲子

liable ['laɪəbl] adj. 有……倾向的

sergeant ['sɑ:rdʒənt] n. 中士

grab [græb] vt. 匆匆拿走

exactly [ɪg'zæktli] adv. 确切地

strike [straɪk] vt. 罢工

Scene 6 意外状况频发

时间： 第 11 集 00:13:37—00:15:19

地点： 木屋

人物： 尼克，奎恩，L. J. 林肯

事件： 尼克等人中计，尼克中枪生死未卜。

精彩亮点

1　尼克，维罗妮卡和 L.J. 为了躲避跟踪他们的人，来到了一间荒野木屋。当他们刚进入木屋后不久就听到门外有人在呼救。这个人是谁呢？

2　敲门的人是副总统卡罗琳的手下奎恩，他一路尾随尼克一行人，装作开车时打盹儿摔伤的样子来到他们面前，还不忘夸大他受伤的严重程度，只为了让他们放松警惕。

3　就在尼克蹲下身去寻找急救箱时，奎恩突然拿出手枪对着尼克的背部就开了一枪，令众人始料未及。

4　奎恩将维罗妮卡绑了起来，将 L.J. 林肯拖到了门外，而此时的尼克则躺在血泊中。奎恩以尼克的性命相威胁，逼迫维罗妮卡说出林肯谋杀案调查的进度。

Nike: What happened?☺1

Quinn: Uh… I must have dozed off①. I was driving for 12 hours.

L.J.: Should I get some water from the well?

Nike: The well's dried up②.

Quinn: Oh, God, my leg.☺2

Nike: I think there's a medical kit over here.

Quinn: No one's going anywhere. All right. Say goodbye to junior.☺3

Nike: No!

Quinn: Do you know how many pints of blood the human body has?③ The answer is ten. How many do you think the Prince Charming④ over there on the floor has left? Eight? Going on seven? Tell you what? I'm gonna take him out to the woodshed, have a little talk. In the meantime, I want you to chew on this. **You tell me everything that you have discovered about the Lincoln case, and who else you have told about it, and there's a chance that I might let you go in time to get Mr. Savrinn to a doctor.**☺4 You decide whose life is more valuable—the guy waiting to die on death row⑤ or the guy wishing he would die out⑥ in the woodshed.

译文

尼　　克：发生什么事了？

奎　　恩：哦……我肯定是打盹了。我连着开了 12 个小时了。

L. J. 林肯：我需要打点儿井水给他吗？

尼　　克：那井已经干了。

奎　　恩：天呐，我的腿。

尼　　克：那边好像有个急救箱。

奎　　恩：谁也不准出去。好了，跟这小子说再见吧。

尼　　克：不要！

奎　　恩：你知道人身上有多少品脱的血吗？答案是十品脱。你觉得地板上的那个帅哥还剩多少血呢？八品脱？快到七品脱了？告诉你，我要带他到木屋里谈话。与此同时，我希望你好好考虑一下这个。告诉我关于林肯的案子你都发现了什么，你都告诉过谁，我或许会放你走，让你及时带萨维恩先生去看医生。由你来决定谁的命更值钱——是那个在死牢等死的家伙，还是希望死在木屋里的这个家伙。

知识点拨

1. doze off 表示"打瞌睡，睡着"。例：He can doze off whenever he gets tired. 无论何时他累了都能睡着。

2. dry up 表示"枯竭，（使……）干涸"。例：Warm breezes from the South dried up the streets. 来自南方的温暖和风吹干了街道。

3. 人体内的血液量大约是体重的 7 ～ 8%，如果失血量较少，不超过总血量的 10%，则通过身体的自我调节，可以很快恢复；如果失血量较大，达总血量的 20% 时，则出现脉搏加快，血压下降等症状；如果在短时间内丧失的血液达全身血液的 30% 或更多，就可能危及生命。

4. Prince Charming 就是我们熟悉的"白马王子"。例：Darling, you're my Prince Charming. 亲爱的，你是我的白马王子。

5. death row 表示"死囚室"。例：He has been on Death Row for 11 years. 他已经在死囚室关了 11 年。

6. die out 表示"（物种、家族、习惯、观念等）绝迹，消失；绝种；绝灭；淘汰"。例：How did the dinosaurs die out? 恐龙是如何灭绝的？

 词汇加油站

doze [doʊz] *vi.* 打盹儿

kit [kɪt] *n.* 成套用品

pint [paɪnt] *n.* 品脱

woodshed ['wʊdʃed] *n.* 柴房

valuable ['væljuəbl] *adj.* 有价值的

well [wel] *n.* 水井

junior ['dʒuːnɪər] *n.* 年少者

prince [prɪns] *n.* 王子

chew [tʃuː] *vt.* 深思

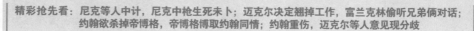

时间： 第 12 集 00:04:20—00:05:20
地点： 监狱里
人物： 迈克尔，林肯，富兰克林
事件： 迈克尔决定翘掉工作，富兰克林偷听兄弟俩对话。

片段二

精彩亮点

1
迈克尔已经找到了通往医务室的路径，现在的难题是如何能让通往医务室的路畅通无阻。于是迈克尔决定翘掉明早的工作溜出去。

2
林肯当然不想让迈克尔溜出去。一旦有狱警前来巡视，发现迈克尔失踪了，整个越狱计划就会毁于一旦。但事到如今，找到这条路就可以使整个越狱计划进行得畅通无阻。迈克尔自然想要放手一搏。

3
韦斯特莫兰德已经上了年纪，行动自然不如年轻人灵活。在林肯看来，必须要让其中一人退出才能保证越狱成功。

4
迈克尔和林肯的话让黑人富兰克林听得一清二楚。现在越狱成员已增加到七人，但越狱时间有限，七个人无法在 18 分钟内冲出那面墙。必须要淘汰一人，那么谁会被淘汰呢？

Michael: I found our access to the infirmary building, but I'm gonna need some time to make it work①. ☺1

Lincoln: How much time?

Michael: Enough for me to find my way up a 20-foot vertical drain pipe② without using a ladder. I'll probably need to skip PI tomorrow if I want to get this thing done.

Lincoln: Can not just skip it. It is not class. What if one of the bulls decide to drop in③?

Michael: Well, I don't have a choice, do I? ☺2 Once we get through the pipe below the guards' room, it will be a whole lot④ easier. I can come and go⑤ without using the door, and with Westmoreland as a lookout, we'll have one more man available for dig.

Lincoln: Westmoreland's gonna be a problem. All seven of us can't break over⑥ that wall in 18 minutes. You said it yourself. It's impossible. Listen, man, I'm telling you, one of us has got to take a hike.⑦ ☺3

Michael: I know.

Franklin: Mind if I share that with the rest of the class? ☺4 Apparently, college boy here did the math. Figured out that we got too many clowns in the car. So, one of us is in here digging, but his seat is not guaranteed.

译文

迈 克 尔：我找到了通往医务室的路径，但我需要点儿时间去"开路"。

林 肯：要多长时间？

迈 克 尔：足够让我不用梯子找到通往 20 尺高的垂直下水管道的路。如果我想做成这件事，可能需要翘掉明早的工作。

林 肯：你不能就这样溜出去，又不是上课。万一有狱警进来怎么办？

迈 克 尔：但我没得选择，对吧？只要我们能从警卫室下的管道经过，事情就容易多了。即使不通过那扇门我也能进进出出，韦斯特莫兰德来放风。我们要再安排一个人去挖掘。

林 肯：韦斯特莫兰德会是个难题，我们 7 个人在 18 分钟内是无法冲出那面墙的。是你自己说的，这是不可能的。听着，我要告诉你，我们当中有一个人退出。

迈 克 尔：我知道。

富兰克林：介意我加入你们的谈话吗？显然，这个上过大学的小子做了道数学题。他算出我们现在这辆车已经"超载"了，所以，在这里挖掘的人中要有一个会被淘汰出局。

知识点拨

1. make it work 表示"使起作用"。例：We know what to do to make it work. 我们知道如何让它起作用。

2. drain pipe 表示"排水管，泄水管"。

3. drop in 表示"投入；顺便拜访；降下"。例：Whenever I'm up there I always drop in. 每次我到那儿都会顺便去看看。

4. a whole lot 表示"相当多"。例：It will free us of a whole lot of debt. 它会使我们摆脱巨额债务。

5. come and go 表示"出没，来来往往，往返"。例：Can I read your letters that come and go between your university and you? 我可以看看你和学校往来的信件吗？

6. break over 表示"吞没，淹没"。

7. take a hike 是"希望别人离开"，有点儿"哪儿凉快去哪儿"的意味。例：I am tired of you all complaining, take a hike. 我听够你的抱怨了，你哪凉快哪待着去吧。

词汇加油站

drain [dreɪn] *n.* 排水

skip [skɪp] *vt.* 不做（应做的事等）

hike [haɪk] *n.* 远足

clown [klaʊn] *n.* 丑角

ladder ['lædər] *n.* 梯子

lookout ['lʊkaʊt] *n.* 警戒

apparently [ə'pærəntli] *adv.* 看来

guarantee [ˌɡærən'tiː] *vt.* 保证

时间： 第 12 集 00:38:23—00:39:53
地点： 监狱里
人物： 帝博格，约翰
事件： 约翰欲杀掉帝博格，帝博格博取约翰同情。

片段三

精彩亮点

1　越狱计划眼看就要到最后关头，但现在的问题是 7 个人无法在 18 分钟内冲出那面墙，所以必须要让其中一人退出。众人都将目标锁定在阴险狡诈的帝博格身上，约翰率领一帮人将帝博格围住，逼迫他退出。

2　狡猾的帝博格怎能让自己连日来的辛苦付诸东流？他故意提到了吉米，吉米是帝博格的表弟，被约翰杀死了，但约翰本意并不想杀他，他也一直在为此事而深感愧疚。帝博格就是想让约翰怀有负罪感，不忍心对自己下手。

3　果然，约翰上当。他本来打算将帝博格杀死，但帝博格的话让他不忍下手，他觉得自己罪孽深重。此外，看到眼前帝博格已无力反抗，他也放松了戒备。

4　帝博格假装答应约翰自己退出越狱计划，但实际上，此时的约翰因为帝博格的一番话情绪十分激动，帝博格瞄准时机，用自己预先准备的一把小刀划破了约翰的喉咙。

T-Bag: **You don't have to do this.** ☺₁

John: You brought it on ① yourself. I'm just an emissary for all the pain and suffering you caused, all the families you ruined, all the kids.

T-Bag: **What about Jimmy?** ☺₂ He had nothing to do with ② this. You didn't need to kill him. And what about his beautiful son? His whole life in front of ③ him. You didn't need to kill a beautiful child. After all I've done, maybe I do deserve to die, maybe I do. But you are no better than ④ me.

John: But I can be, if I want. God has given me the chance to choose. And maybe I should give you a chance as well.

T-Bag: You should. Anything. Anything. Please. Please. Please.

John: **Back out** ⑤. ☺₃

T-Bag: Of the escape?

John: Or die.

T-Bag: I would, I…I wouldn't make it out there, anyway…Not with my proclivities.

John: I want you to give me your word ⑥. You hear me? I want you to give me your word!

T-Bag: **Yeah, you got it, John.** ☺₄

46

译文

帝博格：你不必这么做。

约　翰：这都是你自找的。我只是个传递痛苦的使者，为了所有被你毁了的家庭，还有那些孩子们。

帝博格：那吉米呢？他与这一切无关，你没必要杀了他。还有他漂亮的儿子呢？他还有很长的日子要过，你没必要杀一个漂亮的孩子。我做了那么多坏事，或许罪有应得，但你也好不到哪去。

约　翰：但只要我愿意，我就可以变好。上帝给了我选择的机会，或许我也应该给你一个选择的机会。

帝博格：是的，无论什么，无论什么，求你了，求你了，求你了。

约　翰：退出。

帝博格：退出越狱计划?

约　翰：要不就死。

帝博格：不管怎样，像我这样的人也出不去……从没想过。

约　翰：我要你发誓。你听到了吗？我要你发誓!

帝博格：好，我答应你，约翰。

知识点拨

1. bring it on oneself 表示"自找的"。此外，bring it on 还可表示"把……拿上来"。例：Bring it on! I'm ready to start. 将它拿上来! 我准备要开始了。

2. have nothing to do with 表示"与……没关系，无关"。例：House prices are easily upset by factors which have nothing to do with property. 房价很容易受到与房产毫不相干的因素的干扰。

3. in front of 表示"在……前面"。注意其与 in the front of 的区别。in front of 表示"在……（之外）的前面"；而 in the front of 表示"在……（之内）的前面"。

4. "no+ 比较级 +than" 结构表示该形容词或副词的相反含义，意思是"与……一样不……"。no better than=as bad as，表示"和……一样坏"。

5. back out 表示"不遵守（诺言、合约等），打退堂鼓"。在这里约翰想让帝博格自动退出越狱计划。例：Madonna backed out of the project after much wrangling. 多番争吵之后，麦当娜退出了这个项目。

6. give sb. one's word 表示"向某人保证"。例：Don't do that again. Give me your word. 不要再这样做了。你要向我保证。

 词汇加油站

emissary ['emɪseri] *n.* （外交上的）使者

suffering ['sʌfərɪŋ] *n.* 受苦

deserve [dɪ'zɜːrv] *vt.* 应受

proclivity [prə'klɪvəti] *n.* 癖性

pain [peɪn] *n.* 痛苦

ruin ['ruːɪn] *vt.* 破坏

escape [ɪ'skeɪp] *n.* 逃离

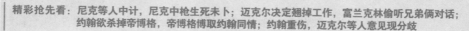
时间： 第 13 集 00:04:21—00:05:16
地点： 监狱草场
人物： 迈克尔，帝博格，富兰克林，苏克雷
事件： 约翰重伤，迈克尔等人意见现分歧。

精彩亮点

1 约翰被帝博格用小刀割破了喉咙，众人看着他被抬走，危在旦夕，这无疑是迈克尔等人始料未及的。原本打算让帝博格退出的他们又该如何计划呢？

2 身为罪魁祸首的帝博格此时却仍假惺惺地询问约翰的情况。同时，也在暗示众人：你们想把我赶走，没那么容易！

3 迈克尔完成了越狱计划的准备工作，未曾想到此时狱警向警卫室废墟走来，为了赢得时间让迈克尔爬出坑道，林肯打伤了狱警，被拖向单独禁闭室。如果不能救哥哥出来，越狱计划就失去了意义。迈克尔又会打算怎么做呢？

4 自私的帝博格当然不会顾及其他人的死活，他傲慢地对迈克尔说即使没有你我也能从牢房溜出去。他能否如愿以偿呢？

Sucre: **The name is John Abruzzi. A-B-R-U-Z-Z...** ☺₁ I don't care what protocol is. I just want to know if he's okay. Hello? Hello? The hospital won't give out① any information.

T-Bag: **Wonder what happened to that boy.** ☺₂ Maybe them mafia chickens came home to roost② after all.

Michael: We got to put this whole thing on hold③.

Franklin: Oh, easy, fish, we're not putting nothing on hold.

Michael: I don't think you heard me. **Until I get my brother out of that hole, no one's doing a damn thing.** ☺₃

Franklin: For God bless sake④, but the man is gone. You go to the tombs, you don't get out. Not until they strap you up⑤.

Michael: If you think I'm going to leave my brother behind, you have massively underestimated me.

Franklin: Really?

Michael: Really.

T-Bag: **Yeah, but that is not my fight. I'm through** ⑥ that hole, pretty, with or without you. Next time I'm on P.I. ☺₄

译文

苏 克 雷：名字是约翰·阿布鲁兹，A-b-r-u-z-z……我才不管你什么规定。我只想知道他现在怎样。喂？喂？医院不肯透露任何信息。

帝 博 格：真想知道那家伙怎么了，或许黑手党的鹰犬都会有这样的报应。

迈 克 尔：我们必须暂停整个计划。

富兰克林：冷静点儿，雏儿，我们不能把计划暂停。

迈 克 尔：我想你没听清我说的话，在救我哥哥出去之前，谁也不许轻举妄动。

富兰克林：我很抱歉，但你哥哥已经回不来了。进了那个禁闭室，你就别想出来了，直到你被绑上电椅。

迈 克 尔：如果你以为我会丢下我哥哥，那你就大大低估我了。

富兰克林：真的吗？

迈 克 尔：真的。

帝 博 格：是的，但这可不关我的事。有没有你我都能漂亮地从牢房里溜出去，就在下次我自由活动时。

知识点拨

1. give out 表示"分发，公布；停止运行，停止起作用"。在片中表示"透露（消息）"。例：He wouldn't give out any information. 他不愿透露任何消息。

2. chickens come home to roost 表面意思是"鸡回家睡觉"，在这里表示"恶有恶报"。由于小鸡们白天在院子里刨食，晚上回到鸡舍里睡觉，这中间隔了一段时间。而如果一个人做了不好的事，也许他不会马上得到报应，但是总有一天他会得到应有的惩罚。

3. put something on hold 是指"暂停一件事情的进行"。例：She will put her star career on hold to become France's first lady. 她将暂停自己的明星事业，努力当好法国第一夫人。

4. for God's sake 表示"看在上帝的份上"=for goodness' sake=for heaven's sake。

5. strap sb. up 表示"给某人扣上皮带"。例：As darkness comes you strap up your basket and drive happily home. 当黄昏降临时，你系好篮子，快乐地驾车回家。

6. be through 表示"结束；友谊破裂"，在片中表示"穿过"。例：If we wanted to isolate our environments, the only way to do this would be through logical partitioning. 如果我们以前希望对环境进行隔离，则唯一的办法就是通过逻辑分区进行。

 词汇加油站

protocol ['prəʊtəkɔ:l] *n.* （数据传递的）协议
roost [ru:st] *vi.* 栖息
tomb [tu:m] *n.* 坟墓
massively ['mæsɪvli] *adv.* 大而重

mafia ['mɑ:fɪə] *n.* 黑手党
bless [bles] *vt.* 保佑
strap [stræp] *v.* 用皮带抽打；约束
underestimate [ˌʌndər'estɪmeɪt] *vt.* 低估

Scene 7 林肯死刑暂缓

时间： 第 13 集 00:22:18—00:23:43
地点： 监狱里
人物： 迈克尔，贝里克，帝博格，富兰克林
事件： 迈克尔故意将水管砸坏，为越狱争取时间。

精彩亮点

约翰被送走后，迈克尔等人的越狱计划仍在有条不紊地实施着。帝博格始终对迈克尔的计划感到怀疑，于是称他为"空头支票先生"，意在表明迈克尔只口头承诺但未见实效。**1**

面对帝博格的咄咄逼问，迈克尔告诉他等到九点。但聪明的帝博格马上就想到他们的工作时间是到晚上 5 点结束，怎么可能让他们等到九点呢？那么，迈克尔有什么计划呢？**2**

迈克尔未与众人商量就拿锤子砸坏了水管，惹得黑人富兰克林大惊失色。但事实上，迈克尔早有计划，他要砸坏水管为越狱争取更多的时间。**3**

迈克尔在此故意向狱警透露石膏遇水会发霉。狱警则不能容忍这类事的发生，于是勒令迈克尔等人留下来把这里漏的水清理干净。这就为迈克尔等人争取了足够多的时间。**4**

T-Bag: So, Mr. Pied piper①, what's the play? ☺1

Michael: We do what we always do: Pretend to be working, being model citizens②…until the time comes.

T-Bag: And that would be…?

Michael: Nine o'clock. ☺2

T-Bag: Seem to be forgetting the fact that P.I. shuts down③ at 5:00, pretty.

Michael: Then we have to make sure it doesn't, don't we? Hammer.

Franklin: Whoa④, whoa! What the hell are you doing, man? ☺3

Bellick: What the hell happened here?

Michael: Messed up⑤, hit a pipe. Should have killed the water before we started.

Bellick: Should have, huh?

Michael: It's not that big a deal. We can fix it in the morning. I don't think mold should be a problem before then. ☺4

Bellick: Mold?

Franklin: Scofield, shut up⑥.

Bellick: No, you shut up. What are you talking about?

Michael: You get drywall and insulation soaked like this, you run the risk of stachybotrys mold.

译文

帝 博 格：那么，空头支票先生有什么计划呢？

迈 克 尔：我们像平常一样：假装工作，装良好市民……直到那一刻到来。

帝 博 格：那是几点呢？

迈 克 尔：9点。

帝 博 格：帅哥，你忘了工作时间就到5点啊。

迈 克 尔：那么我们就要确保它不能在5点结束，不是吗？给我锤子。

富兰克林：喔，喔！你到底在做什么啊？

贝 里 克：这里发生什么了？

迈 克 尔：搞砸了，砸破管子了，应该在我们开始之前就关水阀的。

贝 里 克：应该，啊？

迈 克 尔：没多大关系。我们明天早上就能修好，不过我想那时石膏就该发霉了。

贝 里 克：发霉？

富兰克林：斯科菲尔德，你闭嘴。

贝 里 克：不，你闭嘴。你在说什么？

迈 克 尔：干墙和绝缘线像这样浸在水里的话，葡萄状穗霉有可能发生霉变。

知识点拨

1. Pied piper 通常用来指代"那些善开空头支票的领导者"。它用幽默而有力的方法暗示如果你盲目地跟随、支持这样的政治人物，就会和传说中的老鼠一样，结果只是自寻死路。

2. model citizen 指的是"模范公民，模范市民"。例：Once Carl kicked the drug habit, he became a model citizen. 卡尔自从戒毒之后，他便成了一个模范公民。

3. shut down 表示"停工，完全关闭，停下"。例：Smaller contractors had been forced to shut down. 规模较小的承包商已被迫歇业。

4. whoa 通常表示"停下，住手"，用作对某事很惊讶的情况下要求停止。而 wow 通常表示一种惊叹，或是欢喜。

5. mess up 表示"搞乱，弄乱，弄糟，搅乱"。例：When politicians mess things up, it is the people who pay the price. 政客们把事情搞砸的时候，埋单的是老百姓。

6. shut up 意为"闭嘴"，正式场合少用，一般多为生气时使用，作为一名绅士，最好听完别人所说的话。

词汇加油站

piper ['paɪpər] *n.* 吹笛人

model ['mɑ:dl] *n.* 典型

mold [mould] *n.* 霉

soak [souk] *vt.* 浸泡

pretend [prɪ'tend] *vt.* 假装

hammer ['hæmər] *n.* 铁锤

insulation [ˌɪnsə'leɪʃn] *n.* 绝缘

时间： 第 14 集 00:06:41—00:09:49

地点： 监狱里

人物： 贝里克，苏克雷，帝博格，迈克尔，韦斯特莫兰德，狱警

事件： 韦斯特莫兰德卡在地道有惊无险。

精彩亮点

1 看到门外的石膏板，贝里克不禁起了疑心：弄了一整个晚上，竟然还没有弄好？事实上，迈克尔等人一整晚都在挖地道，根本没有清理漏水。

2 上了年纪的韦斯特莫兰德在看地道时不慎被卡住了，恰巧这时贝里克进来了，这可让众人捏了一把汗，如果此时让韦斯特莫兰德上来，地道的秘密定会让贝里克得知，整个越狱计划就全部泡汤了，于是众人先将门关上。

3 面对贝里克的质问，反应敏捷的帝博格称是风扇总把门吹开，他们才不得不把它关上。于是，大家你一言我一语终于把谎圆过去了。

4 贝里克也狡猾得很，他发现好像屋里少了一个人，话音未落，韦斯特莫兰德刚好从地道爬上来，好在有惊无险。

Bellick: Wuss. Anybody else? <u>Suit yourselves</u>①. Hey, none of the Sheetrock in front of the break room's been touched.

Prison guard: Ah, the P.I. 's letting it dry out.

Bellick: Still? ☺₁

Sucre: Westmoreland!

Westmoreland: I'm caught on something. ☺₂

Sucre: Come on! Come on! Come on! Come on!

Michael: Stay there. Stay <u>down there</u>②.

Bellick: Why was this door locked?

T-Bag: **Wasn't locked, boss. The fan kept pushing it open, so we just had to wedge it closed.** ☺₃

Bellick: You've been in here all night not doing a damn thing.

Sucre: Room is still wet, boss. Nothing we could do. It's not like we were having a picnic.

Bellick: <u>Bunch of</u>③ shiftless, no good convicts. You got something to say, Scofield? <u>Wrap it up</u>④. And all four of you, get your asses back to the block. Get these nitwits back to the <u>cell block</u>⑤. **You seem to be one light.** ☺₄

Westmoreland: Right here, boss.

Franklin: Oh, no. <u>No way</u>⑥! I should be halfway to seeing my family right now!

译文

贝　里　克：胆小鬼，还有别人吗？随便你们。喂，石膏板都还在外面。

狱　　警：我让监狱工厂的人弄干的。

贝　里　克：还在弄？

苏　克　雷：韦斯特莫兰德？

韦斯特莫兰德：我被卡住了。

苏　克　雷：快点儿，快点儿，快点儿！

迈　克　尔：待在那里，再等一会儿。

贝　里　克：为什么门上锁了？

帝　博　格：没锁啊，老大。风扇总是把门吹开，我们只好把它关上了。

贝　里　克：你们待在这儿一晚上什么都没做。

苏　克　雷：屋子还是湿的，老大，我们什么也做不了。我们也没有在这儿野餐。

贝　里　克：偷懒是不行的，没用的犯人们。你好像有话要说，斯科菲尔德？收拾一下，你们四个再滚回牢里。把他们押回牢去，看样子，你们好像少了一人。

韦斯特莫兰德：在这呢，老大。

富　兰　克　林：哦，不！不！我现在应该在见家人的路上了！

知识点拨

1. suit oneself 表示"随你的便吧；想怎样就怎样吧"。例：A: I don't really feel like going out after all. B: Suit yourself. A：我还是不太想出去。B：随你的便吧。

2. down there 表示"在那儿，那里"。例：I don't mind waiting down there for an hour, but I'm not going to stay in this damned hotel shaking with nerves for another minute. 我宁愿在那里等一个小时，也不愿在这个鬼饭店里惶惶不安地再多等一分钟。

3. 准确来讲，这里应该是 a bunch of，表示"一群，一束，一堆"。例：We don't want to look like a bunch of cowboys. 我们不想看上去像一帮奸商。

4. wrap sth. up 可以表示"把某物包起来"，在片中表示"收拾"。例：Okay, everybody! Let's wrap it up and go home. 好的，各位，让我们收工回家吧。

5. cell block 直译为"单元块"，在片中指"监狱牢房"。例：A cell block reserved for convicts awaiting execution. 特别为等待处决的死刑犯设置的牢房。

6. no way 表示"没门儿，不可能"。例：Mike, no way am I playing cards with you for money. 迈克，我是决不会和你玩牌赌钱的。

 词汇加油站

wuss [wʊs] *n.* 无用的人；懦夫

sheetrock [ʃiːtrɑːk] *n.*（建筑用）石膏灰胶纸夹板

wedge [wedʒ] *vt.* 挤进

shiftless [ˈʃɪftləs] *adj.* 没出息的

suit [sjuːt] *vt.* 适合于（某人）

lock [lɑːk] *vt.* 锁上

picnic [ˈpɪknɪk] *n.* 野餐郊游

convict [ˈkɑːnvɪkt] *n.* 罪犯

时间： 第 14 集 00:15:27—00:16:13
地点： 法院门前
人物： 尼克，莱尔，维罗妮卡
事件： 尼克、维罗妮卡请求与法官面谈。

片段三

精彩亮点

正当迈克尔等人在监狱为越狱进行各种准备之际，维罗妮卡和尼克也在搜寻证据，试图通过法律手段帮林肯洗刷冤屈。尼克找到了老同学莱尔，这个莱尔到底是什么来头呢？

1

莱尔是法官的文书，尼克希望他能帮助他们将林肯谋杀案加入诉讼时间表中。但显然，莱尔并不愿意帮这个忙，他一方面为法官着想，一方面也怕引火上身。

2

维罗妮卡提出开棺验尸。对于普通民众而言，为了案情需要，开棺验尸或许并不难批准下来，但对于像副总统弟弟这样显赫的人物是绝不可能的。

3

尼克见莱尔无意帮助他们，决定动之以情，诉说俩人昔日的交情，但莱尔只是冷漠地告诉他，法官今天下午没空。最终，在维罗妮卡和尼克的坚持下，莱尔答应给他们 15 分钟的时间与法官面谈。

4

Nike: **Look, if Terrence Steadman is still alive, Lyle, then it can't be Terrence Steadman buried in the ground.**☺₁

Lyle: Yeah, but a secret informant claims that Steadman is still alive? I don't know, Nick, it all sounds pretty farfetched.

Nike: You're his clerk, just get us on the docket①.

Lyle: **Nick, you're asking him to commit political suicide② by granting a stay of execution③ to Illinois' most notorious death row inmate.**☺₂

Veronica: Officially, all we're asking is for an exhumation order. If he grants it, he can order a stay until the tests are come in④.

Lyle: An exhumation order? **Well that's better digging up the vice president's brother.**☺₃ No way.

Nike: **Lyle, Lyle, look, we took Intro to Civ Pro⑤ together, remember? We studied for the Bar, day and night⑥, in that crappy little apartment of yours, talking about how we're going to make a difference.**☺₄

Lyle: Nick, you filed an eleventh hour motion, and Judge Kessler's docket is full this afternoon…

Nike: Come on, Lyle, everyone knows you run that courtroom. You can't adjust things around a bit?

译文

尼　克： 听着莱尔，如果特伦斯·斯蒂德曼还活着，那他不可能埋在地里。所以，埋在地里的肯定不是他。

莱　尔： 是的，但是一个告密者声称斯蒂德曼还活着？我不知道，尼克，这听起来很不可靠。

尼　克： 你是法官的文书，给我们加进诉讼事件表中就好。

莱　尔： 尼克，你这是要让他断送政治前途，干涉对伊利诺伊州最臭名昭著的囚犯执行死刑。

维罗妮卡： 我们只要求获得挖坟开棺许可。如果他批准了，就可以拖延执行死刑，直到出了验尸结果。

莱　尔： 开棺许可？这下更好，干脆去挖副总统弟弟的坟。没门。

尼　克： 莱尔，莱尔，你看我们过去关系不错，你还记得吗？我们为了考取律师执照，藏身于你的一幢小破公寓里，每日每夜疯狂看书，还说要改变世界。

莱　尔： 尼克，你的动议 11 小时内有效，凯斯勒法官今天下午没空……

尼　克： 得了，莱尔，我知道你操控着法庭。你就不能稍微调整一下？

知识点拨

1. on the docket 表示"在审理中"。The Court has about 800 appeals on its docket. 法庭的备审案件约有 800 宗。

2. commit suicide 指"自杀，自寻了断"。例：There are unconfirmed reports that he tried to commit suicide. 有未经证实的报道说他曾企图自杀。

3. a stay of execution 表示"延期执行"。例：The tobacco companies have demanded a stay of execution before. 烟草公司已经要求在执行前暂时停止该法。

4. come in 意思很多，现归纳如下：1）进入；到达；开始；2）上市；到成熟季节；3）（比赛）获得……名；4）流行；时髦；时兴起来；5）上台；执政；6）（潮水）升涨；7）起作用；做一份工作；8）收入；9）存在；出现。片中取第九个意思。

5. Intro to Civ Pro=Introduction to Civil Procedure 指"民事诉讼的介绍"（书名）。

6. day and night 表示"日日夜夜，白天黑夜，夜以继日地"。例：Dozens of doctors and nurses have been working day and night for weeks. 很多医生和护士已经夜以继日地工作数周了。

词汇加油站

informant [ɪnˈfɔːrmənt] *n.* 告密者

clerk [klɑːrk] *n.* 职员

suicide [ˈsuːɪsaɪd] *n.* 自杀

exhumation [ˌekshjuːˈmeɪʃn] *n.* 掘尸

farfetched [ˈfɑːˈfetʃt] *adj.* 牵强的

docket [ˈdɑːkɪt] *n.* （待判决的）诉讼事件表

notorious [nouˈtɔːriəs] *adj.* 臭名昭著的

crappy [ˈkræpi] *adj.* 没价值的

时间： 第 15 集 00:06:16—00:07:16

地点： 副总统办公室

人物： 卡罗琳，凯勒曼，布林克尔

事件： 林肯未被处决惹卡罗琳不满。

精彩亮点

1 就在千钧一发之际，由于发现了新的证据，林肯的死刑被延期了。但是谁向法官提供的证据呢？是维罗妮卡和尼克他们吗？

2 副总统卡罗琳当即想出是凯勒曼的那个胖子朋友哈尔泄露了信息，但凯勒曼一口否定不是他干的。的确，如果是他干的，维罗妮卡在法庭辩论时肯定会提出来。那么，又会是谁提供的证据呢？

3 副总统的手下起了内讧。双方，即凯勒曼和公司代表布林克尔相互推诿责任。事实上，林肯说，在观刑室里看见了离家出走近 30 年的父亲。而提供证据的也正是自己的父亲，两兄弟的父亲到底有什么来头？

4 布林克尔一直以傲慢的姿态与副总统谈话，在她离开时，副总统警告她说下次要站着和自己说话。布林克尔当然看不惯副总统的姿态，却也无可奈何。

Caroline: Why is he still alive[①]? ☺1

Kellerman: It appears that some information was anonymously slipped to the judge.

Caroline: Anonymously? **It was your fat little friend, Hale.** ☺2 If you had taken care of[②] him sooner.

Kellerman: It wasn't Hale.

Brinker: How do you know that?

Kellerman: If Hale had given[③] veronica Donovan anything that could have gotten a stay of execution, I think she would have brought it up[④] when she made her argument in court. It didn't come from him.

Brinker: Well, who else on your end knows?

Kellerman: Who else on your end knows? Why all the finger pointing at us? Are you sure that the leak didn't come from your end? From the company? ☺3

Caroline: We are all on the same team[⑤], remember?

Brinker: Absolutely.

Caroline: Just find the leak…and plug it.

Kellerman: Thank you, ma'am.

Caroline: One more thing[⑥], the next time you're in my office, I expect you to stand when you're addressing me. ☺4

Brinker: Absolutely.

译文

卡 罗 琳：为什么他还活着?

凯 勒 曼：看起来是有人匿名向法官提供了信息。

卡 罗 琳：匿名? 我想是你那位胖伙伴哈尔干的吧，要是你早点儿解决了他。

凯 勒 曼：不是哈尔。

布林克尔：你怎么知道?

凯 勒 曼：如果哈尔给维罗妮卡·多诺万提供了可以延期执行死刑的信息，维罗妮卡在法庭辩论时肯定会提出来的。所以，不是他提供的。

布林克尔：那么，你这边还有谁知道?

凯 勒 曼：你那边又还有谁知道? 为什么把责任都推到我们身上? 你确定你们公司没有泄露信息吗?

卡 罗 琳：还记得吗? 我们都是同一条船上的。

布林克尔：当然。

卡 罗 琳：找出是谁泄的密……然后堵住他的嘴!

凯 勒 曼：谢谢您，夫人。

卡 罗 琳：还有一件事，下次再来我办公室时，我希望你站着和我说话。

布林克尔：当然。

知识点拨

1. alive 是表语形容词，做"活着的，在世的"解，既可以修饰人也可以修饰物。注意其与 living，lively 的区别。living 意为"活着的"，主要用作定语。live 读作 [laɪv]，意为"活着的"，一般不用来修饰人。lively 意为"生动的，活泼的"，可以用来修饰人或物。

2. take care of 表示"照顾；杀掉，对付；抵消"。例：They leave it to the system to try and take care of the problem. 他们让系统去设法解决这个问题。

3. 与过去事实相反的虚拟语气常用结构为：从句用"had+ 过去分词"，主句用"would / should / could / might+have done"。

4. bring up 表示"提出；养育；谈到；呕出"。片中表示"提出"。

5. on the same team 在片中表示"处于统一战线上"。例：By empathizing with your child's desire to wear the same clothes, you're letting her know that you're on the same team. 理解孩子想穿同样衣服的想法，让孩子知道你也是这样。

6. one more thing 表示"还有一件事"。例：Now there's only one more thing that we have to do. 现在我们只剩下一件事了。

词汇加油站

anonymously [ə'nɑːnɪməsli] *adv.* 匿名地

argument ['ɑːrgjumənt] *n.* 论据

leak [liːk] *n.* 泄漏；泄露

plug [plʌg] *vt.* 以（塞子）塞住

slip [slɪp] *vt.* 松开，悄悄塞

finger ['fɪŋgər] *n.* 手指

absolutely ['æbsəluːtli] *adv.* 绝对地

address [ə'dres] *v.* 向……说话

Scene 8 林肯谋杀案水落石出

时间： 第 15 集 00:17:24—00:19:00
地点： 监狱里
人物： 韦斯特莫兰德，贝里克，富兰克林，苏克雷，迈克尔
事件： 墙上破了一个大洞，众人合力成功瞒过贝里克。

 精彩亮点

1
　　狱警贝里克又来巡视了，但意想不到的是，富兰克林一不小心踩塌了墙壁，墙壁破了一个大洞，露出了水泥。眼看贝里克就来了，狱友们该怎么瞒过去呢？

2
　　富兰克林不得不用一只脚倚在墙上以防水泥掉下，但贝里克命令他去干活，富兰克林只得称自己脚有点儿麻，此时，韦斯特莫兰德赶紧过来救场，他成心呵斥富兰克林，并很自然地跟他换了位置。

3
　　富兰克林明白了韦斯特莫兰德的用意，跟他配合演了一出好戏。他们的表演能否成功骗过狡猾的贝里克呢？

4
　　贝里克果然被蒙骗过去了。几个人总算有惊无险。但现在的问题是，他们又该如何填补这个大洞呢？

Michael: Let's look busy.
Franklin: **What the hell?** ☺₁
Sucre: Damn, what did you do?
Franklin: It's the cement we dug up.
Bellick: My God, you cons① are slower than a Spelling Bee② full of stutterers. You all think you can work this job slowly, play grab ass in here? Drag it out③ for months? Get to work.
Westmoreland: You got it④, boss.
Bellick: How about it, eight ball⑤? Get to work.
Franklin: Oh, you know, boss, my leg just fell asleep⑥.
Bellick: You disobeying me, convict?
Westmoreland: **The man said get to work.** ☺₂
Franklin: **What the hell is your problem, old head?!** ☺₃
Westmoreland: My problem is young con punks who don't know how things work around here. Construction is a sweet gig. You want to clean toilets, be my guest⑦. Otherwise, grab a hammer.
Bellick: **All right. Still got some piss and vinegar in those old veins, Charles? I like it.** ☺₄
Westmoreland: Close one, huh? Oh, man. What we gonna do with this?

译文

迈 克 尔：大家假装忙起来。

富 兰 克 林：怎么了？

苏 克 雷：糟了！你都做了什么？

富 兰 克 林：是我们挖出来的水泥。

贝 里 克：我的天啊，你们这帮囚犯比结巴拼写单词还慢。你们以为能偷懒，磨磨蹭蹭，在这里歇着？拖上几个月？快去干活！

韦斯特莫兰德：知道了，老大。

贝 里 克：说你呢！八号球，干活去！

富 兰 克 林：老大，你知道，我的腿有点儿麻。

贝 里 克：你敢违抗我的命令吗？

韦斯特莫兰德：他说了干活！

富 兰 克 林：老头，你有毛病啊？

韦斯特莫兰德：我就是对你们这些小子有意见！太不懂得这里的规矩了！干工程是轻松的活，你要扫厕所的话，随便，要不就拿锤子干活。

贝 里 克：好了，查尔斯，你的威风不减当年嘛！我喜欢你这点！

韦斯特莫兰德：真险啊，是不是？哦，天呐，接下来怎么办？

词汇加油站

cement [sɪˈment] *n.* 水泥

stutterer [ˈstʌtərər] *n.* 口吃（的人）

drag [dræg] *vt.* 拖拽

punk [pʌŋk] *n.* 年轻无知的人

知识点拨

1. con 是拉丁语 contra 的简写，指 in opposition to, against（"反对"）；其反义词 pro 是指 in favor of（"赞成"）的意思。

2. Spelling Bee 英语拼写大赛源于美国，始于 1925 年。是全球享有盛誉的年度性英文拼字竞赛。随着大赛风靡全美，其独特魅力也随之扩散至更多的国家和地区，数以百万计的青少年逐渐加入到 Speller 的行列中。

3. drag sth. out 表示"把某物拖[拉]出，（使）拖延"。例：Let's get it over as soon as possible, rather than drag it out. 我们尽快把它完成吧，不要再拖了。

4. You got it! 口语中这种回答很常见，但含义并不一样。在片中表示"放心吧"或"没问题"。它是 "You've got it." 的简写。

5. eight ball 源自一种叫作凯利的台球（Kelly Pool），彩色台球按 1 到 15 的数字编号，而八号球（eight ball）是黑色的。

6. fall asleep 表示"睡着，入睡"。片中字面意思是"我的腿睡着了"，实际上是指"我的腿麻了"。例：In case I fall asleep, please wake me up. 如果我睡着了，请叫醒我。

7. be my guest 是口语，意思是"请便"，用于礼貌地同意别人的请求。

spelling [ˈspelɪŋ] *n.* 拼写

grab [græb] *n.* 不法所得

disobey [ˌdɪsəˈbeɪ] *vt.* 不服从

gig [gɪg] *n.* 工作

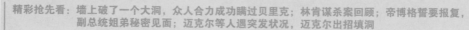
时间： 第16集 00:11:12—00:12:02

地点： 女副总统办公室，迈克尔公司

片段二

人物： 卡罗琳，布林克尔，维罗妮卡，迈克尔，助理

事件： 林肯谋杀案回顾。

精彩亮点

1
这里回溯到故事的开端，副总统和布林克尔正商量着在发布会上的说辞，她必须得到民众的支持以判处林肯死刑。

2
此时的维罗妮卡和迈克尔已得知林肯因谋杀罪而被警方抓获。在林肯被捕前，曾给迈克尔打过一通电话，他因欠下9万美元的债务无力偿还，而被迫成为雇佣杀手。在动手前他致电迈克尔想向他讨个主意，但对哥哥失望的迈克尔却挂断了电话。

3
迈克尔对哥哥怀有成见，他认为哥哥自甘堕落，也相信哥哥可能会为了钱而杀了副总统的弟弟。

4
看到迈克尔对哥哥如此冷淡，维罗妮卡无奈下不得不告诉迈克尔他分到的赡养费是林肯借来的，但林肯却不让维罗妮卡告诉迈克尔。哥哥对自己的恩情让迈克尔对林肯有了重新认识。

Brinker: Here… here is where we want the turn to anger. ☺₁

Caroline: Trust me, that will not be a problem.

Brinker: Now remember to stress his record as a repeat offender. We need the public behind us ① if we want the death penalty ②.

Caroline: And where are we with Governor Tancredi?

Brinker: He has aspirations. He won't be a problem.

Assistant: Uh, 30 seconds, Madam ③ Vice President.

Veronica: The papers have already crucified him. The police say they got a phone call right after ④ the murder, from someone claiming they saw Lincoln running from the garage. ☺₂

Michael: He was into someone ⑤ for 90 grand. What do you need that kind of money for? Drugs? Bribes? Forget about what you want to be true. Let's look at this objectively. ☺₃

Veronica: Maybe you should, too.

Michael: I am.

Veronica: All right, you know what? I promised I would not say anything, but I'm getting tired of ⑥ you talking about him like he's some guy from the neighborhood that you used to know. ☺₄ He's your brother.

60

译文

布林克尔： 这里……这里，我们要表现出愤怒。

卡罗琳： 相信我，这不成问题。

布林克尔： 现在，记住强调他的犯罪记录，他是个惯犯。如果要判他死刑，我们需要公众的支持。

卡罗琳： 谭克雷迪州长对此表现出了什么态度？

布林克尔： 他有野心，不会成为我们的阻碍。

助理： 还有 30 秒，副总统阁下。

维罗妮卡： 媒体已经要求重判林肯，警方说他们在案发后就接到了报警电话，有人说看见林肯从停车场跑了出来。

迈克尔： 他欠别人 9 万块。你需要这么多钱干什么？吸毒？贿赂？把你的期望放在一边，让我们客观点儿看问题。

维罗妮卡： 或许你也应该客观点儿。

迈克尔： 我就是客观地看问题的。

维罗妮卡： 好吧，你知道吗？我保证过什么也不会说，但我实在厌烦你这么说他，就好像他是你以前在社区里认识的某个邻居，但他可是你的哥哥。

知识点拨

1. behind sb.（sth.）指"对某人或某事表示支持或赞同"。例：I also know I'm not in anything alone, I have friends and family behind me. 我也知道我并不是孤单一人，我有朋友与家人支持着我。

2. death penalty 表示"死刑"。例：If convicted for murder, both youngsters could face the death penalty. 如果谋杀罪名成立，这两个年轻人都可能会被判处死刑。

3. madam 主要用作呼语，用于对妇女（已婚或未婚）的尊称，通常用于不相识者，尤其是店主对顾客的称呼），相当于称呼男性的 sir，可译为"夫人，太太，女士，小姐"等。而 madame 主要用于讲法语或非英语民族的已婚妇女姓名前表尊称，有时也用于称呼年长的未婚妇女，其用法相当于 Mrs。

4. right after 表示"刚好在……之后"。例：Doctor Paige will be here right after lunch to see her. 佩奇医生一吃完午饭就会来这儿看她。

5. be into something or someone 意为"喜欢某事或某人，对某事或某人极感兴趣"。例：It's a street artist. Everyone's getting really into him now. 这是一个街头艺术家，最近还挺火的。

6. get tired of 表示"对……厌烦了"。例：You never get tired of hearing this story. 这个故事百听不厌。

 词汇加油站

anger [ˈæŋɡər] *n.* 愤怒

penalty [ˈpenəlti] *n.* 刑罚

crucify [ˈkruːsɪfaɪ] *vt.* 折磨

bribe [braɪb] *n.* 贿赂

offender [əˈfendər] *n.* 罪犯

aspiration [ˌæspəˈreɪʃn] *n.* 强烈的愿望

garage [ɡəˈrɑːʒ] *n.* 车库

objectively [əbˈdʒektɪvli] *adv.* 客观地

时间： 第 16 集 00:38:53—00:42:14
地点： 监狱里，林间小屋（特伦斯藏匿地）
人物： 帝博格，苏珊，特伦斯，卡罗琳
事件： 帝博格誓要报复，副总统姐弟秘密见面。

片段三

精彩亮点

苏珊与帝博格狱中见面，帝博格视苏珊为今生遇到的第一个真爱，他认为自己可以抹杀过去的罪恶，过上崭新的生活，但苏珊却把他再次扔回了黑暗中。

1

苏珊起初并不知道帝博格是一个杀死了 6 个学生的残忍的杀人犯，当她知道了真相后，就报了警，帝博格一直怀恨在心。在苏珊看来，无论他是否痛改前非，都无法抹去过去杀人的事实，他应该为他过去所做的一切负责。

2

当帝博格再次被送到监狱时，他的内心是崩溃的，同时，罪恶再一次在他心中复活了。他威胁苏珊，自己有朝一日出去后一定要找她报仇。

3

卡罗琳和她的弟弟见面了，由此证实了林肯是被冤枉的。但特伦斯也没有好过到哪儿去，他被姐姐"软禁"在林间别墅里，过着与世隔绝的生活。

4

T-Bag: You think you're the only one who feels betrayed? I... loved you, Susan. Real love① for the first time in my life.☺₁ And then to have you do me like that, to just throw me out to the dogs, just toss me out② the back door like...

Susan: You're a murderer, Teddy!

T-Bag: That's not...I have sinned in the past, but when I met you, that person, that one that did all those terrible things, he died, and I was reborn. By the grace of your love, I was a...a new man, a better man.

Susan: No. That doesn't just erase the man who killed 6 students in Alabama.☺₂

T-Bag: I guess that's where you're right. Cause when you sent me here, to this place, with these people, it brought that old, dirty bastard right back home③. In fact, there was a candle in the window, just waiting for me to walk up④ them front steps⑤. You know, I'm gonna...I'm gonna get out of here someday. And when I do... Don't think I won't remember what your front steps look like, Susan.☺₃

Caroline: It's almost over. Lincoln will be dead soon, and then things will start getting back to normal⑥. I know that you've been through a lot, but I promise you, the worst is now behind us.

Terence: My dear sister...you have no idea what I've been through.☺₄

Caroline: Good night, Terrence.

译文

帝博格： 你认为自己是唯一被背叛的人吗？我爱过你，苏珊。你是我人生第一次真爱，而你对我却……把我扔回了黑暗中，撕裂了我……

苏　珊： 你是个杀人凶手，泰迪！

帝博格： 不是……我在过去有罪，但我遇见你后，那个做尽坏事的人，他死了，我重生了。你的爱令我成为……一个新的人，一个好人。

苏　珊： 不，这并不能抹掉那个在阿拉巴马州杀死6名学生的人。

帝博格： 我想你是对的，因为当你把我送进这个地方，和这些人待在一起，让我的罪恶完全复活了。事实上，透过窗户，我看见了一盏蜡烛，等待我走进你家的前门。你知道，我总有一天会出去的。当那天到来……别以为我不记得你家前门的样子，苏珊。

卡罗琳： 就要结束了。林肯很快就死了，这样一来，一切都会恢复正常。我知道你受了很多苦，但我向你保证，最糟的已经过去。

特伦斯： 亲爱的姐姐……你根本不知道我经受了什么。

卡罗琳： 晚安，特伦斯。

 词汇加油站

betray [bɪˈtreɪ] *vt.* 背叛
sin [sɪn] *vt.* 犯罪
grace [greɪs] *n.* 恩泽
bastard [ˈbæstərd] *n.* 态度傲慢且令人讨厌的人

toss [tɑːs] *vt.* （轻轻或漫不经心地）扔
reborn [ˌriːˈbɔːrn] *adj.* 再生的

step [step] *n.* 步；台阶

 知识点拨

1. real love 表示"真实的爱，真爱"。例：When you have real love in your life you have everything. 当你拥有了人生中的真爱，你便拥有了一切。

2. toss out 表示"丢弃，扔掉"。例：You should toss out all those old magazines. 你应该把那些旧杂志都处理掉。

3. back home 表示"回家；真爱守候"。例：Smith changed his mind and moved back home. 史密斯改变了主意，搬回家了。

4. walk up 表示"向上走，沿……走去"。例：The elevator broke down and we had to walk up the tenth floor. 电梯坏了，我们只好走到十楼。

5. front step 表示"前门台阶"。例：I stubbed my toe on your front step; it was very painful. 我一脚踢到你前门的台阶上，痛得要命。

6. get back to normal 指"恢复正常"。例：People want to fix these problems and get back to normal, not take more crisis measures. 人们想要解决这些问题，回到正常状态，而不是采取更多危机措施。

时间： 第17集 00:04:08—00:04:58

地点： 监狱里

人物： 路易斯，迈克尔，韦斯特莫兰德，富兰克林，帝博格

事件： 迈克尔等人遇突发状况，迈克尔出招填洞。

片段四

精彩亮点

1. 看守通知他们这里的活儿要结束了，需要他们马上离开这里。但想到迈克尔等人在这里挖的地道留下了一个大洞极易被发现，众人不禁紧张起来。

2. 虽然富兰克林表示要把地毯弄一下，但监狱看守表示他们会请专业人员过来，而且就在明天，时间紧迫，迈克尔等人有没有什么好办法呢？

3. 帝博格道出了众人心中的忧虑：等专业人员进到这个房间，只要掀开地毯就能看到他们挖的大洞，到时候一切努力都将付之东流。

4. 果然是迈克尔，遇事从容淡定，建筑师出身的他很快就想出了对策：用一块胶合板和几英寸厚的快速定型混凝土先把这个洞填上。

Louis: Time to wrap it up. We're going to have you start① exterminating.

Westmoreland: We're not done in here.

Louis: Well, you look done to me.

Franklin: Nah, co②, we still got the carpet to do, man.☺1

Louis: No, Bellick is going to bring professionals in to do that. Wants the job done right.

Westmoreland: When is that going to happen?

Louis: Tomorrow.☺2

T-Bag: We got a real problem on our hands③, don't we?☺3 Rug monkeys gonna come in here, tear up④ that carpet and that hole's gonna be smiling up at them.

Michael: We'll have to fill it in⑤.

Franklin: We just dug that bitch.

Michael: All we need is a piece of plywood and a couple inches of that fast-setting concrete on top of it.☺4 The carpet guys will never know there's anything beneath it. And the night we break out, we'll just smash through with a sledgehammer. Let's get on⑥ it. We've only got a couple hours to get this thing done.

64

译文

路　易　斯：准备收工吧！你们要开始进行清理工作了。

韦斯特莫兰德：可我们这儿的活儿还没干完呢！

路　易　斯：在我看来已经干完了。

富兰克林：那个，狱警，我们还得把地毯弄一下。

路　易　斯：不，贝利克正准备叫专业人员过来，他想把工作做得更好。

韦斯特莫兰德：什么时候？

路　易　斯：明天。

帝　博　格：我们有麻烦了，是不是？那帮家伙一来，掀开地毯，这个洞就没地方藏了。

迈　克　尔：我们必须把它填上。

富兰克林：可我们刚把这鬼东西挖开！

迈　克　尔：我们只需要一块胶合板，在上面再弄几英寸厚的快速定型混凝土。那些弄地毯的家伙永远不会知道下面有什么东西，到晚上我们只需要个锤子就能把它敲开。我们开始干吧，只剩几小时了。

知识点拨

1. have sb. do sth. 是指"让某人做某事"，强调一次性的动作。而 have sb. doing sth. 是指"让某人一直做某事"，强调动作的持续性、连续性或者动作的反复性。

2. co=correctional officer 表示"监狱看守"。

3. get sth. on one's hands 表示"有……需要处理"。例：I got something urgent on my hands. Will you help me with these documents? 我有些急事要处理，你能帮我整理一下这些文件吗？

4. tear up 表示"撕毁，撕掉，挖开（地面等）"。例：Dozens of miles of railway track have been torn up. 好几十英里的铁轨被毁坏了。

5. fill in 表示"填补；填（写）；代替；淤塞"。片中表示"填补"。例：He helped us to fill in a big gap in our knowledge. 他帮我们填补知识上的空白。

6. get on 表示"上车；进行；变老；对付"。片中表示"进行"。例：I'd better leave you to get on with it, then. 那我还是让你一个人接着干吧。

词汇加油站

wrap [ræp] *vt.* 包
carpet ['kɑ:rpɪt] *n.* 地毯
fast-setting [fæst 'setɪŋ] *n.* 快速固化
sledgehammer ['sledʒhæmər] *n.* 大锤

exterminate [ɪk'stɜ:rmɪneɪt] *vt.* 根除
plywood ['plaɪwʊd] *n.* 胶合板
smash [smæʃ] *vt.* 撞击

Scene 9 越狱小组成员齐聚首

时间： 第 17 集 00:32:52—00:33:54

地点： 副总统办公室，室外马路

片段一

人物： 凯勒曼，卡罗琳，布林克尔

事件： 凯勒曼得知卡罗琳的阴谋，卡罗琳为参议院投票。

精彩亮点

凯勒曼得知当初选择林肯并不是因为他无法为自己辩护，而是因为他的父亲。他的父亲因为厌恶公司的做法就带着他所知道的一切公司内幕逃走了。虽然公司一直在寻找他，但一直无法追查到他的行踪，就用陷害林肯的方式逼他现身，顺便也把副总统弟弟的丑闻遮掩过去。

1

让我们再来看看凯勒曼，他精明能干且心狠手辣，效忠政府，为了心爱的卡罗琳可以不惜一切代价，但得知了卡罗琳的阴谋后，他极其失望。

2

凯勒曼为坚持心中对卡罗琳的爱还是选择相信、追随她。尽管他心里清楚，自己不过是卡罗琳手下的一枚棋子，卡罗琳对自己的承诺也是她为了稳住自己的权宜之计。

3

卡罗琳要为参议院投票，公司代表让她投赞成票，因为这不仅仅是个投票那么简单，如果卡罗琳保持中立，就会赢得中间人士的关键选票当选。

4

Caroline: Make it fast.

Kellerman: I thought we picked Lincoln Burrows off [1] the street because he was some low-life who couldn't defend himself. Now I learn it's all about his father, some old spook the company's trying to settle a score [2] with? ☺1

Caroline: Well, fortunately for us, the company's agenda and our agenda have the same endgame.

Kellerman: Caroline, I've been doing this for 15 years, and it' has never been about anything other than [3] you, your family, and most importantly, this country. I need to know who I'm working for here. ☺2

Caroline: You are working for me.

Kellerman: Promise me that.

Caroline: I promise you, Paul. I got to go [4] now. And to what do I owe [5] this honor? ☺3

Brinker: To the vote on the Senate floor this afternoon.

Caroline: Look, I get it. The vote comes down to [6] me, and I vote no. It'll get done.

Brinker: Well, actually, we are going to need you to vote "yes" on this one.

Caroline: I want to make sure I heard you straight. You want me to vote on the environmentalists' side? ☺4

译文

卡罗琳：快点儿说。

凯勒曼：我以为当初选择林肯·巴罗斯是因为他无法为自己辩护。现在，我才知道原来是为了他老爸公司才做出这样的决定？

卡罗琳：幸运的是，对我们来说公司的决定和我们的决定一致。

凯勒曼：卡罗琳，我干这行15年了，为了你，为了你的家庭，最重要的是为了这个国家。我需要知道自己究竟在为谁卖命。

卡罗琳：你为我一个人卖命。

凯勒曼：向我保证。

卡罗琳：我向你保证，保罗。现在，我要走了，我能有幸为你做什么呢？

布林克尔：为今天下午的参议院投票。

卡罗琳：我明白了。否决权在我手里，我会投否决票的，我会处理好。

布林克尔：事实上，我们需要你投赞成票。

卡罗琳：我没听错吧？你希望我支持那些环保分子？

知识点拨

1. pick off 表示"摘去；逐个毁掉；瞄准射死"。例：Any decent shot with telescopic sights could pick us off at random. 任何借助望远镜瞄准器的像样射手都可以随意把我们逐个干掉。

2. settle a score 表示"清账；报复"。例：Those of you, who have been waiting to settle a score with someone will get an opportunity to do so. 那些等待着与某人合作完成某一项目的人将迎来梦寐以求的机会。

3. other than 表示"除了；不同于；绝不是"。例：There are similar charges if you want to cash a cheque at a branch other than your own. 如果你想在开户行以外的网点兑现支票，也要收取类似的费用。

4. I got to go 其实是 I have got to go 的缩写。口语里 've 发音省略。

5. owe sth. to sb. 表示"欠……（某物），把……归功于某人"。例：We owe to Newton the Principle of Gravitation. 万有引力原理的发现应归功于牛顿。

6. come down to 表示"屈尊做某事；归结起来（为……）"。例：Walter Crowley says the problem comes down to money. 沃尔特·克劳利说，归根结底就是钱的问题。

 词汇加油站

low-life ['loʊ,laɪf] *n.* 卑劣的人

endgame ['endgeɪm] *n.* 最后阶段

senate ['senət] *n.* 参议院

straight [streɪt] *adj.* 直的

environmentalist [ɪn,vaɪrən'mentəlɪst] *n.* 环保人士

spook [spuːk] *n.* 间谍

honor ['ɑːnər] *n.* 光荣

actually ['æktʃuəli] *adv.* 事实上

时间： 第 18 集 00:08:18—00:08:59
地点： 监狱，拘留室

人物： 维罗妮卡，林肯
事件： L.J. 面临指控，林肯欲出狱看儿子。

精彩亮点

1　狱警路易斯告诉林肯有他儿子的电话，且情况紧急。电话那边，儿子 L.J. 丝毫无悔改之意，且誓要与恶势力对抗到底。林肯无奈，只好先让维罗妮卡接电话，了解事情的来龙去脉。

2　林肯得知儿子面临多项指控为此坐立不安。现在，L.J. 的情况并不乐观，且无法假释。

3　维罗妮卡表示 L.J. 唯一的机会就是作为未成年人受审，但现在 L.J. 固执己见，丝毫不将维罗妮卡的话放在心里。林肯想要出狱见儿子。

4　尽管维罗妮卡说林肯不可能见到 L.J.，但林肯坚持要亲自劝说儿子，毕竟 L.J. 还年轻，他面前的路还很长，维罗妮卡答应替他向监狱总局申请。

Veronica: Lincoln?

Lincoln: What are the charges?

Veronica: Attempted murder①. He's also being arraigned for the murder of his mother and his stepfather. ☺1

Lincoln: I guess bail's out of the question②?

Veronica: Exactly.

Lincoln: Anything you can do?

Veronica: Right now, his only shot is if we can get him tried as a minor. But he needs to show some remorse. I need to sell to the court that he was just a scared kid. Where his head's at right now, he won't listen to me.

Lincoln: He'll listen to me. I need to see him. ☺2

Veronica: Lincoln, there's no way③.

Lincoln: He gets tried as an adult, he may as well④ sit in my lap in the chair. ☺3 You got to do⑤ something, Veronica.

Veronica: Okay, I'll petition the D.O.C., but it's a million-to-one shot⑥ they'll let you out to see him. ☺4

Lincoln: All right.

译文

维罗妮卡：林肯？

林　肯：指控是什么？

维罗妮卡：谋杀未遂。他还会因谋杀母亲和
继父的案子被传唤。

林　肯：我猜想不能假释?

维罗妮卡：一点儿没错。

林　肯：你能帮上忙吗？

维罗妮卡：现在，他唯一的机会是看我们能
否让他作为未成年人受审，但他
要表现出一些懊悔。我要让法庭
相信他只是个被吓坏的孩子，但
不论怎样，他现在都不听我的。

林　肯：他听我的话，我要见他。

维罗妮卡：林肯，这不可能。

林　肯：如果他作为成年人受审，就可能
会和我一起坐电椅。你一定要帮
我，维罗妮卡。

维罗妮卡：好，我会找监狱总局，但只有万
分之一的机会允许你出去见他。

林　肯：好。

知识点拨

1. attempted murder 表示"谋杀未遂"。例：
Stewart denies attempted murder and
kidnap. 斯图尔特否认对其谋杀未遂和绑架
的指控。

2. out of the question 表示"不可能"，注意
其与 out of question 的区别，后者表示"毫
无疑问"。例：Is a tax increase still out of the
question? 增加税收仍然是不可能的事吗？

3. no way 表示"没门儿，不可能"。例：
Mike, no way am I playing cards with you for
money. 迈克，我是决不会和你玩牌赌钱的。

4. may as well 主要用于表示提议或劝告，意为
"不妨"。例：I may as well start at once.
我还不妨马上就动身。

5. You got to do sth.=You have to do sth. 意为
"你必须得做些什么"。例：You got to do
something. You can't let bad behavior go
unchecked. 你必须得做些什么，你不能对错
误的行为放任不管。

6. million-to-one 表示"万分之一"，万分之一
的机会即为"不可能"。例：It's a million-
to-one shot he will admit his mistake. 他根
本不可能承认他的错误。

词汇加油站

charge [tʃɑːrdʒ] *n.* 指控
arraign [əˈreɪn] *vt.* 传讯
bail [beɪl] *n.* 保释
scared [skerd] *adj.* 恐惧的

attempted [əˈtemptɪd] *adj.* 未遂的
stepfather [ˈstepfɑːðər] *n.* 继父
remorse [rɪˈmɔːrs] *n.* 悔恨
petition [pəˈtɪʃn] *vt.* （向法庭）申诉

时间： 第 18 集 00:20:10—00:22:10
地点： 精神病区
人物： 迈克尔，海威尔
事件： 海威尔回忆起迈克尔，帮助迈克尔回忆背后地图。

精彩亮点

1
迈克尔为了钻进地洞熟悉新的路线，通过蒸汽室时被烫伤，精神病区部分的管道图被烫毁了。他记得海威尔曾看过他背后的路线图，于是，他决定进入精神病区，找海威尔帮其复原缺损的管道。但由于长期服用药物，海威尔已记不清迈克尔了。通过迈克尔频繁与他接触，海威尔是否能记起什么呢？

2
海威尔回忆起了一切，他清楚地记得自己曾遭到迈克尔陷害，对他顿生恨意。当然，他更关心的还是迈克尔背后的路线图。

3
海威尔将这幅管道图画了下来，以撕毁它做要挟，要求迈克尔告诉他越狱的地点和时间，迈克尔只得一五一十告诉了他。

4
迈克尔此时诚心想跟海威尔合作，虽然海威尔仍对迈克尔曾经陷害过自己耿耿于怀，但摆在面前的获得自由的机会还是使他决定与迈克尔合作。

Michael: Haywire. Haywire…Haywire…Haywire…Did you take your meds① ? Come on. You got something in your teeth again. ☺1

Haywire: You should be careful when you tell people to remember things, Michael. Because I remember everything now. I remember how you set me up② ! **How you smashed your own head…and had me sent back③ here. I also… remember this. The pathway. Your map. Your escape…** ☺2

Michael: Give me that. Don't. Don't.

Haywire: Now, do I tear this up…or do you tell me exactly where and when you're doing this?

Michael: It starts in the basement.

Haywire: Okay.

Michael: This line leads from a hatch in the coal room to④ this pipe system here. And that runs to the infirmary. That's how we'll get out. I just need to get out of psych ward⑤ to set things up. Three days after I'm gone, I'll come back up through the basement and get you out.

Haywire: You're just telling me what I want to hear. ☺3

Michael: No, I'm not. I need you to let me get us out of here. I need you to trust me.

Haywire: If you try to screw me over⑥ again, I'll kill you. ☺4

译文

迈克尔： 海威尔，海威尔……海威尔……海威尔……你把药吃了？好吧，你的牙缝里又有东西了。

海威尔： 当你让别人回忆一些什么的时候你应该小心一点儿，迈克尔。因为我现在想起了一切，我想起来你是怎么陷害我的！你是怎么打破自己的头……让我被送到这里的。我还……记得这个，那条路。你的地图。你逃跑……

迈克尔： 把它给我，不要，不要撕。

海威尔： 现在，我该把它撕了……还是你告诉我你做这些的确切时间和地点？

迈克尔： 是从地下室开始。

海威尔： 好的。

迈克尔： 这条线连接着煤房的舱门口和管道系统，而这里通向医务室，我们就这样出去。我只需要离开精神病区，做点儿准备。我走后的第三天，我会从地下室回来然后带你离开。

海威尔： 你说的正是我想要的。

迈克尔： 不，不是。我需要你帮我们离开这里。我需要你相信我。

海威尔： 如果你试图再骗我一次，我会杀了你。

知识点拨

1. 此处 meds 是 medicines 的缩写，表示"医药"。例：And I got you some meds from the pharmacy. 我从药房拿了些药给你。

2. set sb. up=frame sb. up 表示"陷害某人"。例：Gino, your son stole this money to set me up! 吉诺，你儿子偷了你的钱来陷害我。

3. have sb. done 表示"某人被主语叫去做某事"。例：Lucy has Lily washed clothes. 莉莉被露西叫去洗衣服。

4. from...to 表示"从……到……"。例：I've read the book from beginning to end. 我把这本书从头至尾读完了。

5. psych ward 指"精神病区"。例：Michael sits in the psych ward receiving room. 迈克尔坐在精神病区接待室内。

6. screw someone over 表示"欺负某人"。例：They violate laws, screw over their allies. 他们违反法律，欺负盟友。

词汇加油站

smash [smæʃ] vt. 打碎

tear [ter] v. 撕裂

hatch [hætʃ] n. （船甲板或飞机底部装货物的）舱口

ward [wɔːrd] n. 病房

pathway ['pæθweɪ] n. 道

basement ['beɪsmənt] n. 地下室

screw [skruː] vt. 诈骗

时间： 第 19 集 00:05:38—00:06:59
地点： 监狱里
人物： 迈克尔，约翰
事件： 约翰伤愈归来，迈克尔寻求与约翰合作。

片段四

精彩亮点

正当越狱小组再度聚首时，当初命悬一线的约翰伤愈归来了。众人极度惊讶，罪魁祸首帝博格更是始料未及。

1

约翰一副虔诚信徒的模样跟迈克尔谈话。的确，还有什么比生命还重要呢？实际上，迈克尔十分盼望约翰归来，他的归来到底有何意义呢？

2

约翰这番话略带讽刺，他表示"还以为你们已经走了呢"，事实上，他心里很清楚，没有他提供的飞机，他们怎能顺利越狱呢？

3

迈克尔听出了约翰的话外音，他直接问约翰是否还有越狱的想法。约翰表示"新的灵魂应该得到自由"，就表明他答应迈克尔继续与他合作。

4

Michael: **Hello, John.** ☺1

John: Michael.

Michael: How are you?

John: **Any day** above ground① **is a** blessing. **Thanks be to God**② **. You** mind③ **? Please.** ☺2

Michael: Thank you. Lot of rumors going around④ .

John: Yeah.

Michael: I'm glad you're back.

John: **I'm surprised you're still here. I** **thought you would be gone by now**⑤ **.** ☺3

Michael: Well, we had a few setbacks.

John: Still planning on it?

Michael: That depends. How does the idea of escaping sit with the new you?

John: Oh, the old sinner who was confined to ⑥ these walls, he's dead. The new soul deserves to be free.

Michael: **Well, the old sinner was going to** **have a** jet **ready for us. Is the new soul** **going to be able to pull that off**⑦ **?** ☺4

John: Noah had his ark, did he not? Let's pray.

译文

迈克尔：你好，约翰。

约　翰：迈克尔。

迈克尔：你好吗？

约　翰：活着的每一天都是福分。感谢上帝。你介意吗？请坐。

迈克尔：谢谢你。我听到了很多流言蜚语。

约　翰：是呀。

迈克尔：我很高兴你回来了。

约　翰：我惊讶的是你们怎么还在这里，我还以为你们现在已经走了呢。

迈克尔：嗯，我们遇到了一些麻烦。

约　翰：还在计划？

迈克尔：这要看情况了，全新的你对于越狱有什么看法？

约　翰：噢，那个被高墙关在这里的罪人，他已经死了，新的灵魂应该得到自由。

迈克尔：年长的那位犯人会给我们准备一架飞机，新的灵魂还能做到这一点吗？

约　翰：诺亚有方舟，他没有吗？让我们祈祷吧。

 知识点拨

1. above ground 表示"在世"。例：I have made only one simple rule for my own happiness: Every day above ground is a good day. 我为自己的快乐制定了一个简单的法则：人生在世的每一天都是一个好日子。

2. Thanks be To God 表示"感谢神"。例：Thanks be to God for his word and the answer to all our fears! 感谢神，因为他的话给了我们对所有恐惧的答案！

3. You mind? 是"Do you mind？"省略 do 的口语表达，表示"你介意吗，如果你不介意的话"。例：Do you mind if I ask you one more thing? 您不介意我再问您一个问题吧？

4. go around 表示"参观；转动；走访；相处"。例：There's a nasty sort of rumour going around about it. 关于这件事正有一则恶意的谣言在流传。

5. by now 表示"到如今，到目前为止"。例：By now you will have guessed that I'm back in Ireland. 你现在应该已经猜出我回到了爱尔兰了。

6. be confined to 表示"限于，禁闭"。例：For the time being the call-up will be confined to men under the age of twenty-five. 眼下征召令将限于二十五岁以下的男子。

7. pull off 表示"脱去；胜利完成；捣鬼"。片中表示"胜利完成"。例：The National League for Democracy pulled off a landslide victory. 全国民主联盟获得了压倒性的胜利。

 **词汇加油站**

blessing ['blesɪŋ] *n.* 福分

setback ['setbæk] *n.* 阻碍

confine [kən'faɪn] *vt.* 局限于

jet [dʒet] *n.* 喷气式飞机

rumor ['ruːmər] *n.* 传闻

sinner ['sɪnər] *n.* 罪人

deserve [dɪ'zɜːrv] *vt.* 值得

ark [ɑːrk] *n.* 方舟（《圣经》）

Scene 10 成功越狱

时间： 第 20 集 00:04:16—00:05:12
地点： 监狱草场围栏
片段一
人物： 韦斯特莫兰德，迈克尔，富兰克林，约翰，苏克雷
事件： 贝里克发现地洞，迈克尔决定今晚越狱。

精彩亮点

1 贝里克发现狱警休息室里迈克尔等人挖的地洞惊骇不已，如果他报告这件事，迈克尔等人的越狱计划就会全部泡汤。众人又会采取什么措施呢？

2 贝里克不是一个能轻易被收买的人，于是，韦斯特莫兰德趁贝里克不注意，将其打晕后捆了起来藏在了地道里。

3 现在监狱里的狱警发现贝里克失踪只是时间问题，迈克尔当即决定今晚就越狱。虽然希望将越狱时间提前，但今晚就行动还是令富兰克林心生不安。

4 面对富兰克林的各种担忧，迈克尔用责备的口吻跟他说如果今晚不行动，监狱的狱警发现贝里克失踪，明天一早等待他们的就是加刑。

Westmoreland: I don't know how he found it. He just did. ☺1
Sucre: The hole's just sitting there?
Westmoreland: I covered it the best I could, but it's just a matter of time ① before someone discovers Bellick's missing.
Michael: What do you mean Bellick's missing? ☺2
Sucre: Okay, okay, okay. Fox River ② is a big place.
Franklin: Maybe they won't notice for a while ③. Nothing happens around here without Bellick's say so.
John: Somebody is gonna notice that he's missing. And when they do, they're gonna close this place down ④ until they find him.
Sucre: What are we going to do?
Michael: As soon as it gets dark...we go. ☺3
Franklin: Tonight? Pretty, we ain't ⑤ ready to escape tonight.
Michael: Escape already started. It started the minute Bellick found that hole.
Franklin: It's gonna end the minute they figure out ⑥ that he's missing.
Michael: Then stay! I'll be sure to read the papers in the morning. See how many years you got when they realized which crew was working in that room and dug that hole. ☺4

译文

韦斯特莫兰德：我也不知道他怎么发现的，但他确实找到了。

苏 克 雷：那个洞就在那儿吗？

韦斯特莫兰德：我已经竭尽全力把洞盖住了，不过发现贝里克失踪只是时间问题。

迈 克 尔：贝里克失踪是什么意思？

苏 克 雷：好了，好了，好了。福克斯河监狱是个很大的地方。

富 兰 克 林：或许一时半会儿他们还没注意到。没有贝里克的命令，那些人什么也不会做。

约 翰：有人会发现他失踪了。他们一旦发现就会关闭这里，直到他们找到他。

苏 克 雷：我们要怎么做？

迈 克 尔：天一黑我们就行动。

富 兰 克 林：今晚？帅哥，今晚我们可没准备好。

迈 克 尔：越狱已经开始了，从贝里克发现那个洞时就已经开始了。

富 兰 克 林：他们发现他失踪后并不会怎么样。

迈 克 尔：那你就留下！我一定会看早报，看看你们被发现在那个房间工作过、挖过洞后，要再判多少年。

知识点拨

1. a matter of time 表示"时间问题"。例：It would be only a matter of time before he went through with it. 他完成这件事只是时间问题。

2. Fox River（福克斯河监狱）事实上是位于伊利诺伊州的朱利叶市惩治中心（监狱）。这座维多利亚式建筑建于 1858 年，由芝加哥 Water Tower 的建筑师 William Boyington 设计，该监狱于 2002 年关闭。

3. for a while 表示"暂时"，可与 for a moment 互换。例：She rested for a while, then had a wash and changed her clothes. 她休息了一会儿，然后洗了洗，换了身衣服。

4. close down 表示"（使）停业，（使）停产；（广播电台或电视台）结束当日广播"。片中表示"停业/关闭"。例：The library had to close down for it was too late. 天太晚了，图书馆得关门了。

5. ain't 原本是美国南部一帮文盲、粗人（但非原住民）说的话，现在趋于普遍，并且已经收入到了各类词典当中。最开始它是 am not 的缩写，最初写作 amn't，后由于发音连读问题（省去前一个辅音 m，只发后一个辅音 n），以讹传讹地变成了 ain't。

6. figure out 表示"想出；解决；计算出；弄明白"。例：They're trying to figure out the politics of this whole situation. 他们正试图弄明白整个情形背后的权术争斗。

词汇加油站

hole [hoʊl] *n.* 洞

missing ['mɪsɪŋ] *v.* 失踪（miss 的现在分词）

minute ['mɪnɪt] *n.* 分钟

cover ['kʌvər] *v.* 遮盖

tonight [tə'naɪt] *n.* 今晚

crew [kru:] *n.* 全体工作人员

时间： 第 21 集 00:02:05—00:03:31

地点： 典狱长办公室

片段二

人物： 迈克尔，典狱长，麦克，狱警

事件： 迈克尔绑架典狱长，要求把林肯转到医务室。

精彩亮点

1　　典狱长打算送给妻子做礼物的泰姬陵突然倒塌，事实上，迈克尔提前抽出了泰姬陵的一根木棍才使其坍塌，从而让典狱长不得不立刻召见自己。与此同时，警卫向他报告，贝里克失踪了。

2　　此时的典狱长受到迈克尔的威胁，他要求典狱长一方面帮自己圆谎：称贝里克只是进城去了，稳住了其他狱警；另一方面，他要求典狱长把林肯转到医务室与他们几个人会合。

3　　典狱长面对拿刀指着自己的迈克尔只好要求监狱看守把林肯转到医务室，他对迈克尔十分失望。

4　　迈克尔心地善良，他告诉典狱长他们将贝里克藏在何处，也向他表达了自己的愧疚之情，希望他能体谅自己。最后，迈克尔为了制造一起典狱长遭胁迫的假象，将典狱长打晕，绑了起来，这样事后其他人就不会怀疑典狱长了。

Mack: Sir?

Pope: Mack.

Mack: Yes, sir.

Pope: I just spoke with Bellick. He's walked into town. He's taking some personal time①.☺1

Mack: Is he all right?

Pope: He's fine.

Mack: Copy that②.

Michael: Okay. I just need you to do one more thing. **Have Lincoln transferred to the infirmary.**☺2 And he needs to be there overnight.

Pope: How long have you been planning③ this?

Michael: That is a conversation for another day, warden.

Pope: Pope to base.

Prison guard: Go ahead④, sir.

Pope: Have Lincoln Burrows transferred to the infirmary. I want him held overnight for tests.☺3

Prison guard: Copy that.

Michael: Once we're gone, you'll find Bellick in a hole under the guards' break room. **I'm sorry you got caught in the middle**⑤**, but one day, you'll understand why I did this.**☺4

Pope: You'll never make it⑥ over the wall.

Michael: I'm sorry, Henry.

译文

麦　　克：长官?

波　　普：麦克。

麦　　克：是的，长官。

波　　普：我刚跟贝里克谈过，他进城去了，他要处理些私事。

麦　　克：他还好吧?

波　　普：他很好。

麦　　克：收到。

迈克尔：好了，我需要你再做一件事，把林肯转到医务室，确保他整晚都在那儿。

波　　普：你计划了多久了?

迈克尔：今天我们不谈这个，典狱长。

波　　普：调度室。

狱　　警：长官，请讲。

波　　普：把林肯·巴罗斯转到医务室，我要他在那里过夜，接受检查。

狱　　警：收到。

迈克尔：一旦我们逃脱了，你会发现贝里克在警卫休息室下的洞中。对不起半夜把你抓住，但总有一天，你会理解我为什么这样做。

波　　普：你不可能越过高墙的。

迈克尔：对不起，亨利。

知识点拨

1. personal time 表示"个人时间，私人时间"。例：In the following sections, we will examine the basic methods and functions of Personal Time Management. 在以下部分，我们将审查个人时间管理的基本的方法和作用。

2. copy that 无线电通信俚语，表示"确认"，意思是"我听到你了，我明白"。和 Roger 同义，经常简化为 Copy。

3. have been doing 是现在完成进行时，用来表示过去发生的动作一直在进行到现在。例：We have making our model car since last week. 自从上周以来，我们一直在做我们的汽车模型。

4. go ahead 主要有三种用法：1）表示同意或允许，可译为"说吧；做吧；开始吧；进行吧"。2）表示请对方继续说、继续做等，通常可译为"继续……吧"。3）表示请对方先走或先做某事，可译为"你先走一步，你先请"。片中取第二个意思。

5. in the middle 表示"在中部；正忙于；拦腰；当心"。例：The glass cover for this is cleverly jointed in the middle. 这件东西的玻璃罩子在中间用活动接头巧妙地连接了起来。

6. make it 表示"及时到达；成功；约定时间"。片中表示"成功"。例：So you did make it to America, after all. 那么，你终究还是成功地来到了美国。

 词汇加油站

copy ['kɑːpi] *vt.* 收到

conversation [ˌkɑːnvərˈseɪʃn] *n.* 交谈

base [beɪs] *n.* 基地

transfer [trænsˈfɜːr] *vt.* 使转移

warden [ˈwɔːrdn] *n.* 典狱官

wall [wɔːl] *n.* 墙

片段三

时间： 第 22 集 00:17:36—00:18:57

地点： 逃亡车内

人物： 迈克尔，林肯，苏克雷，富兰克林，帝博格，大卫

事件： 众人越狱遇警方搜查，弃车而逃。

 精彩亮点

1 越狱行动紧张地开始了，老韦斯特莫兰德没有逃出去，不幸身亡。剩下八人成功越狱。贝里克被救出后，立刻带人杀气腾腾地开始追踪越狱者。

2 由于贝里克的搜捕，前往机场的路被封锁了。林肯告诉车上众人："我们遇到麻烦了"。但前往机场的路只有这一条，迈克尔他们又该如何通过关卡呢？

3 逃出来后，约翰本想在车上对付帝博格，但帝博格早有准备，他把自己和迈克尔铐在一起，并吞下钥匙。迈克尔命令帝博格把钥匙交出来！

4 车子突然停止运行，原来是车子陷入了泥潭根本无法启动。为了绕过警方检查，他们只能弃车而逃。

Sucre: All I want to do is touch her belly, feel that he's in there. ☺₁ After that, whatever I got to do, I'll figure it out. I just want to touch her belly. We're close, papi.

Lincoln: We got trouble.

David: Yo①, dawg, man, this is bananas. We got to get off② this road.

Lincoln: Any other way to the airstrip. ☺₂

Michael: This is the only road.

David: Let's just run this bitch.

Franklin: Somebody shut him up③, or I will.

Sucre: Can we go back④?

Michael: That won't do us any good⑤. It'll only get us farther from where we need to be.

Lincoln: Which means we got to bust that roadblock.

Michael: Maybe not. We've got to try and go around. Come on. We're gonna get that key from you. I don't care if you got to crap it out⑥. ☺₃

T-Bag: You got a foul mouth sometimes, pretty.

Michael: What? ☺₄

译文

苏克雷：我只想抚摸她的肚子，感觉肚子里的孩子。只要能这样，不管我做什么，都会应付的。我只想抚摸她的肚子。儿子，我就来了。

林　肯：我们有麻烦了。

大　卫：天啊，这太疯狂了。我们得离开这条路。

林　肯：找一条去飞机场的其他路。

迈克尔：这是唯一的路。

大　卫：我们干脆硬着头皮上吧！

富兰克林：给我闭嘴，不然我可要动手了。

苏克雷：我们能回头吗?

迈克尔：回头没有任何用处。这只会让我们越走越远。

林　肯：意思是我们必须闯过关卡。

迈克尔：或许没这个必要。我们可以试试绕开。来吧。我们会从你身上拿到钥匙的，你就是拉屎也给我拉出来！

帝博格：帅哥，有时候你这张嘴很不干净哦。

迈克尔：怎么了?

知识点拨

1. Yo 是个感叹词，可根据具体语境译为"哟，唷"等。例：Yo, Carl, great outfit man! 哟，卡尔，这身行头很不错嘛!

2. get off 表示"离开；下（车、马等）；发出；（使）入睡"。例：He kept on at me to such an extent that occasionally I wished he would get off my back. 他一直对我唠叨个没完，有时我真希望他不要再烦我了。

3. shut sb. up 表示"使某人安静，闭嘴"。例：A sharp put-down was the only way to shut her up. 对她冷嘲热讽是让她闭嘴的唯一方法。

4. 现在我们来区分一下 go back 和 return 两个表达。以 home 为例，go back home 指的是"说话人不在家，但将要回家去"，而 return home 则是"说话人从别处回来，在家里说这句话"，即 go back 是从出发地说的，而 return 是从到达地说的。

5. do sb. good=do good to sb. 表示"对某人有好处/益处"，其中 good 为不可数名词。例：A week's vacation will do you a lot of good. 休一周的假对你有很多益处。

6. crap out 表示"放弃，退出"。

词汇加油站

belly ['beli] *n.* 肚子
dawg [dɔːg] *n.* <口> 狗
bust [bʌst] *vt.* 突击搜查（或搜捕）
crap [kræp] *vi.* 拉屎

trouble ['trʌbəl] *n.* 麻烦
airstrip ['erstrɪp] *n.* 飞机跑道
roadblock ['roʊdblɑːk] *n.* 路障
foul [faʊl] *adj.* 有恶臭的

时间： 第 22 集 00:27:07—00:27:54
地点： 典狱长办公室，监狱外
人物： 典狱长波普，狱警，贝里克，帕特森
事件： 莎拉遭怀疑，警犬发现迈克尔等人踪迹。

片段四

精彩亮点

1 贝里克带人将迈克尔等人有可能的逃跑路线全部包围，并通知典狱长，估计不久后就可将他们缉拿归案。事实上又如何呢？

2 典狱长怀疑监狱里出了奸细。这时狱警的一个关键信息为他提供了线索：莎拉医生今天提前下班，且行为异常。

3 事实上，迈克尔之前请求莎拉帮他一个小忙：下班时不要锁门。莎拉虽然内心矛盾，但还是给迈克尔留了门，而且为了逃避，提前下了班。狱警让典狱长先通知州长一声，毕竟莎拉是他的女儿，典狱长若有所思。

4 警犬嗅出了迈克尔等人的踪迹。好在迈克尔等人有先见之明：分开逃跑。这也为他们每个人争取了逃亡时间。

Pope: Brad, this could be over quicker than we thought. We've got 'em boxed in[1]. ☺1

Prison guard: Sir, we've got an update on Dr. Tancredi.

Pope: Tell me.

Prison guard: None of the staff had any interaction with[2] her. She left work suddenly in the early afternoon. Returned for maybe an hour, then left again. ☺2 All of it's very erratic.

Pope: Has anyone been able to reach her?

Prison guard: Doesn't have a home line, cell phone seems to be shut off[3]. Chicago PD[4] identified her car outside her residence. They're getting an emergency warrant to go in. Sir, it's none of my business[5], but are you going to call the governor? This is his daughter we're talking about. ☺3

Patterson: Captain, the dogs picked up[6] a trail.

Bellick: Which way?

Patterson: That way and that way.

Bellick: They split up[7]? ☺4

Patterson: Looks like it.

Bellick: What the hell we waiting for?

译文

波　普：布拉德，这件事或许要比我们之前预期的更早结束。我们已经把他们包围了。

狱　警：长官，谭克雷蒂医生有新情况了。

波　普：快说。

狱　警：大家都没跟她有过交流，她下午突然提前下班离开了。然后又回来待了一个小时，然后又走了，非常反常。

波　普：有人能联系到她吗？

狱　警：没有她家电话，手机也似乎关机了。芝加哥警方在她家门口发现了她的车，他们正在申请紧急搜查令进屋。长官，我知道这不是我该管的事，但您为什么不打电话给州长呢？我们谈论的可是他女儿啊！

帕特森：长官，警犬发现踪迹了。

贝里克：哪个方向？

帕特森：这个方向和那个方向。

贝里克：他们分开逃跑了？

帕特森：看上去是这样。

贝里克：那我们还在等什么？

知识点拨

1. box in 表示"如盒子一般地围起来；不让……通过"。例：Armstrong was boxed in with 300 metres to go. 阿姆斯特朗在离目的地还有300米的地方被堵住不能动弹。

2. have interaction with sb.=interact with sb. 表示"与某人相互作用，与某人相互交流，与某人相互配合"。例：Even though I'm supposed to be working by myself, there are other people who I can interact with. 即便是需要我一个人工作，我还是可以和别人进行交流的。

3. shut off 表示"关掉；停止；隔绝，使不进入"。片中表示"关掉"。例：They pulled over and shut off the engine. 他们靠边停车熄火。

4. PD= Police Department 表示"警察局"。

5. none of my business 表示"不关我的事"。例：It has nothing to do with me. It's none of my business. 这事与我无干。

6. pick up 有许多意思："掘地；捡起；获得；使人恢复精神；加快；看到；随便地认识"。片中表示"获得"。例：They've picked up a really nasty infection from something they've eaten. 他们因吃错东西而得了很严重的感染症。

7. split up 可以指"瓜分；劈成；（使）分成若干小部分；（使）断绝关系。片中表示"分成若干小部分"。例：Did the two of you split up in the woods? 你们俩是在树林里分开的吗？

 ### 词汇加油站

box [bɑːks] *vt.* 把……装入盒 [箱，匣] 中
staff [stæf] *n.* 全体职员
erratic [ɪˈrætɪk] *adj.* 行为古怪的
warrant [ˈwɔːrənt] *n.* 许可证

update [ˈʌpdeɪt] *n.* 更新的信息
interaction [ˌɪntərˈækʃn] *n.* 互动
residence [ˈrezɪdəns] *n.* 住处
governor [ˈɡʌvərnər] *n.* 州长

Prison Break

Season 2 迈克尔与马霍

Scene 1 联邦调查局特工马霍出场

时间： 第 1 集 00:08:41—00:09:26
地点： 办公大楼
人物： 典狱长波普，马霍
事件： 马霍出场，与典狱长谈论案情。

精彩亮点

马霍是美国联邦调查局的特工，他受命调查、追踪福克斯河监狱犯人越狱一案，这惹得典狱长很不高兴，因为这本是他负责的事，马霍的出现令他始料未及。**1**

马霍之前已经了解了迈克尔等人越狱一案的概况，对迈克尔的聪明才智极度感兴趣。而他也知道在最后关头助迈克尔等人一臂之力的恰恰就是莎拉医生。因此，他要求与莎拉医生谈谈。**2**

面对马霍的质询，典狱长却守口如瓶，他似乎在隐瞒着什么。为什么典狱长不愿让马霍见莎拉呢？莎拉此时又身在何处呢？**3**

原来莎拉由于注射了过量毒品而陷入深度昏迷，戴着呼吸机生死未卜，自然不能与马霍见面。马霍一出场，就让观众印象深刻——这个人物不简单。**4**

Pope: It's a little early for the FBI to be showing up[1], don't you think? ☺1

Mahone: Look, I get it. It's still your investigation. Once those criminals cross state lines[2], it'll become a federal matter.

Pope: Yeah, well, that is not gonna happen.

Mahone: I hope you're right. That's why I suggest[3] that we cut through[4] any interagency politics from the outset[5]. Full transparency.

Pope: Absolutely.

Mahone: Good. Then maybe you can tell me about Dr. Tancredi. ☺2

Pope: There's nothing to tell.

Mahone: From what I'm hearing, she may have abetted the escapees. Opened the door that allowed them to get out.

Pope: Like I said, there's nothing to tell.

Mahone: You're not being very transparent, warden.

Pope: Look, I don't discuss my staff. ☺3

Mahone: Maybe you should because she may be the key to this thing. ☺4 We need to speak with her.

译文

波普：你不觉得现在由联邦调查局介入还为时尚早吗？

马霍：听着，我明白，调查还是由你主导。只要那些逃犯越过州界，就是联邦事务了。

波普：好吧，不过不会发生这种事的。

马霍：我希望如此。这就是为什么我建议我们先撇开任何政治成见，开诚布公。

波普：当然。

马霍：很好。那么或许你可以跟我谈谈谭克雷蒂医生的事情。

波普：没什么好说的。

马霍：我听说她有可能是逃犯的帮凶，是她打开门让他们逃出去的。

波普：正如我说过的那样，没什么好说的。

马霍：你不太坦白，典狱长。

波普：听着，我不会议论我的下属。

马霍：也许你应该谈谈，因为她可能是整件事的关键。我们需要与她谈谈。

知识点拨

1. show up 表示"显而易见；到场；（使）看得见；羞辱"。片中表示"出面，到场"。例：He did not show up. 他没有出面。

2. 我们一起来看一下各种 line: railway line "铁路线"；telephone line "电话线"；product / assembly line "生产 / 装配线"；county/state line "县 / 州界"；main line "干线"；power line "电源线"；bottom line "概要 / 关键"。

3. suggest 表示"建议"时可接 that 宾语从句，that 从句用 should+ 动词原形，should 可省略。例：She suggested that the class meeting (should) not be held on Saturday. 她建议不要在周六召开班会。

4. cut through 表示"穿过，挤进"。例：The two men broke out of their cells and cut through a perimeter fence. 这两个人逃出牢房，并越过了围墙。

5. from the outset 表示"从……开始"。例：Today's work went smoothly from the outset. 今天的活儿一上手就很顺利。

词汇加油站

investigation [ɪnˌvestɪ'ɡeɪ[n] *n.*（正式的）调查
federal ['fedərəl] *adj.* 联邦的
outset ['aʊtset] *n.* 开端
abet [ə'bet] *vt.* 怂恿

criminal ['krɪmɪnl] *n.* 罪犯
interagency [ˌɪntər'eɪdʒənsi] *adj.* 跨部门的
transparency [træns'pærənsi] *n.* 透明性
transparent [træns'pærənt] *adj.* 透明的

时间： 第 1 集 00:12:36—00:13:43
地点： 林间小屋
人物： 特伦斯，维罗妮卡
事件： 维罗妮卡发现特伦斯并身陷险境。

片段二

精彩亮点

维罗妮卡经过不断调查和搜索，终于找到了总统的弟弟特伦斯藏匿的宅邸，她潜入其中。特伦斯知道她已经进来了，但表示他并没有武器，希望她不要太害怕。

1

维罗妮卡因为追查林肯遭陷害的事情一直被追杀，现在处事谨慎。看到林肯一案的关键人物特伦斯没有死，她又惊又喜。

2

维罗妮卡想说服特伦斯站出来作证，为林肯洗刷冤屈。但殊不知，特伦斯也是阶下囚。由于当初伪造犯罪现场，他也付出了沉重的代价，现在每天都要服用止疼药，这使得他全身无力。

3

维罗妮卡进来时并没有意识到自己身处险境。她没有多想为什么自己这么容易就进来了。而且没有人看管特伦斯，那是因为这里的门只能从外面打开，玻璃是防弹的，根本不可能逃出去。

4

Terence: I'm not armed.☺₁

Veronica: You'll have to excuse me if I'm a little short on① trust at the moment.

Terence: I assure you, young woman, I'm the furthest thing from a threat. I think the Percocet② pretty much③ ensures that.

Veronica: Good. Then you won't mind if I capture this moment for posterity.☺₂

Terence: Won't do you any good.

Veronica: You don't care that somebody's gonna be executed for your murder while you're just sitting here.

Terence: I'm not the one who chose Lincoln Burrows as the fall guy④.

Veronica: Who did? Your sister, the president?

Terence: You don't understand. I'm a prisoner to all of this.☺₃

Veronica: Oh, come on... You could've come forward⑤. You could've stopped this thing before it even got started.

Terence: No, I really am a prisoner. And now you are too.☺₄ The moment you let the door shut behind⑥ you. Didn't it strike you as curious that there wasn't any security out there? The doors only open from the outside. The glass is two inches thick, bulletproof. There's no getting out of here, young woman.

译文

特 伦 斯：我没有武器。

维罗妮卡：请见谅，我最近比较多疑。

特 伦 斯：我向你保证，小姐，我绝对不会对你构成威胁。我吃了止痛药，现在全身无力。

维罗妮卡：很好，那么你应该不介意我拍下证据给后代欣赏。

特 伦 斯：这对你没什么好处。

维罗妮卡：你不关心某人因为谋杀你的罪名要被判处死刑，而你却好端端坐在这里。

特 伦 斯：我不是那个选择让林肯·布鲁斯背黑锅的人。

维罗妮卡：那是谁？是你的总统姐姐?

特 伦 斯：你不明白，我现在也是这一切的阶下囚。

维罗妮卡：哦，得了吧……你本可以站出来。你本可以阻止这一切发生。

特 伦 斯：不，我是真正的囚犯，现在你也是了，从你关上门的那一刻开始。难道你不觉得奇怪吗？这里没有一个保安，门只能从外面打开。玻璃是两英寸厚的防弹玻璃，你逃不出去了，小姐。

知识点拨

1. be short on sth. 表示"短缺……"。例：But, occasionally, through haste or carelessness, mistakes were made, so that at the end of business day one teller would be short on cash, the other long. 但是，偶尔也有这种情况，由于仓促匆忙或者粗心大意而造成错误，结果当天停业结算时，有的出纳少了现金而另一个出纳却会多了现金。

2. Percocet 即"镇痛药"。例：Do you guys know the name of that kid with the percocet addiction? 你们知道镇痛药上瘾的那孩子的名字吗？

3. pretty much 表示"几乎，差不多"。例：A job is pretty much nine-to-five. Is this what you feel would make you happy? 工作时间多数是朝九晚五，你觉得这样会让你感觉愉快吗？

4. fall guy 表示"被牺牲者，替罪羔羊"。例：He claims he was made the fall guy for the affair. 他声称自己是这起事件的替罪羊。

5. come forward 表示"出面；自告奋勇，自愿，主动提供(帮助或服务)"。片中表示"出面"。例：A vital witness came forward to say that she saw Tanner wearing the boots. 一位非常重要的证人站出来说，她看见坦纳穿着那双靴子。

6. shut behind 表示"顺手关上"。例：He slammed the gate shut behind him. 他砰的一声带上了大门。

词汇加油站

armed [ɑːrmd] *adj.* 携带武器的

ensure [ɪnˈʃʊr] *vt.* 确保

posterity [pɑːˈsterəti] *n.* 后代

strike [straɪk] *vt.* 撞

furthest [ˈfɜːrðɪst] *adj.* 最远的

capture [ˈkæptʃər] *vt.* 夺取

prisoner [ˈprɪznər] *n.* 囚犯

bulletproof [ˈbʊlɪtpruːf] *adj.* 防弹的

时间： 第 2 集 00:02:56—00:03:53
地点： 逃亡避难屋
人物： 富兰克林，林肯，苏克雷，迈克尔，陌生男子，约翰
事件： 众人不知何去何从，迈克尔成功拿回食物。

 精彩亮点

1
成功越狱的几个人现在分成几拨逃亡。富兰克林、林肯、迈克尔、苏克雷和约翰现在在一起，他们藏在了一间小黑屋里，不知何去何从。

2
从富兰克林的话语中，我们听出他对兄弟俩的不满：自己辛辛苦苦帮他们挖了洞，现在虽然逃了出来却不知下一步该前往何处。

3
富兰克林所说的五百万美元是这一季的重要线索。这些钱是老韦斯特莫兰德留下的，他把这笔钱藏在了一个地方，但没有人知晓具体的位置。

4
迈克尔乔扮成大学生的模样，坐在公园长椅子上，乘人不备偷回了大包食物。他冒险将这些食物带回来，五个人美餐了一顿，毕竟从监狱中逃出来到现在几个人还没有吃过东西。

Franklin: What's the plan, man?

Lincoln: No bars on these doors. Do what you like. ☺₁

Sucre: With what?

Franklin: We're supposed to① be in Mexico, sipping on margaritas② ...waiting for the heat to dip that was the plan. See? They just used us to dig, right? We're gophers. ☺₂

Sucre: Where's Michael?

Lincoln: He'll be here.

Franklin: Okay. You know what, Sucre? Maybe you and I should go and get that $5 million, you know what I'm saying? ☺₃ It's sitting there in Tooele, ready to get.

Lincoln: You wanna③ stay, shut your mouth④.

Franklin: You've got one more time to touch me.

Sucre: Guys, chill.

Lincoln: What?

Michael: Hey! Relax.

Man: Honey, are you sure you packed everything?

John: Yummy⑥. ☺₄

译文

富兰克林： 哥们儿，我们打算怎么做？

林　　肯： 这里又不是监狱，你们想做什么就做什么。

苏 克 雷： 我们能做什么？

富兰克林： 我们本该现在在墨西哥，喝着鸡尾酒，等风头过去，原本计划是这样子的。看吧？他们只利用我们挖洞，是吗？我们只负责挖地洞。

苏 克 雷： 迈克尔去哪了？

林　　肯： 他待会儿就来。

富兰克林： 好吧。你知道吗，苏克雷？或许你和我该去挖那五百万美元，懂我的意思吗？钱就在图埃勒县，等着出来透透气。

林　　肯： 要是你想留下就闭嘴。

富兰克林： 警告你不准再碰我！

苏 克 雷： 两位，冷静。

林　　肯： 不然怎样？

迈 克 尔： 嘿，怎么了？沉住气。

陌生男子： 老婆，你确定东西都带了吗？

约　　翰： 真好吃。

知识点拨

1. be supposed to... 其中 to 是动词不定式符号，其后要跟动词原形。当 be supposed to... 的主语是"人"时，意为"应该……；被期望……"，它可以用来表示"劝告、建议、义务、责任"等，相当于情态动词 should。主语是"物"时，它表示"本应；本该"，用于表示"某事本应该发生而没有发生"。

2. margaritas 是由墨西哥龙舌兰酒、酸橙或柠檬汁以及橙味酒混合调制而成的玛格丽特酒。例：I went to get us margaritas. 我去拿玛格丽特酒。

3. wanna 是一个非正式的口语化的词。他的意思是"想要，有意愿的"。和 want to 的用法相同，发音一样。相比于 want to 更广泛应用于日常对话。

4. 英文中想要某人"闭上嘴，不要说话"有以下表达：shut up, shut your mouth, bite your tongue, zip/button your lip, hold your jaw。

5. yum 本身是一个象声词，是吃东西嘴唇一张一合发出的声音。yummy 表示"好吃"。

 词汇加油站

bar [bɑːr] *n.* 障碍

sip [sɪp] *vt.* 小口喝

gopher ['goʊfər] *n.* 囊地鼠

honey ['hʌni] *n.* 宝贝

suppose [sə'poʊz] *vt.* 假定

dip [dɪp] *vt.* （使）下沉

chill [tʃɪl] *vt.* 冷静

pack [pæk] *vt.* （把……）打包

时间： 第 2 集 00:17:37—00:19:22
地点： 监狱
人物： 亚里克斯，L. J. 林肯
事件： 马霍欲说服 L. J. 与其合作。

精彩亮点

马霍成功找到切入点，一上来就盛赞迈克尔和林肯聪明过人，他抓住了 L.J. 这个未成年人的心理。如此一来，他与 L.J. 的谈话就可以顺利进行下去了。

1

果然，L.J. 很看好他，也爽快地问他要自己做什么。马霍也毫不遮掩，直接说以和平方式逮捕他们。他特意强调了"和平方式"，因为林肯和迈克尔毕竟是 L.J. 的亲人，这样说来情理上也说得过去。

2

L.J. 毕竟是未成年人，心思当然没有马霍缜密，他直接说出了自己的顾虑：这一切都是高层的设计，而你是政府人员……虽然此时他对马霍的提议无动于衷，那么接下来，马霍又会使出什么招数呢？

3

马霍开始转换思路，从 L.J. 个人利益角度攻陷他：他强调了 L.J. 会被判很久，但他的父亲和叔叔是不会替他去坐牢的，还让他要多为自己打算。L.J. 出于对坐牢的恐惧，果然动心了。

4

Mahone: **The level of planning and sophistication that went into this one… and eight guys got out…**☺1 I really do, professionally speaking…have a lot of admiration for Lincoln and Michael.

L.J: <u>Cool</u>①. Now we're buddies. What do you need?

Mahone: **Help me** <u>**bring them in**</u>② **peacefully.**☺2

L.J: I don't know where they are. I don't know where they're going.

Mahone: There's another way you can help.

L.J: How?

Mahone: Go on TV. I can have a <u>camera crew</u>③ down here in a half an hour.

L.J: You know what, man? The murder charge they put on my dad…the two murder charges they put me…everything's been a setup, coming from way up top. **So the fact that you work for the government…I got nothing to say.**☺3

Mahone: I'll give you the same advice that you'd get from the guy working at the <u>deli</u>④ downstairs. Start thinking about yourself now. In fact, <u>the sooner the better</u>⑤, because no one…not your father, L.J., not your uncle…is going to <u>do your time</u>⑥. **And at 16 years old, you're looking at a long stretch.**☺4 How much time you get, where you serve it…who your cellmate might be? You need to start thinking about yourself now. I want your dad, I want your uncle, and I'm willing to deal. Don't wait and let someone else get the reward.

译文

马　霍：他们计划的缜密周详的程度……加上八个人能一起逃出去……以专业角度来看，我真的……很钦佩林肯和迈克尔。

L. J. 林肯：很好，现在我们是好朋友了。你需要我做什么？

马　霍：帮我以和平的方式逮捕他们。

L. J. 林肯：我不知道他们在哪里，我也不知道他们要去哪里。

马　霍：你还有其他方式可以帮忙。

L. J. 林肯：怎么帮？

马　霍：上电视。我能在半小时内请摄制小组过来。

L. J. 林肯：你知道吗？他们栽赃我爸谋杀罪……还栽赃我两项谋杀罪……这一切都是高层的设计。那么，你为政府卖命……我无可奉告。

马　霍：我给你的建议和楼下餐厅的人一样，现在你要为自己想想。事实上，越快越好，L.J. 你要知道，没有人……无论是你父亲还是你叔叔……都不会替你坐牢。你现在才 16 岁，刑期会非常长。你会被判多少年？要去哪里坐牢？谁是你的狱友？你现在必须开始为自己设想。我要逮捕你的父亲和叔叔，我愿意谈条件，不要等着让大好机会溜到别人手中。

知识点拨

1. 虽然"酷"是"好"的意思，但如果青少年称赞一个人"酷"，那么这个人或者在衣着打扮、或者在言行举止、或者在精神气质上肯定是特立独行、充满个性的，绝对不是老一辈人所欣赏的那种纯朴热情、循规蹈矩的"好"。

2. bring sb. in 表示"把某人带进来；收获（庄稼等）；赚（钱）"。例：The firm decided to bring in a new management team. 该公司决定聘请新的管理团队。

3. camera crew 表示"摄制组"。例：We better get to the airport with a camera crew. 我们最好与摄制组一起到机场去。

4. deli=delicatessen 表示"熟食店，熟肉店"。例：Specialist foods can be found at your local delicatessen. 在你们当地的熟食店可以买到特色食品。

5. the sooner the better 表示"越快越好，尽早，越早越好"。例：Mark, you'd better get cracking, the sooner the better. 马克，你最好尽快开始，越快越好。

6. do time 表示"服刑"。例：He is doing his time in Fox River. 它正在福克斯河监狱服刑。

 词汇加油站

sophistication [sə,fɪstɪˈkeɪʃn] *n.* 精明	professionally [prəˈfeʃənəli] *adv.* 专业地
admiration [,ædməˈreɪʃn] *n.* 钦佩	buddy [ˈbʌdi] *n.* 搭档
crew [kruː] *n.* 一帮	deli [ˈdeli] *n.* 熟食店
stretch [stretʃ] *n.* 一段时间；服刑期	cellmate [ˈselmeɪt] *n.* 同牢室友

Scene 2 迈克尔与妮卡重逢

时间： 第 3 集 00:03:07—00:04:25
地点： 妮卡住处
人物： 迈克尔，妮卡，林肯
事件： 林肯中弹，迈克尔带林肯前往"妻子"妮卡住。

 精彩亮点

在营救儿子 L.J. 的过程中，马霍抓住了 L.J.，不让他逃走。与此同时，马霍通知警卫立刻上楼顶去抓迈克尔和林肯。在逃跑过程中，林肯腿部中弹，流血不止。林肯和迈克尔来到迈克尔的"妻子"妮卡家。 **1**

妮卡是一个舞女，她偷渡到美国，然后和迈克尔结婚，为的是要获得一张绿卡，而迈克尔需要她在自己进监狱之后帮他在外面做准备以此作为交换条件。 **2**

迈克尔不想让妮卡牵扯进来，而且这也不是他们之前的协议内容。虽然妮卡和迈克尔之间并没有爱情，但两个人作为朋友也很为对方着想。 **3**

迈克尔安顿好林肯后想要回去取车，林肯让他不要再管那辆车了，因为再回去一趟十分危险。但迈克尔表示那辆车上有帮助逃亡所需的一切东西。 **4**

Michael: I'm gonna need some rubbing alcohol①, some towels and painkillers. Whatever you got. ☺1

Lincoln: And some booze.

Michael: Please. Easy, easy. Easy, easy. Easy.

Lincoln: It's fine, man. Let's just keep moving.

Michael: We keep moving and that leg keeps bleeding. That leg keeps bleeding and we're not getting out of Illinois. This is gonna hurt. That's good, that's good, that's good. This will seal the capillaries.

Nika: You should not have come here, Michael. The police have been here asking questions. ☺2

Michael: We didn't have a choice.

Nika: I'm thankful for② the help with the green card but I just don't wanna get involved…

Michael: It wasn't part of our deal. I know. I know. I'm sorry. I'm sorry. There was nowhere else to go③. ☺3

Nika: When I saw you on the news, I was worried. I just hoped you'd crossed the border④ by now.

Michael: So did I⑤. Keep giving him these. See if you can find him some clean clothes.

Nika: Okay.

Michael: I gotta go back and get our car. ☺4

Lincoln: Forget the car. We can get another.

译文

迈克尔：我需要一些消毒酒精、毛巾和止痛剂，你有什么都拿来吧。

林　肯：再来一些酒。

迈克尔：拜托了，放松，放松。放松，放松，放松。

林　肯：没事的，我们继续逃。

迈克尔：如果继续逃，你的腿会继续流血。这条腿不止血，我们就逃不出伊利诺伊州，这会很痛的。很好，很好，很好，这样就可以让毛细血管闭合了。

妮　卡：你们不该来这儿的，迈克尔，警察已经来问过我了。

迈克尔：我们没有其他选择了。

妮　卡：我很感谢你帮我拿到绿卡，可是我不想被牵扯进来……

迈克尔：我知道，我知道，协议并不包括这个，对不起。对不起，可是我们没有其他地方可去。

妮　卡：我在新闻上看到你的时候很担心，我真希望你们已经跨越边境了。

迈克尔：我也这么希望，继续给他吃这个。你看看能不能帮他找些干净衣服。

妮　卡：好。

迈克尔：我得回去把车开回来。

林　肯：别管那辆车了，我们再找一辆。

知识点拨

1. rubbing alcohol 表示"外用酒精"。例：Sometimes using the rubbing alcohol feels like ice on my skin. 有时我在皮肤上擦酒精感觉像冰一样的冷。

2. be thankful for 后接 sth. 表示"对某事表示感谢"。例：You should be thankful for all we've done for you. 你应该感谢我们为你所做的一切。

3. nowhere else to go 表示"无处可去"。例：These rootless young people have nowhere else to go. 这些漂泊不定的年轻人没有其他地方可去。

4. cross the border 表示"越界"。例：The authorities had agreed to waive normal requirements for permits to cross the border. 当局已经同意免除跨境所需办理的常规手续。

5. So did I. 表示"我也一样"。"So+do+主语"表示"……也一样"。例：They had a wonderful time and so did I. 他们玩得很开心，我也一样。

词汇加油站

rub [rʌb] vt. 擦
painkiller ['peɪnkɪlər] n. 止痛药
bleed [bli:d] v. 流血
border ['bɔ:rdər] n. 边界

towel ['taʊəl] n. 毛巾
booze [bu:z] n. 酒
capillary ['kæpəleri] n. 毛细血管

时间： 第 3 集 00:23:12—00:24:45
地点： 汽车里
片段二　人物： 迈克尔，林肯
事件： 迈克尔、林肯继续逃亡，迈克尔故意在语音信箱留言。

 精彩亮点

1 林肯和迈克尔再次上路了，林肯刚想打开收音机，迈克尔连忙制止。因为他们的一举一动都有可能受到监视，如果警方收到无线信号就会查出他们的所在地。

2 外面太过安静，林肯不禁开始回忆自己的狱中生活，自己好像已经习惯了狱中的噪音。迈克尔打趣道：既然如此，还是回监狱吧。

3 林肯将话题转到了迈克尔的刺青上。的确，随着剧情的深入，迈克尔身上刺青的秘密也一一被揭晓。除了用来越狱，迈克尔的刺身还记载着他们越狱后的逃亡路线。可以说，迈克尔在进监狱前已经筹划好了一切。

4 迈克尔提到的这个人就是马霍，自从上次营救 L.J. 失败后，迈克尔就对这个在电梯相遇的男人印象深刻。可以说，马霍的才智可以与迈克尔媲美，但两个人最后谁才是赢家呢？

Lincoln: Let's put some music on①.

Michael: Don't. ☺1

Lincoln: I forgot. No radio. Man, it's quiet out here. Inside, there was always noise, you know. Someone yelling, guards making the rounds②. I got used to it.

Michael: You're right. We should go back. ☺2

Lincoln: The tats they weren't just for getting out, were they?

Michael: Breaking out was just the beginning. Now it gets a little more interesting. ☺3

Lincoln: Because me being strapped to the electric chair wasn't interesting enough.

Michael: All I'm saying, is inside, we had the element of surprise. No one knew what we were planning. But there's something about this guy, the one in the elevator. ☺4 It's like…It's like he knows where we're going, what we're thinking. It's a matter of time before he finds out about the money in Utah, Bolshoi Booze, our way into Mexico. Everything. You ready for this?

Lincoln: Make the call③.

Electric Voice (on phone): Please leave a message④ after the beep.

Michael: Hey. It's me. I've got Linc. We're on our way⑤ there. If, for some reason, you can't make it, call me back at 917454…

译文

林　　肯：我们听会儿音乐吧。

迈 克 尔：不行。

林　　肯：我忘记了，不能开收音机。外面真是安静啊，你知道的，监狱里到处都是噪音。我已经习惯听那些喊叫声和狱警巡查声了。

迈 克 尔：说得对，那还是回监狱好了。

林　　肯：你的刺青不只是用来越狱的吧?

迈 克 尔：越狱只是开端，现在事情变得更有趣了。

林　　肯：我被绑在电椅上还不够有趣吗?

迈 克 尔：我只是说在监狱里有意外的惊喜。没有人知道我们的计划，可是电梯里的那个人有点儿意思，就像是……就像是他知道我们要去哪儿，知道我们在想什么。那么他知道犹他州的钱、知道文身的事、知道我们逃到墨西哥的通道是早晚的事。他全都会知道，你准备好了吗?

林　　肯：打电话吧。

语音信箱：请在滴声后留言。

迈 克 尔：是我，林肯在我这儿，我们正要赶过去。如果你因故赶不过来，就给我回电：917454……

知识点拨

1. put on music 表示"放音乐"。例：He'd put on music to lower my blood pressure. 他会放音乐来帮我降血压。

2. make the rounds 表示"串门拜访；四处走动"。例：The minister worked very hard to make the rounds of his parish and visit the homes of the sick. 那位部长工作十分努力，多次对他所管辖的区域进行巡视，到病人家里拜访。

3. make the call 表示"打电话"。例：Green does not give him permission to make the call. 格林不允许他打这个电话。

4. leave a message 表示"留言，留话"。例：You can leave a message on our answering machine. 您可以在我们的答录机上留言。

5. on one's way to 表示"某人在去往……的路上"。例：Whatever happens, we are well on our way to starting the New Year with a victory over the dark ones. 无论发生什么，我们都会带着击败黑暗势力的胜利走向新的一年。

词汇加油站

yell [jel] vt. 叫喊

electric [ɪˈlektrɪk] adj. 电的

elevator [ˈelɪveɪtər] n. 电梯

strap [stræp] v. 用带捆扎

element [ˈelɪmənt] n. 少量，有点，有些

beep [biːp] n. 哔哔声

片段三

时间： 第 4 集 00:03:29—00:05:04
地点： 郊外树林
人物： 贝里克，迈克尔，林肯，吉瑞
事件： 贝里克追赶迈克尔等人，要挟他们助其寻得"宝藏"。

精彩亮点

1
迈克尔和林肯载着妮卡离开，在车上，迈克尔向妮卡保证到下个小镇会把她放下，回头就把许诺她的一万美元给她，但就在这时，贝里克和吉瑞开着车尾随其后。

2
贝里克和典狱长波普因越狱事件受到上级调查。被辞退的狱警高里出面作证，证实贝里克接受了约翰的贿赂，才让几个越狱的犯人有机会在警卫休息室打出地洞。最终，贝里克被革职。

3
就在贝里克因为革职一事一度产生自杀念头时，他偶然得知抓捕迈克尔等人的赏金达数十万美元，他又燃起了斗志，想将他们一网打尽。而芒什曾向贝里克泄密，称老韦斯特莫兰德有一笔巨款，但并没听清他所有的话，这让贪财的贝里克又找到了"奋斗"下去的理由。

4
在贝里克和吉瑞两个人的合作下，迈克尔、林肯和妮卡被抓。贝里克将他们锁在一间小屋里，迈克尔等人又会如何逃脱呢？

Bellick: Nobody move① ! Nobody move! Oh, good to see you again, boy. ☺1

Lincoln: No need for anyone to get hurt, boss.

Bellick: Boss? Oh, there's no need for formalities anymore there, sink. I'm no longer an employee of the state, thanks to② you. ☺2

Michael: I think somebody wants that reward.

Bellick: Oh, it's not about reward③ money, friend. Your pal Manche told me all about your little treasure hunt④ …for Westmoreland's stash. ☺3 Get in the car. We're going to Utah. Cops following you all over the country…when all they had to do was tail the tail, you know. Move that moneymaker, sweetheart.

Geary: Let's move it, convict.

Michael: If you know about the money in Utah, why do you need us?

Bellick: In the excitement of the escape, Manche didn't hear everything Westmoreland said…before he kicked the bucket⑤ , but he heard enough. Utah and five million. You'll fill in the blanks⑥ .

Michael: Hey!

Bellick: Don't even think about getting cute. You and your brother are gonna take me to where that money is… ☺4

译文

贝里克： 不许动！不准动！哦，很高兴再次见到你们。

林　肯： 长官，没必要让人受伤吧？

贝里克： 长官？在外面没必要见外了，水槽。多亏了你们，我已经被开除公职了。

迈克尔： 我看是有人想要赏金吧？

贝里克： 哦，我们要的不是赏金，朋友。你的伙伴芒什告诉我你要去挖韦斯特莫兰德的宝藏，上车吧，我们要去犹他州。警察正在全国范围内追踪你们……你知道的，他们只需要跟住你们的人就行了。快点儿，亲爱的！

吉　瑞： 快点儿，犯人。

迈克尔： 如果你知道犹他州宝藏的事，为什么还需要我们？

贝里克： 在你们兴冲冲地逃亡时，芒什没听清韦斯特莫兰德所有的话，然后那老头就撒手归西了，不过他听到的已经足够了，犹他州、五百万。你来填空吧。

迈克尔： 你要干什么！

贝里克： 别想耍滑头。你们兄弟俩要带我找到钱……

知识点拨

1. nobody move 表示"不许动"。例：And nobody move for five minutes. 五分钟之内不得移动。

2. thanks to 表示"幸亏，多亏，由于"。例：Thanks to that job I became an avid reader. 多亏了那份工作我才成了一个喜欢阅读的人。

3. award，reward 两者的含义基本相同，但在不同语境中表达的含义有所差别。reward 表示"报答，奖赏"，多指对某人的工作或服务等的报答。而 award 指"正式地或官方地颁发，授予，给予"，强调荣誉而不在乎奖品的大小。

4. treasure hunt 表示"寻宝"。例：We should have ourselves a treasure hunt. 我们应该开始一场寻宝行动。

5. kick the bucket 字面上的意思是踢掉水桶，引申为"死掉，一命呜呼，蹬腿"的意思。这是一条带有戏谑口吻的成语，不能用于书面语。

6. fill in the blanks 表示"填空；填充"。例：Fill in the blanks with the words and phrases you have learnt in this unit. 根据本单元学的单词和短语填空。

 词汇加油站

hurt [hɜːrt] *n.* 伤害

sink [sɪŋk] *n.* 水池

pal [pæl] *n.* 朋友

tail [teɪl] *vt.* 跟踪

formality [fɔːrˈmæləti] *n.* 礼节

reward [rɪˈwɔːrd] *n.* 赏金

stash [stæʃ] *n.* 隐（贮）藏物

convict [ˈkɑːnvɪkt] *n.* 罪犯

精彩抢先看： 林肯中弹，迈克尔带林肯前往"妻子"妮卡住处；迈克尔和林肯继续逃亡，迈克尔故意在语音信箱留言；贝里克追赶迈克尔等人，要挟他们助其寻得"宝藏"；贝里克上当，迈克尔等人成功逃脱

时间： 第4集 00:29:36—00:31:14
地点： 林间小屋
人物： 迈克尔，贝里克，林肯，吉瑞
事件： 贝里克上当，迈克尔等人成功逃脱。

精彩亮点

1 妮可使用美人计成功偷到了钥匙，为迈克尔和林肯解开了手铐。

2 由于吉瑞之前没有准备备胎，贝里克命令他去镇上抬一个回来。等到他扛着轮胎回来时，林肯早已举着枪等候他的到来了。

3 连日以来一直躲避追捕、根本无暇看报纸的迈克尔不知道莎拉的近况。听到贝里克所说的莎拉的惨状，迈克尔不敢相信，也不想相信。

4 贝里克一直刺激着迈克尔，事实上，贝里克对迈克尔打从一开始就看不顺眼还有一个重要原因就是，他暗恋的莎拉医生喜欢的是迈克尔这个罪犯。

Bellick: How stupid do you think I am? My daddy always said, "Fool me once, shame on you…fool me twice, and I <u>put you in the ground</u>①." Any more games and I stop the whore's air, understand? Thanks for the dance, <u>sweet pea</u>②.

Lincoln: Fooled you.

Geary: I carried it. The cons can change it. Oh, you really suck, Bellick, you know that? ☺1

Michael: Roll him. Let's go. Hands <u>behind your back</u>③. Thank you.

Bellick: You're as stupid as the prison doc, you know that? ☺2 Ignore him. He conned her too. Made her think he loved her. Look what she got. An overdose and a shot at 30 years inside.

Michael: What are you talking about?

Bellick: <u>You haven't been reading the papers, have you</u>④, college boy? Cops found your girlfriend fish-belly white⑤, gargling her own puke⑥. ☺3

Michael: Shut up.

Bellick: What do you care? <u>As long as</u>⑦ she left the door open for you. ☺4

Michael: Shut up!

Bellick: Hit a sore spot, didn't I?

译文

贝里克：你以为我很蠢吗？我爸总是说："骗我一次，是你不好……骗我两次，我就把你打倒在地。"再耍花招我就杀了这妓女，懂了吗？感谢你的艳舞，美女。

林　肯：骗到你了。

吉　瑞：我扛轮胎来了，那些犯人可以来换轮胎。哦，贝里克，你真的很没用，你知道吗？

迈克尔：绑住他，来吧，手放到背后。谢谢。

贝里克：你和那个监狱医生一样傻，你知道吗？别理他。她也被他骗了，她以为他爱她，看看她又得到什么？用药过量，还可能被判刑 30 年。

迈克尔：你在胡说什么？

贝里克：小子，看来你最近没看报纸吧？警察发现你的女友口吐白沫，命悬一线。

迈克尔：闭嘴。

贝里克：你在乎她吗？还是只要她替你开门就行。

迈克尔：闭嘴！

贝里克：我说到你的痛处了，是吗？

知识点拨

1. put sb. in the ground 表示"把某人给杀死，把某人给弄死"。例：They kept trying to put me in the ground but I wasn't ready. 他们不停地要将我击垮，但我却毫无防备。

2. sweet pea 表示"香豌豆，麝香豌豆花"。例：We have chicken, sweet pea stalks, and fish with bean sauce. 我们有鸡，好吃的豌豆，还有豆瓣鱼。

3. behind one's back 在片中表示"在某人背后"，还可以表示"背着某人"。例：He spoke ill of her behind her back. 他在背后说她坏话。

4. 反意疑问句由两部分组成：前一部分是一个陈述句，后一部分是一个简短的疑问句，两部分的人称时态应保持一致。陈述部分和疑问部分要么前肯后否，要么前否后肯。

5. fish-belly 表示"鱼腹"，fish-belly white 直译为"鱼翻白肚"，即"生命岌岌可危"。

6. gargle 表示"漱口"，puke 为"呕吐物"，gargling her own puke 直译过来表示"漱出了呕吐物"，即"口吐白沫"。

7. as long as 用法很多，片中表示 on condition that, provided that 或 if（"只要，如果"）的含义。例：You can go out, as long as you promise to be back early. 你可以出去，只要你答应早回来。

 词汇加油站

shame [ʃeɪm] *vt.* 使感到羞愧	**pea** [pi:] *n.* 豌豆
fool [fu:l] *vt.* 愚弄	**suck** [sʌk] *n.* 差劲，糟糕
roll [roʊl] *vt.* 滚动	**stupid** ['stu:pɪd] *adj.* 愚蠢的
overdose ['oʊvərdoʊs] *n.* 过量用药	**puke** [pju:k] *n.* 呕吐

Scene 3 巴拿马寻宝之旅

时间： 第 5 集 00:01:23—00:02:18
地点： 车上
人物： 迈克尔，林肯，新闻播报员
事件： 马霍识破迈克尔计谋，兄弟二人前去寻找"宝藏"。

精彩亮点

兄弟二人与妮卡道别后继续踏上逃亡之旅。新闻报道越狱逃犯约翰被击毙，约翰本可以与妻儿一起过上幸福的生活，但当他得到出卖他的人斐波纳契的线索时，他不顾妻子的反对，毅然决定前往汽车旅馆报仇。作为意大利的黑帮老大，有恩必报，有冤必申就是其奉行的宗旨。

1

迈克尔的话语中透露出他的乐观情绪，他想要与阻碍他们越狱的人来一场较量，但哥哥林肯显然没有他那样乐观。

2

之前，迈克尔伪造了一起车祸现场，让警方一度认为他和哥哥已经死于这场车祸，但聪明的马霍最终还是识破了他们的伎俩。

3

林肯一直思念自己的儿子，想要先去救 L.J.，但迈克尔却坚决制止了他，告诉他："没有钱，我们什么都做不了。"现在当务之急是找到藏钱的地点。

4

Announcer: This morning, authorities in Illinois issued an update on the escaped convicts…known ①, until now ②, as the Fox River Eight, **Chicago mob boss John Abruzzi…was gunned down** ③ **outside a Washington D.C. motel** ④ **last night…after investigators received a tip from an informant.** ☺₁ The other seven escapees are still at large ⑤ and considered dangerous. A Florida man wanted in…

Lincoln: I didn't think Abruzzi'd be the first to eat it.

Michael: **I have a feeling we're in for** ⑥ **lots of surprises.** ☺₂

Lincoln: **They said seven are still out there. So much for faking our deaths.** ☺₃

Michael: I bought us some time. That's what counts. How much further?

Lincoln: Seventy, eighty miles.

Michael: Means we should be hitting Double K Ranch by this afternoon.

Lincoln: We could keep driving, pick up L.J. And hit Panama.

Michael: **We can't hit Panama. We can't hit anything. We can't do anything without the money. We need to find Charles' stash.** ☺₄

Lincoln: I know some other guys who are thinking the same thing.

译文

新闻播报员： 今天早晨，伊利诺伊州官方发布了逃犯的最新进展……截至目前，他们被称为"福克斯河监狱八人帮"，芝加哥黑帮老大约翰·阿布鲁兹昨晚在华盛顿特区的汽车旅馆外被击毙，这一切要归功于线人的密告。其余七名逃犯依然在逃并且相当危险。一名佛罗里达州男子遭通缉……

林　　肯： 我没料到阿布鲁兹会是第一个。

迈　克　尔： 我有预感我们会遇到许多惊喜。

林　　肯： 新闻说七名逃犯在逃，诈死似乎不管用。

迈　克　尔： 我已经为我们争取到一些时间，这才是最重要的。还有多远？

林　　肯： 七八十英里。

迈　克　尔： 这意味着我们下午应该就能抵达双 K 牧场。

林　　肯： 我们还可以继续开车去救 L.J.，再去巴拿马。

迈　克　尔： 我们不能去巴拿马，哪都不能去，因为没有钱我们什么都做不了，我们得找到查尔斯藏钱的地点。

林　　肯： 我知道其他人也在想着同一件事。

知识点拨

1. known as 表示"被称为，公认为"。Brindley was known as a very, very fast driver. 众所周知，布林德利是个喜欢飞车的人。

2. until now 表示"到现在为止，迄今"。例：It has taken until now to pin down its exact location. 直到现在才确定了它的准确位置。

3. gun down 表示"用枪击伤，枪杀"。例：He had been gunned down and killed at point-blank range. 他被近距离开枪射杀。

4. motel 中文意为"汽车旅馆"是 motor 和 hotel 的合成词，即"汽车旅馆"，以前是指没有房间的旅馆，可以停车，而人就在汽车内睡，只不过比停在外面多了层保护而已。

5. be at large 表示"逍遥法外；失去控制；在逃"。例：Though there was no knowledge of a specific imminent attack, the officials said maintaining the "critical" alert level was necessary because other unknown people connected to the alleged plot could be at large. 官员们表示，尽管没有得到迫在眉睫的恐怖袭击的消息，但有必要将恐怖袭击警戒级别保持在"危急"级，因为与这起恐怖阴谋有关的其他未知人士可能依然逍遥法外。

6. be in for 表示"必定会遭到，定要受罚"。例: You might be in for a shock at the sheer hard work involved. 所做工作之艰辛可能会让你大吃一惊。

词汇加油站

update ['ʌpdeɪt] *n.* 更新的信息

motel [moʊ'tel] *n.* 汽车旅馆

informant [ɪn'fɔːrmənt] *n.* 提供消息的人

count [kaʊnt] *v.* 重要

convict ['kaːnvɪkt] *n.* 罪犯

investigator [ɪn'vestɪɡeɪtər] *n.* 侦查员

fake [feɪk] *v.* 捏造，假装

stash [stæʃ] *n.* 隐（贮）藏物

时间： 第 5 集 00:08:23—00:09:14

地点： 图勒镇

人物： 林肯，迈克尔，老者

事件： 兄弟俩来到巴拿马，查无所获。

 精彩亮点

1

迈克尔和林肯两个人驱车来到巴拿马以寻找老韦斯特莫兰德藏钱的地点。迈克尔在来的路上一直回忆着韦斯特莫兰德透露的信息：钱就埋在双K牧场的一个地窖里，就在犹他州的图勒镇外。他们能否顺利找到这个地方呢？

2

他们询问了一位当地人，是否听说过双K牧场，但老人却说从没听说过。难道老韦斯特莫兰德欺骗了他们吗？

3

聪明的迈克尔很快想到可以通过查询地产记录得知原委，而这东西在估税员手中，想要拿到这份记录，必须潜入市政大楼，他们又能否成功潜入呢？

Michael: Well, guess what①. No listing for a Double K Ranch.☺1

Lincoln: Excuse me②. You know where I might find the Double-K Ranch?

Old people: What'd you call it?

Lincoln: Double-K Ranch.

Old people: No.

Lincoln: You from around here?☺2

Old people: Yeah, born and raised③. There's no double nothing.

Lincoln: Great. Thank you. Looks like Westmoreland spent his last breath④ blowing smoke⑤ up your ass.☺3

Michael: There's one way to find out. The county keeps property records. Every plot is mapped out with dimensions. It's public record.

Lincoln: But if there is a tax assessor⑥'s office here…it's gonna be in there.

Michael: In the municipal building

Lincoln: Lot of cops in there, Michael.

译文

迈克尔： 你猜怎么着？双K牧场根本没有登记在电话簿上。

林　肯： 打扰一下，你知道双K牧场在哪里吗？

老　者： 你说叫什么名字？

林　肯： 双K牧场。

老　者： 不知道。

林　肯： 你是这里人吗？

老　者： 对，在这儿土生土长。这里没有叫双什么的牧场。

林　肯： 太好了，谢谢你。看来，韦斯特莫兰德用尽最后一口气，蒙了你。

迈克尔： 只有一个方法能查清，这个郡有地产记录。每块土地都有记载面积的地图，这是公开的记录。

林　肯： 如果这里有估税员办公室……东西一定在那里。

迈克尔： 市政大楼。

林　肯： 迈克尔，里面有很多警察。

知识点拨

1. guess what 表示"猜猜看，你猜怎么着"。例：I expect you can guess what follows. 我想你能猜出接下来发生了什么。

2. excuse me 用法有很多，现为大家归纳如下：1）用来向不熟悉的人打听情况或提出请求；2）用来客气地打断别人的话；3）用作从别人面前经过时的礼貌用语；4）表示中途退席或暂时告退；5）表示不同意或不赞成；6）表示事先对自己不礼貌的行为道歉；7）表示有礼貌地询问某事或请求允许；8）用来代替 sorry，表示道歉；9）表示不耐烦或不愿帮忙；10）用来对有失礼仪的行为表示抱歉。片中是其第一个用法。

3. born and raised 表示"土生土长"。例：I was born and raised in Hawaii. 我出生并成长在夏威夷。

4. last breath 表示"临终"。例：For the cause of revolution, he fought till his last breath. 为了革命事业，他战斗到了生命的最后一刻。

5. blow smoke 从字面意义上解释就是"喷吐烟雾"，这个习惯用语被很多政界人士借用，表示"说空话蒙混他人"。例：I have a lot of people who blow smoke at me. 经常有人对我说空口白话。

6. tax assessor 表示"估税员"。

 词汇加油站

listing ['lɪstɪŋ] *n.* 列表
raise [reɪz] *v.* 养育
plot [plɑ:t] *n.* 一块地
municipal [mju:'nɪsɪpl] *adj.* 市政的

ranch [ræntʃ] *n.* 大牧场
property ['prɑ:pərti] *n.* 地产
dimension [daɪ'menʃn] *n.* 面积

时间： 第 6 集 00:05:26—00:09:14
地点： 牧场
片段三 **人物：** 帝博格，迈克尔，林肯
事件： 帝博格为迈克尔和林肯带路，迈克尔分析藏钱地点。

 精彩亮点

迈克尔和林肯与帝博格相遇了，帝博格还记得老韦斯特莫兰德藏钱的具体地点。可是他们来到这儿时牧场已经不见了，但聪明的迈克尔很快发现有两棵树与众不同。 **1**

那两棵树明显比其他同时种下的树要矮，迈克尔当即想到那里应该就是地窖的所在地。 **2**

正当林肯等人准备动手时，从附近的一间房子走出一位妇女，如果此时去挖树势必会引起她的注意与怀疑。别说是钱了，估计几个人都要再被抓回牢里。 **3**

帝博格心狠手辣，为达目的不择手段。他竟然提出要把这位妇女杀死，但迈克尔善良而稳重，与他形成鲜明对比。那么，迈克尔又会想出何种解决方案呢？ **4**

T-Bag: All right, shut it. I think I remember. If I had to bet, I'd lay it all on the silo being on the left of the ranch house… inside the trees.

Michael: No. **It's outside the trees. Right there. You see those two trees? They're shorter than the rest. They were all planted at the same time but those two didn't get as much sunlight.** ☺1

Lincoln: Something was in the way[①].

Michael: **The silo. Our money should be right there, under that garage.** ☺2

T-Bag: You better be right, boy.

Michael: This isn't a high-end[②] subdivision. They slapped this place up[③] overnight. The silo's foundations might still be there. To save money, they probably just laid the concrete[④]…for the garage floor right on top of it. We'll dig straight down. If we hit the foundation, we stay. If not, we go.

Lincoln: Let's do it. **Oh, man**[⑤]. ☺3

T-Bag: Ain't no problem that a screwdriver to her temple won't fix. People die all the time, boys. Five million dollars comes once in a lifetime.

David: Let me out of here, man. Come on, guys.

Michael: **Well, we gotta do something. And it's not gonna involve hurting anyone.** ☺4

译文

帝博格: 好了，别说话，我想我记起来了。如果要我打赌，我赌地窖在房子左边……树的内侧。

迈克尔: 不对，是在树的外侧，就在那边。你看见那两棵树了吗？它们比其他树都矮。树木都是同时种植的，但那两棵树得到的阳光比较少。

林　肯: 有东西挡住了阳光。

迈克尔: 就是地窖。我们的钱应该就在那儿，那座车库下。

帝博格: 最好是你所说的那样，小子。

迈克尔: 这里不是高档的分售土地，建筑商一夜之间就拆掉了原来的建筑，地窖的地基可能还在那里。为了省钱，他们可能只盖了地基……铺了水泥当作车库地板。我们往下挖，如果挖到地基，就留下；否则，就离开。

林　肯: 动手吧。哦，可恶。

帝博格: 拿螺丝刀杀了她就没问题了。人死是很正常的事，两位，五百万美元却是一辈子都难得的。

大　卫: 放我出去，求你们了。

迈克尔: 我们得想个办法，不要伤害任何人。

知识点拨

1. be in the way 表示"挡路，碍手，妨碍，绊手绊脚"。例：This table is too close to the door. It gets in the way. 这张桌子放在门口太碍事了。

2. high-end 表示"高档的"。例：In many foreigners, this is a very high-end brands. 在许多外国人看来，这是一个非常高端的品牌。

3. slap up 表示"仓促做某事"。例：Can you slap up a quick meal for my friend before we rush to the game? 你能在我跟朋友们赶去看比赛之前给我们随便做点儿吃的吗？

4. lay the concrete 表示"铺设混凝土"。例：The developer just asked the workers to lay the concrete a month a ago. 开发商一个月前才让工人们铺设混凝土。

5. Oh, man 表示"惊奇、气愤等"，可以译为"哦，天呐"。例：Oh, man, why is he still here? 哦，天呐，他怎么还在这儿？

词汇加油站

silo ['saɪloʊ] *n.* （危险物品的）地下贮藏库

subdivision [ˌsʌbdɪ'vɪʒn] *n.* 分支

overnight [ˌoʊvər'naɪt] *adv.* 突然，一夜之间

screwdriver ['skru:draɪvər] *n.* 螺丝刀

sunlight ['sʌnlaɪt] *n.* 阳光

slap [slæp] *vt.* 用力放置

foundation [faʊn'deɪʃn] *n.* 地基

temple ['templ] *n.* 太阳穴

时间： 第 6 集 00:22:12—00:23:18

地点： 珍妮特家

人物： 帝博格，迈克尔，珍妮特，林肯，富兰克林，大卫

事件： 众人冒充电工混进女主人家，富兰克林现身。

片段四

精彩亮点

1
　　迈克尔几个人想要在不伤害他人的情况下拿到那笔钱。于是，曾经当过电工的林肯想出了一个主意：让珍妮特家断电，几个人冒充电工进入她家拿走韦斯特莫兰德留下的那笔钱。

2
　　珍妮特还是很有警惕性的，虽然迈克尔劝她可以去打网球躲避噪音，但她执意要盯着迈克尔他们干活，担心他们会偷东西。

3
　　迈克尔跟女主人说故障的线路正好在她家车库下面，需要挖开地板才能修理线路。事实上，那笔巨款就藏在那里。

4
　　富兰克林和苏克雷相遇后两个人直奔图勒镇，没想到还是被迈克尔等人抢先了一步。可是现在他们二人的到来只会把事情搞得越来越糟。归根到底，还是他们对彼此不信任。

Michael: One way or another①, we'll be out of here② today.

T-Bag: Really need to get started, ma'am. Wouldn't want a pretty little thing like yourself sitting…in the dark tonight, now, would we? ☺₁

Jeanette: Well, that depends on③ who I'm sitting with.

T-Bag: Touché④.

Jeanette: Fine. It's okay. Y'all⑤ go ahead and do whatever y'all need to do.

Michael: Jeanette, the noise might be substantial. You might wanna take in that tennis game after all.

Jeanette: Oh, no, it's too hot for that now. Plus, I gotta keep an eye on you⑥ all and make sure you don't steal anything. ☺₂

Lincoln: Ma'am.

Jeanette: How are you?

Lincoln: Good.

Michael: All right, where's Tweener?

Lincoln: He's next door plugging in the extension cord⑦.

Michael: We're gonna have to cut up the cement. ☺₃

David: Yo, we got company.

Franklin: What's up, snowflake? ☺₄

译文

迈 克 尔： 无论如何，我们今天一定能完工。

帝 博 格： 我们真该开工了，女士。我们不希望让你这种美人今晚坐在黑暗中，对吧?

珍 妮 特： 那要看我跟谁坐在一起了。

帝 博 格： 说得对。

珍 妮 特： 好吧，就这样。你们动工做你们要做的事吧。

迈 克 尔： 珍妮特，施工时噪音可能很大，或许你去打网球会好一点儿。

珍 妮 特： 哦，不了，现在打球太热了。再说，我还要盯紧你们，确保你们不会偷东西。

林 　 肯： 女士。

珍 妮 特： 你好吗?

林 　 肯： 很好。

迈 克 尔： 好，特威纳呢?

林 　 肯： 他在隔壁插延长线。

迈 克 尔： 我们必须挖开水泥。

大 　 卫： 各位，有人来了。

富兰克林： 怎么了，小白脸?

知识点拨

1. one way or another 表示"不管怎样"。例：People that are addicted to drugs get help from the government one way or another. 那些吸毒上瘾的人以某种方式获得政府帮助。

2. be out of here 表示"离开这里"。例：She'll be out of here by tonight. 今天晚上，她就会离开这儿。

3. depend on 表示"依赖；相信，信赖；随……而定"。例："You can depend on me." Cross assured him. "你可以信赖我。"克罗斯向他保证。

4. 人们用 Touché 来表示"在辩论中认可对方或者认为对方（对手）在辩论中的论点非常贴切"。现在，touché 在美国变得越来越流行，用它表示"说得好"。

5. Y'all 就是 you all 的意思。很多美国人都会说 y'all! 例：Hey y'all! How you doin'? 大家好! 怎么样啊?

6. keep an eye on sb. 表示"注视某人，监视某人"。例：Why do you think I want to keep an eye on you? 你怎么会认为我在监视你呢?

7. extension cord 表示"延长绳"。例：Our host ran a long extension cord out from the house and set up a screen and a projector. 我们的主人从房里牵出一根延长电线，架起屏幕和投影仪。

 词汇加油站

depend [dɪ'pend] *vi.* 决定于
substantial [səb'stænʃl] *adj.* 大量的
plug [plʌg] *vt.* 插入
cord [kɔːrd] *n.* （细）绳

noise [nɔɪz] *n.* 噪音
steal [stiːl] *vt.* 偷
extension [ɪk'stenʃn] *n.* 延长
snowflake ['snoʊfleɪk] *n.* 雪花，雪片

Scene 4 五百万现金浮出水面

时间： 第 7 集 00:05:26—00:06:49

地点： 珍妮特家中

人物： 迈克尔，富兰克林，帝博格，林肯

事件： 情况突变，迈克尔等人绑架珍妮特母女。

片段一

精彩亮点

迈克尔等人终于挖到了地基，眼看就能拿着那笔钱逃之夭夭了，没想到珍妮特的警官女儿回来了。如果看到他们几个越狱逃犯，身为警察的她怎能放过他们？就在这时，帝博格捂住珍妮特的嘴，让她不要发出声音。

1

迈克尔等人绑架了珍妮特和她的女儿，这无疑又给他们增添了一条罪责。富兰克林虽然不想再生事端，但眼下也只有这一个办法了。

2

迈克尔也不想把情况搞成这样，可不曾想此时的大卫已经被马霍抓住，而马霍试图通过拷问大卫了解其他几个人的去向。

3

林肯似乎打算放弃这笔即将到手的巨款，但迈克尔却带有讽刺意味地说："或许可以再去抢银行。"既然自己曾经抢过银行，这已经是事实，就无法抹去自己犯下的罪行。

4

Michael: **This is going wrong in every possible way.** ☺₁

Franklin: **This is** stupid**, man. We cannot do this.** ☺₂

T-Bag: The hat's over the wall now①.

Franklin: What the hell is that supposed to mean?

T-Bag: I mean we committed. It's time to go get the hat②. We don't have a choice.

Franklin: Yeah, we do. We can walk right up③ out of here right now, man.

T-Bag: And then what? We are already in the house. Those women are bound. We have already committed this crime. **We leave, it ain't④ gonna change any of that.** ☺₃

Michael: Why couldn't there just be a silo in the middle of a field with no one around?

Lincoln: We'll figure it out and get the money another way.

Michael: Yeah, maybe I can rob another bank. You know what Charles once said to me? He said there's no such thing as an excon. Because I used to think there was a way we could wipe the slate clean⑤. Make up for⑥ everything we've done. The hat's over the wall, Linc. For everyone. **Sorry isn't gonna mean anything to you right now. But I wanna say it anyway**⑦. ☺₄

译文

迈 克 尔： 能出差错的都出了差错。

富兰克林： 这样做很愚蠢，我们不能这样做。

帝 博 格： 现在我们收不了手了。

富兰克林： 你这话到底是什么意思？

帝 博 格： 我的意思是我们既然已经犯罪了，那该是拿钱的时候就拿，我们没有退路。

富兰克林： 不，我们有退路，我们现在就可以离开这里。

帝 博 格： 然后呢？我们已经进屋了，还绑了这些女人，我们已经犯罪了，就算离开也不会改变情况。

迈 克 尔： 为什么这个地窖不能出现在无人的地方？

林　　肯： 我们可以想别的办法筹钱。

迈 克 尔： 对，或许我可以再去抢银行。你知道查尔斯曾经对我说过什么吗？他说犯了罪，一辈子都是犯人。因为我曾经认为我们可以洗清犯下的罪行，弥补我们做过的事，但林肯，我们现在回不了头了，大家都是这样。"对不起"现在对你毫无意义，但我还是要说。

知识点拨

1. The hat's over the wall. 表示"犯罪已成事实"。

2. get the hat. 中 hat 不是"帽子"的意思，而是表示"非法所得的收入"。

3. right up 表示"一直等到，直到"。例：She was in this right up to the hilt. 她已经完全卷入了此事。

4. ain't =am not 表示"不是"，也可用作 are not, is not, has not, will not 和 have not 的缩略语。它经常被使用在非正式书面文字中。

5. wipe the slate clean 表示"一笔勾销"。例：Why not wipe the slate clean and start all over again? 为什么不洗心革面，从头来过呢？

6. make up for 表示"补偿，弥补"。例：Ask for an extra compensation payment to make up for the stress you have been caused. 为补偿你为此承受的压力，你要申请额外的补偿金。

7. anyway 和 anyhow 同义，anyway 在句中用作副词和连接词，表示"无论如何，不管怎样"，相当于 in any case 和 at any rate。

 词汇加油站

stupid ['stu:pɪd] *adj.* 愚蠢的

bind [baɪnd] *vt.* 捆绑；系

rob [rɑ:b] *vt.* 抢劫

slate [sleɪt] *n.* 行为记录

commit [kə'mɪt] *vt.* 犯罪

silo ['saɪloʊ] *n.* （危险物品的）地下贮藏库

wipe [waɪp] *vt.* 消除

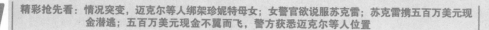

时间： 第 7 集 00:39:18—00:40:05

地点： 珍妮特家

人物： 女警官，苏克雷，迈克尔

事件： 女警官欲说服苏克雷去自首。

精彩亮点

女警官突然跟苏克雷说要喝药，还特意强调是预防流产的药。苏克雷一听就想到自己即将出世的孩子，果然心软。女警官见势想要继续说服苏克雷。

1

苏克雷因抢劫罪被判了 5 年刑，现在还有 18 个月就要刑满释放。但他的妻子已经怀有身孕，他越狱是想陪在妻子身边看着孩子出生。

2

女警官进一步利用孩子说服苏克雷，而且她分析得很在理：如果苏克雷不想听她的话，早就应该堵住她的嘴。因为她说的每句话都说到了苏克雷心里。

3

女警官的一番话的确打动了苏克雷。而此时，另一间屋内迈克尔等人终于挖到了那五百万美元，正在大家欢呼雀跃时，苏克雷却拿着枪对准了他们，然后独自拿着五百万美元跑掉了。苏克雷真的背叛了迈克尔吗？

4

Police-woman: You walk out① with those guys now…it's only a matter of time before you get caught.☺₁ You realize that? You're not just dealing with② escape charges. Assault, unlawful imprisonment, kidnapping…

Sucre: I don't need to hear this.

Police-woman: No, you do. How much longer do you really think you can stay ahead of③ the cops?☺₂ Look, if you turn yourself in④ … I will testify at the sentencing, I will say that you cooperated. That can make a difference⑤.

Sucre: Shut up.

Police-woman: Be smart. You have a baby on the way⑥. Wanna be around for its second birthday? Or its 22nd?☺₃

Sucre: Shut up.

Police-woman: If you didn't wanna hear what a big mistake you were making… you would've put that gag back on...

Michael: Fernando! It's time to go!

Police-woman: You can still do the right thing, Fernando.☺₄

译文

女警官：你现在和那些人一起逃走……你被逮住是迟早的事，你明白吗？你不仅要面临越狱的刑罚，还有攻击、非法挟持、绑架……

苏克雷：我无须听你这么说。

女警官：不，你要听。你认为警察能让你逍遥法外多久？听着，如果你自首……我会出庭作证，说你愿意合作。这会有很大的帮助。

苏克雷：闭嘴。

女警官：聪明一点儿，你的孩子就要出生了，你只想要看着他长到 2 岁，还是 22 岁？

苏克雷：闭嘴！

女警官：如果你不想听自己犯下的错误……你早该堵住我的嘴……

迈克尔：费尔南多，我们该走了！

女警官：现在回头还来得及，费尔南多。

知识点拨

1. walk out 表示"罢工；突然离开；出走；退场"。例：Several dozen councilors walked out of the meeting in protest. 几十名议员愤然从会场退席以示抗议。

2. deal with 表示"应付；对待；惠顾；与……交易"。例：In dealing with suicidal youngsters, our aims should be clear. 在对待有自杀倾向的青少年时，我们的目标应当很明确。

3. stay ahead of sb. 表示"领先于某人，走在某人前面"。例：If I can only stay ahead of the other runners, now that I am in the lead, I can win this race! 既然我现在已跑在所有人的前头了，如果我能保持住，我就胜利了。

4. turn yourself in 表示"自首"。例：This is out of control; you've got to turn yourself in. 局面已经失控，你自首吧。

5. make a difference 表示"有影响；起（重要）作用"。例：Does where the start and the finish are in relation to each other make a difference? 起点和终点的位置和它们的相互关系是否会使得结果不同？

6. on the way 表示"沿途，在途中；接近；（孩子）已成胎而尚未出生"。例：She is married with twin sons and a third child on the way. 她已经结婚，有一对双胞胎儿子，第三个宝宝也即将出世。

 词汇加油站

escape [ɪˈskeɪp] *n.* 逃走
imprisonment [ɪmˈprɪznmənt] *n.* 监禁
testify [ˈtestɪfaɪ] *vt.* 作证
gag [gæg] *n.* 塞口物

unlawful [ʌnˈlɔːfl] *adj.* 不合法的
kidnapping [ˈkɪdnæpɪŋ] *n.* 诱拐，绑架
sentence [ˈsentəns] *v.* 宣判

时间： 第8集 00:01:07—00:02:14
地点： 珍妮特家
人物： 富兰克林，苏克雷，迈克尔
事件： 苏克雷携五百万美元现金潜逃。

片段三

精彩亮点

1
经过几小时的辛苦挖掘，迈克尔等人终于挖到了五百万美元，他们每个人脸上都洋溢着喜悦之情，甚至还规划起美好的未来。

2
就在众人畅想美好未来之际，苏克雷拿着枪闯了进来。他勒令在场的所有人不许动，将装满五百万美元的背包交给他。

3
迈克尔虽然震惊，但表现得十分平静。难道苏克雷真的背叛了迈克尔吗？从之前苏克雷的表现来看，他并不是重利忘义之人，这到底是怎么一回事呢？

4
面对三个人，苏克雷仍有自信能逃出去。原来，这都是他和迈克尔之前商量好的，两个人配合演了一场好戏，目的就是为了不让帝博格拿到这笔钱，但事实果真如此吗？

Franklin: Charles Westmoreland, God bless you and your wrinkled old sack.☺1

Michael: It's all here.

Franklin: Where's Sucre?

Sucre: Drop the pack. No one's going anywhere.☺2

Franklin: What the hell are you doing, man? Sucre, whatever it is you want…

Sucre: I want the money. All of it.

Franklin: What? Are you robbing us?

Sucre: The money was never yours to begin with ① . This is about business. Five million dollars worth ② of business.

Michael: So this is how it's gonna go down ③ , huh? After everything? Once a thief, always a thief ④ .☺3

Sucre: You just figuring that out. The backpack. Now!

Michael: Don't do this, buddy.

Franklin: Yo, take a look ⑤ around you, papi. There's three of us. There's one of you. You are outnumbered, man, and we will come after you ⑥ .

Sucre: It'll be the last thing you do.☺4

译文

富兰克林：查尔斯·韦斯特莫兰德，愿上帝保佑你还有你褶皱的旧麻袋。

迈 克 尔：钱都在这里。

富兰克林：苏克雷在哪里？

苏 克 雷：放下袋子，都别想离开。

富兰克林：你到底想做什么？苏克雷，不管你想要干什么……

苏 克 雷：我要钱，全部的钱。

富兰克林：什么？你要抢我们的钱？

苏 克 雷：这钱打一开始就不是你们的，这只是交易，价值五百万美元的交易。

迈 克 尔：你真的要这么做？在这么多事情之后？做一次贼，一辈子都是贼。

苏 克 雷：你现在才想通吗？把背包给我！快点儿！

迈 克 尔：兄弟，别这么做。

富兰克林：你自己看看四周，我们有三个人，你只有一个人。你一个人寡不敌众，我们不会放过你的。

苏 克 雷：你不会的。

知识点拨

1. begin with 表示"以……开始，从……开始"。例：It was great to begin with but now it's difficult. 一开始非常好，但现在可就难了。

2. be worth 后面一般有三个结构：be worth of sth. / be worth doing sth. / be worth+money，均表示"做某事 / 某物有价值"。

3. go down 表示"停止；被接受；沉下；被打败"。例：Her excuse didn't go down well, no one believed it. 她的借口不能使人信服，没有一个人相信它。

4. Once a thief, always a thief. 表示"偷盗一次，做贼一世"。

5. take a look 表示"注视"。例：In case you think I was incautious, take a look at the map. 如果你认为我不够仔细，就自己看看地图。

6. come after sb. 表示"跟着……来，跟在……后面"。

词汇加油站

wrinkle ['rɪŋkl] *vt.* 使起褶皱
pack [pæk] *n.* 包裹
figure ['fɪgjər] *vt.* 估计
backpack ['bækpæk] *n.* （指登山者、步行者使用的或背小孩时使用的）背包
outnumber [,aʊt'nʌmbər] *vt.* 数量多于

sack [sæk] *n.* 麻袋
thief [θi:f] *n.* 小偷

时间： 第8集 00:10:17—00:11:16

地点： 树林

人物： 迈克尔，苏克雷，接线员

事件： 五百万现金不翼而飞，警方获悉迈克尔等人位置。

精彩亮点

苏克雷与赶来的迈克尔在树林中汇合。原来，苏克雷与迈克尔早就商量好这笔钱由他们三个人均分。但迈克尔坚持还要留一份给老韦斯特莫兰德的女儿。正当他们高兴地打开背包分钱时，却发现里面没有一分钱，都是一些杂志。

1

聪明的迈克尔很快就将目标锁定在帝博格身上，当他和富兰克林离开前，帝博格已不见了踪影。事实上，当他们挖出这笔钱时，帝博格就已经将这笔钱和一堆旧杂志调包了。此时的他，正带着五百万美元，在高速路上疾驶着。

2

迈克尔临走时拿走了女警官的通话设备，从而得知警方已经追查到了他们的行踪。因为苏克雷威胁这几个人时开了枪，枪声惊扰了邻居，邻居报了警。

3

苏克雷和迈克尔只有一辆摩托车，这辆摩托车虽然能坐下他们两个人，但速度如何呢？他们能否成功躲过警方的追击呢？

4

Michael: We can't go back. ☺1

Sucre: You said it: Without the money, we're screwed①. We can't…

Michael: Just let me think. Maybe there's… Just let me think.

Sucre: Maybe it's still back at the house.

Michael: The money's not back at the house unless T-Bag is. He must've switched the packs. ☺2

Sucre: What…? What do we do…? What do we do now?

Michael: We still got the 5 grand② we took when we pocketed the money. It's not gonna be 5 million…but it might be enough to get us where we're going.

Operator: All units be advised, escaped convicts from Fox River…have been positively ID'd at 1131 Monterey Lane. We have dogs being dispatched to the location, I want every road in or out of town blocked off③, I don't care if it's on wheels④, rails or hooves. I want it stopped and searched.

Sucre: You said we would have a head start⑤.

Michael: It was the gunshot, buddy. One of the neighbors must've heard⑥. ☺3 How fast can that thing go?

Sucre: I don't know. Both of us, it could probably, I don't know… ☺4

114

译文

迈克尔： 我们不能回去。

苏克雷： 你说过，没有钱我们就死定了。我们不能……

迈克尔： 让我想想。或许……让我想想。

苏克雷： 钱可能还在房子里。

迈克尔： 除非帝博格在里面，否则钱不会在房子里，他肯定把背包调包了。

苏克雷： 那……我们该怎么办……？现在我们该怎么办？

迈克尔： 装钱的时候我们还留了五千美元，虽然不是五百万美元……但或许足够让我们抵达目的地了。

接线员： 各小队注意，福克斯河越狱逃犯已确定其藏身地点，在蒙特雷路1131号。我们已派警犬前往该地，我要封锁镇上所有的出入通道，无论是什么交通工具，全都要拦截下来搜查。

苏克雷： 你不是说我们有很宽裕的时间吗？

迈克尔： 老兄，是枪声，一定是有邻居听到了。这台机车能跑多快？

苏克雷： 我不知道。可能能坐下我们两个人，我不知道……

知识点拨

1. be screwed 表示"喝醉，醉得晕头转向；完蛋了"。例：And then you're really gonna be screwed. 你就真的完蛋了。

2. grand 做形容词表示"宏大的，宏伟的"；做名词表示"一千美元"。例：They're paying you ten grand now for those adaptations of old plays. 他们打算付你一万美元，作为改编老剧本的报酬。

3. block off 表示"关闭，封闭，封锁"。例：They had blocked off the fireplaces to stop draughts. 他们已经封住了壁炉，以阻挡通风。

4. on wheels 表示"（开车，骑车）旅行；（用于强调厌恶某人）该死的"。例：We did excellent business; everything went on wheels. 我们的生意兴隆，一切顺利。

5. a head start 表示"优势，有利条件"。例：A good education gives your child a head start in life. 良好的教育会让你的孩子在人生的起跑线上比别人领先一步。

6. must have done 表示"对过去某事的肯定猜测"，其否定或疑问形式都用 can / could 来表示。例：Since the road is wet, it must have rained last night. 路是湿的，所以昨天晚上一定下雨了。

 词汇加油站

screw [skru:] *vt.* 诈骗
pocket ['pɑːkɪt] *vt.* 私吞
lane [leɪn] *n.* 车道
block [blɑːk] *vt.* 阻止

switch [swɪtʃ] *vt.* 转换
advise [əd'vaɪz] *vt.* 通知
dispatch [dɪ'spætʃ] *vt.* 派遣
hoof [huːf] *n.* 马蹄

Scene 5 五百万的诱惑

时间： 第 9 集 00:06:15—00:06:46
地点： 小餐馆
片段一
人物： 记者，马霍，迈克尔
事件： 迈克尔获悉硬盘被马霍找到。

 精彩亮点

1 马霍的确找到了迈克尔的硬盘，那张硬盘里记录着迈克尔所有的计划。此时的迈克尔坐在一个小餐馆的角落里，听到大卫的死和马霍找到自己硬盘的事不禁坐直了身子。

2 马霍不希望自己找到迈克尔硬盘的事被媒体公之于众，因为他不想让迈克尔知道，不想打草惊蛇。这样迈克尔就会放松警惕，自己也能控制迈克尔的一举一动。

3 今早在植物园发生的事件是：迈克尔溜进植物园的后勤区域，没想到在这附近溜达的义工就是伪装埋伏的警员。迈克尔知道自己中了圈套，慢慢从那棵植物旁退开。最终穿过一队参观的小学生，飞奔出去。

4 迈克尔回忆着自己先前对哥哥说过，马霍这个人似乎知道自己的一举一动，看透了他的想法。现在他终于明白了原因：马霍找到了他的硬盘。但迈克尔不能坐以待毙，他开始着手调查马霍。

Journalist: Sources claim that you have recovered Scofield's hard drive[1]. Obtained substantial data from it.☺1

Mahone: What sources?

Journalist: Retrieved information detailing not only how Scofield broke out, …but how he plans to stay out[2]. Comment.

Mahone: No.☺2

Journalist: The event at Blanding Botanical Gardens earlier today, … that was a result of[3] hard drive data you collected[4].☺3

Mahone: No comment[5].

Journalist: Have you found other locations where Scofield might be?

Mahone: I believe I said no comment.

Michael: There's something about this guy. It's like he knows where we're going, what we're thinking.☺4

Journalist: Tell us where you're heading, what role will the hard drive play[6]?

Mahone: Details of this investigation are extremely confidential.

译文

记　者：有消息称你已经找到了斯科菲尔德的硬盘，并且获得了其中的大量信息。

马　霍：哪来的消息？

记　者：据说你不仅已经知道斯科菲尔德是如何越狱的，还知道他的逃亡计划，请对此作出解释。

马　霍：我不知道。

记　者：今早在布兰丁植物园发生的事件，正是你从硬盘里收集的资料带来的结果。

马　霍：我不做评论。

记　者：你有发现斯科菲尔德可能去的其他地点吗？

马　霍：我想我已经说过无可奉告了。

迈克尔：这家伙不简单，似乎他知道我们要去哪儿，看透了我的想法。

记　者：请告诉我们接下来你的计划，硬盘还有什么用？

马　霍：整个调查的细节都是高度机密的。

知识点拨

1. hard drive 表示"硬盘驱动器"。例：If the problem still occurs, your hard drive may be broken. 如果问题持续出现，你的硬盘驱动器可能是坏了。

2. stay out 表示"留在户外，不在家中；避开；不插手"。例：We couldn't stay out there in that desolation another day. 在那个荒凉的地方我们一天也待不下去了。

3. a result of 表示"是……的结果"。例：Foreign currency depreciation is a result of economic depression in the country concerned. 外汇贬值是有关国家经济不景气的结果。

4. collect data 表示"数据 / 资料搜集"。例：In this example, you collect data on network packet receipt and transmission. 在这个例子中，您可以收集关于网络包接收和发送的数据。

5. no comment 表示"无可奉告；拒绝评论，不说"。例：There's been no comment so far from police about the allegations. 到目前为止，警方对这些指控还没有发表任何评论。

6. play...role 表示"扮演……角色，起……作用"。例：She would only play a role if she could identify with the character. 她只愿扮演她能认同的角色。

词汇加油站

claim [kleɪm] *vt.* 声称
substantial [səbˈstænʃl] *adj.* 大量的
botanical [bəˈtænɪkl] *adj.* 植物学的
confidential [ˌkɑːnfiˈdenʃl] *adj.* 机密的

recover [rɪˈkʌvər] *vt.* 找回
retrieve [rɪˈtriːv] *vt.* 恢复
investigation [inˌvestɪˈɡeɪʃn] *n.* （正式的）调查

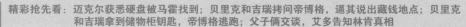

时间： 第 10 集 00:01:10—00:02:49
地点： 奥朗德太太家
人物： 贝里克，吉瑞，帝博格
事件： 贝里克和吉瑞拷问帝博格，逼其说出藏钱地点。

片段二

精彩亮点

吉瑞和贝里克两个人本来已经放弃了希望，决定各奔东西了，但一则新闻为他们指明了前进的方向。他们询问了珍妮特后，得知是帝博格拿走了这 500 万美元，所以一路尾随帝博格。

1

帝博格被贝里克和吉瑞绑在椅子上，遭到一夜毒打后头垂在胸前。吉瑞把音响开得很大以掩盖拷打的声音。

2

贝里克和吉瑞拷问了帝博格一夜后，帝博格什么都不说。吉瑞劝贝里克改变方法，但贝里克仍不肯善罢甘休。

3

帝博格费尽心机搞到了这笔钱，怎么可能轻易就给他们呢？正当气急败坏的贝里克想把他放下来的时候，从帝博格的袜子里掉出了一把储物柜的钥匙。

4

Bellick: Now, you're gonna tell me where you stashed Westmoreland's money… or **I'm gonna pluck you like a chicken, stitch by stitch** [1]. ☺1

Geary: **For a millionaire, you travel light** [2]. **Hey. Hey, what is this?** ☺2

T-Bag: It's for my blood pressure [3].

Bellick: Lookee [4] what I found. Guess Ms. Hollander liked to beat some meat. A couple whacks with this would help you remember where you put the money.

Geary: Hey, we've been beating his ass all night. He ain't coming off [5] the goods. We need to do something different. ☺3

T-Bag: It doesn't matter [6] what you do to me. I ain't talking.

Bellick: Well, I ain't stopping till I get what I came for. How about we listen to that again?

T-Bag: Please.

Bellick: Tell me where that money is or I'm gonna read it on your tombstone.

T-Bag: Okay, I will give you a little clue. It ain't here. ☺4

译文

贝里克：现在，告诉我你把韦斯特莫兰德的钱藏在哪儿了，否则我会一下一下地把你像一只鸡一样拆掉。

吉　瑞：对于你这个百万富翁来说，你的行李还真轻便。喂，这是什么？

帝博格：是我用来量血压的。

贝里克：看看我找到了什么，我猜测奥朗德太太喜欢敲肉。用这个敲你几下也许就能想起把钱藏在哪儿了。

吉　瑞：喂，我们已经揍了他一整晚了，他什么都不说，我们得换别的方法。

帝博格：不管你们对我做什么，我都不会说。

贝里克：达到目的之前我是不会善罢甘休的。我们再听一次歌怎么样？

帝博格：请吧。

贝里克：告诉我钱在哪里，否则你就等着受死吧。

帝博格：好吧，那我告诉你一个线索。钱不在这里。

知识点拨

1. stitch by stitch 表示"一针一线"。例：She put on her spectacles, threaded a needle, and stitch by stitch sewed up the rent in the sleeve. 她戴上眼镜，穿好针，然后一针一针地把衣袖上的裂缝补好。

2. travel light 表示"轻装旅行"。例：When the Cossacks are chasing you around Europe you need to travel light. 当哥萨克人追着你满欧洲跑的时候，你需要轻装上路。

3. blood pressure 表示"血压"。例：Your doctor will monitor your blood pressure. 医生会监测你的血压。

4. lookee 表示"（用以唤起注意）看呐！你注意！"

5. come off 表示"成功；举行；表现；能被去掉（或除去）"。例：It was a good try but it didn't quite come off. 这是一次不错的尝试，但效果欠佳。

6. It doesn't matter… 表示"没关系，没什么"。例：It doesn't matter to me whether you go or not. 你去或不去，对我都没关系。

 词汇加油站

stash [stæʃ] v. 贮藏

stitch [stɪtʃ] n. （缝纫或编织中的）一针

whack [wæk] n. 重击

clue [klu:] n. 线索

pluck [plʌk] vt. 拔掉

millionaire [ˌmɪljəˈner] n. 百万富翁

tombstone [ˈtu:mstoʊn] n. 墓碑

时间： 第 10 集 00:28:32—00:29:43

地点： 奥朗德太太家

片段三

人物： 贝里克，帝博格，吉瑞

事件： 贝里克和吉瑞拿到储物柜钥匙，帝博格逃跑。

 精彩亮点

> 贝里克将帝博格举起时，一把储物柜的钥匙掉了出来，这就是藏五百万美元那个储物柜的钥匙。狡猾的帝博格将钥匙吞到了肚子里，但贝里克是不会善罢甘休的，他会想出什么主意呢？
>
> **1**

> 贝里克命令吉瑞去买些泻药回来，逼帝博格吞下。果然，不一会儿，帝博格就拉肚子了，这一拉便把钥匙拉了出来。
>
> **2**

> 贝里克和吉瑞成功拿到了钥匙，但贝里克并不放心，他马上拨通了911报警电话，还将帝博格铐了起来，帝博格会这样坐以待毙吗？
>
> **3**

> 被绑在电暖气上的帝博格大声尖叫，眼看警察就要破门而入，但是当警察攻入房间时却发现帝博格已经逃得无影无踪了，原来在最后关头他砍断了自己的手才得以逃脱。
>
> **4**

Bellick: Yeah, this is it right here, seventy-five foot, twin diesel Azimut[①] …fly bridge, panoramic. Pull up[②] in a boat like that, you're somebody[③].☺1

Geary: Let me see.

Bellick: Hey, get off.

T-Bag: No.☺2

Bellick: How you doing[④], Bagwell? Get the stool.

Geary: What stool?

Bellick: The stool.

Geary: It's from one of the lockers in a bus station.

Bellick: I'll try not to think about where it's been.

Announcer: 911 operator[⑤], what's your emergency?☺3

T-Bag: Don't do that. Come on.

Bellick: Hey there, send the police. Some scumbag broke into my house.

Announcer: Your address.

Bellick: Yeah, 1605 Midberry Hill.

Announcer: Is he still there?

Bellick: Yeah, you better come quickly.

Geary: Let's hit it[⑥], Roy.☺4

译文

贝里克： 是的，就是这艘，高 75 英尺，双柴油机阿兹慕游艇……即飞桥游艇，还有全景窗户。开这种游艇的肯定是大人物。

吉 瑞： 让我看看。

贝里克： 喂，把手拿开。

帝博格： 不要。

贝里克： 你还好吗，巴格威尔？去拿粪便。

吉 瑞： 什么粪便？

贝里克： 这家伙的粪便。

吉 瑞： 这是巴士站的储物柜钥匙。

贝里克： 我会尽量不去想钥匙是从哪里出来的。

接线员： 911，有何紧急状况？

帝博格： 拜托，别这样。

贝里克： 请派警员来，有个浑蛋闯进了我家。

接线员： 请告诉我地址。

贝里克： 米德贝瑞山庄 1605 号。

接线员： 他还在那里吗？

贝里克： 还在，你们最好快点儿来。

吉 瑞： 走吧，罗伊。

知识点拨

1. Azimut（阿兹慕）是全球顶尖的休闲游艇品牌，其摩登先锋的创新、锐意进取的研发和意大利卓越的工艺，一同构筑了品牌今天的辉煌成就。无论是经典的飞桥游艇还是时尚的运动艇，其设计和生产都代表着全球的顶尖潮流，是欧美和亚洲地区最畅销的意大利游艇品牌之一。

2. pull up 表示"（使）停下（住）；责备；（使）名次提前；从土里拔出来"。例：The cab pulled up and the driver jumped out. 出租车减速停下，司机跳了出来。

3. you're somebody 表示"你是个重要人物"。除了 somebody，表示"重要人物"还有以下几种说法：bigwig；big wheel；big cheese；big shot。

4. How are you doing?=How're you doing? 美国口语（尤其是黑人口语）习惯把 are 省略而说成："How you doing?"

5. 911 是美国通用的报警电话号码。消防电话、急救电话、警报电话都是 911。2001 年 9 月 11 日美国发生了 9·11 事件，使 911 报警电话更加出名。

 词汇加油站

diesel ['diːzl] *n.* 柴油机

pull [pʊl] *vi.* 划（船）

locker ['lɑːkər] *n.* 储物柜

scumbag ['skʌmbæg] *n.* 卑鄙的家伙

panoramic [ˌpænəˈræmɪk] *adj.* 全景的

stool [stuːl] *n.* 粪便

emergency [ɪˈmɜːrdʒənsi] *n.* 紧急情况

时间： 第11集 00:04:17—00:05:37

地点： 艾多办公室

人物： 艾多，林肯

事件： 父子俩交谈，艾多告知林肯真相。

精彩亮点

1
林肯的父亲终于正式出场了。先前，林肯带着儿子 L.J. 逃跑时险些被捕，营救他们父子俩的正是林肯的父亲艾多。

2
艾多向林肯解释说，他所在的组织为一些大机构工作，目的是要揭穿总统的真面目。总统就是"公司"的傀儡，他们的最终目的就是搞垮"公司"。

3
林肯自认为自己被诬陷入狱，还险些被处以死刑，与总统和"公司"一点儿关联都没有，自己就是一个普通百姓，也不曾与这些人有过往来或利益纠纷，但事实果真如此吗？

4
艾多告诉林肯他们的组织曾与一位分析师密切合作，而这位分析师已经拿到了能够证明林肯无辜的证据，但这个人失踪了。作为录音的证据还在，艾多认为这份证据在莎拉手里。

Aldo: It's corporate interests taking over… buying elections, fighting wars. People dying so they can turn a profit①. We're trying to stop it. ☺1

Lincoln: What are you, a bunch of spies?

Aldo: Just a handful of② senators, congressmen. People like me that once worked for The Company. People willing to expose the president for what she is. A shill③ working for these corporations. We bring her down, we bring them down. ☺2

Lincoln: What's it got to do with me?

Aldo: Because the way we'll bring her down is also what we're gonna use to set you free. ☺3 About a week ago, we finally got a break④. An NSA analyst sympathetic to our cause…finally worked his way up and got clearance into the Echelon program, Emails, cellphone calls all across this country. If it's transmitted, it goes through Echelon. It's cataloged, interpreted, and then stored for Homeland Security. Nothing is missed by them. Nothing. Including, by accident⑤, for a few months after 9/11…the White House. The analyst got his hands on a phone conversation the president had…with Terrence, two weeks after you supposedly killed him. The analyst tried to get this information out of the building,… ☺4

译文

艾多： 财团利益控制了政府……选举贿选、引发战争。他们用人命去换商业利益，我们要阻止他们。

林肯： 那你们是谁？间谍吗？

艾多： 只是几个参议员和众议员。像我这样的"公司"前员工愿意揭发总统的真面目，她是这些企业的傀儡，我们要把她搞垮，他们就会瓦解。

林肯： 那这跟我有什么关系？

艾多： 因为我们可以利用搞垮她的方式让你获得自由。就在约一周前，我们终于有了进展。一位对我们目的有同感的国家安全局分析师终于升职通过安全检查进入梯队系统，全国的电子邮件、手机通话，只要是通讯都会经过梯队系统。通讯经过分类、编译再存档，供国土安全部参考。什么都躲不过他们的耳目，什么都逃不过，包括9·11事件后的几个月间意外截取到的白宫通话记录。这位分析师发现就在称你谋杀了特伦斯的两周后，总统和特伦斯通过话。这位分析师想将这个信息放出去……

知识点拨

1. turn a profit 表示"获利；盈利；赚到一笔"。例：To turn a profit, he needs to produce more than four million chopsticks a day, which he is on track to do in the next month or two. 为了获取利润，他需要一天生产四百万双筷子，这就是他接下来这一两个月要做的。

2. a handful of 表示"一把；少数，几个，不多"。例：Only a handful of firms offer share option schemes to all their employees. 只有少数几家公司向所有员工提供股票期权方案。

3. shill 表示"雇用的骗子"，即"托儿"。例：And this is one reason that shill bidding is more rampancy in auction. 这也是"托儿"在拍卖中更加猖獗的原因之一。

4. get a break 表示"时来运转"。例：It would be good for you to get a break, they said. 他们说，换换环境对我有好处。

5. by accident 表示"偶然地，不经意地"。例：She discovered the problem by accident. 她偶然发现了这个问题。

 词汇加油站

bunch [bʌntʃ] *n.* 大量
handful ['hændfʊl] *n.* 少量
clearance ['klɪrəns] *n.* 空隙
interpret [ɪn'tɜ:rprɪt] *vt.* 诠释

spy [spaɪ] *n.* 间谍
sympathetic [ˌsɪmpə'θetɪk] *adj.* 赞同的
transmit [træns'mɪt] *vt.* 传输

Scene 6 父子团聚

时间： 第12集 00:09:42—00:10:47
地点： 室外空地
人物： 迈克尔，艾多，林肯
事件： 迈克尔与父亲见面，父亲告知当年离开的原因。

精彩亮点

1　迈克尔从小是由母亲一手带大的，所以他对父亲没什么印象，对于抛弃他们的父亲一直怀恨在心。在迈克尔看来，父亲为了事业抛弃了家庭。

2　父亲也一直很愧疚，但他认为自己的选择是正确的，只有这样才能保护他的家人。他为"公司"工作，而且自己在"公司"还是一个重要人物，后来因为背叛"公司"而成为目标。为了防止"公司"通过他的家人找到他，他要与家人断绝联系。

3　由于看不惯公司的腐败作风，艾多离开了"公司"，自己又成立了一家与"公司"对着干的组织。如果当年不离开家人，就会让他们深陷危机，所以艾多选择离开。

4　与艾多密切合作的那位分析师失踪前留下了一个录音带，里面记录着所有证据，而这盒带子就在迈克尔的女友莎拉身上。

Michael: Yes, Linc told me about The Company①. You were some kind of analyst. **That's the job you chose over your family.** ☺1

Aldo: **I thought I was doing the right thing,** protecting **you.** ☺2

Michael: From what, Dad? From who?

Aldo: The Company had enemies. I was important to② The Company. I became a target. **Easiest way to get to me would be to get to you.** ☺3 I left as soon as I realized how corrupt it was. How they were buying the government.

Michael: You could've come back.

Aldo: No, I couldn't! Michael, turning on③ The Company put me and you at even greater risk④. I had to stay away⑤.

Michael: We were your sons.

Aldo: And you still are, Michael. We can fix this. I came back⑥ so that we could fix this.

Michael: This can never be fixed.

Aldo: There's a tape. It gives us everything we need. Linc will be set free if we find it.

Lincoln: You're not gonna believe who he thinks has it.

Michael: Who?

Lincoln: Sara. ☺4

译文

迈克尔：是的，林肯告诉过我"公司"的事。你也是分析师，而你为了工作抛弃了家庭。

艾 多：我认为自己这样做是对的，这样才能保护你们。

迈克尔：谁会危害我们，爸？

艾 多：公司有很多敌人，而我对公司又至关重要，后来我成为目标，通过你们就能轻松逮到我。当我发现公司是多么腐败，发现他们是如何收买政府的以后，我就马上离开了。

迈克尔：你本可以回到我们身边。

艾 多：不，我不可以！迈克尔，我背叛公司让我们都深陷更大的危机，我必须得离开你们。

迈克尔：我们是你的儿子！

艾 多：迈克尔，你现在仍然是我的儿子，我们可以解决这件事，我回来就是为了解决这件事。

迈克尔：永远不可能解决。

艾 多：有一段录音，里面有我们所需的全部证据。如果我们能找到它，林肯就能重获自由。

林 肯：你一定想不到他认为东西在谁手上。

迈克尔：谁？

林 肯：莎拉。

知识点拨

1. tell sb. about sth. 表示"讲述，告诉（某人）有关……的情况，谈及"。例：Women usually want to know about you, but even more they would like to tell about themselves. 女人通常都想了解你，但她们更愿意谈论自己。

2. be important to sb./sth., 表示"对某人/事物很重要"，强调对某人/事物很重要的东西。而 be important for sb. 是说"某事对某人的重要性"，强调做某事对某人的重要性。

3. turn on 表示"打开（水、电视、收音机、灯、煤气等）；（使）感兴趣；（使）兴奋；发动；攻击"。例：Demonstrators turned on police, overturning vehicles and setting fire to them. 示威者们攻击警察，推翻车辆并将其纵火焚烧。

4. put sb. at risk 表示"让某人处于危险中"。例：Exchanging vows with a junk food addict could put you at risk of developing the same vice. 比如说，如果你的另一半喜欢吃垃圾食品，你也很有可能受他影响喜欢上垃圾食品。

5. stay away 表示"躲开，离开；缺席"。例：A lone mother Canada goose honked a warning to stay away from her nest. 一只孤独无伴的雌性加拿大黑雁鸣叫了一声，警告别人不要靠近它的巢。

6. come back 表示"回来；记起；强烈反驳；重复说"。偏重表示"回来"。例：When I thought about it, it all came back. 当我回想起来，往事全都涌上了心头。

 词汇加油站

analyst ['ænəlɪst] *n.* 分析家
corrupt [kə'rʌpt] *adj.* 腐败的
fix [fɪks] *vt.* 修理
gonna ['ɡɔːnə] *n.* 将要

protect [prə'tekt] *vt.* 保护
risk [rɪsk] *n.* 危险
tape [teɪp] *n.* 带子

片段二

时间： 第13集 00:01:00—00:02:36

地点： 室外空地

人物： 迈克尔，马霍，林肯，警察，莎拉

事件： 马霍欲枪杀兄弟俩，边境巡警队逮捕兄弟俩。

 精彩亮点

1 　　迈克尔好不容易发现附近有座电视塔，可以接收到信号。因为先前父亲告诉他，记录林肯一案关键证据的录音带在莎拉手中，他要与莎拉通话。但没想到，马霍却一路尾随他们。

2 　　马霍得意扬扬地跟迈克尔和林肯说："你们差一点儿就成功了"。受伤的迈克尔和林肯从车里爬出来，马霍的枪口正对着他们。

3 　　迈克尔手上握有对马霍不利的证据：马霍杀了连环杀人犯，把尸体埋在了自己家的花园中，至此，他的心理就出现了很大问题，必须服用药物保持镇静。

4 　　就在马霍要向迈克尔和林肯开枪时，边境巡警队来了。对于马霍而言，他没有办法枪杀兄弟俩，而对于兄弟俩来说，又不得不被抓回监狱。

Michael: If we're gonna go down①, might as well② go down swinging. Sara.☺1

Sara: Michael?

Mahone: Almost made it③.☺2

Sarah: Hello? Hello, Michael? Is that you?

Mahone: Get up. Turn around. Turn around!

Michael: If you're gonna murder us, Alex, you'll have to look us in the eyes④ while you do it.

Mahone: Shut up.

Lincoln: You want me, you got me. Let my brother go!

Mahone: I don't want either of you. I just want my life back!

Michael: You're gonna kill two innocent men to get it?

Mahone: Absolutely.

Police: This is the United States Border Patrol. Drop the weapon and remain where you are. Drop the weapon, United States Border Patrol! Drop your weapon! All agents hold your positions.

Mahone: I'm FBI. These men are in my custody⑤.☺3

Police: I don't care who you are. Until we verify, you will drop your weapon or we will drop you. You choice. Move in! Hands on your head now! Don't move.☺4

译文

迈克尔：就算我们要死，也要死得轰轰烈烈。莎拉。

莎 拉：迈克尔？

马 霍：你们只差一点儿就成功了。

莎 拉：喂？喂，迈克尔，是你吗？

马 霍：站起来，转过去，转过去！

迈克尔：马霍，如果你打算杀我们，你就看着我们的眼睛开枪。

马 霍：闭嘴！

林 肯：你已经逮住我了，让我弟弟走！

马 霍：你们俩我谁都不想要，我只想找回我的人生！

迈克尔：为了你的目的，你要杀死两个无辜的人？

马 霍：那当然！

警 察：我们是美国边境巡警队，放下武器，待在原地。放下武器，我们是美国边境巡警队，放下武器！所有人各就各位。

马 霍：我是联邦调查局探员，他们已被我逮捕。

警 察：我不管你是谁，在确认身份前放下你的武器，否则我们会开枪。你自己选择！往前走！双手抱头，快点儿！不准动！

知识点拨

1. go down 表示"停止；被接受；沉下；被打败"。片中表示"牺牲"。例：They went down 2-1 to Australia. 他们以1比2输给了澳大利亚队。

2. might as well 表示"还是……的好；不妨，莫如，何妨"。例：I'll come with you if you like. I might as well. 如果你想的话，我会和你一起来，我无所谓。

3. make it 是美国俚语，其常见用法如下：1）用来表示规定时间，常与 can，let 等词连用；2）用来表示达到预定目标，"办成，做到；成功；发迹"；3）用来表示及时抵达，"赶上"；4）用来表示（疾病）等得到好转，"得救"；5）用来表示相处得很好，"受欢迎（或尊重），被接受（与 with 连用）"；6）用来表示预定小吃。

4. look sb. in the eyes=look sb. in the face 表示"直视某人（因觉得惭愧，尴尬等）"。例：Can you look me in the eyes and say you didn't break the window? 你能直视我的眼睛说，窗户不是你打碎的吗？

5. be in custody 表示"在押"。例：To say the least, even if the appeal succeeded, the case may probably continue to be in custody to face the embarrassing situation. 退一步讲，即使上诉胜利了，绝大多数情况下也得面临被继续羁押的尴尬局面。

 词汇加油站

swing ['swɪŋ] v. （使）摇摆
shut [ʃʌt] vt. 关闭
absolutely ['æbsəluːtli] adv. 绝对地
custody ['kʌstədi] n. 拘留

murder ['mɜːrdər] vt. 凶杀
innocent ['ɪnəsnt] adj. 无辜的
patrol [pə'troʊl] n. 巡查
verify ['verɪfaɪ] vt. 证明

时间： 第 13 集 00:05:18—00:06:34
地点： 酒吧
片段三
人物： 帝博格，长官
事件： 帝博格与长官交谈，欲获知安装假手途径。

精彩亮点

坐在酒吧里的帝博格看到电视里在报道迈克尔和林肯被抓捕的消息高兴得合不拢嘴。他环顾四周，酒吧里许多人也都安了假手，他能否找到安装假手的方法呢？

1

满嘴谎言的帝博格说，自己从沙漠报效祖国刚回来，但军方安排治疗的医生治疗得很毛躁，长官不由得有些同情他。

2

帝博格想要向那位长官炫一下富，前些日子，虽然被贝里克和吉瑞整得很惨，但最终他还是杀了吉瑞，抢回了那五百万美元。

3

长官讽刺地跟帝博格说：既然你能把头发染成那样，也一定能想办法安上假手。这番讥讽让帝博格心里很不是滋味，他望向了长官的手，暗下决心，要把长官的手安到自己的断手上。

4

T-Bag: Excuse me, sarge①. I was wondering if you could help a brother out②. ☺₁

Sarge: With what?

T-Bag: I only recently returned from delivering democracy to the desert… and I was wondering if you could tell me…how a guy goes about getting one of those prosthetic jobbies?

Sarge: Didn't they make you whole before they shipped you?

T-Bag: Well, let's just say the doctor made the bed③, he just neglected to tuck in④ the sheets.

Sarge: Best thing for you to do is go on down there to the VA, get in line⑤.

T-Bag: That simple?

Sarge: Yeah. Till they send you the bill, and you gotta pay it. Those bastards in Washington send us to fight for them. Not a damn one of them fights for us.

T-Bag: Man, that is a crime. But luckily for me…money is not the issue. ☺₂

Sarge: Is that right?

T-Bag: Any particular forms I might need in order to qualify?

Sarge: You know what, Mr. Don't Ask Don't Tell⑥? You figured out how to dye that hair of yours…up like a nancy all by yourself. You sure as well can figure out how to get a prosthetic…for that stump of yours by yourself. ☺₃

T-Bag: Yeah, I think I got a pretty good idea where to start. ☺₄

译文

帝博格： 打扰一下，长官。我在想您是否可以帮弟兄个忙？

长　官： 什么忙？

帝博格： 我最近刚从沙漠报效国家回来……我在想你可否告诉我……要去哪里才能装假肢？

长　官： 你被送回国前军方没帮你治疗吗？

帝博格： 是这样，我只能说那个医生治疗得毛躁。

长　官： 你最好去荣民医院排队等待。

帝博格： 就那么简单？

长　官： 是的，但过后他们会给你寄账单，然后你要支付医药费。华盛顿的那些坏蛋送我们去替他们打仗，他们却没人愿意帮我们。

帝博格： 这简直是犯罪啊，但我还算幸运……钱不成问题。

长　官： 是吗？

帝博格： 我需要填哪些表格吗？

长　官： 你知道吗，同性恋先生？你既然知道如何把你的头发染得这么女性化，你肯定可以自己想办法弄到假肢，装在你的断手上。

帝博格： 没错，我想我知道该从哪里下手了。

知识点拨

1. "沙展"（sergeant）是一种音译，职级也就是一个小队的队长，sarge 是俚语表达。

2. help sb. out 表示"帮助某人解决难题，帮助某人摆脱困境，帮助某人完成工作"。例：Help sb. out of pity, kindness, generosity, etc. 出于怜悯、好意、慷慨等帮助某人。

3. make the bed 表示"铺床"。例：I have to make the bed and do the laundry. 我得整理床铺和洗衣服。

4. tuck in 表示"把……掖进去"。例："Probably." I said, tucking in my shirt. "大概吧。"我边说边把衬衫掖了进去。

5. get in line 表示"排队"。例：Listen carefully! When I call you please get in line. 听仔细着！当我叫你的名字时，请过来站到队里。

6. don't ask, don't tell 表示"不许问，不许说"。

词汇加油站

prosthetic [prɑːsˈθetɪk] *adj.* 假体的
bastard [ˈbæstərd] *n.* 态度傲慢且令人讨厌的人
qualify [ˈkwɑːlɪfaɪ] *vt.* （使）具有资格
stump [stʌmp] *n.* 假肢

tuck [tʌk] *vt.* 裹起
crime [kraɪm] *n.* 罪行
dye [daɪ] *vt.* 给……染色

时间： 第 14 集 00:02:37—00:03:48

地点： 凯勒曼车中

片段四

人物： 迈克尔，凯勒曼，亨弗里斯，警官

事件： 凯勒曼帮助迈克尔和林肯躲避追捕。

精彩亮点

林肯和迈克尔在被押往另一处的过程中，马霍故意将手铐的钥匙放在兄弟俩面前。聪明的迈克尔知道这其中一定有诈，马霍是想要在他们逃出去的时候枪杀他们。虽知有诈他们两个人还是决定冒险一试。就在马霍和凯勒曼将兄弟俩包围时，凯勒曼却击中了马霍。他为什么要这么做呢？**1**

凯勒曼曾经爱慕副总统卡罗琳，愿意为她做任何事。但最近来了一个叫金的家伙，对他颐指气使，这让他心里很不舒服。于是，他决定给副总统他们一点儿颜色瞧瞧。**2**

发现兄弟俩逃跑后，各处警力集结，誓要抓捕这两名逃犯。在凯勒曼的帮助下，兄弟俩能否顺利逃过警方的搜查呢？**3**

亨弗里斯是位十分负责的小队长，面对凯勒曼的权势威胁，他丝毫没有动摇。凯勒曼表示：如果耽误了他追捕两名逃犯的时间，后果由你们这些人承担！亨弗里斯的上级不想惹事，就命令亨弗里斯放行了。**4**

Michael: Who are you?☺1

Kellerman: I used to work for the president.

Michael: Why are you helping us?

Kellerman: Lay down① on the floor. Now. Federal agent②, let me through.☺2

Humphries: Air support is telling us that they saw your vehicle traveling down Route 46.

Kellerman: Forty six is a possible exit route for the convicts. I was securing it.

Humphries: No offense③, sir, but we're searching every vehicle.

Kellerman: No offense. Either you let me through or you get me a supervisor.

Humphries: I'm supervising this roadblock, Agent Kellerman. I'm sorry, but I need you to get out of the vehicle.

Kellerman: Sergeant Humphries. Lincoln and Scofield have been loose for less than 10 minutes. That means every second is critical. So if you detain me… for one moment more, I will have all of your jobs. Do you understand me?☺3

Police: Go ahead④.

Humphries: What?

Police: Just let him go⑤.☺4

译文

迈 克 尔：你是谁？

凯 勒 曼：我曾为总统效力。

迈 克 尔：为什么你要帮助我们？

凯 勒 曼：趴下去，快点儿！我是联邦探员，让我过去。

亨弗里斯：空中小队说看见你的车子沿着四十六号公路前进。

凯 勒 曼：逃犯可能会从四十六号公路逃走，我负责搜查。

亨弗里斯：无意冒犯，先生，请别介意我们要检查每一辆车。

凯 勒 曼：无意冒犯，让我过去，否则就请你的长官来。

亨弗里斯：凯勒曼探员，这条路障由我负责。抱歉，但是请你下车。

凯 勒 曼：亨弗里斯小队长，林肯和斯科菲尔德脱逃还不到十分钟，这意味着每一秒都很重要。如果你再拖延我……哪怕是一秒钟，我也会让你们全部失业。听懂了吗？

警　　官：你走吧。

亨弗里斯：什么？

警　　官：就让他走吧。

知识点拨

1. lay down 表示"放下；规定；放弃；建造"。例：Daniel finished the article and laid the newspaper down on his desk. 丹尼尔看完文章后把报纸放在他的书桌上。

2. federal agent 表示"联邦探员"。例：I already got you for killing a federal agent. 我知道你杀了一个联邦探员。

3. no offense 表示"无意冒犯"。例：No offense, but you make an unlikely dove. 无意冒犯，但你成了一个不可靠的天真的人。

4. go ahead 的意思很多，主要有三个用法：1）表示同意或允许，根据情况可译为"说吧，做吧，开始吧，进行吧"；2）表示继续或持续，通常可译为"继续……吧"；3）表示请对方先走或先做某事，其意为"你先走一步，你先请"。

5. let sb. go 表示"让某人走"。例：Since someone has to go anyway, let me go. 反正得去一个人，就让我去吧！

 词汇加油站

vehicle ['vi:hɪkl] *n.* 交通工具

exit ['egzɪt, 'eksɪt] *n.* 出口

offense [ə'fens] *n.* 攻势

roadblock ['roʊdblɑ:k] *n.* 路障

route [ru:t, raʊt] *n.* 路

secure [sə'kjʊr] *vt.* 使安全

supervisor ['su:pərvaɪzər] *n.* 管理者

detain [dɪ'teɪn] *vt.* 拘留，扣留

Scene 7 凯勒曼的转变

片段一

时间： 第 14 集 00:10:28—00:11:24
地点： 凯勒曼的车上
人物： 迈克尔，凯勒曼，金，林肯
事件： 凯勒曼向金谎报迈克尔和林肯已死。

精彩亮点

1
迈克尔用颇带讽刺的口吻说：一群身着西装的小鬼在到处乱窜互相残杀。这其中含有太多利益纠葛，也不乏情感纠葛。

2
林肯说话直爽，他没有想过要感谢凯勒曼，毕竟先前要不是副总统命令他做出了那些伤天害理的事，他和迈克尔也不至于沦落到今天四处逃命的地步。

3
此时的金还不知道到底发生了什么。凯勒曼心情大好，欺骗金说马霍是林肯开枪打中的，甚至还虚情假意地称赞起金来。

4
凯勒曼声称林肯兄弟已经死了，自己正在埋尸体。但金坚持要看到他们的尸体，凯勒曼说可以给他看照片，但金一再强调不要埋尸体。曾经凯勒曼说杀死了莎拉，但事后证明莎拉并没有死，这让金对凯勒曼心生戒备，更何况是如此聪明的迈克尔及其哥哥，又怎会轻易死在他手中？

Michael: So, this is the conspiracy, huh? A bunch of little boys in suits① running around② trying to kill each other. It's pathetic. ☺1

Kellerman: Well, you were a little more formidable than we anticipated.

Lincoln: We don't need compliments out of you, jackass③. ☺2

Kellerman: Oh, yes, there it is. The winning Lincoln personality.

Lincoln: Shut your mouth and drive.

Kellerman: The one we really knew would win over④ a jury. Good work⑤. Mr. Kim.

Kim: What the hell is going on out there? ☺3

Kellerman: It was touch and go⑥ for a minute. but I got everything handled.

Kim: Mahone's been shot.

Kellerman: Yes, I know, Bill, I was there. I saw Lincoln pull the trigger. We lost a valuable asset, but… ☺4

Kim: Mahone's alive.

Kellerman: That's good. It looked bad, so...

Kim: Where are Lincoln and Scofield?

Kellerman: Lincoln and Scofield are dead. And they're in my SUV⑦. I'm heading out to bury them. Right now.

译文

迈克尔： 所以说，这就是阴谋，不是吗？一堆穿着西装的小鬼到处乱窜互相残杀？多么可悲啊。

凯勒曼： 老实说，我们没想到你们会那么难对付。

林　肯： 浑蛋，我们不需要你称赞。

凯勒曼： 哦，看吧，出现了，林肯讨人喜欢的个性。

林　肯： 闭上你的嘴，开车。

凯勒曼： 我们知道你会讨陪审团的欢心，干得好！金先生。

金： 到底出了什么事？

凯勒曼： 刚刚一度有些混乱……但一切都在我的掌控中。

金： 马霍中弹了。

凯勒曼： 是的，我知道，比尔，我在场，我看见林肯扣下了扳机。我们失去了宝贵的一员，但……

金： 马霍还活着。

凯勒曼： 那真是太好了，因为伤势看来不轻。

金： 林肯和斯科菲尔德现在在哪儿？

凯勒曼： 他们已经死了，在我的运动型多用途跑车上，我现在正要去埋尸体。

知识点拨

1. in suits 表示"西装革履的"。例：The young women are dressed in kimonos and the young men are in suits and ties. 这个年轻的女人穿着和服，这个年轻的男子穿着西装、系着领带。

2. run around 表示"东奔西跑，奔忙，（尤指孩子）到处玩耍游逛"。例：No one noticed we had been running around emptying bins and cleaning up. 没有人注意到我们一直都在东奔西跑地倒垃圾，打扫卫生。

3. jackass 表示"公驴；愚人，傻子"。例：You made yourself look like a jackass. 你令自己看起来像个傻瓜。

4. win over 表示"争取，赢得……的支持（赞同）；胜诉；收揽"。例：He has won over a significant number of the left-wing deputies. 他争取到了相当数量的左翼代表的支持。

5. good work=good job 表示"（工作）做得好；善事，好行为"。例：Provide constructive feedback and acknowledged good work. 给予有建设性的回馈和优秀的工作表现。

6. touch and go 最初为航空专用术语。指的是飞机着陆时刚接触到地面就立刻拉升起飞。即连续起飞。现在已经引申为"危险的，不稳定的，无把握的"。

7. SUV 的全称是 Sport Utility Vehicle，即"运动型多用途汽车"；称之为 Suburban Utility Vehicle，即"城郊多用途汽车"。

 词汇加油站

conspiracy [kən'spɪrəsi] *n.* 阴谋
formidable ['fɔːrmɪdəbl] *adj.* 难以对付的
compliment ['kɑːmplɪmənt] *n.* 恭维
jury ['dʒʊri] *n.* 陪审团

pathetic [pə'θetɪk] *adj.* 令人同情的
anticipate [æn'tɪsɪpeɪt] *vt.* 预料
personality [,pɜːrsə'næləti] *n.* 个性
trigger ['trɪgər] *n.* （枪）扳机

时间： 第 15 集 00:02:02—00:03:00

地点： 特伦斯藏身小木屋

人物： 林肯，凯勒曼，迈克尔，巡警，记者

事件： 特伦斯自杀身亡，迈克尔等人躲避警察追捕。

精彩亮点

1 迈克尔等人从凯勒曼那里得知了特伦斯的藏身地点，他们前往小木屋，找到了特伦斯。迈克尔想要说服特伦斯站出来，澄清事实，特伦斯果断拒绝。迈克尔拨通了电视台电话，表明接下来会证明林肯的清白，但随后特伦斯就举枪自尽了。

2 现场留下了林肯等人的指纹，这下就算林肯是无辜的，也会被怀疑是他枪杀了特伦斯，那么，接下来他们该怎么办呢？

3 这间小木屋只有正门一个出口，迈克尔当即决定就从这扇门走出去，当然要利用凯勒曼联邦调查局专员的身份，那他们具体要怎么做呢？

4 一个巡警询问凯勒曼是谁，凯勒曼一边压着迈克尔和林肯，一边往门外走，告诉他自己是联邦调查局的。就在这时，凯勒曼用枪对准摄像师的头，林肯则拿枪对准巡警，迈克尔命令女记者去拿车钥匙，三人各有分工，最后顺利驾车逃跑。

Patrol: **This is the Montana Highway Patrol**①, **Michael Scofield and Lincoln Burrows, … you need to exit with your hands in the air**②. ☺₁ This is a warning. You got line of sight③ from there? Exit with your hands up.

Lincoln: What about him?

Kellerman: **Him? He's useless. Dead body**④. ☺₂

Lincoln: We got fingerprints everywhere.

Kellerman: You worried someone will pin a murder on you⑤?

Lincoln: What's your plan? Leave the body, walk out the door?

Michael: **Yes. That's exactly what we're gonna do.** ☺₃

Patrol: Michael Scofield and Lincoln Burrows, you need to exit with your hands up.

Kellerman: FBI, hold your fire⑥.

Journalist: FBI?

Kellerman: I have Lincoln and Scofield. Start rolling. We're coming out. Hold your fire.

Patrol: Hold up⑦, who are you?

Kellerman: **Federal Bureau of Investigation. We're going to Billings.** ☺₄

译文

巡 警：我们是蒙大拿公路巡警，迈克尔·斯科菲尔德，林肯·巴罗斯，请把双手举高走出来，这是警告。你可以看到里头吗？举起双手出来。

林 肯：他怎么办？

凯勒曼：他？他毫无用处。只是一具尸体罢了。

林 肯：到处都是我们的指纹。

凯勒曼：你担心会被控谋杀？

林 肯：你有什么计划？还是说你想丢下尸体从前门走出去？

迈克尔：对，我们就要这么做。

巡 警：迈克尔·斯科菲尔德，林肯·巴罗斯，把双手举高走出来。

凯勒曼：我是联邦调查局的，不要开枪。

记 者：联邦调查局？

凯勒曼：我已制伏了他们两个，快滚出去。我们要出来了，不要开枪。

巡 警：等一下，你是谁？

凯勒曼：我是联邦调查局的，我们要去比灵斯市。

知识点拨

1. highway patrol 表示"公路巡逻队"。例：He saw the flashing lights of the highway patrol car in his driving mirror. 他从后视镜中看见公路巡逻车闪烁的车灯。

2. in the air 表示"悬而未决；（谣言等）传开，流行开来；半空中"。例：This may provide a quick and accurate way of monitoring the amount of carbon dioxide in the air. 这也许能提供一个监测空气中二氧化碳含量的既快又准的方法。

3. line of sight 表示"视线，瞄准线"。例：Claire positioned herself so as not to obstruct David's line of sight. 克莱尔为了不挡住大卫的视线挪了一下位置。

4. dead body 表示"尸体，死尸"。例：He dived into the water to look for the dead body. 他潜入水底找寻尸首。

5. pin sth. on sb. 表示"钉上，别上；把（某事）归咎于（某人），把（责任等）强加于（某人）"。例：The bank manager was really to blame, though he tried to pin it on a clerk. 真正受责备的应该是银行经理，可是他却想把责任推到一个职员身上。

6. hold your fire 表示"别开枪"。例：Hold your fire! We got hostages, so back off! 别开枪！我们有人质，退后！

7. hold up 表示"举起，支撑；耽搁；持械抢劫"。例：Why were you holding everyone up? 你为什么要耽搁大家？

词汇加油站

highway ['haɪweɪ] *n.* 公路

exit ['egzɪt] *v.* 退出

fingerprint ['fɪŋgərprɪnt] *n.* 指纹

roll [roʊl] *vt.* 滚动，翻滚

patrol [pə'troʊl] *n.* 侦察队

warning ['wɔ:rnɪŋ] *n.* 警告

pin [pɪn] *vt.* 牵制

时间： 第 15 集 00:04:43—00:06:01
地点： 汽车内
人物： 凯勒曼，迈克尔，林肯，雷诺兹，播音员
事件： 迈克尔等人驾车逃亡，迈克尔另有计划。

精彩亮点

1
林肯驾车，迈克尔坐在副驾驶的位置，凯勒曼则坐在后面用枪顶住摄像师的头。现在，特伦斯真的死了，无法作证；莎拉也不知所踪，关键的证据在她的手里。林肯为此感到一片茫然。

2
广播里播放了一则关于特伦斯的新闻，从中得知副总统正忙于为竞选总统寻求各州支持，这不由得让迈克尔计上心来。

3
林肯认为迈克尔让他停车是想要放了摄影师，此外，他还建议迈克尔赶快甩掉凯勒曼，但迈克尔又做何打算呢？

4
迈克尔表示那个摄影师还有用途：他想让那个摄影师拍摄一段视频，他要和林肯在视频中说出副总统的阴谋。看了电视的金坐不住了，要求在这则消息上头条前立刻将其封杀。

Kellerman: I'll make you a deal①. You don't move a muscle; I won't blow your head off.☺1

Michael: No one's gonna hurt you, Greg.

Lincoln: Where are we going, Michael? We can't keep driving. Lost Steadman. Sara's in the wind…☺2

Kellerman: Turn it up②.

Announcer: Murder of Terrence Steadman, President Reynolds' brother. The president could not be reached as she continues to tour the Midwest, shoring up③ support in key states.

Reynolds: For entrepreneurs and orange growers, iron workers and artists, the American dream is alive and well for all of us.

Announcer: Reynolds travels to Colorado today, for a scheduled appearance in Denver that…☺3

Michael: Pull over④.

Lincoln: What for?

Michael: Just pull over.

Kellerman: Get out. Over here.

Lincoln: You want to drop off⑤ this kid?

Michael: Later.☺4

Lincoln: We should get rid of⑥ Kellerman too. We don't need him.

Michael: Actually, we do. We still have assets. It's just a question of how we use them.

译文

凯勒曼： 我跟你做笔交易，只要你乖乖不动我就不割掉你的头。

迈克尔： 我们不会伤害你的，格雷格。

林　肯： 我们要去哪儿，迈克尔？我们不能就这样一直开下去，斯蒂德曼死了，莎拉又不知所踪。

凯勒曼： 把音量调高点儿。

播音员： 雷诺兹总统的弟弟特伦斯·斯蒂德曼遭谋杀。总统目前尚未发表声明，她正在中西部进行访问，在关键的几个州寻求支持。

雷诺兹： 对企业家、橘子种植者，钢铁工人和艺术家来说，美国梦仍然为我们存在。

播音员： 雷诺兹今天前往科罗拉多州，预计莅临丹佛市。

迈克尔： 停车。

林　肯： 怎么了？

迈克尔： 停车就是了。

凯勒曼： 出来，过来。

林　肯： 你想放了那小子？

迈克尔： 待会吧。

林　肯： 我们也应该把凯勒曼甩掉，我们不需要他。

迈克尔： 事实上，我们还需要他。我们手上还有王牌，只是看我们如何使用了。

知识点拨

1. make sb. a deal=make a deal with sb. 表示"成交；达成交易"。例：You're not going to get out of here unless we make a deal. 除非我们达成协议，否则你就别想从这儿出去。

2. turn up 可以指"出现；翻起；（声音）开大，（尤指失去后偶然）被发现"。片中表示"将音量调高"。例：Bill would turn up the TV in the other room. 比尔会把另一个房间里的电视声音开大。

3. shore up 表示"支撑住"。例：But this was partly to shore up support for the North American Free Trade Agreement. 但是这在一定程度上扶持了它对北美自由贸易协定的支持。

4. pull over 表示"靠边停车"。例：He noticed a man behind him in a blue Ford gesticulating to pull over. 他注意到身后一个开蓝色福特车的男人正打手势要靠边停车。

5. drop off 可以表示"减少；落下；送下车；不知不觉入睡"，偏重表示"送下车"。例：I'll drop off at the corner of Zhongshan street. 我在中山路拐角处下车。

6. get rid of 表示"除掉，去掉；涤荡；革除，摈除"。例：I began to have a sinking feeling that I was not going to get rid of her. 我开始有一种永远也摆脱不了她的沮丧情绪。

 词汇加油站

muscle ['mʌsl] *n.* 肌肉

tour [tʊr] *vt.* 到……旅游

entrepreneur [ˌɑ:ntrəprəˈnɜ:r] *n.* 企业家

schedule ['skedʒu:l] *vt.* 安排

blow [bloʊ] *vt.* 使爆炸

shore [ʃɔ:r] *vt.* 支持

iron ['aɪərn] *n.* 铁器

时间： 第 16 集 00:06:59—00:08:06
地点： 联邦调查局办公室
人物： 马霍，惠勒，金
事件： 惠勒对马霍转变态度，马霍不满。

精彩亮点

1　马霍现在的全部精力都放在迈克尔和林肯身上。他推测既然他们是驾车逃跑的，车子总会有没油的时候，这样一来加油站就是逮捕他们的最佳地点。

2　原来马霍的手下惠勒却表示先不要管迈克尔和林肯，因为又有一起杀人案就在不久前发生了。凶手是精神病患者帕特斯科，他残忍地杀死了一位老妇人。

3　马霍却表示这件事可以叫麦迪逊分局的特工支援，但惠勒却一口回绝，坚持要报告总部。马霍觉察出惠勒态度的转变，他马上拨通了金的电话。

4　马霍向金表示帕特斯科并不具有威胁性，他就是一个精神病罢了，但金却坚持说帕特斯科与迈克尔曾处于同一牢房，而迈克尔还将他列入到越狱名单中，谁知道他是否了解迈克尔的一些秘密。然后便以命令的口吻告诉马霍先不用管迈克尔和林肯，现在只需办好帕特里科的案子就行。马霍不禁怒火中烧。

Mahone: All gas stations. On 80, 30, 77. I want Scofield and Lincoln' pictures on each and every gas pump①. If they have no fuel, they can't get anywhere. ☺₁

Wheeler: Sir.

Mahone: What?

Wheeler: We might need to divert our attention away from② Scofield and Lincoln.

Mahone: Why would I do that?

Wheeler: One of the escapees just killed a civilian. Patoshik. A man fitting his description was spotted running from the scene of a brutal homicide. ☺₂ It happened in Algoma, Wisconsin. It's less than four hours from the president.

Mahone: Call the field office③ in Madison and have them get some agents out there.

Wheeler: I'll notify headquarters.

Mahone: I didn't say headquarters. Are you not following direct orders④?

Wheeler: Oh, I'm following direct orders, sir. Just not from you anymore. ☺₃ Everything goes through⑤ headquarters from now on⑥. May I⑦?

Mahone: Yeah?

Kim: You heard about Patoshik?

Mahone: Just now. ☺₄

译文

马霍：所有的加油站。八十、三十、七十七号公路上，我要所有的加油泵上都贴上斯科菲尔德和林肯的照片。如果他们没油了，他们哪都去不了。

惠勒：长官。

马霍：什么事？

惠勒：我们可能得从斯科菲尔德与林肯身上分点儿心。

马霍：为什么我要这么做？

惠勒：有个逃犯刚杀了一位平民，是帕特斯科。有人看到一位符合描述特征的男子从残暴的凶杀案现场逃跑了，事发地点在威斯康星州阿尔戈马，距离总统所在处不到四小时的车程。

马霍：联络麦迪逊的分局，叫他们派特工过去支援。

惠勒：我会通知总部。

马霍：我没说总部，你不听我的直接指示吗？

惠勒：哦，我听指示，长官。但再也不听你的了。从现在起，一切都要呈报总部，我可以走了吗？

马霍：什么事？

金：你听说帕特斯科的事了吗？

马霍：刚听说。

知识点拨

1. gas pump 表示"气体泵，气泵；加油站"。例：Many families are feeling the pinch at the grocery store and the gas pump. 许多家庭在杂货店和汽油站都会感到手头拮据。

2. divert one's attention from sth. 表示"将某人的注意力从……转移开"。例：His mother try to divert his attention from the mobile game. 他的母亲想把他的注意力从游戏中转移出来。

3. field office 表示"（管理）外地办事处；分局；外勤人员"。例：A random security check was triggered from our field office. 随机安全检查是由我们分局启动的。

4. direct order 表示"直接命令"。follow direct order 则表示"听从直接命令"。例：The president has given me a direct order. 总统已给我下了直接的命令。

5. go through 表示"（法律、合同等正式）通过；用完；检查；完成"。例：The bill might have gone through if the economy was growing. 要是当时经济在增长的话，该法案或许也就获得通过了。

6. from now on 表示"从现在开始，从此，从今以后，往后"。例：It's getting colder and colder from now on. 往后的天气越来越冷了。

词汇加油站

gas [gæs] *n.* 气体

divert [daɪ'vɜːrt] *vt.* 使转移

civilian [sə'vɪliən] *n.* 平民

homicide ['hɑːmɪsaɪd] *n.* 杀人犯

pump [pʌmp] *n.* 泵

escapee [ɪˌskeɪ'piː] *n.* 逃亡者

brutal ['bruːtl] *adj.* 残忍的

notify ['noʊtɪfaɪ] *vt.* 通知

Scene 8 与典狱长的重逢

时间： 第 16 集 00:24:15—00:27:40
地点： 火车车厢内
片段一 **人物：** 迈克尔，莎拉，林肯，凯勒曼
事件： 迈克尔安慰莎拉，火车遇路障。

精彩亮点

1 看到要与曾经试图杀死自己的凯勒曼合作，莎拉的内心难以平静。她拿起一根绳子，勒住了凯勒曼的脖子，迈克尔和林肯马上赶来将莎拉和凯勒曼分开。

2 莎拉回想着自己三周前还是名医生，现在却沦落到要四处逃亡，甚至就在刚才，还产生了杀人的冲动。迈克尔安慰她，告诉她要相信自己能够找回一切。

3 支撑迈克尔走下去的是信念，而支撑莎拉活下去的：一是为他的父亲报仇；二是她爱上了迈克尔，一个她本不应该爱上的人。

4 就在这时，火车遇到了路障。多辆警车停靠在隧道附近，林肯等人不禁紧张起来。几个人能否躲过警察的搜查呢？

Michael: Hey, Sara. ☺1

Sara: Come on in①. I've been sitting here, evaluating. I jumped bail②, I'm on the run③...and I just tried to take a man's life④. I'm not using. Which is actually quite an accomplishment. **But three weeks ago, I was a doctor.** ☺2

Michael: You can get that back. All of it. You need to believe that.

Sara: You believe that? You think you can get it all back?

Michael: **I choose to have faith⑤. Because without that, I have nothing. It's the only thing that's keeping me going.** ☺3

Sara: Well. I got two things keeping me going. The first is that I want the people who took my dad. And actually the second...ironically, I probably wouldn't even say if I hadn't lost it. But...you should know that...The first thing they tell you when you take the job is...never to fall in love with an inmate⑥.

Kellerman: What's going on?

Lincoln: Roadblock.

Michael: Linc.

Lincoln: It's locked. ☺4

140

译文

迈克尔：嘿，莎拉。

莎 拉：进来。我刚才坐在这儿一直想。我在保释期间脱逃，现在又在逃亡……我刚刚还企图杀人。我没有吸毒，事实上，这是一大成就，但就在三周前我还是个医生。

迈克尔：你可以找回一切，你要相信这一点。

莎 拉：你相信吗？你觉得你可以找回你的人生？

迈克尔：我选择拥有信念，因为失去信念，我就一无所有，这是唯一让我活下去的力量。

莎 拉：有两件事给我力量活下去：第一件事是我要替父亲报仇。至于第二件事……讽刺的是，我应该还没有失去。不过……你应该知道……接下这工作后他们告诉我的第一件事是……永远不要爱上犯人。

凯勒曼：怎么回事？

林 肯：有路障。

迈克尔：林肯。

林 肯：门被锁住了。

知识点拨

1. come on in 表示"进来，请进，快进来"。例：All right, come on in, help yourself, there you go. 好吧，来吧，请自便，可以开始了。

2. jump bail 表示"弃保潜逃，保释中逃跑"。与 bail 相关的其他短语包括：bail out "帮助摆脱困境；舀出；保释"；bail handle "横木把手"。

3. be on the run 表示"忙来忙去；正在逃离中"。例：He could be on the run, we're not sure. 他可能正在逃离，我们不得而知。

4. take one's life 表示"取某人的命，杀掉某人"。例：But as far as I know that's just speculation, whatever has lead Gary to take his life is probably more personal than illness. 但据我所知这只是一种推测，让加里选择结束自己生命的也许是更加私人的原因而不是病痛。

5. have faith 表示"相信"，后面一般加介词 in。例：We must have faith in the masses. 要相信群众。

6. fall in love with someone 表示"爱上 / 倾心于某人"。例：Slowly but surely she started to fall in love with him. 虽然过程缓慢，但她无疑开始爱上他了。

 词汇加油站

evaluate [ɪˈvæljueɪt] *vt.* 评价
accomplishment [əˈkɑːmplɪʃmənt] *n.* 成就
ironically [aɪˈrɑːnɪkli] *adv.* 具有讽刺意味地
roadblock [ˈroʊdblɑːk] *n.* 路障

bail [beɪl] *n.* 保释
faith [feɪθ] *n.* 宗教信仰
inmate [ˈɪnmeɪt] *n.* （监狱里的）犯人
lock [lɑːk] *vt.* 锁上

时间： 第 17 集 00:04:51—00:06:24

地点： 波普家

片段二

人物： 波普，莎拉，迈克尔

事件： 莎拉和迈克尔冒险与典狱长见面，希望他帮忙拿出钥匙。

精彩亮点

1 莎拉和迈克尔来到雪茄俱乐部，莎拉望着会员的私人抽屉，不知道哪个才是自己父亲的。迈克尔在翻阅俱乐部宣传册时看到了波普的名字，于是计上心来。

2 莎拉的一句"我们"让波普不免心中一惊，果然，那个他不想看到的人还是来了。没错，这个人就是他曾经信赖却在最后让他大失所望的迈克尔。

3 因为时间有限，迈克尔一上来就直接进入话题。莎拉等人曾去过会员俱乐部，如果对手一旦发现他们去过那里，马上就会利用他们的权势把那里的证据消灭掉，所以他们必须马上找到莎拉父亲的抽屉。

4 莎拉诚恳地告诉波普：钥匙是父亲留给她唯一的东西，这把钥匙背后的线索至关重要，一方面，林肯可以洗刷冤屈，另一方面，自己也能找到父亲的死因。

Pope: What are you doing here? Aside from① jumping bail and evading the authorities. ☺1

Sara: There's something that you need to hear. But first, I need to know if you'll listen.

Pope: Sara, we've got nothing to discuss.

Sara: Please, I need five minutes. After that, if you want us to, we'll leave.

Pope: Who's us? I don't want any trouble. ☺2

Michael: Good. Because that's not why we're here.

Pope: What the hell are you thinking about, waltzing in here? You're a wanted criminal②. In case③ you've forgotten, I dedicated my career…my entire life, to④ keeping people like you behind bars⑤.

Michael: You're talking about guilty people. My brother is innocent. We have the evidence to prove it.

Pope: I don't care. I want you out.

Michael: It's in a locked box at the Corona De oro Club and you're a member. ☺3

Pope: Out.

Sara: Henry, please listen.

Pope: Sara, I'm tempted to⑥ say you should've known better. But after what you did…

Sara: My father was looking into the Lincoln case when he was murdered. This key is the only thing I could recover from his body. ☺4

142

译文

波 普：你来这里干什么？你这是弃保潜逃，是逃避司法处罚，还不够吗？

莎 拉：有件事你需要听我说，但首先，我要知道你是否愿意听。

波 普：莎拉，我们没有什么好谈的。

莎 拉：求求你，我只要五分钟。听完了你要我们走，我们就走。

波 普：我们是指谁？我不想惹麻烦。

迈克尔：很好，因为我们不是来找麻烦的。

波 普：你到底想干什么？大摇大摆地走进来吗？你可是通缉犯。我看你忘了，我整个事业生涯……我的一生都致力于将你们这样的人关在牢里。

迈克尔：你说的是有罪的人，我哥哥是无辜的，我们有证据可以证明。

波 普：我不在乎，让你们出去。

迈克尔：东西就在金皇冠俱乐部的箱子里，而你是那里会员。

波 普：出去。

莎 拉：亨利，请听他说。

波 普：莎拉，我很想说你早该学到教训了。但你做的事……

莎 拉：我父亲在调查林肯的案子时遭遇谋杀。这把钥匙是我在他的尸体上找到的唯一的东西。

知识点拨

1. aside from 表示"除……之外"，有三层意思：1）表示排除，即表示"除……之外不再有"；2）表示累加，表示"除……之外尚有"；3）表示条件，即所表示的"除……外"指的是"如果不考虑"。

2. a wanted criminal 表示"通缉犯"。例：We're looking for a wanted criminal, please do not be alarmed. 我们正在寻找一名通缉犯，请不要担心。

3. in case 表示"万一"，是连词，引导条件状语从句。in case of 的 of 是介词，后面只能带名词性质的词，比如名词、代词等，也表示万一。

4. dedicate to 表示"宣告……是供奉（上帝）的；献（身）于……；把（时间、精力等）用于……；写（某作品）以献给某人"。

5. behind bars 表示"关在监牢里"。例：Nearly 5,000 people a year are put behind bars over motoring penalties. 每年有近5,000人因违章驾车而入狱。

6. be tempted to do sth. 表示"受诱惑做某事"。例：The president has gone along with the hardliners lest they be tempted to oust him. 总统同意了强硬派的意见，以免他们产生赶他下台的念头。

词汇加油站

evade [ɪˈveɪd] vt. 逃避
dedicate [ˈdedɪkeɪt] vt. 献身
guilty [ˈgɪlti] adj. 内疚的
recover [rɪˈkʌvər] vt. 找回

waltz [wɔːlts] vi. 大摇大摆地走
bar [bɑːr] n. 障碍
evidence [ˈevɪdəns] n. 证据

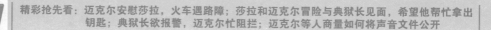

片段三

时间： 第 17 集 00:10:36—00:11:38
地点： 波普家
人物： 典狱长波普，迈克尔
事件： 典狱长波普欲报警，迈克尔忙阻拦。

精彩亮点

1 典狱长曾经很感激迈克尔帮助他制作了建筑模型以讨好妻子，甚至将迈克尔视作自己的亲人。但没想到迈克尔导演了越狱计划，甚至还逼迫自己帮助他越狱，他对其失望至极。

2 现在，特伦斯已经自杀了，能拯救林肯，证明其无罪的希望就只剩下莎拉手中的这把钥匙，因此，迈克尔等人可以说是被逼到了绝路。

3 波普想要通知警方逮捕迈克尔，但迈克尔拿着枪对准了他，这也是无奈之举。倔强的波普表示拿枪对着他是无济于事的，看到这里着实令人心焦。

4 迈克尔表示这一切都不是他真正期望看到的。如果可以，他也希望一切可以重来，但事已至此，现在说什么都来不及了，他只想竭尽全力让波普信任自己。

Pope: I don't give a rat's ass① about you or your brother. I trusted you. I took you under my wing②. I treated you like my own son. I believed you. Day after day③, you lied to me④.☺1 What kind of a man does that?

Michael: A desperate one. Yeah.☺2

Pope: Well, you two made a big mistake coming here today. You gave me no choice. I'm gonna notify the authorities right now.

Michael: I'm sorry…but I can't let you do that. I don't wanna hurt you, Henry.

Pope: Said by the man with the gun.☺3

Michael: If it's the way I can convince you, so be it⑤.

Pope: Well, you're not gonna convince me by doing that.

Michael: I'm not the man you think I am.

Pope: I have a pretty good idea⑥ who you are.

Michael: If that's true, then you already know I never wanted to be in Fox River. I never wanted to meet you, Henry. I certainly didn't wanna ruin your life.☺4

Pope: Yeah? You've done a pretty damn good job.

144

译文

波　普：我才不在乎你或是你哥的死活。我信任你，保护你，把你当儿子看待。我那么相信你，可你日复一日地欺骗我，谁会做出这种事？

迈克尔：一个绝望的人，是的。

波　普：那你们今天来这里算是犯下大错了。你让我别无选择，我现在就要通知警方。

迈克尔：对不起……但我不能让你这么做。我不想伤害你，亨利。

波　普：这是一个拿着枪的人说出的话吗？

迈克尔：只要能说服你，我会这样做。

波　普：拿枪指着我是无法说服我的。

迈克尔：我不是你想的那种人。

波　普：我很清楚你是怎样的人。

迈克尔：如果你真了解，你就应该知道我根本不想进福克斯河监狱。我根本不想认识你，亨利。当然，我也不想毁了你的人生。

波　普：是吗？那你所做的可真了不起。

 知识点拨

1. 俚语 not give a rat's ass=not care at all，也就是说"一点儿也不在乎、不感兴趣"。例：I don't give a rat's ass about other things once I start eating. 我一吃起来就什么都不管不顾了。

2. take someone under your wing 表示"指导、保护和照料某人"。例：But, it's so nice of you to take her under your wing. 但是，保护她说明你人很好。

3. day after day 表示"一天又一天地，日复一日地，连日，累日"。例：The newspaper job had me doing the same thing day after day. 这份在报社的工作让我日复一日地做着同样的事。

4. lie to sb. 表示"对某人撒谎，对某人说谎"。例：I forgive you this time, but you can't lie to me again. 这次我原谅你，但你不能再对我撒谎了。

5. be it 表示"存在；是这样的"。例：Far be it from me to criticise, but shouldn't their mother take a share of the blame? 不是我要挑理，他们的母亲难道就不应该负点儿责任吗？

6. have a pretty good idea 表示"肚里有数"。例：But I do have a pretty good idea of where you can stick these. 但在哪儿可以贴这些东西，我倒是有好的建议。

 词汇加油站

wing [wɪŋ] *n.* 翅膀
lie [laɪ] *v.* 说谎
convince [kən'vɪns] *vt.* 使相信
pretty ['prɪti] *adv.* 相当

treat [triːt] *v.* 对待
desperate ['despərət] *adj.* 绝望的
ruin ['ruːɪn] *vt.* 破坏

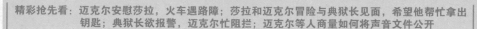

片段四

时间： 第 18 集 00:04:16—00:05:09
地点： 酒店
人物： 迈克尔，林肯，莎拉
事件： 迈克尔等人商量如何将声音文件公开。

精彩亮点

1
迈克尔等人终于拿到了莎拉父亲临终时留下的遗物——U 盘。他们用计算机播放声音文件。几个人屏住呼吸，专心地听着，而里面的内容让莎拉吓得目瞪口呆，林肯在房间里踱来踱去，思考着如何利用这份声音文件。

2
林肯听到迈克尔要将这个 U 盘交给政府的人，他大为恼怒。当初陷害他入狱的就是政府，如果把这份证明他无罪的文件交给政府，岂不是让他们之前的努力付之东流？

3
迈克尔深知即使在政府内，也存在派系纷争。现在的问题是：找谁来承担公开这份录音文件的任务？

4
林肯想到了与父亲共事的简，她现在是 L.J. 的监护人，而在她的保护下，L.J. 换了名字，又可以像以前一样上学、交朋友了。

Lincoln: We give this to the press, the government will discredit it. Just like they did with the tape we made.☺1

Sara: Okay. So, what do we do with① it?

Michael: There are people in the administration Dad was working with. If we give it to them, they'll finally have the smoking gun② they need…to bring Caroline Reynolds down③. But they'll release the tape, not us.

Sara: And how can she discredit④ her own appointees?

Michael: Sure.

Lincoln: We're gonna give the only thing that can exonerate me…to someone who works for⑤ the government? The same government that set me up?☺2

Michael: We'll have to find someone we can trust. Someone honest.☺3

Lincoln: Jane Phillips. She'll know someone that can help us. She worked with Dad. She's watching L.J.☺4 I trust her, Michael. She'll do it. She'll find someone.

Michael: Well, I hope you're right. Because this is our last shot⑥.

译文

林 肯： 如果把这个（录音）交给媒体，政府是不会承认的，就像他们对我们拍的影带一样。

莎 拉： 好吧，那我们该怎么做？

迈克尔： 爸说他在政府里还有共事的人。如果我们把录音交给他们，他们就有如山的铁证……就能搞垮卡罗琳总统，但要由他们把录音公开，不能由我们来。

莎 拉： 她怎么会怀疑自己任命的人呢？

迈克尔： 当然会。

林 肯： 我们要把唯一能赦免我的证据……交给政府的人？就是那个陷害我的政府？

迈克尔： 我们必须要找一个值得信任的人，一个正直的人。

林 肯： 简·菲利普，她知道谁可以帮助我们。她和爸共事过，现在正在照顾L.J.，我信任她，迈克尔，她可以帮忙找人。

迈克尔： 好吧，我希望你是正确的。因为这是我们最后的希望了。

知识点拨

1. do with 表示"处理；需要；与……相处"。例：This has nothing to do with you. 这与你不相干。

2. smoking gun 表示"确切的证据"。例：The search for other kinds of evidence tying him to trafficking has not produced a smoking gun. 还没有找到其他能够证明他参与了毒品交易的确凿证据。

3. bring sb. down 表示"把（某物，某人）抬下（楼、山）；使（某物或某人）掉下 [倒下]；击败某人"。例：They were threatening to bring down the government by withdrawing from the ruling coalition. 他们威胁要退出执政联盟，让政府垮台。

4. discredit sb. 表示"诋毁某人"。例：Sylvia does not get on with the supervisor and the danger is that he will trump up some charge to discredit her. 西尔维娅与主管相处得不好，因而害怕他会捏造一些罪名使她名誉扫地。

5. work for sb. / sth. 表示"受雇于，为……而工作 / 效劳"。例：I still do a certain amount of work for them. 我仍然为他们做一些工作。

6. last shot 表示"最后一搏，最后的机会"。例：I do not know if you can say the last shot, it will. 我不知道你是否能说这是最后的一次机会。

词汇加油站

press [pres] *n.* 新闻报道
tape [teɪp] *n.* 带子
exonerate [ɪgˈzɑːnəreɪt] *vt.* 使免罪
shot [ʃɑːt] *n.* 努力；尝试

discredit [dɪsˈkredɪt] *vt.* 使被怀疑
appointee [əˌpɔɪnˈtiː] *n.* 被任命者
honest [ˈɑːnɪst] *adj.* 诚实的

Scene 9 卡罗琳与迈克尔会面

时间： 第 18 集 00:26:06—00:27:36
地点： 贝克博物馆
人物： 迈克尔，假格林，莎拉，林肯
事件： 迈克尔与假格林会面。

精彩亮点

1 假格林终于与迈克尔见面了，林肯用望远镜在一座大楼里观察着他的一举一动。为了摆脱假格林身后人的跟踪，林肯可是让假格林吃了不少苦头。

2 就在迈克尔与假格林会面的同时，莎拉给林肯打来电话，告诉他现在和迈克尔见面的是假格林，林肯听罢，冲向贝克博物馆告诉迈克尔这个消息。

3 经历过无数次欺骗的迈克尔警惕性很高，他没有立马将 U 盘交给面前的这个人，反复向他核对信息，而指示这位假格林的正是诡计多端的金先生。

4 假格林催促着迈克尔跟他到停车的铜像附近，事实上，金先生早已在那里埋伏了人手。假格林谎称自己有哮喘病，聪明的迈克尔巧妙地识破了面前的这个人是假格林，一拳将他打晕在地。

False Green: Well, it's nice to finally meet you. Do you have the tape? ☺1

Michael: It's right here.

Lincoln: Yeah?

Sara: Lincoln, it's Sara, Listen to me. The man Michael's with is not Cooper Green. You hear me? The man that Michael's with right now is not Cooper Green. ☺2

False Green: We should hurry. We're in Chicago. Won't be long before the Company knows you're in town.

Michael: Where are we going?

False Green: Well, we're gonna make sure that that tape goes into the right hands①.

Michael: Whose?

False Green: A friend.

Michael: What kind of friend?

False Green: He's a federal judge②. Is that good enough for you?

Michael: Well, this tape is my brother's life and mine. And consequently, I need a name. ☺3

False Green: Judge Scott Warren. A lifetime appointee…who was put on the bench③ by President Mills. He has no job to lose, no loyalty to④ Reynolds. Wants to see her gone⑤, just like us. Well, let's go. I left my car over⑥ by the statue. ☺4

译文

假格林：很高兴终于见到你了，录音带在你手上吗？

迈克尔：就在这里。

林 肯：什么事？

莎 拉：林肯，是我，莎拉，听我说，和迈克尔见面的人不是库珀·格林，你听见了吗？现在和迈克尔见面的人不是库珀·格林。

假格林：我们得要快点儿了，这里是芝加哥。公司很快就会发现你来了。

迈克尔：我们要去哪里？

假格林：我们要确保录音交到对的人手上。

迈克尔：谁的手上？

假格林：一个朋友。

迈克尔：什么样的朋友？

假格林：他是联邦法官，这样你满意了吗？

迈克尔：这段录音是我哥和我的命，因此，我要知道名字。

假格林：是斯科特·沃伦法官，他是前总统米尔斯任命的终身制法官。他不会失业，也无须效忠雷诺兹。他和我们一样希望她下台，我们走吧，我的车停在铜像附近。

知识点拨

1. go into the right hands 表示"落到适当的人手里"。例：He wants to get some device into the right hands by finding Michael and Linc, and then he'll get their records clean. 他想找到迈克尔和林肯，把设备交给信得过的人，然后他会帮他们把过去的记录抹去。

2. federal judge 表示"联邦法官"。

3. on the bench 表示"任法官"。例：Allgood served on the bench for more than 50 years. 奥尔古德当了五十多年的法官。

4. loyalty to 表示"对……的忠诚"。例：His loyalty to his friends was never in doubt. 他对朋友的一片忠心从来没受到怀疑。

5. see sb. done 中 done 在这个结构中做宾补，即表示和宾语之间的被动关系。例：We often see her surrounded by her friends. 我们常常看见她被朋友环绕。

6. leave over 表示"留下，剩下；延后，推迟"。例：Similarly the output messages will leave over a channel. 类似地，输出消息将通过频道发出去。

 词汇加油站

hurry ['hʌri] *vt.* 仓促（做某事）

judge [dʒʌdʒ] *n.* 法官

lifetime ['laɪftaɪm] *n.* 一生

loyalty ['lɔɪəlti] *n.* 忠诚

federal ['fedərəl] *adj.* 联邦（制）的

consequently ['kɑ:nsəkwentli] *adv.* 因此

bench [bentʃ] *n.* 法官席；法官的职位；法官

statue ['stætʃu:] *n.* 雕像

149

时间： 第 19 集 00:14:33—00:16:23

地点： 酒店

片段二

人物： 金，迈克尔，助理

事件： 迈克尔故意让自己被捕，迈克尔与金见面。

 精彩亮点

迈克尔等人来到芝加哥，在那里，卡罗琳正在为她的竞选做演讲。在卡罗琳与群众握手时，迈克尔故意紧紧抓住她的手不放，递给她一张纸条。警卫们逮捕了迈克尔。迈克尔来此有何意图呢？ **1**

迈克尔递给卡罗琳的纸条上写着：我们有磁带，卡罗琳不免有些惊慌。谨慎的金先生让政府人员查看是否有人拍了他们逮捕迈克尔的照片，并在必要时没收那些人的相机，还让他们在谣言散布前发表声明。 **2**

迈克尔是来和卡罗琳谈条件的。但阴险狡诈的金先生怎么可能让他去见总统？他命令政府人员都离开，自己单独和迈克尔谈话。为何金先生有如此大的权力？事实上，他是公司的最高执行者。 **3**

尽管金先生百般逼问，但迈克尔对哥哥的去向守口如瓶，这让金恼怒不已。他嘴角露出狡黠的笑容，脱下外套，对迈克尔一通暴打。 **4**

Kim: **You and I both know that this situation requires us to abandon protocol.**① ☺1 I don't know what you need to tell them, but I need your men to leave. Now.

Assistant: Yes, sir. ☺2

Kim: Where's your brother?

Michael: I need to see the president.

Kim: **Really? And you think that's a possibility?** ☺3

Michael: She'll want to hear what I have to say.

Kim: Oh, I highly doubt that. The only person you get to talk to…is me. And the only way you're gonna live through② the next hour…is if you tell me where to find your brother.

Michael: Okay. He's in a safe place.

Kim: Be more specific③.

Michael: Specifically…a place you will never find him.

Kim: I had the honor…to attend Mountbrook Military Academy④ …whose mission it is…to ensure the greatness of this country, its future leadership…encouraging patriotism…building a strong moral foundation⑤ and providing the service of men…committed to⑥ the values of honor, freedom and country. **But, first and foremost**⑦ **…they taught you this.** ☺4

知识点拨

1. require sb.to do sth. 表示"需要某人做某事，命令某人做某事"；require doing sth. 表示"需要做某事"。

2. live through 表示"经历过,经历……而未死"。例：We are too young to have lived through the war. 我们太年轻，没经历过那场战争。

3. be specific 表示"具体一些"。例：To be specific, the argument in your thesis is logical. 具体地说，你的毕业论文逻辑性很强。

4. Military Academy 表示"军校,陆军军官学校"。例：He passed into the Military Academy with to ditficulty. 他毫无困难地考上了军事学院。

5. moral foundation 表示"道德基础"。例：Integrity is the moral foundation for the development of all athletic sports. 诚信是竞技体育赖以生存和发展的道德基础。

6. commit to 表示"把……送交,托付给……；对……做出承诺，承担义务；使（自己）致力于……；把……固定在……"。例：How can you commit to a company where the major shareholders might be against you? 在主要股东可能反对你的情况下，你怎么对一家企业投资？

7. first and foremost 表示"首要的，第一"。例：I see myself, first and foremost, as a working artist. 我首先还是把自己看作一名艺术工作者。

译文

金： 你我都知道在这种情况下，我们必须抛开正常程序。我不知道你怎么呈报，但我需要你们的人离开。马上。

助 理： 好的，长官。

金： 你哥在哪里？

迈克尔： 我要见总统。

金： 是吗？你觉得有这个可能吗？

迈克尔： 她会想听我要说的话。

金： 哦？我很怀疑呀。你唯一能见的人就是我。你下一个小时能活命的唯一方式就是告诉我你哥在哪里。

迈克尔： 好吧，他在一个安全的地方。

金： 说具体一点儿。

迈克尔： 具体来说，他在你永远找不到的地方。

金： 我很荣幸……能够上蒙布克军事学校，该校的使命在于……确保本国的伟大，确保其未来领导人的伟大……倡导爱国主义……打下坚实的道德基础并为人民提供服务……这些为荣耀、自由和国家效命的人。但是，首先……学校会先教你这招。

词汇加油站

protocol ['prəʊtəkɔ:l] *n.* 礼仪；条约草案

doubt [daʊt] *vt.* 怀疑

mission ['mɪʃn] *n.* 使命

moral ['mɔːrəl] *adj.* 道德的

possibility [ˌpɑːsəˈbɪləti] *n.* 可能性

specific [spəˈsɪfɪk] *adj.* 具体的

patriotism ['peɪtriətɪzəm] *n.* 爱国主义

foremost ['fɔːrmoʊst] *adj.* 最重要的

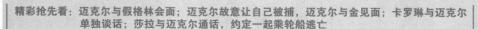

时间： 第 19 集 00:20:43—00:23:21

地点： 酒店

人物： 卡罗琳，迈克尔，金

事件： 卡罗琳与迈克尔单独谈话。

片段三

精彩亮点

1 此时的迈克尔已经被金先生打得鼻青脸肿，金告诉迈克尔他和马霍不同点是：马霍根本不知道迈克尔的价值。就在金先生举枪要杀死迈克尔的一刹那，卡罗琳来了，告诉金自己要单独和迈克尔谈话。

2 金虚情假意地表示出于对总统安危的考虑，自己应该留在她旁边保护，但卡罗琳坚决让金出去，甚至用命令的口吻强制让他出去。

3 卡罗琳知道迈克尔手上有录音文件，但相关人员已经在搜查，所以他认为迈克尔并不会对自己产生威胁。

4 迈克尔告诉卡罗琳，这份录音文件是她和弟弟在弟弟"死后"的一段对话，这让卡罗琳不禁有些惊慌。这份录音文件已经有 20 份拷贝，分布在 20 个不同的地方。且迈克尔提出卡罗琳只能通过电话或是通过新闻听到这份录音文件。

Caroline: I need to talk to Mr. Scofield. Alone.☺₁

Kim: Madam President. Could I…have a word①? It wouldn't be prudent for me to leave you alone with Mr. Scof②…

Caroline: My men are right outside this door. I have a right to③ privacy.

Kim: Your rights…aren't my first concern.

Caroline: Do I need to remind you who you are talking to? Step outside and close the door behind you④.☺₂ The things you do for your brother. It's impressive.

Michael: I could say the same for you. But I won't.

Caroline: Bear in mind⑤ … your opinion means little to me. This tape…You have it with you?☺₃

Michael: No. But I can arrange for you to hear it.

Caroline: You don't make arrangements for me⑥, Mr. Scofield. I have people for that. I'm not exactly sure what is on this tape… but I doubt it's of any interest to me.

Michael: It's a recorded conversation between you and your brother.

Caroline: Well, out of millions of conversations that I had with my brother during his lifetime…

Michael: I'll narrow it down⑦ for you. It was recorded sometime after his death.☺₄ And this…particular conversation…you might wanna keep in the family.

译文

卡罗琳：我要和斯科菲尔德先生谈谈，单独谈。

金：总统女士，可否借一步……跟您谈谈？让您单独和他谈不妥当……

卡罗琳：我的手下就在门外，我有保有隐私的权利。

金：您的权利……不是我最关心的。

卡罗琳：我需要提醒你现在正跟谁说话吗？出去时把门关上。你为了你哥做的事令人难忘。

迈克尔：我想说你也一样，但我不会说。

卡罗琳：记住，你的意见我毫不在乎。这段录音……你带在身上了吗？

迈克尔：没有，但我可以安排让你听。

卡罗琳：斯科菲尔德先生，你无须替我安排。有人会替我安排的。我不太确定录音的内容……但我想对我应该不会有什么用。

迈克尔：这里面是你和你弟的对话录音。

卡罗琳：我和我弟在他生前通过无数次电话……

迈克尔：我说具体一点儿，录音是在他"死后"录到的。这段……特别的录音……你可能不想让外人听到。

知识点拨

1. have a word with sb. 表示"简短地和某人说话"。例：I wonder if I might have a word with. Mr. Abbot? 请问我能否和阿博特先生说几句话吗？

2. leave sb. alone 表示"不理 / 不管 / 不烦扰 / 不干涉某人"。例：I wish everyone would stop interfering and just leave me alone. 我希望大家都别再来干涉我，让我一个人静一静。

3. have a right to sth. 表示"拥有某方面的权利"。to 后也可跟 do sth. 表示"拥有做某事的权利"。例：Well, you have a right to your career. 喔，你有权选择自己的职业。

4. close the door behind you 表示"请随手关门"。例：Please close the door behind you, will you? 请随手把门关上，好吗？

5. bear sth. in mind 表示"记住；考虑"（=remember, consider）。例：You must bear in mind that contradictions exist everywhere. 应当记住，矛盾是普遍存在的。

6. make arrangements for sth. 表示"安排，部署某事"。例：Our college is to make arrangements for the meeting. 我们学院负责筹办这次会议。

7. narrow down 表示"（使）变窄，（使）减少，（使）缩小"。例：I've managed to narrow the list down to twenty-three. 我已设法把清单上的项目压缩到了 23 项。

 词汇加油站

prudent ['pru:dnt] *adj.* 慎重的
remind [rɪ'maɪnd] *vt.* 使想起
arrange [ə'reɪndʒ] *vt.* 安排
particular [pər'tɪkjələr] *adj.* 特别的

privacy ['praɪvəsi] *n.* 隐私
impressive [ɪm'presɪv] *adj.* 给人印象深刻的
lifetime ['laɪftaɪm] *n.* 一生

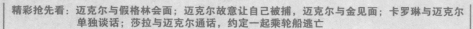

片段四

时间： 第 20 集 00:03:09—00:04:02
地点： 莎拉车上，大街上
人物： 莎拉，迈克尔，播音员
事件： 莎拉与迈克尔通话，约定一起乘轮船逃亡。

 精彩亮点

1

迈克尔和林肯守在电视机前，等待着卡罗琳总统给他们两个人的总统特赦。事实上，卡罗琳本来是打算这么做的，听了迈克尔描述弟弟的自杀，她也有所触动。但金先生怎能允许他们的计划就此落空？他手上也握有对卡罗琳不利的证据，卡罗琳无奈，只得宣布辞去总统一职。

2

此时莎拉开着车，从广播中听到了总统辞职的消息，恰巧此时迈克尔给她打来了电话，告诉她现在他们要准备逃亡。

3

迈克尔觉得很对不起莎拉，因为林肯的事连累了莎拉一家，本来莎拉可以过着稳定的生活，但现在迫不得已也要和迈克尔他们走上逃亡之路。

4

莎拉丝毫也不责怪迈克尔，她觉得只要能和迈克尔在一起，她什么也不怕。她答应迈克尔与他一会儿见，但没有料想到的是，联邦调查局的人早已悄悄跟踪在莎拉的车后。

Announcer: Continuing with our top story ①, Caroline Reynolds made the announcement, just a short while ago ② that she is stepping down ③ ...as president of the United States. ☺₁ We'll be bringing you more information…

Sara: Hello?

Michael: Hey, are you all right?

Sara: Yeah, I'm fine. I just heard about the president. What does it mean? ☺₂

Michael: It means it's time to go.

Sara: Okay. When?

Michael: Ten minutes. How far away are you?

Sara: Five.

Michael: Listen, Sara, Linc and I are on the ship. This is it ④. There's no turning back now, so…I know it's not what you wanted from your life…but in case you're interested, there is room for one more. ☺₃

Sara: Michael Scofield, you asking me to sail off ⑤ into the sunset with you?

Michael: Well, it's more of ⑥ a freighter, but yes.

Sara: I'll be there.

Michael: I'll see you soon. ☺₄

译文

播音员：继续来看焦点新闻，卡罗琳·雷诺兹不久前宣布她要卸下……美国总统的职位。我们将提供最新消息……

莎　拉：喂？

迈克尔：嘿，你还好吧？

莎　拉：我没事，我刚听说总统的事。这是什么意思？

迈克尔：意思是我们该走了。

莎　拉：好，什么时候？

迈克尔：十分钟，你还要多久才到？

莎　拉：五分钟。

迈克尔：听着，莎拉，林肯和我已经上船了，时候到了，已经没路可退了。我知道你不想过这种日子……不过如果你有兴趣的话，还有一个位子。

莎　拉：迈克尔·斯科菲尔德，你在邀请我与你扬帆迎向夕阳吗？

迈克尔：其实是艘货轮，不过的确如此。

莎　拉：我会去的。

迈克尔：一会儿见。

知识点拨

1. top story 表示"头条新闻，头条故事"。例：The disaster was a top story in Dutch newspapers. 这场灾难是当时荷兰报纸的头条新闻。

2. a short while ago 表示"方才"。例：He went back for his coat a short while ago. 刚才他回去拿他的上衣了。

3. step down 表示"退休，辞职"。例：Judge Ito said that if his wife was called as a witness, he would step down as a trial judge. 伊藤法官说，如果他的妻子被传作证，他将不再担任初审法官。

4. this is it 表示"这正是所需的，这正是未能成功的原因"。例：This is it, folks, the best record guide in the business. 就是这个，伙计们，业内最好的唱片指南。

5. sail off 表示"出海，出航"。例：The boat sailed off into the blue. 小船已驶出海。

6. more of a / an + n. 指数量或程度上"更（像／是）……"，表示"更具有某种特质"，相当于 more like a (n)…，常做宾语或表语。more of a(n) A than a(n) B 表示否定 B，肯定A 或在肯定 B 的基础上，更强调A，意为"与其说是 B，还不如说是 A；不是 B，而更像是 A；与 B 相比，更像 A"。

 词汇加油站

continue [kən'tɪnjuː] *vt.* 使持续
step [step] *vi.* 行走
sail [seɪl] *vi.* 起航
freighter ['freɪtər] *n.* 货船

announcement [ə'naʊnsmənt] *n.* 宣告
ship [ʃɪp] *n.* 船
sunset ['sʌnset] *n.* 黄昏

Scene 10 莎拉被捕

片段一

时间： 第 20 集 00:07:27—00:10:09

地点： 大街上，轮船甲板

人物： 马霍，莎拉，迈克尔，林肯，朗，播音员

事件： 莎拉被捕，拒绝说出迈克尔的下落，马霍几近崩溃。

精彩亮点

莎拉通过后视镜看到了自己被尾随了，她望向了轮船，知道自己无论如何也无法与迈克尔他们一起逃亡了。莎拉不由得眼角湿润了，她擦了擦眼泪，毅然走出车门，高举双手投降，跟来的马霍看到只有莎拉一个人，知道自己的抓捕计划又失败了。**1**

马霍询问莎拉迈克尔他们在哪儿，莎拉自然不会说。马霍知道莎拉是为了去见迈克尔，因为他认为莎拉一开始并不知道有联邦调查局的人在跟踪她。**2**

迈克尔焦急万分，就在这时，响起的警笛声吸引了他们的注意。迈克尔看到了莎拉被捕的画面，他想要下船营救莎拉，但林肯拉住了他。迈克尔知道自己如果现在过去，非但救不了莎拉，自己也会被捕。迈克尔只能望着心爱的人坐船离开。**3**

迈克尔和林肯再次逃脱，马霍一周都没有出现在联邦调查局里，他望着满屋贴满的逃犯的资料，整个人陷入了精神恍惚的状态。**4**

Lang: You have the right to an attorney. If you cannot afford an attorney… one will be provided for you. ☺₁

Mahone: Where is he?

Sara: I don't know. ☺₂

Mahone: No more games ①, Sara. You were on your way to see ② him.

Sara: No, I wasn't.

Mahone: You were just compelled to ③ flee the custody of a federal agent?

Man: All lines astern are loose. Prepare for cast off ④.

Michael: I couldn't find her. Sara.

Lincoln: We gotta go back. There's nothing you can do. ☺₃

Michael: Always something we can do.

Lincoln: Not this time. Not this time. It's done. I'm sorry.

Mahone: Scofield or prison?

Sara: I just wanted a doughnut.

Mahone: Get her a doughnut. Can we get her one? Get her a doughnut. Get her a dozen ⑤ doughnuts. Lock her up ⑥. May, May, May, New Mexico. Don't, don't, don't. Where the hell did you go, Michael? ☺₄

译文

朗： 你有权聘请律师，如果负担不起……法院会提供给你。

马 霍： 他在哪儿？

莎 拉： 我不知道。

马 霍： 别跟我耍心眼儿了，莎拉。你正要去见他。

莎 拉： 不，我没有。

马 霍： 难道你只是想逃离联邦探员的追捕？

播音员： 所有围栏线已松开，准备开船。

迈克尔： 我找不到她，莎拉。

林 肯： 我们得回去，你做不了什么。

迈克尔： 我们总能做些什么的。

林 肯： 这次不行，这次你帮不了她，没戏了，我很遗憾。

马 霍： 要么说出斯科菲尔德在哪，要么坐牢？

莎 拉： 我只想吃甜甜圈。

马 霍： 给她一个甜甜圈，给她一个好吗？给她一个甜甜圈，给她买一堆甜甜圈！把她关起来。五月，五月，五月，新墨西哥。不要，不要，不要。你到底跑哪儿去了，迈克尔？

知识点拨

1. No more games 表示"不再是游戏，别再玩游戏了"。例：No more games with me, okay? 别再和我玩游戏了，听到吗？

2. on one's way to do 中的 to do 做目的状语，表示"在去做某事的路上"，这里的"路"是真实的路，土路、水泥路、柏油路等。on one's way to doing 中的 to doing 引出的是某个过程的结果，表示"接近做某事"，这里的路是抽象意义上的路，是一个过程。

3. be compelled to do sth. 表示"迫不得已做某事"。例：People cannot be compelled to accept one particular style of art or school of thought. 不能强制人们接受一种艺术风格或一种学派。

4. cast off 表示"摆脱，抛弃，脱下，解开"。例：He cast off, heading out to the bay. 他解开缆绳，往海湾驶去。

5. a dozen of 的意思是"十二个，一打"，后接代词或名词。后接名词时，of 可省略，如：a dozen of apples 或 a dozen apples（十二个苹果）。

6. lock sb. / sth. up 表示"将某人 / 物锁住（关押）"。例：Give away any food you have on hand, or lock it up and give the key to the neighbors. 把手头的所有食物都送给别人，或者把食物藏好锁起，然后将钥匙交给邻居。

词汇加油站

attorney [əˈtɜːrni] *n.* 律师

flee [fliː] *vt.* 逃离

federal [ˈfedərəl] *adj.* 联邦（制）的

loose [luːs] *adj.* 未系住的

compel [kəmˈpel] *vt.* 强迫

custody [ˈkʌstədi] *n.* 拘留

astern [əˈstɜːrn] *adv.* （指船）向后

doughnut [ˈdoʊnʌt] *n.* 炸面圈

时间： 第 21 集 00:33:37—00:36:57
地点： 巴拿马树林小屋
人物： 迈克尔，帝博格
事件： 迈克尔找到帝博格并将其刺伤。

片段二

精彩亮点

迈克尔先前在寻找 500 万美元时曾告诉苏克雷如果以后有什么事可以上一个网站上留言，迈克尔在留言板上看到苏克雷留言说帝博格现在就在巴拿马的一个酒店里。本来林肯想直接告诉警察帝博格的具体位置，但迈克尔说巴拿马这里没有引渡法，警察也对帝博格无可奈何。

1

迈克尔和苏克雷押着帝博格前往大使馆，希望将帝博格绳之以法。但狡猾的帝博格用车上的利器刺伤了苏克雷。在迈克尔为苏克雷简单包扎的过程中，帝博格带着那 500 万美元逃跑了，迈克尔追上了帝博格。

2

帝博格以为迈克尔找他就是为了那 500 万美元，事实上，迈克尔主要的目的就是为了将帝博格绳之以法。他回想起一个个无辜的人都因帝博格而死去，不禁为自己没能及时制止帝博格而深感内疚。

3

狡猾的帝博格被迈克尔按倒在地，迈克尔手拿小刀，帝博格深知迈克尔不敢杀人，故意刺激他，致使迈克尔一刀向帝博格的右手刺过去。

4

Michael: Pressure. Pressure. ☺1

T-Bag: What exactly is it that you want, pretty?

Michael: I'm turning you in①. ☺2

T-Bag: Is that it②, really? It ain't about the money? ☺3 Because if it is, you can tell me. Ain't nobody here but us cons.

Michael: You can walk or get dragged… but it's up to you③.

T-Bag: No, see, when you had the gun on me, I afforded you a certain respect. But here, well, the scales are tipped back my way. So I'm gonna spell out④ the present options. Either we split this money…and you can go get your legs tattooed, or whatever the hell it is that you want. Or they're gonna find your corpse over that chair…with your pants down around your ankles because it's been a long time coming. Well, I got my answer.

Michael: Whenever you're done yakking⑤.

T-Bag: Bring it, bitch. Who are you fooling? You ain't gonna kill me, Mr. Michelangelo. You ain't got it in you. So why don't we⑥ just let me… ☺4

译文

迈克尔：压住伤口，压住。

帝博格：你到底想要什么，帅哥？

迈克尔：我要将你绳之以法。

帝博格：就这样，真的吗？不是为了钱？如果是，你可以告诉我，这里只有我们两个罪犯。

迈克尔：你可以自己走还是被我拖着……你自己定。

帝博格：不，知道吗？当你拿枪指着我时，我还会多少向你表示尊重。但现在，掌控权在我手上，所以我要说出现在的想法。要不我们把钱分掉……你就能在腿上做刺青或是爱干什么干什么。否则，你就去那把椅子上找你的尸体吧，并且裤子还被我脱下，因为我觊觎你很久了。好了，我得到我的答案了。

迈克尔：我等你把废话说完。

帝博格：来吧，贱人。你骗谁啊？你不会杀我的，白面书生。你没这胆量。那么，为什么不让我……

知识点拨

1. turn sb. in 表示"交出某人；告发某人"。例：Did he know that you tried to turn him in? 他知道你想举报他吗？

2. that is it 表示"就是这样，就这样"。

3. it s up to you 表示"由你决定，取决于你"。例：Of course, it's up to you to decide whether I am suitable for the job. 当然，我是否适合这份工作，只有你能做出决定。

4. spell out 表示"拼出，读出；阐明"。片中表示"阐明"。例：Be assertive and spell out exactly how you feel. 要自信点儿，把自己的感受讲清楚。

5. yakking 为贬义词，表示"没完没了地谈些无关要紧的事，喋喋不休，唠叨"。例：She just kept yakking on. 她只是一个劲地东拉西扯。

6. why don't we do sth. 表示"建议"，意为"为什么我们不……呢？"例：Why don't we talk it through? 为什么我们不把这事谈开呢？

 词汇加油站

pressure ['preʃər] *n.* 压（迫）感

scale [skeɪl] *n.* 比例（尺）；范围；程度

split [splɪt] *vt.* 分担

corpse [kɔːrps] *n.* 尸体

drag [dræg] *vt.* 拖拽

tip [tɪp] *vt.* 倾覆

tattoo [tæ'tuː] *n.* 文身

ankle ['æŋkl] *n.* 踝

159

时间： 第 22 集 00:02:58—00:03:59

地点： 仓库，轮船上

人物： 马霍，迈克尔，林肯

事件： 马霍与迈克尔通话，迈克尔决定去找马霍。

精彩亮点

1
拿到 500 万美元后的迈克尔在轮船的上层甲板上踱步，焦虑不安地考虑着马霍的条件。就在此时，他的电话响了。马霍提出如果他们愿意提供船只和钱给他，就会放了林肯，迈克尔将信将疑。

2
马霍表示现在他和他们兄弟俩有了共同的敌人——公司，只有他们两个人共同合作才能渡过难关。

3
迈克尔果然心动了，但他也知道这是他现在面对的唯一选择，只能选择信任马霍。但是，事实真能如迈克尔所愿吗？

4
挂掉电话后，马霍就拨通了金先生的电话。他告诉金先生两个兄弟现在的藏身地点，还告诉金最好乘飞机来，等他到来，自己就会抓住他们，一切都会结束。

Mahone: Yeah, the people I was working for, they kind of sold me down the river①. Now, I just wanna go out to sea②. ☺1

Michael: That's funny. I'll have to remember that one.

Mahone: I face more prison time than you. Sort of jumped ahead of you a few spots on the public enemy list. You're my way to freedom, Michael, and I'm yours. We both know what the other one's capable of. Let's treat each other with respect③ here. No games, no bluffing. **Just two guys doing each other a favor④. What do you say⑤?** ☺2

Michael: **Where are you?** ☺3

Mahone: Mira Flores shipping docks,⑥ just outside of Panama City. It's a big warehouse right on the water.

Michael: That's a long ways. It'll take me at least 24 hours to get there.

Mahone: Well, then, I'd get moving.

Lincoln: How's it feel being on the run?

Mahone: I'll survive.

Lincoln: Not if they catch you. They'll send you to the chair.

Mahone: **You think that's ironic?** ☺4

160

译文

马　霍：是的，我以前为之效力的人们，他们算是把我卖到下游了。现在，我只想出海。

迈克尔：这可真好笑，我得把它记住。

马　霍：我面临的刑期比你还长，我在公敌名单上的排位突然领先了你，迈克尔，你我要获得自由需要彼此，我们都清楚对方的能力，让我们给予彼此一些尊重。不要花招、不玩伎俩，就是两个人互相帮忙，你觉得怎么样？

迈克尔：你在哪里？

马　霍：米拉佛瑞斯码头，巴拿马市郊，河边的一间大仓库。

迈克尔：那可真远，我至少要 24 小时才能到。

马　霍：好了，那就快出发吧。

林　肯：逃亡的感觉如何？

马　霍：我会活下来的。

林　肯：被逮到你就不会这么说了，他们会送你上电椅。

马　霍：你觉得很讽刺吗？

知识点拨

1. sell sb. down the river 表示"出卖某人"。

2. go out to sea 表示"出海"。例：Even in the dirtiest weather, they were driven to go out to sea. 即使是最恶劣的天气，他们也被迫出海。

3. with respect 表示"尊敬地，怀有敬意地"。例：With respect, Minister, you still haven't answered my question. 部长，恕我冒昧，您还没有回答我的问题。

4. do sb. a favor 表示"帮某人一个忙，帮助某人，帮某人忙"。例：Could you do me a favor and lend me some money? 你能帮我个忙，借我一些钱吗？

5. what do you say 表示"你说什么，你有何意见"。

6. shipping dock 表示"装运台，装卸码头"。例：Are Closed Circuit Television cameras used to monitor the shipping dock and container loading areas? 是否采用闭路电视摄像机监控运输区和集装箱装货区？

 词汇加油站

enemy ['enəmi] *n.* 敌人
bluff [blʌf] *v.* 虚张声势；唬人
dock [dɑːk] *n.* 码头
survive [sər'vaɪv] *vt.* 幸存

capable ['keɪpəbl] *adj.* 有才能的
favor ['feɪvər] *n.* 恩惠
warehouse ['werhaʊs] *n.* 仓库
ironic [aɪ'rɑːnɪk] *adj.* 具有讽刺意味的

时间： 第 22 集 00:31:10—00:32:38

地点： 轮船上

人物： 迈克尔，林肯，金

事件： 迈克尔和林肯欲庆祝重获自由，金找到他们却惨遭灭口。

片段四

精彩亮点

1 　迈克尔和林肯带着 500 万美元从大仓库中逃出来，迈克尔先前早已找好当地人准备了轮船。更让他惊喜的是，从轮船舱内走出的正是他日思夜想的女友莎拉。莎拉告诉他们再也不用逃亡了，凯勒曼已经出庭作证供认了所有罪行，证明林肯是无辜的，而莎拉父亲的朋友也表示会负责迈克尔的案子。

2 　就在兄弟俩在为莎拉带来的这个好消息庆祝时，金先生突然出现，用枪对着他们。原来，他从大仓库出来后一直尾随着迈克尔他们，既然林肯已经被无罪赦免了，他又有何目的呢？

3 　来巴拿马之前，公司董事就交代金先生要将兄弟二人其中一人送入索纳监狱。林肯让金放了迈克尔，称这一切都是他引起的，和弟弟无关，但"公司"的目标却是迈克尔。

4 　就当金想要开枪时，金却突然中枪落入河中身亡。到底是谁开的枪呢？原来，开枪的是莎拉，她战战兢兢，为了迈克尔杀了人，迈克尔告诉她自己已经害了她一次，这一次就让他来报答莎拉。

Lincoln: Here. Help me out of① this.☺₁

Michael: We did it, Linc.

Lincoln: We did it. Yeah.

Kim: No. You almost did it.☺₂

Lincoln: You want the money? Take the money. Take it.

Kim: You think this is about the money? Pocket change②? Like 5 million?

Michael: Then what is it about? My brother's been exonerated. The president stepped down. We're not a threat anymore. It's over.

Kim: You may be done with us③, but that doesn't mean we're done with you. The police are on their way.☺₃

Lincoln: This started with④ me. Let my brother go.

Kim: Oh, that's sweet, that's sweet. You don't hear that much⑤ anymore, that sort of fidelity in families. Two brothers who will go to the ends of the earth⑥ for each other. Too bad only one of you will survive.

Michael: No! We gotta go.☺₄

知识点拨

1. help sb. out of sth. 表示"帮助某人干某事"。

2. pocket change 表示"零钱，小钱"。例：It was a lot of money to me but pocket change to him. 对我来说，这是很大的一笔的钱，可对他而言只是一点儿小钱而已。

3. be done with 表示"完结，结束某事"。后面如果是 sb. 表示"与某人的恩怨了结"。例：And we can be done with all of this finally. 我们就可以结束这一切。

4. start with 表示"以……开始"。例：Success was assured and, at least to start with, the system operated smoothly. 成功有保证了，至少该系统一开始运行得挺顺利。

5. that much 表示"这（那）么多，这（那）么些"。例：I'm quite pleased that we do have the capacity to produce that much food. 我很高兴我们确实有能力生产这么多粮食。

6. go to the ends of the Earth 表示"走遍天涯海角"。例：I would go to the ends of the earth to find you. 走遍天涯海角，我也要找到你。

译文

林　肯：来，帮我把这个解开。

迈克尔：我们成功了，林肯。

林　肯：是的，我们成功了。

金：　　不，你们差一点儿就成功了。

林　肯：你想要钱是吗？把钱拿走，拿去。

金：　　你们以为这跟钱有关？就五百万这种零钱？

迈克尔：不然你想怎么样？我哥已经被赦免无罪了，总统已经下台了，我们不再是威胁了，一切都结束了。

金：　　你们可能和我们了结了，但这不意味着我们和你们了结了，警察在来的路上。

林　肯：这一切都始于我，放我弟弟走。

金：　　哦，真是温馨，真是温馨呀！很少能见到家人之间的这种忠诚，兄弟俩人肯为彼此付出一切，不幸的是，只有一个人能活命。

迈克尔：不，我们快走。

词汇加油站

pocket ['pɑːkɪt] *n.* 口袋
exonerate [ɪɡ'zɑːnəreɪt] *vt.* 使免罪
threat [θret] *n.* 威胁
fidelity [fɪ'deləti] *n.* 忠诚

change [tʃeɪndʒ] *n.* 零钱
step [step] *vi.* 走
sweet [swiːt] *adj.* 亲切的

Prison Break

Season **3** 索纳监狱

Scene 1 索纳监狱初探

时间： 第 1 集 00:07:46—00:08:50
地点： 索纳监狱
人物： 马克尔，马霍
事件： 马霍欲与迈克尔合作，迈克尔拒绝。

 精彩亮点

上一季结束时，马霍和迈克尔同时被送到了索纳监狱。这里关押的都是些穷凶极恶之徒，没有法律效力，犯人死亡在这里是常有的事。**1**

马霍之所以也被关在索纳监狱是因为先前自己曾与迈克尔通话，以释放林肯为条件，让迈克尔答应把钱和轮船给他，但聪明的迈克尔留了一手，他从巴拿马当地一个小伙手中买了两包毒品藏在船上，等马霍赶到，宣称这艘船是他的时，不仅船被扣留，马霍也被带到索纳监狱。**2**

迈克尔认为马霍和公司的人是一伙的，正是因为他的陷害自己才会被关在这里。但马霍说公司只命令他去巴拿马逮捕迈克尔和林肯并把他们移送回来，现在因为迈克尔的栽赃陷害，本来与妻儿团聚的计划又泡汤了。**3**

马霍希望迈克尔与他合作离开索纳监狱，但迈克尔却表示自己不会和一个杀父仇人一起合作的。**4**

Mahone: How are you doing [1] ? ☺1
Michael: What do you want, Alex?
Mahone: You're so cleverlike planting the drugs on the boat. That's a big irony. Lawman in jail [2]. You are exactly where you belong. No, that's where you're wrong. And that's where you're gonna help me. I will have a court date [3] one of these days, and you will be there on the stand [4]. And you will tell the truth that you planned this and you set this up, and I'm gonna go home.
Michael: That's funny, I could have sworn you set this up. ☺2
Mahone: I set this up? I'm in here.
Michael: What does the Company want with me? Why Panama? ☺3
Mahone: What, you think I know what they wanted? They had me. I did what they asked me to do, arrest you in Panama hand you over. That's it. That's, that's… That's old news [5], huh? This is the first day of the rest of our lives. How about we work together, you know? Help each other out.
Michael: Except [6] every time I look at you, all I can see is the man who killed my father. You're on your own [7]. ☺4

 知识点拨

译文

马　霍：你怎么样？

迈克尔：亚力克斯，你想怎么样？

马　霍：你太聪明了，竟然想出在船上放毒品栽赃我，这实在太嘲讽了，罗曼现在也被关在监狱里，你现在是罪有应得。不，这就是你错误的地方，而我需要你的帮助。这几天我就要接受庭审了，你到时也会出庭。你会告诉大家真相：你计划了这一切，是你设计的栽赃，这样我就可以回家了。

迈克尔：真有意思，我对天发誓这是你栽赃陷害。

马　霍：我栽赃陷害？我也在这儿。

迈克尔：公司到底对我有什么企图？为什么要在巴拿马？

马　霍：你觉得我像是知道这一切的人吗？我也受他们控制。我曾经听命于他们，在巴拿马逮捕你并移送回来，就是这样。这……这……这一切都是过去的事了，不是吗？今天是我们共度余生的第一天。不如我们合作，你觉得呢？互相帮助，一起逃出去。

迈克尔：我每次看到你只能想起那个杀我父亲的凶手，你自求多福吧。

1. How are you doing？表示"你好吗？"。例：You're so grown-up, how are you doing? 你都长这么大了，你好吗？

2. in jail 表示"在狱中服刑"。例：He picked a fight with a waiter and landed in jail. 他找碴儿跟服务生打了一架，最后进了监狱。

3. court date 表示"开庭日期"。例：To do so you need to contact the courthouse and set up a court date. 这样做你需要联系法院，并安排出庭日期。

4. on the stand 表示"在法院的证人席"。例：I had to put him on the stand. 我得把他放在被告席上。

5. old news 表示"旧闻，旧新闻"。例：That's old news. I knew it long ago. 你这是"旧闻"我早知道了。

6. except 用于表示"同类事物之间的关系"，其意为"除……以外；除去"。而 except for 用于表示"对主要部分的肯定和对局部的否定"。它不表示同类事物之间的关系，意为"除了……以外"。

7. on your own 表示"独立地；自愿地"。例：When push comes to shove, you are on your own. 如果形势糟糕，你就只能靠自己了。

 词汇加油站

drug [drʌg] n. 毒品
jail [dʒeɪl] n. 监狱
stand [stænd] n. 台
arrest [ə'rest] vt. 逮捕

irony ['aɪrəni] n. 具有讽刺意味的事
court [kɔːrt] n. 法院
swear [swer] v. 发誓要

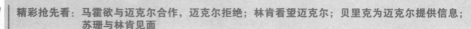

时间： 第 1 集 00:09:22—00:10:25
地点： 索纳监狱
人物： 迈克尔，林肯，士兵
事件： 林肯看望迈克尔。

片段二

 精彩亮点

1

　　林肯前来索纳监狱看望弟弟迈克尔，看守的士兵让他签字，声明一旦在里面遇到任何意外，都要自己承担责任，足以看出索纳监狱的恐怖。有人将其比喻为"单行道"，只有进，没有出，除非罪犯在里面死亡。

2

　　林肯感激迈克尔为自己做的一切，如果没有迈克尔，自己现在早已经不在人世了。而如今迈克尔却被关在索纳监狱，自己怎么可以弃他不顾？

3

　　从林肯的话中，我们可以看出他已厌倦过着逃亡的生活，每天战战兢兢。此外，在领事馆的律师告诉了他一个好消息，这条好消息是什么呢？

4

　　来之前，林肯已经和领事馆的律师面谈过。律师告诉他，已经在案发现场找到了金先生携带的特工手枪，他们可以以正当防卫为由申请为迈克尔洗脱罪责。此外，领事馆还准备将迈克尔转移到更安全的地方，听起来一切如果按照计划进行，将是最完美的结局，但事实又如何呢？

Soldier: Sign here to say that once inside, you're on your own by the law[1], that you're not protected by the military in case of an assault. ☺1 And any attempt to assist an inmate trying to escape will be met with[2] a lethal response.

Lincoln: Wouldn't dream of[3] it. So…

Michael: So…

Lincoln: Feel like I'm on the wrong side[4]. ☺2

Michael: You're on the right side.

Lincoln: You're not.

Michael: Gonna break me out?

Lincoln: Too tiring. All that[5] running. ☺3

Michael: Yeah, well, maybe you should have lost the cowboy boots.

Lincoln: You scared? I'm getting you out of here, man. Listen, the Consulate's arranged to transfer you to a safer facility until the trial which is about a month. They say you got a good shot[6] of walking out of here a free man. ☺4

Michael: When's the transfer?

Lincoln: Tomorrow.

译文

士　兵： 在这里签字，进去后，根据我国法律你就要对自己负责了，发生任何突袭事件，你都不受军方或者法律保护，任何协助在押犯越狱的企图都以死罪论处。

林　肯： 我从来就没想过，怎么样？

迈克尔： 不怎么样。

林　肯： 感觉我站错队了。

迈克尔： 你没站错。

林　肯： 但是你不在。

迈克尔： 要帮我越狱吗？

林　肯： 太累了，一路上都在逃亡。

迈克尔： 是呀，或许你已经把逃亡靴弄丢了。

林　肯： 你害怕了？兄弟，我现在就把你救出来。听着，领事馆准备把你转移到安全的地方。大约一个月后，你就有重获自由的机会。他们说你有很大机会无罪释放。

迈克尔： 什么时候转移？

林　肯： 明天。

知识点拨

1. by the law 表示"依法治国，根据法律"。例：Marriages in proximity of blood are forbidden by the law. 法律规定禁止近亲结婚。

2. be met with 表示"遇到，遭受"。例：To his friends this was a scandal, an outrage that had to be met with resistance. 他的朋友们认为，那是一桩丑闻，一桩必须加以抵制的暴行。

3. dream of 表示"梦想，梦见，渴望；考虑"。例：I shouldn't dream of doing such a thing. 我不该梦想做这样的事。

4. be on the wrong side 表示"站错队"。例：We'll be the ones on the wrong side of the law. 我们在法律上的地位将会很被动。

5. all that 表示"到那种程度（地步）"。例：He said all that remained was to agree to a time and venue. 他说剩下的只是商定一个时间和集会地点。

6. a good shot 可以表示"照相的取景很出色"或"神枪手"，在片中表示"有很大可能"。例：She's got a good shot at recovery. 她有很大的希望恢复健康。

 词汇加油站

assault [ə'sɔːlt] *n.* 袭击
lethal ['liːθl] *adj.* 致命的
cowboy ['kaʊbɔɪ] *n.* 牛仔
consulate ['kɑːnsələt] *n.* 领事馆

inmate ['ɪnmeɪt] *n.* （监狱里的）犯人
tiring ['taɪərɪŋ] *adj.* 令人疲倦的
boot [buːt] *n.* 长靴
transfer [træns'fɜːr] *vt.* 使转移

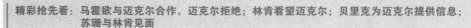

时间：	第 2 集 00:04:42—00:06:44
地点：	索纳监狱，下水道
人物：	贝里克，迈克尔
事件：	贝里克为迈克尔提供信息。

片段三

精彩亮点

上一季，在贝里克、迈克尔和苏克雷三个人去找帝博格"算账"时不料被警察跟踪。帝博格在巴拿马酒店杀死了一位女性，听闻警察来了他马上逃跑，而且还开枪射中了贝里克的腿，迈克尔和苏克雷则去追赶帝博格，留下中枪的贝里克成了"替死鬼"，最后也被送到索纳监狱。 **1**

贝里克在监狱的日子一点儿也不好过，他被逼去清理厕所，并得到躲在通风管内的神秘人分给他的食物，条件是要帮神秘人传纸条，而贝里克在昨天将这张纸条递给了迈克尔。 **2**

在塞纳监狱，犯人们的食物很有限，尤其是水源，这里没有干净的饮用水，而且每次每人只能分得一杯，根本不足以解渴。贝里克以提供水为机会提供给迈克尔一些信息。 **3**

迈克尔收到的纸条上写有两个地名及一个时间，而这张纸条也同时传给了马霍。两个人谁能将惠斯勒带出索纳监狱，谁就能活着出去，而另一个人就要死在索纳监狱里。一场激动人心的营救大战正式上演！ **4**

Bellick: Spare a little? ☺₁

Michael: I need some information.

Bellick: Absolutely.

Michael: You slipped this note in my pocket yesterday. Why? ☺₂

Bellick: My memory's a little foggy on account of① this thirst. Yeah, it's starting to come back to me now. A little more agua② there. ☺₃

Michael: The note.

Bellick: This guy gave me some rat meat in exchange for③ putting that in your pocket and the pocket of the guy you were set to④ fight.

Michael: Why?

Bellick: He's nuts, that's why. Anybody who can live down in those sewers doesn't have all his faculties.

Michael: Where in the sewers? Whistler! Whistler. My name is Michael Scofield. I was here to get you out of here. I'm going to assume they told you I was coming. Or that someone was coming. Whistler. Last chance⑤. I'm not coming down⑥ here again. ☺₄

170

译文

贝里克：能给我点儿吗？

迈克尔：我需要点儿消息。

贝里克：当然可以。

迈克尔：你昨天把这张纸条塞进我口袋里，你为什么要这么做？

贝里克：我渴得有点儿记不清了。是的，现在有点儿回忆起来了，再来一点儿就全记起来了。

迈克尔：纸条。

贝里克：有个家伙给了我点儿鼠肉让我把这个塞进你和你对手的口袋里。

迈克尔：为什么？

贝里克：他是个怪人，这就是原因。能住在下水道这种地方的人都有点儿不正常。

迈克尔：下水道的什么地方？（镜头切换至下水道）惠斯勒，惠斯勒，我叫迈克尔·斯科菲尔德，我来这儿就是为了把你弄出去，我想他们已经告诉你了我会来或是有人要来，惠斯勒，这是最后的机会，我不会再来这儿了。

知识点拨

1. account of sth. 表示"关于……的记述"。例：The preface of the book includes an account of the author's life. 该书前言记述了作者生平。

2. agua 为西班牙语，表示"水、泉"。例：Here's your daily drought reminder to conserve agua. 这里是节约用水的每日干旱提醒。

3. in exchange for sth. 表示"交换某物"。例：It is illegal for public officials to solicit gifts or money in exchange for favors. 公务员通过索要礼物或钱财作为为他人提供便利的交换是违法的。

4. be set to 表示"被定在；被设为"。

5. last chance 表示"最后的机会"。例：This is positively the last chance for the industry to establish such a system. 这绝对是该产业建立这样一个体系的最后机会了。

6. come down 有以下几种含义"下来，下落；着陆；崩塌；决定并宣布（支持或反对）"。例：The curtain came down after the first act. 第一幕过后，幕布落了下来。

 词汇加油站

slip [slɪp] vt. 悄悄塞，偷偷放

rat [ræt] n. 大老鼠

sewer ['su:ər] n. 下水道

assume [ə'su:m] v. 假定

foggy ['fɔ:gi] adj. 模糊的

nuts [nʌts] adj. 发疯的

faculty ['fæklti] n. 官能，天赋

时间： 第2集 00:08:33—00:09:44
地点： 咖啡厅
人物： 苏珊，林肯
事件： 苏珊与林肯见面。

片段四

精彩亮点

1. 苏珊是公司的代表，为人阴险狡诈。她拿林肯儿子和莎拉的生命威胁林肯，使本来有望被转移的迈克尔再一次陷入帮助他人越狱的窘境。

2. 苏珊约林肯在咖啡厅见面，以一副命令的口吻对林肯说话。因为公司已经抓住了对这兄弟俩最重要的两个人，他们别无选择只能听命于自己。

3. 可以看得出来，公司将几个关键人物紧密地联系在一起：迈克尔、林肯、马霍还有本季的线索人物惠斯勒。这其中到底隐藏着公司的什么阴谋呢？

4. 据苏珊所说，惠斯勒的犯罪性质在政界备受关注。惠斯勒到底是为何入狱的呢？狱中有人告诉马霍：惠斯勒因为谋杀市长的儿子被捕入狱，市长敕权索纳监狱头领路赛罗，只要能抓住并杀死惠斯勒，就可以得到上庭重审的机会。

Susan: In an effort to save[1] some time, I'm gonna have to insist that we just skip right past all the threats I know you're prepared to lay out. ☺1 Should anything happen to Sara to L.J., you will scour the Earth and hunt me down[2] and rip my heart from my chest and bup, bup, bup. I absolutely know how you feel, as would I, okay? So that's done. On to business. **Did you brother get the message?** ☺2 Good. You and I will meet here every day. I'll want a full report of the prior day's progress. When I call your cell phone, answer. Don't ask me stupid questions. Don't waste my time. Get a plan together. Execute it. L.J. and Sara will be traded for[3] Whistler. Are we clear[4]?

Lincoln: I want a picture of my son and Sara to prove they're alive.

Susan: Fine. I can do that, next.

Lincoln: Why us? ☺3

Susan: I'll answer that question, so we can put it to bed[5] and you can focus on your work. **There's a political spotlight on Whistler due to the nature of his crime.** ☺4 Raids, bribes, what have you, are not an option. We have to go in through the back d oor, so to speak[6].

Lincoln: This can't be done in a week.

译文

苏珊： 为了节省时间，我还是要强调，跳过那段你我都明白的你先前准备好的威胁论。要是莎拉和 L.J. 有什么三长两短，你会追我到天涯海角，抽我的筋，扒我的皮……我绝对知道你的感受，行吗？那就这么说好了。现在来说正事，你弟弟得到消息了吗？很好，以后每天我们都会在这里碰头，我需要一份详细的越狱进度报告。我给你打电话，你就接听，不要问我愚蠢的问题，也别浪费我时间。计划周全了，然后就开始干，拿惠斯勒来换 L.J. 和莎拉。听清楚了吗？

林肯： 我要看儿子和莎拉的照片证明他们都活着。

苏珊： 可以，我能办到，还有呢？

林肯： 为什么是我们？

苏珊： 我会告诉你答案了结此事，这样我们就能让你专心做事了。惠斯勒的犯罪性质使他备受政界的关注，劫掠，贿赂，随便什么招都行不通。这么说吧，我们必须得走后门。

林肯： 这在一周内不可能搞定。

知识点拨

1. in an effort to do 表示"努力（做）某事"。
   例：It is intended to reduce the burden of students in an effort to do something good for new curriculum. 减轻学生的负担，为新课程做一些力所能及的工作。

2. hunt sb. down 表示"搜索直至找到某人"。
   例：Last December they hunted down and killed one of the gangsters. 去年 12 月他们追捕到其中一名匪徒并将其击毙。

3. A be traded for B 表示"用 A 交换 B"。例：Can money be traded for happiness? 钱能换来幸福吗？

4. Are we clear? 可以表示"我们的债两清了吗？"在片中表示"我说清楚了吗？/ 你明白我说的意思了吗？"

5. put sth. to bed 表示"关于某事的讨论到此结束，结束某个话题"。例：The only thing I'll say, and then we can put it to bed, is everyone at the football club is totally and utterly behind Luis Suarez. 总之，到此为止，我唯一想说的就是现在我们的俱乐部里的每一个成员都会全力支持路易斯·苏亚雷斯！

6. so to speak 表示"可以说，可谓"。例：I ought not to tell you but I will, since you're in the family, so to speak. 我本来不该告诉你的，但我还是要这么做，因为好歹你是家里的一员。

 词汇加油站

skip [skɪp] vt. 跳过
rip [rɪp] vt. 撕裂
stupid ['stu:pɪd] adj. 愚蠢的
raid [reɪd] n. 抢劫

scour [skaʊər] v. 四处搜索
chest [tʃest] n. 胸部
spotlight ['spɑ:tlaɪt] n. 公众注意或突出显著

Scene 2 鸟的指南成为关键线索

时间： 第 2 集 00:40:47—00:41:42
地点： 林肯临时居所
人物： 苏珊，林肯
事件： 林肯拿走关于鸟的指南被发现，苏珊逼其交出来。

 精彩亮点

1 苏珊得知林肯从惠斯勒女友手中拿走了一本关于鸟的指南，恼怒不已，这本指南正是公司的目标。那么这本指南里到底有什么秘密呢？

2 惠斯勒的女友看到了惠斯勒纸条上写的地名，林肯跟踪她来到指定地点，等到她出来时，从她的包里抢走了那本指南。

3 林肯想假装不知道，但苏珊怎么可能没有识破他的谎言？看来不威胁一下林肯他是不会交出那本指南的。于是，她威胁林肯自己的车上有所有能毁尸灭迹的工具，如果林肯不交出指南，她就可以把林肯杀死。

4 林肯一向头脑简单，不像迈克尔一样做事考虑周全，但这一次，林肯竟然留了一个心眼，他把假指南交给了苏珊，而把真正的指南藏在了裤脚里。

Susan: **You know, they told me that your brother got all the brains**①**, but I didn't realize you were this stupid.**☺₁

Lincoln: What do you want, Susan?

Susan: No sooner② do I tell you to stick to③ the plan, than you go and hassle Whistler's girlfriend. **You need to quit playing Sherlock Holmes**④ **and leave her alone.**☺₂

Lincoln: Why?

Susan: 'Cause I said so. How about that?

Lincoln: All right. How about you beat it⑤, so I can get to work?

Susan: I will as soon as you give me what you took from her.

Lincoln: **I took nothing from her.**☺₃

Susan: I got a gallon of bleach, a tarp and a hacksaw in the trunk of my car. One hour, tops—you're off the face of the earth⑥.

Lincoln: It's just a bird guide.

Susan: **I am not going to ask you again. Toss it.**☺₄ Tomorrow — bar. Progress report. I will be waiting.

译文

苏珊： 你知道，他们告诉我你弟弟十分聪明，但我没想到你居然这么愚蠢。

林肯： 你想要什么，苏珊？

苏珊： 我刚让你去实施计划你就马上去骚扰惠斯勒的女友，你别再扮演福尔摩斯了，离她远点儿。

林肯： 为什么？（苏珊用手枪指着林肯）

苏珊： 因为我这么说了。怎么样？

林肯： 好，你何不把枪放下，让我好去做事？

苏珊： 我会的，只要你给我从她那儿得到的东西。

林肯： 我没拿她什么东西。

苏珊： 我的车厢里有一加仑漂白剂，一块防水布和一把钢锯。最多一小时你就人间蒸发了。

林肯： 只是一本关于鸟的指南。

苏珊： 我不会问你第二遍，把它放下，明天在酒吧见，我等着你的进展报告。

知识点拨

1. the brains 表示"智力超群的人"。例：Some investigators regarded her as the brains of the gang. 一些调查员认为她是该团伙的决策者。

2. no sooner... than... 表示"一……就……"，引导时间状语从句，主句用过去完成时，than 后面的从句用一般过去时。

3. stick to 表示"遵守；保留；坚持；忠于"。后面加名词或动名词。例：I tend to stick to fresh fruit for pudding. 我一直坚持用新鲜水果做甜点。

4. 大家对夏洛克·福尔摩斯一定不陌生，他是由 19 世纪末的英国侦探小说家阿瑟·柯南·道尔所塑造的一个才华横溢的虚构的侦探，足不出户就能解决许多难题。

5. beat it 表示"逃走，滚开，立即走开"。例：This is private land, so beat it! 这是私人地产，请走开。

6. off the face of the earth 表示"完全彻底地（消灭）"。例：If a nuclear war breaks out, every living thing will be wiped off the face of the Earth. 如果爆发核战争，地球上的所有生物都将灭绝。

词汇加油站

stupid ['stuːpɪd] *adj.* 愚蠢的

hassle ['hæsl] *vt.* 不断烦扰

gallon ['gælən] *n.* 加仑（容量单位）

tarp [tɑːrp] *n.* 防水布

stick [stɪk] *vt.* 容忍

quit [kwɪt] *vt.* 中断

bleach [bliːtʃ] *n.* 漂白剂

hacksaw ['hæksɔː] *n.* 钢锯

时间： 第 3 集 00:08:15—00:09:02

地点： 索纳监狱，咖啡厅

人物： 迈克尔，苏珊，林肯，犯人

事件： 迈克尔欲与莎拉通话，林肯与苏珊为此周旋。

片段二

精彩亮点

1
苏珊按照约定派人把 L.J. 和莎拉的照片拿给林肯，林肯去监狱看望迈克尔时，将这两张照片给迈克尔看，照片中的莎拉在指着某个地方，是想告诉迈克尔他们她的所在地。迈克尔迫不及待地想跟莎拉通话。

2
迈克尔在狱中想办法与莎拉通话的同时，林肯正与苏珊见面，要求他们同意迈克尔与莎拉通话。迈克尔将监狱内的水管打通，帮助监狱头头路赛罗排解了一大难题，从而换来路赛罗的一句：现在，惠斯勒清白了，这也就意味着路赛罗可以不用在狱中东躲西藏了，没有人敢杀他了。

3
苏珊告诉林肯，有两件事可以向他保证：一是莎拉没事，二是就算林肯把她打倒，也不可能让莎拉和迈克尔通话。但她也明白迈克尔很倔强，如果因为这一点耽误了帮助惠斯勒越狱的时机就得不偿失了，

4
在索纳监狱，犯人是不允许与外界通话的，不仅电话线全部被切断，外面来探视的人也不允许带电话进来。而在这里，只有一个人有权使用手机，他就是索纳监狱的头头——路赛罗。

Prisoner: **Government rip out**① **all the phones when they find out bad men in Sona still setting up deals.** ☺₁ Making bang-bangs just like before. They just did it over the phone.

Michael: Well, if they cut the lines, maybe we can fix 'em.

Prisoner: There's nothing to fix, bro. There used to be a whole row of② them all along the wall, but they're gone now.

Susan: If you have no more questions I'm just gonna get going.

Lincoln: **Michael got the bounty off Whistler's head in two days.** ☺₂ That's more than your people could do in two weeks. Show some goodwill.

Susan: He'll get his goodwill when Whistler's out.

Lincoln: One thing you should know about my brother, he's very stubborn. You want him to fetch, you throw him a bone③ .

Susan: **How does Michael think he's gonna get his hands on a phone inside Sona?** ☺₃

Michael: What about cell phones? With all the traffic④ moving in and out of here.

Prisoner: Cell phone big no-no. **Only one man has access to**⑤ **it, and he would never let a zanahoria**⑥ **like you...** ☺₄

Michael: Let me guess.

译文

犯　人：政府把这里的电话都拆了，因为他们发现这帮犯人在索纳监狱依然恶性不改，还像过去那样闹个不停。所以他们就把电话线切断了。

迈克尔：如果他们切断了线路，或许我们还能修复。

犯　人：大哥，没什么好修理的。从前这里沿着墙都是成卷的电话线，但是现在都没有了。

苏　珊：如果你没有问题，我就走了。

林　肯：迈克尔两天内就救下了惠斯勒的命，那是你们的人两周都办不到的，表现出你的诚意吧。

苏　珊：当他救出惠斯勒后我们会表现诚意的。

林　肯：关于我弟弟有一点你应该了解，那就是他很顽固。要想有收获，必须先付出。

苏　珊：让迈克尔在索纳监狱里通个电话如何？

迈克尔：那手机呢？这边人来人往的可以带个进来。

犯　人：手机？不可能。只有一个人有权用手机，但他一定不会给你这样的家伙用……

迈克尔：让我猜猜。

知识点拨

1. rip out 表示"狠狠地拔出；拿走"。

2. a row of 表示"一排"。例：The dead elms have been replaced by a row of saplings. 枯死的榆树已被移去而换栽了一排幼树。

3. You want him to fetch, you throw him a bone. 表示"欲有所求，必先所施"。例：If you want him to fetch and carry for you, you throw him a bone. 如果你想要差遣他，就要给他点儿好处。

4. traffic 我们很熟悉，知道它可以表示"交通；运输量"，此外，它还可以表示"（非法的）交易；通信量；交际；流量"。

5. have access to 表示"使用，接近；利用"。例：They now have access to the mass markets of Japan and the UK. 他们现在进入了日本和英国的大众市场。

6. zanahoria 是西班牙语，表示"胡萝卜"。

词汇加油站

rip [rɪp] vt. 扯破
row [roʊ] n. 排
goodwill [ˌɡʊdˈwɪl] n. 亲善
fetch [fetʃ] vt. （去）拿来

fix [fɪks] vt. 修理
bounty [ˈbaʊnti] n. 慷慨之举
stubborn [ˈstʌbərn] adj. 固执的

时间： 第3集 00:15:39—00:18:50
地点： 索纳监狱
人物： 迈克尔，帝博格，惠斯勒
事件： 迈克尔向帝博格寻求帮助，惠斯勒向迈克尔索要书。

精彩亮点

帝博格进入索纳监狱后，马上摸清形势，得知路赛罗是这里的老大，就对他卑躬屈膝并效忠于他。为了在索纳监狱如此恶劣的环境中生存，他这样做也是可以理解的。 **1**

迈克尔找到帝博格，想要他帮自己一个忙，他想要与莎拉通话，但索纳监狱里唯一一个被允许使用电话的人就是路赛罗，但自从惠斯勒事件后，路赛罗认为没必要和迈克尔纠缠下去，他也按照约定"赦免"了惠斯勒，迈克尔想找他借电话，并通过帝博格为自己牵线搭桥。 **2**

惠斯勒的女友探视惠斯勒时告诉他那本关于鸟的指南被林肯拿走了。惠斯勒找到迈克尔，想让他说服他哥哥把那本书还给他。 **3**

对于迈克尔而言，拿到这本书可以牵制公司，既然书在他们手上，公司自然也不敢对 L.J. 和莎拉下手。那么，这本书对惠斯勒又有何意义呢？里面到底记录着什么呢？ **4**

T-Bag: Careful, Pretty. Don't bite the hand you trying to get fed out of. ☺1

Michael: I'm not looking for food, I'm looking for a favor. ☺2

T-Bag: Why the hell① should I do you a favor, huh?

Michael: Cause unlike your new compadres, I know who you are, what you've done and who you've done it to.

T-Bag: Let me get this straight②. You're saying you gonna tell on③ me?

Michael: What I'm saying is this here is a religious country, and I'm willing to bet the good folks down in Panama don't take too kindly to rapists and pedophiles. You want to bet against④ me?

Whistler: Listen, mate. Here's what I know so far. I know you've got a brother helping on the outside, I know he ran into⑤ my girlfriend, and I know he took a book from her that belongs to me. I'd like it back. ☺3

Michael: What's so special about this book?

Whistler: Well, unless it has directions out of this prison, I don't think it should really matter to you.

Michael: You don't know what matters to⑥ me. ☺4 You can get that book back when we get out of Sona.

译文

帝博格：小心点儿，帅哥。别惹祸上身。

迈克尔：我没有在找麻烦，而是在寻求帮助。

帝博格：我为什么要帮你啊？

迈克尔：我不像你那些新伙伴，我了解你，知道你都干了什么，对谁干的。

帝博格：让我直说了吧。你是说你想要告发我？

迈克尔：我要说的是，这是个信教的国家，我宁可赌一把看看巴拿马良民会如何善待强奸犯兼恋童癖的。你愿意和我赌一把吗？

惠斯勒：听着，兄弟。这是我目前知道的情况。我知道你哥哥在外面想办法把我们弄出去，我还知道他跑去见我女朋友了，还从她那里拿走了一本我的书。我想让他把书还给我。

迈克尔：那本书有那么特别的吗？

惠斯勒：除非能想办法出去，否则这本书对你来说还是没用。

迈克尔：你不知道这本书对我而言有什么意义，等我们出去了我自然把书还给你。

知识点拨

1. the hell 没有什么实际意思，主要用于加强语气。例：Where the hell have you been? 你到底去哪里了？

2. get sth. straight 表示"矫正……，确认……是不是事实"（make sure sth. is true）。多用成 Let me get sth. straight 的形式，主要使用在未能理解对方的意思或想要重新确认一下的情形中。

3. tell on sb. 表示"告发某人；产生（坏的）影响"。例：Never mind, I won't tell on you. 别担心，我不会告发你。

4. bet against sb. 表示"与某人打赌，打赌断定（某事）不可能发生"。例：Are you asking me to bet against my own man? 你是叫我对自己人下注吗？

5. run into 表示"快速进入……；（使）碰撞；驱车造访……，碰到某人"。例：He ran into Krettner in the corridor a few minutes later. 几分钟之后他在走廊里意外碰到了克雷特纳。

6. matters to sb. 表示"对某人很重要"。例：It matters to me a great deal that this project finishes on time. 对我来说，这项计划按时完成很重要。

 词汇加油站

bite [baɪt] **vt.** 咬

compadre [kəmˈpɑːdreɪ] **n.** 伙伴

religious [rɪˈlɪdʒəs] **adj.** 宗教的

pedophile [ˈpiːdoʊfaɪl] **n.** 恋童癖者

favor [ˈfeɪvər] **n.** 帮助

straight [streɪt] **adj.** 直率的

rapist [ˈreɪpɪst] **n.** 强奸犯

special [ˈspeʃl] **adj.** 特殊的

时间： 第3集 00:19:10—00:20:25

地点： 索纳监狱

人物： 马霍，劳尔

事件： 律师与马霍见面，马霍希望其帮助自己带一些药物被拒绝。

片段四

精彩亮点

1

自从进入索纳监狱以来，马霍一直没有服用镇定药物。现在，他的药瘾已经开始发作，自己平日里不得不依靠对妻儿的想念对抗药瘾。就在他一筹莫展时，他等来了劳尔，劳尔是被委派来为马霍辩护的律师。

2

一开始，当劳尔告诉马霍他的开庭期已经定下来时，马霍无比激动，对未来充满了希望，但当他听说自己还要等上一年时，他又陷入了绝望之中。

3

真正的原因就是在索纳监狱找人作证这种手段根本行不通，马霍此时不禁情绪变得异常暴躁。

4

既然不得不等上一年，现在当务之急是解决自己的药瘾问题。他希望律师帮自己找一种名为 Varatril 的药物，不曾想律师以为他想让自己帮忙贩毒，让马霍恼怒不已。

Raul: Looks like I have some great news. We got you a trial date. ☺₁

Mahone: That's really… th…thank God. Thank God…When?

Raul: June 13.

Mahone: Oh, no, no, wait, wait, wait, th…the…13th, 13th, that was last week. What, we missed it?

Raul: June 13 of next year, Mr. Mahone.

Mahone: Next year. How the hell is that great news? ☺₂

Raul: It usually takes two and a half years for a non-citizen to get before a judge.

Mahone: I've got a guy in, in here, his name is Michael Scofield and, and he will testify that he set me up and that he put the drugs on the boat.

Raul: Which will all be taken into consideration① …

Mahone: A year from now!

Raul: I'm going to have to ask you to calm down②, Mr. Mahone.

Mahone: It's open and shut③. It's a no-brainer④ for you. I got a guy who can cop to… ☺₃

Raul: The notion of one inmate taking the fall⑤ for another is not exactly fresh and usually means someone was pressured into⑥ the confession.

Mahone: Well, here's the thing, Raul. I require a certain medication that they, well, they just don't provide here, and I am…Let's just say that would be good for everybody. If, um, if I got this medication. ☺₄

译文

劳尔：我有好消息要告诉你，我们定下了你案子的开庭时间。

马霍：那可真的要……感谢上帝，感谢上帝。什么时候？

劳尔：6 月 13 日。

马霍：哦，不，不，等等，等等，等等，是……13 日，13 日？那是上个礼拜啊。什么？我们错过了？

劳尔：马霍先生，是明年的 6 月 13 日。

马霍：明年，这究竟是什么好消息？

劳尔：通常情况下，外国公民要等两年半才能开庭。

马霍：我这里有个叫斯科菲尔德的人，他愿意证明是他嫁祸我的，是他把毒品放在船上的。

劳尔：我们会考虑这些情况的……

马霍：一年之后！

劳尔：马霍先生，请您冷静。

马霍：这简直是一目了然的事事！你有没有脑子！现在有人可以证明我……

劳尔：你所说的某个犯人试图代另一个犯人承担罪责这种方法在这里并不新鲜，这通常意味着那个人被迫承认这些事情。

马霍：好吧，还有件事，劳尔。我需要一些药，但这里无法提供给我，而我……让我们这样说吧，这对大家都好，如果，嗯，我可以得到这种药。

知识点拨

1. take sth. into consideration 表示"考虑某事"。例：Well there are many factors to be taken into consideration in deciding which type you want. 嗯，在你们决定采用哪一款之前，有很多因素都必须予以考虑。

2. calm down 表示"（使）平静，镇静，安静"。例：Calm down for a minute and listen to me. 你安静一会儿，听我说。

3. open and shut 表示"一目了然的"。例：It's an open and shut case. The hospital is at fault. 这件事一目了然，责任在医院一方。

4. no-brainer 表示"傻瓜都知道的问题"。例：If it's illegal for someone under 21 to drive, it should be illegal for them to drink and drive. That's a no-brainer. 如果不满 21 岁开车是违法的，那他们酒后驾车也应是违法的，这非常容易理解。

5. take the fall 表示"替别人承担责任，做替罪羊，代人受过"。例：See, now you gonna have to take the fall for this bullshit. 看，你现在得收拾这些烂摊子了。

6. be pressured into doing sth. 表示"被逼迫做某事"。例：Some young people are pressured into staying on at school. 有些年轻人是在压力下才继续留在学校里上学的。

词汇加油站

miss [mɪs] v. 错过（机会）

testify ['testɪfaɪ] vt. 作证

consideration [kən,sɪdə'reɪʃn] n. 考虑

cop [kɑːp] vt. 获得

judge [dʒʌdʒ] n. 法官

drug [drʌg] n. 毒品

shut [ʃʌt] adj. 关闭，合拢

medication [,medɪ'keɪʃn] n. 药物

Scene 3 迈克尔计划帮惠斯勒越狱

时间： 第4集 00:01:45—00:02:33

地点： 索纳监狱

人物： 迈克尔，惠斯勒

事件： 惠斯勒劝迈克尔把书还给他，迈克尔拒绝。

片段一

精彩亮点

1 　　迈克尔正透过狱室望向窗外，他看到了一位掘墓人。出逃人还活着，说明围墙没有电，但惠斯勒表示即使这样，犯人一出去就会被击毙，所以想要越狱根本不可能。

2 　　惠斯勒来找迈克尔主要目的还是想要回林肯手中的鸟的指南。这本指南中藏有公司一心营救他的秘密。但迈克尔是否会答应呢？

3 　　此前，林肯根据迈克尔提供的与莎拉通话的信息找到了儿子和莎拉的所在地，但他晚了一步，在他冲进去时，眼睁睁地看着儿子和莎拉被带上车，再一次消失得无影无踪。林肯的这一举动惹恼了公司,他们杀了莎拉，割下她的头，警告林肯不要再尝试营救儿子。

4 　　不管惠斯勒如何威胁迈克尔，迈克尔都无动于衷，因为这本书关乎莎拉和 L.J. 的性命，是他和林肯手上唯一能威胁公司的筹码，怎能说给他就给他呢？

Whistler: **What's so interesting out there, other than our freedom?** ☺₁

Michael: Finds ① are alive, so the fence is dead.

Whistler: Yeah? Everyone in here knows is that fence doesn't work, and it doesn't mean a bloody thing ②, because there are soldiers out there that'll shoot you dead ③ before you get within 30 yards of it.

Michael: Well, I guess I got a lot of work to do, don't I?

Whistler: **Listen, mate, I get what you're doing with my book.** ☺₂ They hold your girlfriend, you hold what they want. Countering needs. Churchill 101. Soon those bastards are going to ask me what progress I've made ④ in figuring out what they want, and I'm going to say nil, 'cause Lincoln Burrows has the book.

Michael: You know what? **Threatening the brother of the guy who's supposed to get you out of here might not be the smartest move.** ☺₃

Whistler: I'm not threatening, we're on the same team. But if we play games with that book, people who want me out of here will take action ⑤.

Michael: **"I never worry about action, only inaction." Churchill 101. Now, like I said, I got a lot of work to do.** ☺₄

译文

惠斯勒：窗外有什么比自由更吸引人的东西吗？

迈克尔：出逃者还活着，因此围墙上没电。

惠斯勒：是吗？这里的每个人都知道那围墙形同虚设，但这没有任何意义。因为只要你在 30 码内，外面的士兵就会把你击毙。

迈克尔：我得好好规划一下了，是不是？

惠斯勒：听着，伙计，我知道你抢了我的书。他们挟持了你的女友而你抢走了他们要的东西。互惠互利，丘吉尔教的，不久后，那些杂种就会来问我他们所要的我了解了多少，而我会说完全不了解，因为林肯·布鲁斯把书抢走了。

迈克尔：你知道吗？威胁一个要帮你越狱的人的哥哥或许不是明智之举。

惠斯勒：我没有威胁你，我们在同一条船上。但如果我们因为那本书纠缠不清，那些想让我出去的人会采取行动。

迈克尔：丘吉尔还说过："我不在乎你们做什么就怕你们什么也不做"。现在，正如我所说，我还有很多事要做。

知识点拨

1. find 一般做动词，表示"找到，发现，查明，发觉"。但在片中它做名词，表示被发现的人。

2. bloody 表示"该死"，或者 bloody hell。例：Why don't we push the bloody thing off the branch with our nets and catch it on the ground? 为什么我们不用网把那该死的家伙从树杈上推下来，再在地上逮住它呢？

3. shoot dead 表示"枪杀 / 击毙某人"。例：They don't shoot people dead. I found that out. 我发现他们不对死人开枪。

4. make progress 表示"前进，进步，向上"。例：But assuming that the talks make progress, won't they do too little, too late? 就算会谈取得了进展，也未免太微不足道，且为时太晚了吧？

5. take action 表示"采取行动，行动起来"。例：We had to take action to protect the proprietary technology. 我们必须采取措施保护专利技术。

词汇加油站

fence [fens] n. 围墙
soldier ['souldʒər] n. 士兵
mate [meɪt] n. 伙伴
bastard ['bæstərd] n. 态度傲慢且令人讨厌的人

bloody ['blʌdi] adj. 血腥的
yard [jɑ:rd] n. 码
counter ['kaʊntər] adj. 相反的
nil [nɪl] n. 无

时间： 第 4 集 00:09:50—00:10:25
地点： 马霍狱室
人物： 迈克尔，马霍
事件： 迈克尔寻求与马霍合作，马霍入伙。

片段二

 精彩亮点

1
　　马霍因为停了药精神开始越来越恍惚，甚至出现了幻觉。他感觉到有一只手搭在自己的肩膀上，正当他惊恐地四处张望时，迈克尔出现了，他来寻求与马霍合作。

2
　　马霍毫不犹豫地答应了迈克尔的合作请求，迈克尔也明白这是他们现在唯一的选择，迈克尔需要马霍帮他找一支黑色钢笔，他要钢笔干什么呢？

3
　　迈克尔告诉马霍只是用钢笔修改一些文件，事实上，迈克尔计划导演一场停电假象。先前，他还向狱友麦迪借用了他的十字架，这一切都是为了断电所做的准备。

4
　　迈克尔早就注意到了马霍的精神状态，他提醒马霍控制好自己，不要误了大事。马霍当然明白这一点，如果能成功越狱，什么困难都能克服。

Mahone: I'm in. Okay. Just like that? ☺1

Michael: Right. I really don't have a choice, do I?

Mahone: What's the plan?

Michael: I'm working on① it. Meanwhile, I could use your help.

Mahone: What do you need?

Michael: A black felt-tipped pen②. ☺2

Mahone: A pen?

Michael: Yeah.

Mahone: Why?

Michael: Some documents that need altering③. I'll explain it to you later, but right now, I need that pen. Okay? ☺3

Mahone: Yeah.

Michael: And I'll tell you what else I need. I need you to get your act together④. I need you to bring yourself under control⑤, because you're attracting attention⑥, and that we don't need. ☺4

Mahone: I'm under control.

Michael: Of course you are.

译文

马　霍： 我加入，好吧，就这么简单？

迈克尔： 是的。我没有选择，不是吗？

马　霍： 你有什么计划？

迈克尔： 我正在想办法，与此同时，我需要你的帮助。

马　霍： 你需要什么？

迈克尔： 一支黑色毡头笔。

马　霍： 一支钢笔？

迈克尔： 没错。

马　霍： 为什么？

迈克尔： 有些文件需要做些改动。我过后会跟你解释，但现在，我需要那支笔。可以吗？

马　霍： 好的。

迈克尔： 我还要告诉你，我需要你行动也跟上。我需要你控制好自己，因为你正在引起别人的注意，那是我们不想看到的

马　霍： 我能控制好自己。

迈克尔： 你当然可以的。

知识点拨

1. work on sth. 表示"从事于某事，继续工作；努力影响（说服）；致力于"。例：I could do all my work on the computer. 我所有的工作都能在计算机上完成。

2. felt-tipped pen 表示"标签笔，毡头墨水笔"。例：First of all use a black marker or a felt-tipped pen to draw your characters. 首先使用一个黑色记号笔或毡头笔绘制字符。

3. need，want，require，worth 后面接 doing 也可以表示被动，相当于 to be done。例：Your hair needs cutting. 你的头发该剪了。

4. get together 表示"聚会，联欢；收集；整理"。例：This is the only forum where East and West can get together. 这是东西方可以聚首的唯一论坛。

5. under control 表示"被控制住，处于控制之下"。例：Firemen said they had the blaze under control. 消防队员说他们已经控制住了火势。

6. attract attention 表示"引起注意，醒目，打眼"。例：These tracks were calculated to be controversial and attract attention to the album. 这些曲子意在引起争议，吸引人们关注这张专辑。

meanwhile ['mi:nwaɪl] *adv.* 同时
document ['dɑ:kjumənt] *n.* 文件
explain [ɪk'spleɪn] *vt.* 解释
attract [ə'trækt] *vt.* 吸引

tip [tɪp] *v.* 尖端，尖儿
alter ['ɔ:ltər] *vt.* 改变
control [kən'troʊl] *n.* 控制

时间： 第 4 集 00:25:46—00:26:43
地点： 路赛罗狱室
人物： 路赛罗，贝里克
事件： 贝里克向路赛罗告密。

片段三

精彩亮点

1. 贝里克看到迈克尔在路赛罗的带领下前去修理电路，他察觉出这其中一定有阴谋，于是找到迈克尔让他带上自己，但迈克尔完全没有打算拉他入伙，给了他一把铁铲让他铲土。

2. 贝里克气愤不已，既然迈克尔无心捎上自己越狱，他也要让迈克尔计划落空，于是贝里克找到路赛罗，想向他告密。

3. 路赛罗一直看不惯贝里克，自然也不相信他说的话，而且铁铲是自己给迈克尔的，照理说迈克尔应该不会预料到这一步。

4. 贝里克道出自己原来的身份以及迈克尔的所作所为后，路赛罗的表情立马变了，内心也开始动摇。作为索纳监狱的老大，任何人胆敢欺骗他都不会有好下场。迈克尔又会面临何种命运呢？

Bellick: Listen, I heard him talking about escape yesterday — about breaking outta① here.☺₁

Lechero: If he's talking about escape, why are you here telling me and you're not going with him, eh②?

Bellick: I would if he'd let me, but he's already cut me out③.☺₂ He says he's square, but I know the son of a bitch is up to something④. So I figured, if I ain't running, I might unless tell you and make my time in here a little bit easier.

Lechero: Every man fantasizes about escaping from Sona.

Bellick: Yeah, but they aren't all in no-man's-land⑤ with shovels.

Lechero: I gave him the shovels. Get him out.☺₃

Bellick: I gave him shovels too, and guys to work with, just like you. I worked in the prison he broke out of.☺₄ He said he was doing me a favor — fixing damage from a fire, he started. And you know what I got? Hog-tied and left in a pipe under my own prison.

Lechero: There's nothing he can do. The soldiers are watching him.

Bellick: That's what I thought, until he tunneled out of my guard's room. He's buried something in a junction box⑥ out there and covered it with dirt — I saw him. Go see for yourself.

译文

贝里克： 听着，昨天我听他说关于越狱的事——关于逃离这里。

路赛罗： 如果他说要越狱，为什么你要来这儿告诉我而不是跟他一起逃走？

贝里克： 如果他肯让我跟他一起越狱，我当然愿意，但是他已经抛弃我了。他不承认有这事，但是我知道那个混蛋在计划着什么。因此，我想如果我不能逃跑，我或许应该告诉你这个消息，这样你可以让我在这里的日子好过点儿。

路赛罗： 每个人都幻想逃出索纳监狱。

贝里克： 是的，但是不是谁都可以在无人区用铁铲铲地。

路赛罗： 铁铲是我给他的，让他出去。

贝里克： 我也像你一样，也给过他铁铲，还有其他跟他合作的人，我曾在他越狱的监狱工作。他说他在给我帮忙——修理火灾带来的损害，但正是他点的火。你知道我得到什么了吗？四肢并捆，然后被他们扔在了我自己监狱的管子里。

路赛罗： 他做不了什么的，有士兵在监督他。

贝里克： 我也曾那么想，直到他挖地道一直挖到我的保卫室。他在外面的接线盒里埋了些东西，然后用土盖住了——我看见他这么做的。你可以自己去看。

知识点拨

1. outta 是 out of 的简写体。例：All right, that's it! We're outta here. 好了，我们得出去了。

2. eh 表示"啊（请求重复；表惊奇）"。例："So you're going to start next week, eh?""那么你们下星期要出发了，是吗？"

3. cut sb. out 表示"撇开某人，出卖某人"。例：You want to take it all for yourself and cut me out. 你想自己取得一切，将我撇开。

4. be up to something 表示"策划某事"。例：I heard you two whispering so I know you must be up to something. 我听见你们俩嘀嘀咕咕的就知道你们没做什么好事。

5. no-man's-land 表示"无主土地；所有权争议未决的土地；荒地"。

6. junction box 表示"接线盒，分线箱"。例：Where there is distortion, crack or damage on the junction box, it must be stopped using. 发现接线盒外壳有变形、裂痕和损坏，应停止使用。

 词汇加油站

square [skwer] *adj.* 彼此无欠账的；两清的

shovel ['ʃʌvl] *n.* 铁锹

hog [hɔ:g] *n.* 像猪一般的人

bury ['beri] *vt.* 埋藏

fantasize ['fæntəsaɪz] *vt.* 幻想

fix [fɪks] *vt.* 修理

tunnel ['tʌnl] *vt.* 挖掘隧道

junction ['dʒʌŋkʃn] *n.* （电缆等的）接合点

时间： 第 5 集 00:05:00—00:05:54

地点： 索纳监狱

人物： 迈克尔，林肯

事件： 迈克尔向林肯诉说越狱计划。

片段四

 精彩亮点

1

林肯来探视迈克尔，他一直没敢告诉迈克尔莎拉已被杀的消息，他担心如果迈克尔深陷失去莎拉的悲痛中就无心越狱，这样一来，他的儿子，甚至他们兄弟俩都会没命。

2

迈克尔善于察言观色，最近他发现林肯探望他时有意回避他，他察觉出林肯好像瞒着他什么。他很怕莎拉会出事，追问林肯有没有莎拉近期的照片。

3

林肯假装淡定自若，告诉迈克尔自己现在没办法和他们谈条件，当下的主要任务就是帮助惠斯勒越狱，其他一切事宜等越狱成功了再说。

4

迈克尔没办法，只得答应了林肯，通过几天的观察，他想出了越狱计划。但由于整个晚上索纳监狱都有吉普车巡逻，不便于他们行动，所以只能选择在白天越狱。

Lincoln: **She's got the book, man, the bird guide. She worked it out**[①]. ☺₁

Michael: So we have no leverage.

Lincoln: No.

Michael: Tell me when you were handing over[②] the book, did you ask for a recent photo of L.J. and Sara?

Lincoln: Yeah.

Michael: And where is it? ☺₂

Lincoln: She showed me the pictures, but she wouldn't let me keep them. Man, I'm not in a position[③] to bargain with[④] these people. I mean, they're pissed. You break out tomorrow. Let's just focus on that. **Let's keep on track**[⑤]. ☺₃

Michael: All right. While I'm working from the inside, I need you to take care of what happens once we're outside. We're going to need a getaway vehicle, something inconspicuous. Whatever you find, it has to be parked a half mile from here by 3:00 p.m. tomorrow.

Lincoln: You mean a.m.

Michael: No, I mean p.m. We don't have a choice, Linc. I ran some tests[⑥] last night. Military jeeps patrol the perimeter at night. There's no way of telling where they're going to be in the dark. **They were out there all night.** ☺₄

译文

林　肯： 兄弟，她拿走了那本书，鸟类指南。她发现了。

迈克尔： 也就是说我们手上没有筹码了。

林　肯： 没了。

迈克尔： 告诉我当你递上那本书的时候，你有向他们要 L.J. 和莎拉的最新照片吗？

林　肯： 是的。

迈克尔： 那照片呢？

林　肯： 她给我看了照片，但是不肯给我，兄弟，我没办法和他们谈条件，我的意思是他们已经被激怒了。你明天就得越狱出来，我们就先集中全力越狱吧，回到正题上。

迈克尔： 那好吧。当我在狱内开工时，我需要你准备一下我们逃出来后的事。我们需要辆专供逃亡的车，不惹眼的那种。不管你找到什么车，明天下午 3 点必须把车停在离这 1 英里半的地方。

林　肯： 你是说凌晨 3 点？

迈克尔： 不，我是说下午。林肯，我们别无选择。我昨晚做了些测试，军方吉普车晚上在周边巡逻，晚上根本无法分辨他们的方位，整晚他们都在外面巡逻。

知识点拨

1. work out 表示"解决；做出；锻炼；了解某人的本质"。例：Negotiators are due to meet later today to work out a compromise. 谈判人员定于今天晚些时候进行会谈，商定一个折中方案。

2. hand over 表示"交出，交付，交给，让与"。例：He also handed over a letter of apology from the Prime Minister. 他还递交了一封首相写的道歉信。

3. be in a position to do sth. 表示"有资格做某事"。例：In either case, the persons conducting the audit should be in a position to do so impartially and objectively. 无论哪种情况，从事审核的人员都应做到公正，客观。

4. bargain with sb. 表示"与某人讨价还价"。例：They prefer to bargain with individual clients, for cash. 在现款方面，他们更愿意同散户打交道。

5. keep sth. on track 表示"正确的方向 / 想法 / 做法"。例：A flexible routine can keep everyone on track and give children structure and a sense of security. 一个有弹性的规定可以使人们有条不紊，同时能够合理地规范孩子们，给他们一种安全感。

6. run tests 表示"运行测试，游程检验"。例：Use this window to manage and run tests and test lists. 使用此窗口可以管理和运行测试及测试列表。

词汇加油站

leverage ['levərɪdʒ] *n.* 优势

bargain ['bɑːrgən] *vt.* 达成协议

inconspicuous [ˌɪnkən'spɪkjuəs] *adj.* 不引人注目的

patrol [pə'troʊl] *vt.* 巡逻

recent ['riːsnt] *adj.* 最近的

getaway ['getəweɪ] *n.* （尤指犯罪后的）逃跑

jeep [dʒiːp] *n.* 吉普车

perimeter [pə'rɪmɪtər] *n.* 边界

Scene 4 惠斯勒的身份

时间： 第 5 集 00:07:59—00:09:10
地点： 索纳监狱
人物： 迈克尔，惠斯勒
事件： 迈克尔告诉惠斯勒第二天的越狱计划。

精彩亮点

1 迈克尔来到惠斯勒的牢房，此前，他小心翼翼地环视四周，就是担心他们的谈话会被人监听。他来找惠斯勒就是为了告诉他第二天越狱的方案。

2 看到迈克尔前来告诉自己越狱的计划惠斯勒兴奋不已，认真聆听着迈克尔说的每一句话。但当他听说他们要在白天越狱时，惠斯勒表示难以置信。

3 迈克尔所说的那个家伙是站在塔楼上的一个警卫，经过观察，每当太阳照到他时，他就会转身，而下午两点正是太阳最刺眼的时候，也是他们越狱的最好时机。

4 现在的问题是塔楼上有两个警卫，其中一个警卫的习惯已经被迈克尔参透了，但另一个警卫还有待观察，留给迈克尔他们的时间不多了，他们能否成功越狱呢？

Michael: **We leave tomorrow.**☺₁ This… This is how we're getting out of Sona. Getting out of the cell block① shouldn't be a problem. The grate and bars are weak, but we're going to need some kind of rope, some kind of ladder, to let us down on the other side②. That's why I figured out the safest line from here to the hole in the fence. We do it in the day③, we'll only be visible to the two guard towers. The perimeter guards are less predictable, but they're only on at night.

Whistler: **Scurrying across**④ **the field in the middle of the day**⑤**?**☺₂

Michael: It's the only way to avoid the jeep patrol. Now, in the yard tomorrow, there's a soccer game at 2:00. That should prove some distraction inside. And yesterday when we were digging, I saw the glare from the sun hit this guy in the late afternoon. **Looked like he turned away**⑥**, like maybe his vision was blocked.**☺₃

Whistler: It's not much of a break.

Michael: No, but it is one way to do what we need to do. **As far as this other guard, his weakness has yet to be de termined.**☺₄ If we're going to get around these guys, we've got to get to know them.

190

译文

迈克尔：我们明天行动。这是……这是我们逃离索纳监狱的方案。逃出监狱障碍栏应该不成问题，围壁栅栏很脆弱，但是我们需要些绳索，还有梯子，让我们可以从另外一侧下去。因此，我标出最安全的线路是从这里到栅栏的那个洞。我们白天行动，只有塔楼上的两个警卫能看到我们。周边警卫情况难以预测，但是他们只在晚上出没。

惠斯勒：大中午的穿越监狱逃跑？

迈克尔：这是避开巡逻吉普车的唯一方法。听着，明天下午两点，监狱大院里会有场球赛，应该会吸引狱内很多人的注意力。昨天我们挖洞的时候，我看到太阳光在下午晚些时候照到这个家伙。看上去他会转身，好像他的视线会受阻。

惠斯勒：这样还不足以越狱。

迈克尔：不，但这是我们唯一需要做的。还有个警卫，我还没找出他的弱点。如果我们要和这帮警卫周旋就必须得了解他们。

知识点拨

1. cell block 字面意思是"单元块（组）"，表示"牢房"。例：A cell block reserved for convicts awaiting execution. 特别为等待处决的死刑犯设置的牢房。

2. on the other side 表示"另一边；对侧；在另一边"。例：She turned over on her stomach on the other side of the bed. 她翻了个身趴在了床的另一边。

3. in the day 表示"在白天"。例：What with one thing and another, it was fairly late in the day when we returned to Shrewsbury. 忙完这个又忙那个，等到我们回到什鲁斯伯里的时候，天色已经很晚了。

4. scurry across 表示"匆匆走过/穿过"等。例：As we walked along, we saw a rabbit pop up from its burrow and scurry across the field. 我们正在向前走着，看到一只兔子突然从洞里跳出来，穿过田野。

5. in the middle of the day 表示"在一天的中间，在中午"。例：But I have my untimely leave in the middle of the day, in the thick of work. 但我已经在正午，在繁重的工作中不合时宜地离开。

6. turn away 表示"转过脸去，拒绝（某人）进入；辞退"。例：Kennedy exhorted his listeners to turn away from violence. 肯尼迪劝诫听众远离暴力。

 **词汇加油站**

block [blɑːk] *n.* 大楼
rope [roʊp] *n.* 绳索
perimeter [pəˈrɪmɪtər] *n.* 边界
patrol [pəˈtroʊl] *n.* 巡逻

grate [greɪt] *n.* 炉格
ladder [ˈlædər] *n.* 梯子
predictable [prɪˈdɪktəbl] *adj.* 可预料的
distraction [dɪˈstrækʃn] *n.* 注意力分散

时间： 第 5 集 00:37:51—00:38:35

地点： 索纳监狱

人物： 惠斯勒，迈克尔

事件： 迈克尔越狱计划受阻，惠斯勒催促迈克尔想办法。

精彩亮点

迈克尔发现狱警之一是个体育迷，在值班的时候有时还看电视，他想利用微波炉的 EMP 脉冲来干扰狱警的视线，但是却弄巧成拙被发现。狱警蜂拥而入发现迈克尔等人的望远镜，惠斯勒巧妙地用鸟类指南解释自己利用望远镜来观察鸟，帮助迈克尔逃过了一劫，但是他们的计划却泡汤了。

1

眼看时间越来越少，明天就要越狱了，迈克尔又何尝不想早点儿出去？但现在自己先前的计划全部被打乱，迈克尔心中乱作一团。

2

惠斯勒十分焦急，他一直强调自己没有时间了。到底是为什么呢？这也其实是迈克尔一直疑惑的原因：为什么公司的人必须让他明天越狱？

3

惠斯勒前两天收到了一张公司的人递来的纸条，上面写着：你没有时间了。就在惠斯勒被捕前，公司的人偷走了他的通讯录，找到了所有与他有关系的人，这些人的生命就掌握在公司手中。因此，惠斯勒迫不及待要越狱。

4

Whistler: So what do we do now? ☺1

Michael: I don't know. ☺2

Whistler: Well, I'm afraid that's not good enough ① .

Michael: Please just give me a moment ② to think.

Whistler: Wasting time is not an option for me, Michael. I need to be out of here by tomorrow ③ . ☺3

Michael: I know, just in time ④ for be out your next fishing trip, tomorrow. Or is it a bird-watching trip? I forget.

Whistler: That's my trip log, I've told you. I need to retrace my steps ⑤ . I'm doing everything they tell me, the same thing you are.

Michael: Just, just leave me alone, please.

Whistler: You know, before I was arrested, a man came to my flat and took my addresses. ☺4 They know the name of everyone I care about ⑥ and how to find them.

Michael: Well, they already found everyone I care out. Okay?

Whistler: If you can't get me out of here, tell me now because time is running out.

译文

惠斯勒：那我们现在该怎么办？

迈克尔：我也不知道。

惠斯勒：恐怕这个回答可不怎么样。

迈克尔：求你了，给我时间想一想。

惠斯勒：迈克尔，我不能在这里浪费时间了，我明天必须得出去。

迈克尔：我知道，你就是为了赶紧出去钓鱼，或是赏鸟，我记不清了。

惠斯勒：那是我的航海日志，我跟你说过，我必须按图索骥。我现在要听他们吩咐，你也一样。

迈克尔：你让我一个人待会儿吧，求你了。

惠斯勒：你知道吗？我被抓起来之前，有一个人闯进我的公寓，拿走了我的通讯录。他们知道我所关心的所有人的名字以及如何找到他们。

迈克尔：事实上他们已经找到了我所在意的每个人，好吗？

惠斯勒：如果你不能把我弄出去，现在就告诉我，因为我没有时间了。

知识点拨

1. good enough 表示"足够好，够好了，够好"。例：It's not good enough just to blame the unruly children. 对难管教的孩子只是责备是不够的。

2. 我们一起来看几个与 moment 相关的词组。例：in a moment 表示"马上"，跟 in a minute 一个意思；for a moment 表示"（做什么事）一会"；at the moment 表示"当时"，通常是指过去。

3. by tomorrow 表示"到明天（晚上十二点）之前"。例：Please return the book to me by tomorrow. 到明天之前，请把那本书还给我。

4. in time 表示"及时；迟早；最后；经过一段时间之后"。例：Leonard made a rapid calculation: he'd never make it in time. 莱纳德快速盘算了一下：他肯定赶不上了。

5. retrace one's steps 表示"折回原来走过的路"。例：We were lost and decided to retrace our steps. 我们迷路了，决定沿原路返回。

6. care about sb./sth. 表示"关心/在乎/关怀/担忧某人（某事）"。例：He really cares about his parents. 他非常关心他的父母。

 词汇加油站

moment ['moʊmənt] *n.* 片刻
fishing ['fɪʃɪŋ] *n.* 钓鱼
retrace [rɪ'treɪs] *vt.* 回忆
flat [flæt] *n.* 公寓

option ['ɑːpʃn] *n.* 选项
log [lɔːg] *n.* 日志
arrest [ə'rest] *vt.* 逮捕
address ['ædres] *n.* 地址

193

时间： 第 6 集 00:02:13—00:03:00

地点： 索纳监狱

片段三

人物： 迈克尔，蒂格，惠斯勒

事件： 迈克尔欲调查惠斯勒，惠斯勒追问迈克尔越狱进展。

 精彩亮点

1

新来的囚犯蒂格见到惠斯勒时叫他麦克法登，但惠斯勒矢口否认，说自己从来没有见过他，他肯定认错人了。这引起了迈克尔的怀疑，他趁没人注意，找来蒂格，向他打听惠斯勒的情况，以便弄清楚为什么公司的人这么想让他出来。

2

虽然蒂格一副吊儿郎当的样子，但他十分确定自己曾见过惠斯勒，他曾是大使酒店的门卫，知道惠斯勒在那里工作过几个月。迈克尔显然相信他说的话，但他疑惑的是：惠斯勒去尼斯干什么呢？这也为后面的故事情节做了铺垫。

3

就在迈克尔想进一步了解惠斯勒时，惠斯勒出现在他的身后，他想询问迈克尔越狱的事情准备得怎么样了。

4

迈克尔让苏克雷冒着生命危险去喷栅栏，但仅喷一次确实不能有十足的把握，但时间紧迫，迈克尔认为只能先这样了。但身后的马霍提出或许可以让苏克雷再进来一次，苏克雷现在的身份是掘墓人，让他再进来一次就意味着要有一个人牺牲。

Michael: The Australian. You said you knew him from Nice. Is that true? ☺1

Tyge: You calling me a liar now?

Michael: He says you're full of① it. He said he was never an ambassador.

Tyge: No, not an ambassador, the Ambassador. I was concierge at the Ambassador Hotel. I could've sworn he worked there for a few months. ☺2 Who the hell knows, huh? I was high half the time②. Kind of③ why I got fired. Kind of why I'm in here.

Michael: What was he up to④ in Nice?

Tyge: What? You writing a book?

Whistler: We're leaving at 3:13 — that gives us three hours 41 minutes. ☺3 And we still don't have a way into no-man's-land⑤.

Michael: I'll take care of that. I just need to check it out⑥ first.

Whistler: And the fence? Your grave digger friends only sprayed the thing once, and I'd just as soon not get electrocuted today.

Michael: Would I feel better if Sucre had sprayed the fence again? Yes. Is that an option? No. ☺4

译文

迈克尔： 那个澳大利亚人，你说你在尼斯见过他。是真的吗？

蒂 格： 你是在说我是骗子吗？

迈克尔： 他说你满嘴谎话，他说他从没当过大使。

蒂 格： 不，不是一个大使，那地方叫大使。我曾在国宾大饭店的服务台工作。我可以发誓他在那里工作过几个月，谁知道呢？一半的时间我都在嗑药。所以我才被炒了，这也是我会在这里的原因。

迈克尔： 他在尼斯做什么？

蒂 格： 什么？你是要出书吗？

惠斯勒： 我们要在 3:13 离开，他们留给我们 3 个小时零 41 分钟，我们还没法去无人监管的地带。

迈克尔： 我会处理的，我只是想要先搞清楚。

惠斯勒： 那栅栏呢？你的掘墓朋友只往那喷了一次，但愿我今天不会被处死。

迈克尔： 你说如果苏克雷再喷一次栅栏的话我会不会觉得好点儿？是的。但这种方法可行吗？不可行。

 知识点拨

1. be full of=be filled with 表示"充满……"。
例：Your life will be full of love and joy if you are joyful and happy. 倘若你是喜悦和快乐的，那么你的生活也会充满喜悦和快乐。

2. half the time 表示"一半时间，过长的时间，相当长的时间"。例：Half the time, I don't have the slightest idea what he's talking about. 我经常一点儿都听不懂他在说什么。

3. kind of 表示"稍微，有点儿，有几分"。例：This kind of problem frequently crops up. 这类问题是经常发生的。

4. be up to 表示"胜任，从事于；取决于"。例：The exercises in this chapter can guide you, but it will be up to you to do the actual work. 这一章的练习能给你指导，但实际的工作还得靠你自己完成。

5. no-man's-land 表示"无主土地；所有权争议未决的土地；荒地"。

6. check out 表示"检查；合格；看看"。例：Maybe we ought to go down to the library and check it out. 或许我们应该去趟图书馆，查个明白。

 词汇加油站

Australian [ɔːˈstreɪliən] *n.* 澳大利亚人

ambassador [æmˈbæsədər] *n.* 大使

sworn [swɔːrn] *v.* 郑重承诺

digger [ˈdɪɡər] *n.* 挖掘者

liar [ˈlaɪər] *n.* 说谎者

concierge [kɔːnˈsjerʒ] *n.* 看门人

fire [ˈfaɪər] *vt.* 解雇

spray [spreɪ] *vt.* 喷

时间： 第 6 集 00:21:41 — 00:22:38
地点： 走廊
人物： 林肯，苏珊
事件： 苏珊、林肯会面再次确认越狱事宜。

片段四

精彩亮点

1
　　林肯与迈克尔见过面后，迈克尔说如果他看不到莎拉的照片就不会实施越狱计划，这可急坏了林肯。林肯找到苏珊，先是找她要了麻醉剂，这是为了麻醉塔楼守卫的。

2
　　林肯没有告诉苏珊惠斯勒的女友现在跟他一起行动，如果跟苏珊说，不仅惠斯勒的女友会深陷危险，而且自己也会因未向她如实汇报而遭到非难。

3
　　聪明的苏珊一下子便明白了为什么林肯找她索要莎拉的照片，因为林肯并没有告诉迈克尔莎拉已死的消息。苏珊面露满意的微笑，这正合她意，因为迈克尔一直不信任她，这样一来就能稳住迈克尔，让他帮助实施越狱计划。

4
　　迈克尔和林肯约定的是下午三点多越狱，他们并没有把这一计划告诉苏珊，而是跟她称晚上九点，因为，他们不想让公司完全控制他们的一举一动。但林肯若有所思的样子引起了苏珊怀疑。

Susan: Zylafol. It's used to anesthetize dogs. **Two drops, and the guard should be out within an hour.** ☺₁ I was expecting Whistler's girlfriend to join you. Where is she? Around the corner① in the car?

Lincoln: **She came to me**②. ☺₂

Susan: I don't mind③ that she's helping you. I mind that you kept it from me④.

Lincoln: What difference does it make⑤? I mean, we're done by tomorrow, right?

Susan: No more surprises, Lincoln. What? Say it.

Lincoln: Can you get any more pictures of Sara?

Susan: **Alive? No. You didn't tell him. You didn't tell Michael that Sara's dead.** ☺₃

Lincoln: Can we get pictures or not?

Susan: I'm sure we can cobble something together, but smart move⑥ not telling your brother. He seems a little sensitive to me. This is the exchange point, L.J. and I will be waiting. You, Michael and Whistler will meet us there. **Everything goes as planned, you'll have your son back by 9:00. Lincoln?** ☺₄

Lincoln: 9 o'clock.

196

译文

苏珊：Zylafol，用来麻醉狗的。只要两滴就能让守卫一小时内不省人事。我还以为惠斯勒的女友会跟你一起干。她现在在哪？拐角的车里？

林肯：她来找过我。

苏珊：我不介意她帮你，我介意的是你对我隐瞒。

林肯：这有什么不同吗？我的意思是，我们明天就各奔东西了，不是吗？

苏珊：别再让我吃惊了，林肯。什么？说出来。

林肯：你能给我来几张莎拉的照片吗？

苏珊：活着的？不行。你没告诉他，你没告诉迈克尔她死了。

林肯：到底能不能弄到照片？

苏珊：我肯定我们能拼一张出来，但没告诉你弟弟算你聪明，他看起来对我还挺敏感的。这是交换点，L.J. 和我会在这里等。你，迈克尔和惠斯勒去那儿跟我们会面。一切按计划进行，不到9 点你们父子就能团聚。林肯？

林肯：知道了，九点。

知识点拨

1. around the corner 表示"在拐角处"，也可用作形容词词组，表示"迫在眉睫的"。例：In running around the corner, John collided with another boy. 约翰跑到拐角处时和另一个男孩相撞。

2. come to sb. 表示"突然进入脑海，突然出现在某人面前"。例：They come to me to whine about their troubles. 他们到我这儿来不停地唠叨他们的烦恼。

3. I don't mind 表示"不介意，没关系"，语气较客气。与其意思相近的一个词组 I don't care 则表示"我不在乎，与我无关"，语气较为冷淡。

4. keep sth. from sb. 表示"向某人隐瞒某事"。例：He had written something and hidden it away to keep it from the jailer. 他写了些什么，瞒着狱卒把它藏了起来。

5. make a difference 表示"有影响，起（重要）作用"。例：We should make a difference between new word and coinages. 对新词和新造词要区别对待。

6. smart move 表示"明智之举"。例：Not a smart move to piss off Britney's fans, even if it wasn't your intent! 撵走布兰妮的歌迷不是明智之举，即便你本不想这样。

 词汇加油站

anesthetize [ə'niːsθətaɪz] *vt.* 使麻醉

guard [gɑːrd] *n.* 警卫

surprise [sər'praɪz] *n.* 惊喜

sensitive ['sensətɪv] *adj.* 敏感的

drop [drɑːp] *n.* 滴

corner ['kɔːrnər] *n.* 角落

cobble ['kɑːbl] *vt.* 胡乱拼凑

exchange [ɪks'tʃeɪndʒ] *n.* 交换

Scene 5 越狱初试失利

时间： 第 6 集 00:34:24—00:35:10

地点： 索纳监狱

片段一

人物： 迈克尔，帝博格

事件： 惠斯勒被扣留，帝博格为迈克尔出主意。

精彩亮点

眼看就要到计划的越狱时间了，但迈克尔和惠斯勒俩人却频频受阻。先前认出惠斯勒的新人蒂格被发现惨死在楼梯口。因为有人发现惠斯勒和蒂格曾在楼梯口起过争执，惠斯勒便成了最大嫌疑人，现在被路赛罗扣留。 **1**

帝博格的一番话吸引了迈克尔的兴趣。阴险狡诈的帝博格到底有什么计谋呢？他不断地给迈克尔暗示，聪明的迈克尔又怎会不知道他的用意？ **2**

原来，帝博格想让迈克尔找一只替罪羊，这个人不是别人，正是他怀恨在心的萨米。萨米是路赛罗得力的手下，但帝博格的出现威胁到萨米的地位，于是萨米处处刁难帝博格。而帝博格想要利用蒂格的死铲除自己的心头之患。 **3**

迈克尔内心十分矛盾，他不想冤枉一个好人，但眼看距离越狱时间越来越近，他不得不做出一个抉择。他会怎么做呢？ **4**

T-Bag: My condolences. You finally make a friend, and now he's about to① die.☺₁ Damn shame. You can stop it, you know. If you hadn't noticed, my position enables me to hear② things.

Michael: I'm listening.

T-Bag: The only proof Lechero's got is that your man went down that staircase, right? What if③ you had more compelling evidence?☺₂

Michael: Well, I don't.

T-Bag: But if you did…

Michael: You're suggesting I make something up④?

T-Bag: If it makes your conscience feel better, then blame it on somebody⑤ who deserves it. Someone who's killed before and gone unpunished.

Michael: Yeah-like you maybe.

T-Bag: Sammy.☺₃

Michael: You want me to tell Lechero that his right hand⑥ man should die?

T-Bag: You don't tell Lechero squat. Lechero knows this is Sammy's ring. If you drop it in the blood by the staircase, then yell up to Lechero what you've found…the whole entire prison will hear clear-cut⑦ evidence of Sammy's guilt. Lechero will have no choice but to comply.☺₄

198

译文

帝博格：我深表哀悼。你好不容易交了个朋友，现在他却要死了，真遗憾。你能阻止这种事，你知道的。也许你还没留意，我的地位能让我耳听八方。

迈克尔：我在听。

帝博格：路赛罗唯一的证据就是你朋友下楼梯了，对吗？要是你有更令人信服的证据呢？

迈克尔：我并没有。

帝博格：但如果你有 ...

迈克尔：你是想让我编造证据？

帝博格：如果这样能让你良心好受些，那么就去责怪活该的人吧，某个曾经杀过人却没有受到惩罚的人。

迈克尔：是啊，好比你。

帝博格：萨米。

迈克尔：你想让我告诉路赛罗他的得力助手该死？

帝博格：你什么都不要告诉路赛罗，路赛罗知道这是萨米的戒指，如果你把它扔到楼梯的血泊里，然后向路赛罗嚷嚷自己发现了什么……整个监狱都会听到萨米犯罪的确凿证据，路赛罗没有办法只能妥协。

 知识点拨

1. be about to 表示"即将，就要，将要，正打算"。例：A new era seemed to be about to dawn for the coach and his young team. 对于那名教练和他的年轻球队来说，一个崭新的时代似乎即将到来。

2. enable sb. to do sth. 表示"让某人做某事"。例：This piece of paper won't enable me to do anything worthwhile. 凭这一张纸，办不了什么事。

3. what if 表示"要是……又怎样"。例：What if relations between you and your neighbour have reached deadlock, and their behaviour is still unacceptable? 如果你和你的邻居已闹僵了，而他们的行为还是令人难以接受，那怎么办？

4. make something up 表示"编造某事，组成/合成/补充某物"。例：Why would you make something like that up? 你为什么编那种故事呢？

5. blame sth. on sb. 表示"把责任推给某人"。例：We can't put all the blame on him alone. 不能把一切错误都归咎于他。

6. right hand 直译为"右手"，还可以表示"得力助手"。例：I think he ought to be at the right hand of the president. 我想他应该成为总统的得力助手。

7. clear-cut 表示"清晰的；轮廓鲜明的"。例：On matters of principle we should be clear-cut in attitude, and by no means be equivocal. 在原则问题上，我们必须态度鲜明，决不能模棱两可。

 词汇加油站

condolence [kən'doʊləns] *n.* 同情
enable [ɪ'neɪbl] *vt.* 使能够
staircase ['sterkeɪs] *n.* 楼梯
conscience ['kɑːnʃəns] *n.* 良心

shame [ʃeɪm] *n.* 遗憾
proof [pruːf] *n.* 证明
compelling [kəm'pelɪŋ] *adj.* 不可抗拒的
deserve [dɪ'zɜːrv] *vt.* 应受

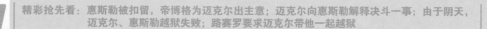

片段二

时间： 第 7 集 00:05:06—00:05:44
地点： 索纳监狱
人物： 迈克尔，惠斯勒
事件： 迈克尔向惠斯勒解释决斗一事。

 精彩亮点

1 　迈克尔事先并没有与惠斯勒商量决斗一事，当众向他发出决斗邀请。实际上，迈克尔心中另有谋划。蒂格的死扰乱了原来的越狱计划，本来应在下午举行的踢球比赛也取消了，所以，迈克尔必须再找一个契机引开公众的注意。

2 　惠斯勒气愤地来找迈克尔，希望让他取消决斗，迈克尔将他的计划告诉惠斯勒时，惠斯勒深感震惊，但更多的还是感谢与愧疚。

3 　在此之前，林肯与迈克尔见面时，虽然林肯手中拿着一张合成的莎拉的照片，但他没有给迈克尔看，一方面他知道弟弟一定一眼就能识别出这是假的，另一方面，他不忍心再隐瞒下去了。当他告诉迈克尔莎拉的死讯后，迈克尔如发疯般地找到惠斯勒，向他提出决斗，从而让惠斯勒误会他真的想和自己决斗。

4 　迈克尔虽然为莎拉的死深感悲痛，但他仍是一个分得清事情轻重的人，他计划在越狱后就去查明杀死莎拉的凶手，并以牙还牙。

Whistler: Look, I don't know what you're thinking, but killing me is not going to solve your problem.☺₁

Michael: Relax. I'm not going to kill you.

Whistler: Then what the hell was all that about?!☺₂

Michael: You want to make it ① out of here without being seen, you need a diversion. Now we have one.

Whistler: You're off your head ②. Do you know that? They're waiting…

Michael: We don't have time for this. It's almost 3:00, and that means the tower guard should be drugged by now. At 3:13, the sun's going to hit the other guard tower. We'll have the cover we need. It's now or never.

Whistler: Listen, Michael, I, uh…I meant what I said about Sara.☺₃

Michael: If I were you I wouldn't ③ mention that name again. We're getting out of here now, and then I'm trading you for ④ my nephew. And then I'm going to find out who's responsible for ⑤ taking her life ⑥ …and I'm taking theirs.☺₄

200

译文

惠斯勒：听着，我不知道你在想什么，但是，杀了我并不能解决你的问题。

迈克尔：放轻松，我不会杀了你的。

惠斯勒：那这一切到底都是为了什么？

迈克尔：你要想躲开众人耳目逃跑就需要转移视线。现在我们有办法了。

惠斯勒：你疯了，你知道吗？他们正在外面等着……

迈克尔：我们没时间了，已经快 3 点了，这就表明塔楼上的警卫们应该都被下了药。在 3:13，太阳会照射到另一个警卫塔，我们就有了所需要的掩护，现在不逃，以后就没机会了。

惠斯勒：听着，迈克尔，我……嗯……我是指莎拉的事。

迈克尔：如果我是你，就不会再提那个名字。我们现在要努力离开这里，然后，我会用你来交换我的侄子。然后，我会去查明是谁该对她的死负责，然后杀了他们。

知识点拨

1. make it 表示"及时到达，成功做某事"。例：So you did make it to America, after all. 那么，你终究还是成功地来到了美国。

2. be off one's head 表示"某人发疯了"。例：You must be off your head going out in weather like this! 你一定疯了，这种天气还出去！

3. 这是表示与现在事实相反或不可能发生的虚拟条件句，句型为：If+ 主语 + 一般过去时，主语 + would (should, might, could)+do。例：If I were you, I would accept his invitation. 我要是你就接受他的邀请。

4. trade...for... 表示"用……交换……"。例：He traded his watch for Ade's basketball. 他用手表来换艾德的篮球。

5. be responsible for 表示"为……负责；形成……的原因"。例：I sometimes find it a strain to be responsible for the mortgage. 我有时觉得背负这笔抵押贷款很有压力。

6. take one's life 表示"取某人的命，杀掉某人"。例：And in the end this system may take his life on some distant battlefield. 这一制度最终可能使他丧生于遥远的战场。

词汇加油站

solve [sɑːlv] vt. 解决

guard [gɑːrd] n. 看守

hit [hɪt] vt. 碰撞

mention ['menʃn] vt. 提到

diversion [daɪ'vɜːrʒn] n. 分散注意力

drug [drʌg] vt. 使服麻醉药

cover ['kʌvər] n. 掩护

nephew ['nefjuː] n. 侄子

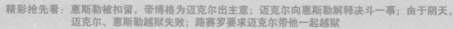

时间： 第 7 集 00:12:08—00:16:34

地点： 索纳监狱

片段三

人物： 迈克尔，惠斯勒，路赛罗

事件： 由于阴天，迈克尔、惠斯勒越狱失败。

 精彩亮点

1

终于到了惊心动魄的越狱时刻了，迈克尔向惠斯勒解释他的越狱计划后，两个人来到萨米的房间准备越狱。但时间紧迫，他们能否越狱成功呢？

2

惠斯勒一直担心塔楼上的守卫会发现他们的行踪。一旦行迹暴露，他们将功亏一篑。但事已至此，迈克尔也只能做到这里了，其他的就只能听天由命了。

3

迈克尔清楚，自己的存在就是为了帮助惠斯勒越狱，如果惠斯勒在越狱过程中中枪身亡，那么，就算他越狱成功，侄子的命，甚至包括林肯和自己的命都将不保。既然如此，他决定打头阵，如果塔楼守卫发现，开枪打死的也是他，而不是惠斯勒。

4

然而，天公不作美，迈克尔怎么也没算到今天阴天，所以塔楼守卫不会像平常那样因阳光刺眼而放松戒备，但这是今天越狱的唯一机会，否则等待他们的只有俩人的决斗。

Michael: Now, remember, we'll only have four minutes of cover, so once you hit the ground you run straight to the fence.☺₁ Don't look up①, don't look back②, don't say a word.

Whistler: What if they see us?☺₂

Michael: If someone yells stop, you stop.

Whistler: That's it?

Michael: That's it.

Lechero: It's time③. Where's Sammy?

Whistler: So, who goes first?

Michael: Right now my life isn't worth a damn④ without yours. If this doesn't go as planned, the first guy through that window's gonna get shot. That guy can't be you.☺₃ I'll go.

Whistler: I got it⑤.

Michael: Come on, come on, come on. This is it⑥. Five, four, three, two, one.

Whistler: The glare. Where's the glare?

Michael: I don't know.

Whistler: This is it. Someone's coming. Good luck.

Michael: You, too. We're losing the light.☺₄ Go back, go back. Go back. Come on! Come on !That was our only chance.

译文

迈克尔：现在，记住我们只有 4 分钟做掩护，所以你一旦到地面就径直跑向围栏。不要向上看，也不要向后看，一句话也不要说。

惠斯勒：他们要是看到我们了呢？

迈克尔：如果有人喊停下，你就停下。

惠斯勒：就这样？

迈克尔：就这样。

路赛罗：时间到了，萨米呢？

惠斯勒：谁先？

迈克尔：现在，没有你我的生命毫无意义。如果事情没能像预计的那样发展，那么第一个人穿过窗子的时候就会被击中，但那个人不能是你。我去。

惠斯勒：我明白了。

迈克尔：快点儿，快点儿，快点儿。就是现在。五，四，三，二，一。

惠斯勒：耀眼的光，耀眼的光在哪？

迈克尔：我不知道。

惠斯勒：就是这样，有人来了。祝你好运。

迈克尔：你也是。没有光了，回去，回去，回去。快点儿！快点儿！这是我们唯一的机会！

知识点拨

1. look up 可以表示"查找；向上看；改善；拜访（某人）"。片中表示"向上看"。例：I look up in the sky, it's my clouds. 我抬头看天，那依旧是我的云。

2. look back 表示"回顾；倒退；追忆；回头看"。例：He turned to look back, but by then she was out of sight. 他转头看去，但那时她已经不见了。

3. It's time 表示"是时候了"。例：It's time you went to school. 你该去上学了。

4. not worth a damn 表示"一文不值，毫无用处"。例：The man who is always worrying whether or not his soul will be damned generally have a soul that is not worth a damn. 老是担心自己的灵魂是否会被打入地狱的人，其灵魂大抵不值分文。

5. got it 表示"知道了，明白了"，此外，还可以表示"拿到 / 得到了"。例：I wasn't qualified to apply for the job really but I got it anyhow. 实际上我并不具备申请这份工作的资格，但不管怎样，我还是被录用了。

6. This is it. 表示"这正是所需的；这正是未能成功的原因"。例：This is it, folks, the best record guide in the business. 就是这个，伙计们，业内最好的唱片指南。

词汇加油站

cover ['kʌvər] *n.* 掩护
yell [jel] *vt.* 叫喊
shot [ʃɑːt] *n.* 射击
chance [tʃæns] *n.* 机会

straight [streɪt] *adj.* 直的
guy [gaɪ] *n.* 家伙
glare [gler] *n.* 强光

时间： 第 7 集 00:38:32—00:39:38
地点： 索纳监狱
人物： 迈克尔，路赛罗
事件： 路赛罗要求迈克尔带他一起越狱。

精彩亮点

1
迈克尔和惠斯勒第一次越狱失败。但由于路赛罗一直催促他们俩出来决斗，眼看萨米就要找到他们了，却没想到露在外面的绳梯引起了塔楼守卫的注意。路赛罗猜出两次计划越狱的那个人就是迈克尔。

2
路赛罗支走了萨米，只留下他和迈克尔俩人单独对话。路赛罗两次询问迈克尔是否试图越狱，但迈克尔矢口否认。

3
迈克尔心生疑惑，他觉得要是按照往常讲求公正的路赛罗早就把自己杀死了，为何现在不仅没动手，还和自己单独谈话？路赛罗到底有何用意呢？

4
自从发现绳梯后，监狱长紧急召集所有囚犯，此事一出，大大降低了路赛罗在监狱中的声望。所以，路赛罗决定与其等着自己被其他人替换，不如自己跟着迈克尔他们一起越狱。

Lechero: I believe in your country they call it, *The Boy Who Cried Wolf*①. **You know it?**☺₁ Well, then you know the moral of that story is even when liars tell the truth②, they can never be believed. But your life's on the line③, boy. Are you trying to break out of④ this prison, Mr. Scofield?

Michael: No.☺₂

Lechero: Are you trying to break out of this prison?

Michael: We both know that's not possible.

Lechero: Answer me!

Michael: What do you want me to say?

Lechero: I want you to tell me the truth. I want to hear it.

Michael: You want a reason to kill me.☺₃

Lechero: No, boy... I have good reason to⑤ kill you. Because of you, it's no longer possible for me to effectively govern this prison. Justified or not, the men no longer has faith in me. That leaves only one thing for me to do to guarantee my survival. You are breaking out of this prison, Mr. Scofield. **And you're taking me with you**⑥.☺₄

译文

路赛罗： 我相信在你的国家，人们称之为《狼来了》。你知道这个故事吗？那么，你知道那个故事给我们的教训是即使骗子说实话，也没人相信他们。但是你已经命悬一线了，小子。斯科菲尔德先生，你是不是正打算从这里越狱？

迈克尔： 没有。

路赛罗： 你是不是打算从这里越狱？

迈克尔： 我们都知道这是不可能的。

路赛罗： 回答我！

迈克尔： 你要我说什么？

路赛罗： 我要你告诉我实话，我想听事实。

迈克尔： 你想找个杀我的理由？

路赛罗： 不是的，小子……我完全有理由杀你，因为你，我再也无法有效地管理这个监狱了。无论是否公正，这里的人都不再信任我了，那样的话只有一条路能确保我自己的安全。斯科菲尔德先生，你要越狱，就要带我一起走。

知识点拨

1. *The Boy Who Cried Wolf* 是指《狼来了》的故事。例：The boy who cried wolf said something bad would happen, and it did not. 嚷嚷着狼来了的男孩说有坏事发生，结果没有。

2. tell the truth 表示"说实话，真言实语，老实相告"。例：To tell the truth, I don't know if I can handle the job. 说实话，我不知道自己是否能做好这份工作。

3. life on the line 表示"命悬一线"。例：Remember last week, I put my life on the line. 记得上周，我孤注一掷。

4. break out of... 表示"逃出……"。例：It's taken a long time to break out of my own conventional training. 我花了很长时间才摆脱掉自身所受的传统训练的羁绊。

5. have good reason to do sth. 表示"有很好/充足的理由做某事"。例：You have good reason to feel hopeful for yourself. You will weather well through the seasons of love. 你有足够的理由对自己充满希望，你会对爱情的四季适应得很好。

6. take sb./sth. with 表示"将某人/物带上"。例：Many websites offer free printable coupons you can take them with you to the grocery store. 很多网站都提供免费的可打印出来的优惠券，你可以带着这些优惠券去杂货店消费。

词汇加油站

wolf [wʊlf] *n.* 狼
liar ['laɪər] *n.* 说谎者
justified ['dʒʌstɪfaɪd] *adj.* 合理的；事出有因的
guarantee [ˌgærən'tiː] *vt.* 保证

moral ['mɔːrəl] *n.* 寓意
govern ['gʌvərn] *vt.* 管理
faith [feɪθ] *n.* 信任
survival [sər'vaɪvl] *n.* 生存

Scene 6 公司亲自出马

时间： 第 8 集 00:01:57—00:03:00

地点： 索纳监狱

人物： 迈克尔，林肯

事件： 迈克尔、林肯见面，林肯向迈克尔道歉。

精彩亮点

1 林肯来见迈克尔时，俩人都很尴尬。迈克尔担忧地询问侄子 L.J. 的情况。林肯说公司又给了他们四天时间。L.J. 现在平安无事。

2 当初迈克尔和惠斯勒越狱失败，林肯和苏克雷准备营救 L.J. 失败，林肯请求苏珊再给他们一些时间，说罢，苏珊开着车带走了 L.J. 走了，只留下地上三只裹尸袋，原来，他们早就计划要毁尸灭迹。

3 迈克尔没有跟林肯多说什么，转身欲离开，林肯叫住了迈克尔，向他道歉。迈克尔表示对林肯很失望，因为他没想到林肯会欺骗自己。

4 林肯内心也做了长时间的斗争。他一方面担心如果告诉迈克尔莎拉死亡的消息，迈克尔会放弃越狱计划；另一方面，他也不愿意欺骗迈克尔。但儿子的安危是林肯最担心的事，所以为了保全儿子，只得欺骗迈克尔。

Michael: L.J. Is he…☺₁

Lincoln: Alive. Giving us four more days.

Michael: Okay, good.

Lincoln: Listen, back at① the exchange point, I saw three body bags②. **You, me and L.J., we weren't getting out of there alive.**☺₂ That's the last time I get caught flatfooted.

Michael: Then do what you got to do③, Linc. As long as I take care of④ my end, right?

Lincoln: Michael, I know you're angry with me about⑤ Sara, but…

Michael: You lied.

Lincoln: I had to lie.

Michael: Your son is my nephew, and there's nothing I wouldn't do for him. But apparently… apparently you only think I only care about myself.

Lincoln: I know you don't care about yourself, but you cared about Sara. You loved her. And I'm sorry. **But L.J.'s my son. I…I couldn't let anything happen to him.**☺₃ You know that.

Michael: **You used me, Linc.**☺₄ So I guess you and the company have something in common⑥.

译文

迈克尔： L.J. 他……

林　肯： 还活着，又给了我们四天时间。

迈克尔： 好的，很好。

林　肯： 听我说，在交换地点我看见了三只裹尸袋。当时，你、我和 L.J. 不可能活着离开那里。我不会再鲁莽行事了。

迈克尔： 林肯，把你要做的事做好吧。我也会做我这边的准备，好吗？

林　肯： 迈克尔，我知道你还在为莎拉的事生我的气，但是……

迈克尔： 你说谎了。

林　肯： 我不得不撒谎。

迈克尔： 你儿子是我侄子，为了他，我可以做任何事。但显然……显然你认为我只在乎我自己。

林　肯： 我知道你不在乎你自己，但你在乎莎拉，你爱她，我很抱歉，但 L.J. 是我儿子。我……我不能让他再发生意外了。你知道的。

迈克尔： 林肯，你利用了我。这让我认为在某些方面你跟公司一样。

知识点拨

1. back at 表示"回顾"。例：I caught Chrissie's eye, but she only smiled back at me innocently. 我与克丽茜对视了一眼，但她只是一脸天真地对我微笑。

2. body bag 表示"带有拉链的装尸袋"。例：The stretcher had an open body bag on it, and they zipped it up around the body. 担架上有个开着的尸体包，他们顺着尸体将包的拉链拉上。

3. 本句中省略了 have，完整的句式为：have got to do 表示"必须做某事"。例：We have got to do something to help these small business people. 我们必须做点什么来帮助这些小企业主。

4. take care of sb. / sth. 表示"照顾……；对付……"。例：Don't worry yourself about me, I can take care of myself. 你别担心我，我能照顾好自己。

5. be angry with sb. about / for sth. 表示"因某事生某人的气"。例：Don't be angry with me for not having written. 别因为我没有写信而生我的气。

6. have something in common 表示"有共同之处（或兴趣、特征）"。例：He's a bartender, so you have something in common. 他是个酒吧男招待，所以你们可能有共同的兴趣爱好。

 词汇加油站

alive [əˈlaɪv] *adj.* 活着的

flatfooted [ˈflætfʊtɪd] *adj.* 无准备的

angry [ˈæŋɡri] *adj.* 生气的

apparently [əˈpærəntli] *adv.* 看来

exchange [ɪksˈtʃeɪndʒ] *n.* 交换

end [end] *n.* 端

lie [laɪ] *v.* 说谎

common [ˈkɑːmən] *adj.* 共有的

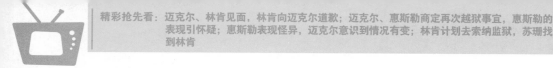

时间： 第 8 集 00:10:00—00:02:17

地点： 惠斯勒牢房

片段二

人物： 迈克尔，惠斯勒，犯人

事件： 迈克尔、惠斯勒商定再次越狱事宜，惠斯勒的表现引怀疑。

 精彩亮点

1
迈克尔来找惠斯勒，告诉他公司愿意再给他们 4 天时间，但惠斯勒看来无精打采，惠斯勒到底怎么了呢？

2
迈克尔已经和路赛罗商量好一起越狱，但是，惠斯勒一直心不在焉，刚才苏珊来索纳监狱找惠斯勒，正巧被迈克尔看见，他们说了什么呢？

3
原来，苏珊告诉惠斯勒公司决定由他们自己去解救惠斯勒，不再需要迈克尔的帮助了，而惠斯勒问该怎么处置迈克尔时，苏珊说杀了他。

4
惠斯勒找到狱中的一名犯人，给了他一些钱让他帮助自己买一把小刀，目的就是要趁机杀掉迈克尔。迈克尔能否躲过这一劫呢？

Michael: Hey. The company's giving us four more days①. 🔵1

Whistler: Okay.

Michael: Problem is I, uh, I don't know how we're getting out of here. Lechero might have some ideas, but I'm still waiting to hear from him②. **I'm sorry, is this a bad time for③ you?** 🔵2

Whistler: It's been an intense 24 hours. I have things on my mind④.

Michael: Yeah, like your last trip to visitation maybe.

Whistler: **What, you're a spy now?** 🔵3

Michael: Forgive me if I'm wrong, but she didn't really strike me as the girlfriend type.

Whistler: She was company. After your failed escape, she came to remind me that I have a stake in⑤ this, too, which you seem to have forgotten. So forgive me if I don't jump for joy⑥ when you say you're working on a plan that may very well⑦ fail again. I've got to get out of here, and it's getting to the point where I don't care how. **Got what we talked about?** 🔵4

Prisoner: You never met me.

译文

迈克尔： 嘿，公司又多给了我们 4 天的时间。

惠斯勒： 好的。

迈克尔： 问题是，我，呃，我不知道我们如何从这里逃出去。路赛罗好像有些主意，但我还在等他的消息。不好意思，现在你是不是不方便和我说话？

惠斯勒： 过去的 24 小时让我很紧张，我脑子里在想很多事。

迈克尔： 是啊，比如你刚才去见的访客。

惠斯勒： 什么？你现在变成间谍了？

迈克尔： 如果我说错了请原谅我，但她真的一点儿也不像是你的女朋友。

惠斯勒： 她是公司的人。昨天你越狱失败后，她过来提醒我，我也有把柄落在他们手上，而你们可能已经忘了。所以当我听说你们又在准备新计划时，无法欢呼雀跃，还请你们原谅我。这个新计划很可能会再次失败，我必须离开这里，我已经不在乎用什么办法了。搞到我们说要的东西了吗？

犯　人： 你从没见过我。

知识点拨

1. another+ 数字 + 名词 = 数字 +more+ 名词。

    例：I want to borrow five more books from the library. 我想再从图书馆借五本书。

2. hear from sb. 表示"收到某人的来信；从某人那里听到；受到（某人）责骂 [警告]"。

    例：You won't hear from Gaston ever again. 你再也不会收到加斯顿的来信了。

3. a bad time 表示"不是时候；艰难的时光"。

    例：I'm sorry but I just cannot say anything. You've caught me at a bad time. 对不起，我真的没什么好说的。你问得不是时候。

4. on one's mind 表示"萦绕在某人心头，使某人挂念"。例：This game has been on my mind all week. 整整一个星期，我都在为这次比赛紧绷着一根弦。

5. have a stake in sth. 表示"与……利害攸关"。

    例：This means that you have a stake in the development and prosperity of the wider world. 这就是说，全世界的发展与繁荣与你们利害攸关。

6. jump for joy 表示"雀跃，欢欣鼓舞，欢跃"。例：What a great chance! I want to jump for joy! 真是一个极好的机会，我高兴得要蹦起来了！

7. very well 可做副词，表示"很，非常"。

    例：I knew very well that the problem was more complex than he supposed. 我很清楚那个问题比他料想的要更复杂。

词汇加油站

intense [ɪnˈtens] *adj.* 紧张的

spy [spaɪ] *n.* 间谍

strike [straɪk] *vt.* 让（某人）觉得

stake [steɪk] *n.* 重大利益

visitation [ˌvɪzɪˈteɪʃn] *n.* 访问

forgive [fərˈgɪv] *vt.* 原谅

remind [rɪˈmaɪnd] *vt.* 使想起

时间： 第 8 集 00:35:17—00:36:55

地点： 索纳监狱，街道

人物： 迈克尔，林肯，惠斯勒，帝博格，路赛罗

事件： 惠斯勒表现怪异，迈克尔意识到情况有变。

精彩亮点

1

　　惠斯勒一直在找机会杀死迈克尔，但总是不凑巧。后来在隧道里又遇到了路赛罗，如果这时动起手来，肯定不是他们的对手，于是，惠斯勒假称自己患有幽闭恐惧症，竭力要上去。

2

　　迈克尔早就看出惠斯勒表现得异常，惠斯勒之前在下水道躲了那么长时间，怎么可能有幽闭恐怖症。现在，眼看距离公司营救惠斯勒的时间越来越近，惠斯勒能否成功出狱呢？

3

　　林肯给路赛罗的手机打了电话，但接电话的却是萨米，萨米一脸疑惑，路赛罗抢过他手中的电话，吩咐帝博格把迈克尔叫来，毕竟现在索纳监狱里他还是老大。

4

　　迈克尔和林肯通话，了解到林肯刚刚遇险，聪明的迈克尔当即就明白了一切，也知晓惠斯勒为何表现怪异，公司不再需要他们了，所以要赶尽杀绝。为了保住性命，只有阻止他们解救惠斯勒。

Whistler: I came looking for scrap metal[①] for the support brace for the tunnel. ☺₁

Michael: Really? Looks like a pretty tight squeeze up there. ☺₂ You sure there's enough fresh air, or does the claustrophobia come and go[②]?

Whistler: What's it like going through life always distrustful?

Michael: You tell me, James.

T-Bag: Ate to break up the brouhaha[③], gentlemen, but Lechero would like to see you. Ays it has something to do with your big brother.

Lechero: Leave us a moment, will you, Teodoro? If your brother should ever call my cell phone again, you tell him you're the one that's gonna pay. ☺₃

Lincoln: Yeah?

Michael: You got the message.

Lincoln: Yeah, you were right. They just tried to take us out[④].

Michael: I know. Whistler got a visit from the company. He's been acting strange ever since. I'm telling you, Linc, something's up[⑤].

Lincoln: Doing more than acting strange, man. He just told Sofia not to be near me 'cause it's dangerous. The company's coming after us.

Michael: They don't need us anymore. Here we go[⑥]. They're breaking him out on their own. ☺₄

译文

惠斯勒： 我去找些废铁来支撑隧道。

迈克尔： 真的吗？看起来上面空间很窄啊。你确定上面有足够的空气，还是你的幽闭恐怖症又犯了？

惠斯勒： 一辈子都被人怀疑是什么感觉呢？

迈克尔： 你来告诉我，詹姆斯。

帝博格： 不好意思打扰你们，先生们，但路赛罗想见你，可能是跟你哥哥有关。

路赛罗： 帝博格，让我们单独待会可以吗？要是你哥哥再给你打电话，你就告诉他由你来付这笔账。

林　肯： 喂？

迈克尔： 你收到消息了。

林　肯： 是啊，你说的没错。他们刚刚想干掉我们。

迈克尔： 我知道，公司的人去找惠斯勒了，打那以后，他就有点儿不对劲。我跟你说林肯，肯定出事了。

林　肯： 已经不仅仅是有事了，兄弟。他刚告诉索菲娅不要接近我，因为会很危险，公司盯上我们了。

迈克尔： 他们不再需要我们了，要开始了，他们打算自己把他弄出去。

知识点拨

1. scrap metal 表示"废金属"。例：A lorry piled with scrap metal had shed its load. 一辆载满废金属的卡车掉货了。

2. come and go 表示"出没，来来往往，过往，往返"。例：Can I read your letters that come and go between your university and you？我可以看看你和学校往来的信件吗？

3. brouhaha 可以表示"喧闹；混乱；激动；暴动"。例：Meanwhile, the brouhaha is bringing what some locals consider to be unwelcome attention to the laid-back canton. 与此同时，这场暴动致使一些当地人认为对于管理松散的州，反响并不好。

4. take sb. out 表示"邀请（某人）外出；除掉某人"。例：We're sitting ducks until we take them out. 在搞定他们之前，我们都是靶子。

5. Something is up. 表示"有麻烦了，出事了"。例：Something's up. I'm alerting the guards. 有麻烦了，我要去警告一下警卫。

6. here we go 表示"我们开始吧"。例：At first, he was told he was too young and I thought, "Oh, boy, here we go again." 起先，他被告知他太年轻了，我心想："哎，又是老一套。"

词汇加油站

scrap [skræp] *n.* 废料，废品
tunnel ['tʌnl] *n.* 隧道
squeeze [skwi:z] *n.* 挤，狭小空间
distrustful [dɪs'trʌstfl] *adj.* 不信任的

brace [breɪs] *n.* 支柱
tight [taɪt] *adj.* 紧凑的
claustrophobia [ˌklɔ:strə'fəʊbɪə] *n.* 幽闭恐怖症
message ['mesɪdʒ] *n.* 消息

时间： 第 9 集 00:04:03—00:05:10
地点： 大街上
人物： 林肯，索菲娅，苏珊，保镖
事件： 林肯计划去索纳监狱，苏珊找到林肯。

精彩亮点

林肯和索菲娅遭到公司的人追击，公司已经决定自己营救惠斯勒了，所以林肯和迈克尔已经没有了利用价值，但跟踪的人发现索菲娅也和林肯在一起，苏珊决定把她也一起杀掉，林肯为了救索菲娅不幸受伤。

1

此时的林肯更担心自己的弟弟，就在刚才，公司的人已经对惠斯勒展开了营救，但迈克尔拼命阻拦，最终，公司营救失败。

2

之前一位房东给索菲娅打来电话，那是惠斯勒租住的另一间公寓，而索菲娅并不知情。就在索菲娅进入那间公寓时，她找到了惠斯勒的护照，但护照上写的名字却不是惠斯勒，索菲娅茫然了，她不知道惠斯勒还有多少秘密没有告诉自己。

3

当初索菲娅进入惠斯勒的另一间公寓时，苏珊就曾出现并警告她快点儿离开，希望以后不要再看到她，否则性命不保，随即便将公寓里与惠斯勒有关的一切全部销毁。没想到，在这里，她又看到了索菲娅。

4

Lincoln: I hope my brother's all right.☺₁
Sofia: Does it hurt?
Lincoln: It's fine. I'm gonna get to the prison.☺₂
Sofia: I was watching the news in the waiting room①. They identified a few bodies, but…It wasn't them.
Lincoln: I'll find out when I get there. You want to come?
Sofia: I don't, I don't know.☺₃ After everything that's happened, I don't know what to think anymore.
Lincoln: What more is there② to think about?
Sofia: James has an answer for everything, and nothing ever makes sense③.
Lincoln: You need to stop asking questions and just look at the facts.
Sofia: I wanted to believe everything he was saying, and I still want him to get out.
Lincoln: I want him out as well④. Trust me, I've been working on this every single day⑤.
Sofia: Lincoln, I really appreciate everything you have done. You saved my life. You didn't have to help me like that.
Lincoln: Yeah. I did.
Susan: Get in the car.
Man: Come on.
Susan: Everywhere I go, there you are⑥. Go home, Sofia.☺₄

译文

林　肯：我希望我弟弟一切顺利。

索菲娅：疼吗？

林　肯：还好，我要去趟监狱。

索菲娅：我在等候室看了新闻。他们确认了几具尸体的身份，但是……没有他们。

林　肯：等我到那儿会查清楚，你想跟我一起吗？

索菲娅：我不，我不知道。发生了这么多事后，我都不知道该去想什么了。

林　肯：还有什么可想的？

索菲娅：詹姆斯知道一切问题的答案，但说这也没意义。

林　肯：你别再问那么多问题了，面对现实吧。

索菲娅：我想相信他说的一切，我仍然希望他可以出来。

林　肯：我也希望他能出来，相信我，我每天都在为此努力。

索菲娅：林肯，我真的很感谢你做的一切。你救了我的命。你其实不用那样帮我的。

林　肯：话虽如此，但是我做了。

苏　珊：上车。

保　镖：快点儿。

苏　珊：无论我去哪儿，都能看到你。回家去，索菲娅。

知识点拨

1. waiting room 表示"等候室；候诊室；候车室"。例：The only magazine in the waiting room was a scientific journal full of technical jargon above my head. 候诊室里唯一的一本杂志是一份全是术语的科学期刊，我看不懂。

2. What more is there 表示"还有什么（多出来）要做的事儿？"例：A: I told you I wasn't done, didn't I? 我不是告诉你，我还没做完吗？ B: What more is there? 还有什么（多出来）要做的事儿？

3. make sense 表示"有意义；理解；讲得通；是明智的"。例：On the face of it that seems to make sense. But the figures don't add up. 乍一看，似乎讲得通，但这些数字对不起来。

4. as well 常用作状语，做"又；也"解，相当于 too 或 also，常位于句末，无须用逗号与句子分开。as well 在口语中也可用于句中，做"也好，也行"或"倒不如"解，用来缓和语气。

5. every single day 表示"每一天"。例：I practise gratitude for my life every single day and I feel the abundance in everything I have now. 每一天，我满怀对生活的感激之情，我满足于我现在拥有的一切。

6. there you are 表示"这就是你要的东西；我早就这样说过"。在片中表示"你都在"。例：It's the wages that count. Not over-generous, but there you are. 重要的是工钱，不要过于慷慨，但也没办法。

词汇加油站

hurt [hɜːrt] *vt.* 感到疼痛
sense [sens] *n.* 意义；含义
single [ˈsɪŋgl] *adj.* 单一的
save [seɪv] *vt.* 解救

identify [aɪˈdentɪfaɪ] *vt.* 识别
fact [fækt] *n.* 事实
appreciate [əˈpriːʃieɪt] *vt.* 感激

Scene 7 越狱人数增加

时间： 第 10 集 00:03:35—00:04:52
地点： 索纳监狱
人物： 迈克尔，帝博格，路赛罗，马霍
事件： 帝博格加入越狱队伍，迈克尔部署越狱准备。

精彩亮点

先前帝博格跟惠斯勒说自己可以帮助他们处理掉萨米，而且他表示，自己早就知道路赛罗和他们成为一伙了，而且准备越狱。帝博格告诉惠斯勒，处理掉萨米的条件就是事成之后带上他跟他们一起越狱。 **1**

此时，迈克尔刚回到牢房。先前，因为公司准备营救惠斯勒失败，迈克尔被当作策划这一切的主谋被狱长拘留。迈克尔交代了一切，惠斯勒在酷刑下承认帮助自己越狱的是苏珊。狱长逮捕苏珊后，让她带他们去找 L.J.，没想到苏珊设计杀死了狱长和随从，迈克尔和惠斯勒也因而得以回到牢房。 **2**

迈克尔说这句话实际上是在讽刺帝博格，因为帝博格失去了一只手，所以，迈克尔以此刺激他，让他留在下面。帝博格虽心有不甘，但迈克尔是整个越狱计划的策划者，而自己只有听从他的话才行。 **3**

迈克尔他们在挖地道，但这也很危险，如果找不到合适的支撑物，地道就会坍塌，这样一来，所有人都会葬身于此。 **4**

T-bag: I am coming with① you. ☺₁
Michael: Okay by me②. ☺₂
T-bag: Everyone here hear that, lawman?
Michael: But you're staying up③ here.
T-bag: Maybe I didn't enunciate myself.
Michael: The work downstairs requires two hands. ☺₃
Lechero: Hey. We need somebody to stay outside in case Sammy returns.
Alex: I thought we couldn't dig through④ this stuff.
Michael: The bracing's gonna be tricky. Unless the tunnel gets the proper support, it's all going to come down⑤ on our heads. ☺₄ We should have the materials for the braces, but we'll need a saw to cut them to size. And a hammer. Can you help us out?
Lechero: Yeah. I can do that.
Michael: Two days.
Mahone: And if not?
Michael: Two days.
Lechero: Guillermo should have everything we need. You know where he is, right?
T-bag: I think it's, uh…
Lechero: It's down this corridor on the left. Halfway down⑥. Cell 40.

译文

帝博格： 我要跟着你走。

迈克尔： 我看可以。

帝博格： 大家都听到了吗？你听到了吗，警官？

迈克尔： 但是你要待在这里。

帝博格： 或许我刚才还没有说清楚。

迈克尔： 楼下的工作需要有两只手的人。

路赛罗： 嘿。我们需要来个人待在外面以防萨米回来。

马　霍： 我还以为我们不可能凿穿这东西。

迈克尔： 找根柱子撑住是关键，除非地道有合适的支撑物，否则会全部塌下来，砸中我们的头。我们该找些做支撑的材料，但是我们需要拿锯把它们锯成合适的大小，还要一把锤子，你能帮我们解决这问题吗？

路赛罗： 好的，没问题。

迈克尔： 只有 2 天。

马　霍： 如果不行呢？

迈克尔： 只有 2 天。

路赛罗： 吉列尔莫应该备好了我们需要的一切。你知道他在哪儿，对吗？

帝博格： 我觉得，呃……

路赛罗： 在这条走廊的左边，走到走廊中间部分，40 号牢房。

知识点拨

1. come with sb. 表示"与某人一起"。例：I'll come with you if you like. I might as well. 如果你想的话，我会和你一起来。我无所谓。

2. Okay by me 表示"我看可以"。例：A: What about paying a visit to Sam's? B: Okay by me. A：我们要不要去看看山姆？B：我看可以。

3. stay up 表示"熬夜；悬在原位上"。例：If necessary, the airship can stay up there for days to keep out of danger. 必要时，飞艇能在那里停留数天以躲避危险。

4. dig through 表示"挖穿，挖通（隧道等）"。

5. come down 可以表示"下来；下落；（价格、温度、比率等）下降；崩塌"。例：If you do something awful they all come down on you like a ton of bricks. 如果你做了错事，他们全都会对你大发雷霆。

6. halfway down 表示"向下走到一半"。例：About the time the three climbers were halfway down, clouds blotted out the sun. 当这 3 个登山者下到半山腰的时候，云层遮住了太阳。

词汇加油站

lawman ['lɔ:mæn] *n.* 执法官，警察，警官

downstairs [ˌdaʊn'sterz] *ad.* 在楼下

brace [breɪs] *vt.* 支撑

hammer ['hæmər] *n.* 铁锤

enunciate [ɪ'nʌnsieɪt] *vt.* 确切地说明

stuff [stʌf] *n.* 原料

tricky ['trɪki] *adj.* （形势、工作等）复杂的

corridor ['kɔ:rɪdɔ:r] *n.* 走廊

时间： 第 10 集 00:08:32—00:09:23
地点： 酒店
人物： 林肯，苏克雷
事件： 苏克雷助力林肯兄弟，林肯深表感激。

片段二

精彩亮点

1 林肯拜托苏克雷帮忙联系卖炸弹的人，这个人帮助苏克雷安排索纳监狱的一系列事宜，相对靠谱，现在不管怎么说，距离越狱时间越来越近，只有拼死一搏了。

2 为了帮助林肯兄弟，苏克雷冒险与苏珊做起了交易，他假装帮苏珊盯着林肯他们的一举一动，实际上是为他们争取时间。

3 苏克雷一直以来没少帮助迈克尔和林肯，实际上，当初要不是迈克尔舍身相救，苏克雷早就被淹死在河中，或是被重新带回监狱，面临更长的刑期。

4 林肯表示只要等迈克尔他们成功越狱，救出儿子 L.J.，他一定会好好报答苏克雷，但苏克雷表示，他做这一切都是心甘情愿的，他现在唯一的愿望就是回家与玛丽·克鲁兹母子团聚。

Sucre: Don't worry. We'll be there with all the cash. ☺1 Okay? Gracias ①. Osberto. That's who you want to talk to.

Lincoln: This guy on the up-and-up ② ?

Sucre: The guy I was running things into Sona for arranged this, so it's as up as it's gonna get for this kind of deal. So, yes. Osberto doesn't speak English, though, so how do you want to work it? I need to meet with ③ Susan. ☺2

Lincoln: I'll take Sofia. She can translate for me. Don't worry about it.

Sucre: So when I meet with Susan, what do you want me to tell her?

Lincoln: Tell her whatever you think she wants to hear. Just buy us enough time to do our thing, all right ④ ?

Sucre: Home stretch ⑤, papi.

Lincoln: Listen, man. I want to thank you for everything.

Sucre: Oh, Linc, please.

Lincoln: When we get home, I got your back ⑥ —whatever you need, whatever you want. ☺3

Sucre: That won't be necessary. When I'm back home, I'm a saint. ☺4 I'm not even jaywalking.

译文

苏克雷： 别担心，我们会带着钱去那儿的。好了吗？谢谢，奥斯博尔托是你们要找的人。

林　肯： 这个人可信吗？

苏克雷： 我给索纳监狱安排的事是这个人帮忙弄的，所以应该信得过，应该是这样。不过奥斯博尔托不会说英语，你想好怎么办了吗？我要去见苏珊。

林　肯： 我带索菲娅一起去，她能给我翻译，别担心。

苏克雷： 那么我见到苏珊的时候，你想让我跟她说什么？

林　肯： 告诉她任何她想听的，只要留给我们足够的时间让我们做事就行，好吗？

苏克雷： 最后一搏了，兄弟。

林　肯： 听着，伙计，对于发生过的一切我都非常感谢你。

苏克雷： 林肯，别这么客气。

林　肯： 等我们到家了，我会回报你的。不管你要什么，我都给你。

苏克雷： 没这个必要。等我回到家，我就是圣人了，我甚至都不会违反交通规则。

知识点拨

1. gracias 是西班牙语，表示"谢谢"。例：Gracias, but I'm not sure I'm old enough to drink, senior. 谢谢，但我还不到喝酒的年龄，先生。

2. up-and-up 表示"诚实的行为；向上；越来越好"。例：That raised three questions for me: First, is bribery on the up-and-up? 这让我想到了三个问题：首先，贿赂是否为一种诚实的行为？

3. 我们一起来看一下 meet 与 meet with 的区别：表示"约见某人，迎接某人，认识某人"等，通常要用 meet。表示"偶然遇到某人"，可用 meet 或 meet with；表示"偶然遇到某物"，通常用 meet with。表示"满足需要，符合要求，达到希望"等，通常用 meet；表示"受到欢迎，得到支持，获得批准"等，通常用 meet with。

4. all right 表示"尚可，（确保对方同意或理解）如何，可允许（的），正确的"。例：All she's worried about is whether he is all right. 她所担心的只是他是否安然无恙。

5. home stretch 表示"终点直道，最后冲刺"。例：He has reached the home stretch on his thesis with two weeks to spare. 他提前了两周进入了写论文的最后阶段。

6. get one's back 表示"罩着某人；支持某人"。例：People often thinks, love is a kind termless, the dedication that does not seek get one's own back. 人们常认为，爱是一种无条件的、不求回报的奉献。

 词汇加油站

cash [kæʃ] *n.* 现金	**arrange** [ə'reɪndʒ] *vt.* 安排，筹备
translate [træns'leɪt] *vt.* 翻译	**enough** [ɪ'nʌf] *det.* 足够的
stretch [stretʃ] *n.* （终点）直道	**necessary** ['nesəseri] *adj.* 必要的
saint [seɪnt] *n.* 圣徒	**jaywalk** ['dʒeɪwɔːk] *vi.* 擅自穿越马路

时间： 第 10 集 00:13:02—00:14:27

地点： 酒吧

人物： 苏珊，苏克雷

事件： 苏克雷向苏珊汇报林肯兄弟情况以争取时间。

精彩亮点

> 苏克雷和林肯俩人演了一场戏，故意让监视他们的人误以为他们俩不和，于是，苏珊打算利用苏克雷监视林肯兄弟的一举一动，并承诺给他 5 万美元做酬劳。

1

> 苏克雷按照之前和林肯计划的那样去找苏珊汇报情况，他隐瞒了林肯和迈克尔的计划，聪明的苏珊能否识破他的谎言呢？

2

> 苏克雷故意说他没有骗苏珊来让苏珊解除对自己的怀疑，事实上，狡猾的苏珊怎么可能不留一手，她一直在派人盯着苏克雷和林肯。

3

> 苏克雷向苏珊表了忠心，苏珊自然要表现出她的诚意，于是支付了他一半酬金。同时也警告苏克雷要眼观六路，耳听八方，否则后果不堪设想。

4

Susan: **So every time I say your name, I'm calling you "sugar".** ☺₁

Sucre: Basically.

Susan: I like that.

Sucre: **Look, I don't have a lot of information. Which, I guess, that's good news for you, right?** ☺₂

Susan: You care to① elaborate?

Sucre: Lincoln isn't cooking anything up②. He's still planning on③ exchanging Whistler for④ L.J. He hasn't been talking about running any games.

Susan: And did he become an Eagle Scout last night, too?

Sucre: Lady, he got the message. He knows he doesn't have a choice, he has to play it straight. Look, I could have come up here and made something up just to get paid, but…I'm not trying to get on your bad side either.

Susan: **You know what? I believe you.** ☺₃

Sucre: So, I'll call you if anything comes up.

Susan: Whoa, whoa! What am I, a toothless crack whore? Sit down. I keep my promises. Le I work for, they don't like to deal in greenbacks; it's just too bulky. Cashier's check payable to cash. Same thing. **Half now and half when you're done. Keep your ears open⑤, sugar.** ☺₄

译文

苏 珊：因此，每次呼唤你的名字，我都叫你甜心。

苏克雷：可以理解。

苏 珊：我喜欢那样。

苏克雷：听着，我的情报不多。我猜这对你来说是好消息吧？

苏 珊：你介意给我仔细说说吗？

苏克雷：林肯没什么鬼点子，他仍打算用惠斯勒换 L.J.。他没跟我说过什么策略。

苏 珊：他昨晚也成了雄鹰童子军了？

苏克雷：小姐，他收到消息了。他知道他别无选择，他只能乖乖服从你们的命令。听着，我完全可以胡编乱造来糊弄你以拿到我的报酬，但……我也不想加入你那一方。

苏 珊：你知道吗？我相信你。

苏克雷：那有情况我就给你打电话。

苏 珊：哇噢，哇噢，你难道觉得我是个卑鄙无耻的小人吗？坐下，我信守诺言。而我的上司，他们不喜欢钞票，因为体积大，银行支票可兑换现金，一样的。先付你一半，其他的事成付清。耳朵机灵点儿，甜心。

知识点拨

1. care to do sth. 表示"想要做某事；愿意做某事"。例：If I care enough to do anything for my birthday this year, which I doubt, I wouldn't be surprised if none of my friends showed up. 如果我因为重视今年的生日而去做一些事的话，我怀疑，万一没有一位朋友来，我也不会很惊讶。

2. cook up 表示"编造；快速做（饭等）；胡诌"。例：He must have cooked up his scheme on the spur of the moment. 他肯定是一时冲动策划了这个阴谋。

3. plan on 表示"打算，指望"。例：They are planning on a trip to Guyana next month. 他们计划下个月去圭亚那旅行。

4. exchange for 表示"用……换取"。例：Refugees also complain that soldiers steal food and personal property from them and demand bribes in exchange for food or shelter. 难民们同时抱怨说士兵偷他们的食品和私人财物，而且借提供食物和住处之机向他们索贿。

5. keep one's ears / eyes open 表示"留心听（看），密切注意"。例：You can often pick up useful tips if you keep your ears open. 如果你留心细听，常常能获得一些有用的消息。

词汇加油站

sugar ['ʃʊgər] *n.* 食糖

elaborate [ɪˈlæbərət] *vt.* 详尽阐述

scout [skaʊt] *n.* 搜索

crack [kræk] *n.* 裂缝

basically ['beɪsɪkli] *adv.* 从根本上说

eagle ['iːgl] *n.* 鹰

toothless ['tuːθləs] *adj.* 无齿的

greenback ['griːnbæk] *n.* 美钞

时间： 第 11 集 00:02:27—00:03:06

地点： 索纳监狱

人物： 迈克尔，林肯

事件： 林肯询问迈克尔越狱进展，迈克尔告诉林肯越狱人数增加。

精彩亮点

1 迈克尔看到林肯的车里坐着惠斯勒的女友索菲娅，聪明的迈克尔马上就意识到哥哥爱上了她。索菲娅不知道该以什么样的心情面对惠斯勒，她觉得自己距离惠斯勒越来越远。而就在这个时候，林肯走进了她的生活，安慰着她，还送给她一个巴黎埃菲尔铁塔的挂饰，因为惠斯勒曾向她承诺等到出狱后两个人就去巴黎。林肯告诉索菲娅：如果他不能带你去，我带你去。

2 迈克尔想让林肯想清楚再做决定，毕竟索菲娅还是惠斯勒的女友，林肯一直否认自己和索菲娅的关系，甚至干脆把话题转移开。

3 铁丝网的工作已经交由苏克雷做得差不多了，现在唯一的问题就是塔楼守卫。迈克尔又会想到什么主意呢？

4 迈克尔的"老朋友"纷纷加入了越狱队伍。帝博格曾让贝里克与萨米决战，结果贝里克大败，还险些丧命，贝里克威胁帝博格说，如果不让他加入，就去把他们要越狱的事告诉所有人。

Michael: **Is that Whistler's girlfriend? Why is she staying in the car?**☺1

Lincoln: Guess she thinks she'll see him tomorrow.

Michael: You've been spending a lot of time together, huh?

Lincoln: And?

Michael: **You sure that's wise?**☺2

Lincoln: Where are we①?

Michael: Behind schedule②. But we should be on the same side of the fence by tomorrow afternoon.

Lincoln: What do you mean, "should"?

Michael: The tunnel gets us into no-man's-land③. **To get to the fence, we're going to④ need a new diversion of the tower guards.**☺3

Lincoln: What time?

Michael: Daytime's still our best option⑤. They double the guards at night.

Lincoln: And the jeep patrols?

Michael: Yeah. And, uh…there's something else.

Lincoln: What?

Michael: **T-bag's coming. And Mahone. Bellick. Oh, yeah, there's a drug lord⑥, too.**☺4

译文

迈克尔：那是惠斯勒的女朋友吗？她怎么待在车里？

林　肯：估计她想明天见他吧。

迈克尔：你们在一起很久了吧，哈？

林　肯：那又怎样？

迈克尔：你觉得这么做明智吗？

林　肯：咱们进展得如何？

迈克尔：比计划落后，但我们明天下午应该都在铁丝网外了。

林　肯：你说"应该"是什么意思？

迈克尔：隧道通往禁区，为到达铁丝网，我们需要用新招对付塔楼守卫。

林　肯：什么时候？

迈克尔：最好还是白天，他们晚上增加了一倍守卫数量。

林　肯：还有巡逻车？

迈克尔：对，嗯……还有……

林　肯：什么？

迈克尔：帝博格也加入了，还有马霍和贝里克。哦，对了，还有毒枭老大。

知识点拨

1. Where are we？表示"我们在哪里？发展到哪一步了？"。例：Women like to ask like where are we or where is this relationship going? 女人总喜欢问男人我们的关系到底到哪里了？

2. behind schedule 表示"晚点，落后于预定计划，误期，误点"。例：We were two months behind schedule, and already over budget. 我们的进度晚了两个月，而且已经超出了预算。

3. no-man's-land 表示"无主土地；所有权争议未决的土地；荒地"。

4. 我们一起来看一下 will 和 be going to 的区别：两者均可用来表示将来的意图，但"be going to"结构语义稍强些，对于"事先经过考虑的打算、计划、意图"，应使用 be going to；对于"未经过考虑的打算，计划"，只是"临时之意"，则用 will 结构；在表示"即将发生某事"时，两者区别意义不大，多可互换。

5. best option 表示"最佳选择，最佳方案"。

6. drug lord 表示"毒枭，毒品之王"。例：The drug lord had his muscleman to protect him. 毒枭雇了保镖保护自己。

词汇加油站

spend [spend] *vt.* 花钱

schedule ['skedʒuːl] *n.* 预定计划

tunnel ['tʌnl] *n.* 地道

option ['ɑːpʃn] *n.* 选项

wise [waɪz] *adj.* 有智慧的

fence [fens] *n.* 围墙

diversion [daɪ'vɜːrʒn] *n.* 分散注意力

patrol [pə'troʊl] *n.* 巡逻队

Scene 8 越狱进行时

片段一

时间： 第 12 集 00:14:40—00:16:12
地点： 树林
人物： 迈克尔，林肯，惠斯勒，马霍，麦克格莱迪
事件： 众人越狱成功，但一路被狱警追赶。

精彩亮点

1　路赛罗、帝博格和贝里克抢在迈克尔他们前面走,不想电源正好接上,塔楼守卫喝令他们停下,路赛罗不顾一切往前冲,结果身中一枪。他们都被逮捕了,只有迈克尔等待时机,趁着巡警们的注意力都在路赛罗他们这三个逃犯身上,带领惠斯勒、马霍和麦克格莱迪顺利越狱。

2　惠斯勒跑得太急,在树林中被绊倒后扭伤了脚踝,但眼看士兵们就要追上来了,迈克尔等人拖着他前行,始终没有放弃他。

3　迈克尔指的是氧气瓶,因为他们准备游泳渡河,在途中等待苏克雷开船来接应他们。但没想到年纪最小的麦克格莱迪不通水性,善良的迈克尔让他和自己共用氧气瓶,并让他抱紧自己。

4　惠斯勒此时有些畏惧,他知道如果自己到了公司手上肯定没有什么好下场,他打算趁着迈克尔他们不注意时逃走,他能否成功呢?

Michael: What's wrong?① ☺1

Whistler: My ankle! I've torn it apart②! ☺2

Michael: Come on. It's not that far. Help me up③!

Alex: Mr. Whistler, we'll drag you by your hair because we got to go!

Whistler: I'll slow you down④. Just go! Just leave me!

Michael: We both know that's not an option. It's only a quarter of a mile to the beach. If we stick to⑤ the bush, we can make it. Alex, a little help? Go. Come on! We only have a few minutes. We got soldiers right behind us.

Lincoln: Cops as well.

Michael: We got what we need?

Lincoln: Yeah, we got what we need.

McGrady: What do we need? ☺3

Lincoln: Always picking up the strays, huh? This way.

Whistler: Listen, Michael, if you think the company's just going to let you swap me for your nephew, you're mistaken.

Lincoln: Shut up.

Whistler: Once they get hold of⑥ me, they're gonna kill all of you, and I don't want Sofia caught in the crossfire⑦. Listen, just let me go. ☺4

译文

迈 克 尔：怎么回事？

惠 斯 勒：我的脚踝！我崴着了！

迈 克 尔：来，不远了，加把劲！

马　　霍：惠斯勒先生，我们就算拽着你头发也得走！

惠 斯 勒：我会拖累你们的，快走吧！别管我了！

迈 克 尔：我们都知道这不可能，离沙滩只有四分之一英里了。只要我们沿着灌木丛跑，就能成功。亚历克斯，帮下忙。走，快走！我们只剩几分钟，士兵马上就要追上来了。

林　　肯：还有警察。

迈 克 尔：我们该带的都带齐了吧？

林　　肯：嗯，都带齐了。

麦克格莱迪：我们需要什么？

林　　肯：总是收留些迷路的小动物，是不是呀？这边。

惠 斯 勒：听着，迈克尔，如果你觉得公司会拿我换你外甥你就错了。

林　　肯：别说了。

惠 斯 勒：只要他们得到我，就会把你们都杀了，而我不想让索菲娅在交火中出事。听我的，让我走吧。

知识点拨

1. What's wrong？表示"怎么了？"。例：What's wrong with you is that you think you can get something for nothing. 你的问题是你认为自己可以不劳而获。

2. tear apart 表示"撕裂"。例：He had been all but torn apart by a shellburst in France. 在法国他几乎被炮弹炸得四分五裂。

3. help sb. up 表示"把某人扶起来"。例：She put out a hand to help me up. 她伸出手来帮我上去。

4. slow down 表示"（使）慢下来，（使）生产缓慢；（使）变得迟钝"。例：The car slowed down as they passed Customs. 过海关的时候，车速慢了下来。

5. stick to 表示"遵守；保留；紧跟；忠于"。例：There are interesting hikes inland, but most ramblers stick to the clifftops. 内陆地区有一些很有意思的徒步远足路线，但多数徒步者都去爬悬崖陡壁。

6. get hold of sth. / sb. 表示"找到某物以供使用；找到某人"。例：Tell Richard I'm going to kill him when I get hold of him. 告诉理查德，一旦抓住他，我要杀了他。

7. crossfire 的原意是"交叉火力"，caught in the crossfire 表示"被夹在交叉火力中间"，即"受到两面夹击，陷入困境"。例：They say they are caught in the crossfire between the education establishment and the government. 他们称自己被卷进了教育机构与政府之间的争端。

词汇加油站

ankle [ˈæŋkl] n. 踝

drag [dræg] vt. 拖拽

bush [buʃ] n. 灌木（丛）

swap [swɑːp] vt. 用……替换

apart [əˈpɑːrt] adv. 分离；成碎片

mile [maɪl] n. 英里

stray [streɪ] n. 走失的宠物（或家畜）

crossfire [ˈkrɔːsfaɪər] n. 交叉火力

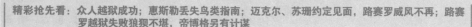

时间： 第 12 集 00:17:27—00:18:15

地点： 海滩

人物： 迈克尔，林肯，惠斯勒，马霍，麦克格莱迪

事件： 惠斯勒丢失鸟类指南，众人决定渡河。

片段二

精彩亮点

1 为了逃避狱警的追捕，迈克尔等人来到了当初兄弟俩约定的海边。林肯把氧气瓶埋在了沙堆里，这是为了让他们一会儿游泳用的，因为这样可以使他们不易被狱警发现。

2 惠斯勒看林肯把怕水的东西塞进塑料袋也想把鸟类指南交给林肯，没想到一摸口袋，那本书不见了。原来在他们越狱时，那本书恰好掉在了地上，但现在关键的是要先躲避狱警的追捕，根本不可能再让他回去找那本书。

3 马霍拿出了儿子的照片，在狱中没有药物控制时，他就是靠着思念儿子、妻子这样的意志力熬过来的。他想让林肯帮自己把这张照片也放进塑料袋，但他是林肯的杀父仇人，林肯对他恨之入骨，自然拒绝了他的请求。

4 麦克格莱迪不会游泳，在这种情况下，唯有游泳渡河才能躲过狱警的追捕，否则只能等着被狱警带回索纳监狱。体贴的迈克尔让他不要害怕，让他紧紧抓住自己和自己共用一个氧气瓶。

Whistler: Hey, I need to put my book in there. The book? My book! It must have fallen out of[1] my pocket. ☺1

Michael: I thought you already figured out[2] the coordinates.

Whistler: Well, I didn't memorize them! I wrote them in the book! ☺2

Michael: I'm pretty sure[3] they're still looking for us, guys.

Lincoln: It's gone. Now get the damn water.

Alex: Would you please[4]? It's a picture of my son. Can you, uh… put it in the bag? ☺3

Lincoln: Screw you, Mahone. Let's go.

Michael: McGrady.

Lincoln: McGrady?

McGrady: I don't swim so good. ☺4

Lincoln: What? Too bad, kid, you're getting wet. Get in.

Michael: Look it's all right. We'll share tanks. Just hold onto[5] me and we'll switch off[6] back and forth[7], ten seconds apiece. Come on. Let's go.

译文

惠 斯 勒：嘿，我必须把我的书放进去。书呢？我的书！它肯定从我的口袋里掉出来了。

迈 克 尔：我以为你已经得到那个坐标了。

惠 斯 勒：但我没把它记住！我记在书上了！

迈 克 尔：我确定他们还在搜寻我们，伙计们。

林 肯：好了，结束了，现在我们快下水吧。

马 霍：帮个忙好吗？这是我儿子的照片。你能，嗯……把它放到袋子里吗？

林 肯：去你的，马霍。我们走吧。

迈 克 尔：麦克格莱迪。

林 肯：麦克格莱迪?

麦克格莱迪：我不太会游泳。

林 肯：你说什么？这可真是太糟了。孩子，你必须下水，进到水里来。

迈 克 尔：来吧，没事的。我们共用一个氧气罐，紧紧抓着我，我们 10 秒钟一换。来吧，我们走。

知识点拨

1. fall out of 表示"从……掉了下来"。例：If you fall out of that tree and break your leg, don't come running to me. 如果你从树上掉下来摔断了腿，别跟我这哭哭啼啼的！

2. figure out 表示"想出，解决；计算出；弄明白"。例：It took them about one month to figure out how to start the equipment. 他们花了大约 1 个月的时间才搞清楚如何启动设备。

3. pretty sure 表示"相当肯定，很确定，确信，非常肯定"。例：I'm pretty sure you have guessed what I drew. 我想你们一定猜到了我画的是什么。

4. would you please 表示"麻烦你"。例：Would you please correct any wrong spellings that you find? 请改正你发现的拼写错误好吗？

5. hold onto sb. / sth. 表示"紧紧抓住某物（某人）"。例：It was so windy that I had to hold onto my hat all the way along the street. 风很大，走在街上我只好一路抓住帽子。

6. switch off 表示"关闭，切断；（使）没兴趣；使停止谈话"。例：Thankfully, I've learned to switch off and let it go over my head. 谢天谢地，我已经学会了释然，随它去吧。

7. back and forth 表示"来回地，一来一往"。例：They swayed back and forth, more or less in sync with the music. 他们来回摇摆，基本上与音乐同步。

 词汇加油站

pocket ['pɑːkɪt] *n.* 口袋

memorize ['meməraɪz] *vt.* 记住

tank [tæŋk] *n.* （贮放液体或气体的）箱，槽，罐

switch [swɪtʃ] *vt.* 转换

coordinate [koʊˈɔːrdɪneɪt] *n.* 坐标

wet [wet] *adj.* 湿的

apiece [əˈpiːs] *adv.* 每个

时间： 第13集 00:06:41—00:08:48

地点： 大街，索纳监狱

人物： 迈克尔，苏珊，贝里克，帝博格，路赛罗

事件： 迈克尔、苏珊约定见面，路赛罗威风不再。

精彩亮点

1 脚扭伤的惠斯勒很快就被林肯兄弟俩抓住了。他们要拿他交换L.J.，迈克尔打电话给苏珊约定会面地点。

2 苏珊决定得到惠斯勒后就杀掉迈克尔和林肯，但迈克尔很聪明，他早料到苏珊会设下埋伏。事实上，法兰西广场并不是真正交换人质的地点，迈克尔将最终地点选在了博物馆，一来人多，二来博物馆的安保较完善。

3 贝里克、帝博格和路赛罗三人越狱失败。路赛罗在越狱途中不幸身中一枪后，索纳监狱其他囚犯都对路赛罗拳打脚踢，唯有帝博格不惜性命前去帮助他，没想到一向残酷的帝博格也有这样的一面。

4 贝里克和帝博格搀着路赛罗回到了他的牢房，昔日光景不再，满屋一片狼藉，还有两个犯人正在偷窃路赛罗房间内的东西。路赛罗拼尽全力拿出自己藏好的手枪，吓跑了两个犯人。

Michael: There's been a change in venue.☺1

Susan: Oh, well, well, well. I finally get to talk to the brains of the outfit.

Michael: We're at the plaza de Francia.

Susan: So you're thinking public place, safety in numbers, plenty of① witnesses to protect you. I'm thinking public place, wanted men, police, lots of witnesses to identify you.

Michael: Plaza de Francia. Ten minutes. Be on your own②.

Susan: Round everyone up③.☺2

Bellick: It's anarchy in here! We gotta hide!

T-bag: I gotta — I gotta help him.☺3

Bellick: He's the most hated person in here. If we start rubbin' elbows④ with him again, then we're gonna…

T-bag: He gave me a home!

Bellick: He gave me third-degree burns down my back! He can go to hell⑤!

T-bag: I owe him this much. You don't want to help, then don't. Get outta here! Shoo fly… Just a few more steps. It's only a few more. Then it's home, sweet home.

Lechero: This is my house!☺4

译文

迈克尔：我们换一个地方。

苏　珊：哦，好好好，我终于跟军师说上话了。

迈克尔：我们在法兰西广场。

苏　珊：因此，你觉得去公共场所人多，目击者也多，这样就可以保护你。可我觉得公共场所会有很多警察和证人会认出你是通缉犯。

迈克尔：法兰西广场，10分钟，你自己来。

苏　珊：把所有人都带上。

贝里克：这里一片混乱，我们得躲起来。

帝博格：我得……我得去帮帮他。

贝里克：他现在是这里最受憎恨的人。如果我们再次跟他扯上关系，我们就要……

帝博格：他给了我一个容身之处。

贝里克：我后背的3级烧伤就是拜他所赐，他可以去死了。

帝博格：我欠他很多，你不想帮忙就算了。滚，赶紧滚。就剩几步了，就几步了，然后就到家了，温暖的家。

路赛罗：这是我的房子！

知识点拨

1. plenty of 表示"很多，大量的"，用来修饰可数名词和不可数名词。例：Are there plenty of fresh fruits and vegetables in your diet? 你的饮食中新鲜果蔬充足吗？

2. on one's own 表示"独立地，独自地"；例：The success or failure of the matter depends on your own effort. 事情的成败在于你自己的努力。

3. round up 表示"使聚拢，围捕；积攒；综述"。例：The police rounded up a number of suspects. 警方围捕了一些嫌疑犯。

4. rub elbows 表示"出去和别人接触和交际"。例：If you travel across America by bus, you rub elbows with all sorts of people. 要是你乘长途汽车到美国各地旅行的话，你就会接触到各种人。

5. go to hell 表示"完蛋，毁灭；滚开"。例：Peter can go to hell. It's my money and I'll leave it to who I want. 让彼得见鬼去吧。这是我的钱，我想留给谁就留给谁。

词汇加油站

venue ['venjuː] *n.* 犯罪地点

plaza ['plæzə] *n.* （西班牙城镇的）广场

identify [aɪ'dentɪfaɪ] *vt.* 识别

elbow ['elboʊ] *n.* 肘部

outfit ['aʊtfɪt] *n.* 组织

witness ['wɪtnəs] *n.* 目击者

anarchy ['ænərki] *n.* 混乱

owe [oʊ] *vt.* 应归功于

时间： 第 13 集 00:15:32—00:17:02

地点： 索纳监狱

片段四

人物： 贝里克，帝博格，路赛罗

事件： 路赛罗越狱失败狼狈不堪，帝博格另有计谋。

 精彩亮点

路赛罗中枪后，索纳监狱失去控制，犯人们聚集在一起声讨路赛罗，胆小的贝里克担心自己帮助路赛罗会受到连累。但帝博格却告诉他路赛罗不仅不会连累他们，如果他们想逃出索纳监狱，还要依靠路赛罗。帝博格到底有什么计划呢？

1

帝博格利用酒精帮助路赛罗处理了伤口，这让路赛罗很感动，但警惕心极强的路赛罗手里始终拿着枪。

2

帝博格谎称守卫说只要交钱就能获得自由，他还劝说路赛罗把钱拿出来，但路赛罗根本不相信拿钱就能换来自由。

3

帝博格终于露出了真面目，他要亲手杀死路赛罗，然后宣布索纳监狱从此人人平等，还将大把大把的钞票分发给每一位犯人。最终，他放了一把火，烧了索纳监狱，并趁机和贝里克等人成功越狱。

4

Bellick: There's a storm brewing out there in the yard.☺1

Lechero: You tell them…come in. I'm not scared.

Bellick: Well, I am.

T-bag: You might want to put that down①.

Lechero: Oh, Teodoro. You're the last one I'd expect to see at my side②.☺2

T-bag: I take offense③, patron.

Lechero: I've had many foot-washers. Many men have come in with sheep's clothing④, only to let the wolf come out.

T-bag: I am not trying to hurt you. I am trying to save you.

Lechero: Save me? I'm gonna die here. Your life is in jeopardy⑤ just being with me.

T-bag: Not necessarily. As I was being escorted back inside today, one of the guards offered us a chance to buy our freedom.

Lechero: If a guard spoke to you, he was lying. It's impossible to get out.

T-bag: Maybe you've been too busy dying to notice⑥, but there's a new colonel outside those gates. Little Suzy Sona ain't playing so hard to get no more. She has her price. And we gonna need some money.☺3

Lechero: No. No.

T-bag: Then you will die in here.☺4

译文

贝里克：院子里开始暴动了。

路赛罗：你告诉他们……进来，我不怕。

贝里克：我怕啊。

帝博格：或许你把枪放下比较好。

路赛罗：哦，帝博格，我从没想到你居然还会在我身边。

帝博格：我可要生气了，老大。

路赛罗：很多人以前都依附在我身边，都是些披着羊皮的狼。

帝博格：我不想伤害你，我只是想救你。

路赛罗：救我？我就要死在这儿了，你跟我在一起是不会有好结果的。

帝博格：那可不一定。今天我被抓回来的时候，一个守卫给了我们一个赎回自由的机会。

路赛罗：如果守卫跟你这么说，他就是在撒谎，我们不可能再出去了。

帝博格：或许你快入土了没注意到外面来了一位新将军。他没有那么严格，开出了价码，而我们只需要一些钱。

路赛罗：不行，不行。

帝博格：那你就死在这儿吧。

知识点拨

1. put sth. down 表示"放下；镇压；记下；估计"。例：Never put anything down on paper which might be used in evidence against you at a later date. 一定不要写下任何书面的东西，以免日后被用作对你不利的证据。

2. at one's side 表示"在某人身边；支持某人"。例：They remain with him throughout life, staying ever at his side even during sin. 他们一生都与他在一起，甚至是在有罪的时候，也站在他的那一边。

3. take offense 表示"介意；生气；见怪；动怒；感到自己受到了侮辱"。例：I hope you won't take offense at my frankness. 我希望你不会对我的坦率生气。

4. a wolf in sheep's clothing 表示"披着羊皮的狼，披着羊皮，面善心恶"。例：He is a wolf in sheep's clothing, outwardly kind but inwardly vicious! 他是个披着羊皮的狼，外貌仁慈，内心狠毒！

5. be in jeopardy 表示"处于危险状态"。例：A series of setbacks have put the whole project in jeopardy. 一系列的挫折使整个项目面临失败。

6. too busy to do sth. 表示"太忙以至于不能做某事"。例：I'm too busy to help you. 我太忙了，不能帮你了。

词汇加油站

brew [bruː] *vt.* （不愉快的事）即将来临，酝酿

scared [skerd] *adj.* 恐惧的

patron ['peɪtrən] *n.* 保护人

jeopardy ['dʒepərdi] *n.* 危险

yard [jɑːrd] *n.* 场地

offense [ə'fens] *n.* 攻势

wolf [wʊlf] *n.* 狼

escort [ɪ'skɔːrt] *vt.* 护送

Prison Break

Season **4** 公司与锡拉

Scene 1 迈克尔获知莎拉消息

时间： 第 1 集 00:00:50—00:01:29
地点： 会议大厅
人物： 迈克尔，苏珊，惠斯勒
事件： 迈克尔来找苏珊算账，惊闻莎拉还活着。

精彩亮点

1　迈克尔等人成功从索纳监狱越狱后，迈克尔告诉林肯自己必须为莎拉报仇，他已经做好准备要杀了苏珊。苏珊和惠斯勒来参加一个会议，在这里他们要拿走一个决定公司命运的锡拉芯片，惠斯勒完成任务后看到了迈克尔，他想告诉迈克尔自己和苏珊不是一伙的。

2　迈克尔等待苏珊现身，不久，苏珊来叫惠斯勒离开，她意外地看到迈克尔此时正拿着枪对着她。而当她知道迈克尔杀她的原因竟是为了莎拉时，她不禁吃惊于惠斯勒没有告诉他莎拉的消息。

3　原来莎拉并没有死，当时，他们将莎拉和 L.J. 共同作为人质以威胁迈克尔兄弟，让他们救出惠斯勒，没想到莎拉竟自己逃了出去，苏珊手上少了一个筹码，只能谎称莎拉已死。

4　眼看迈克尔就要扣动扳机，苏珊十分惊慌，让迈克尔询问哥哥林肯，看他到底看到了什么。事实上，林肯只是在黑暗中看到了一颗放在盒子里的头，那是他们为了掩盖莎拉逃走这一事实故意拿死尸替代的。

Michael: Call Gretchen, get her in here now. ☺₁

Whistler: You have to trust me. I'm not your enemy, Michael.

Susan: James. We need to leave.

Michael: You know, despite① everything… If Sara could weigh in② right now③, she'd tell me not to kill you. That's the kind of person she was. That's the kind of person you took from me④.

Susan: James, didn't you tell him? ☺₂

Whistler: He walked in five…

Michael: Shut up! Gretchen, look at me. This is for Sara.

Susan: I never killed Sara. ☺₃

Michael: I wouldn't expect someone like you to take this with dignity⑤.

Susan: I swear to God⑥ she's alive.

Michael: Don't insult me and don't insult her.

Susan: She escaped. We knew if you found out we wouldn't have any leverage. I fabricated the whole thing.

Michael: My brother saw…

Susan: A head in a box! From a cadaver. You ask Lincoln what he really saw. ☺₄

译文

迈克尔：给格雷琴打电话，让她来这里。

惠斯勒：你一定要相信我，迈克尔，我不是你的敌人。

苏　珊：詹姆斯，我们得走了。

迈克尔：你知道，无论如何……要是莎拉现在在这儿，她会劝我别杀我，她就是那样的人，而你从我身边把她夺走了。

苏　珊：詹姆斯，你没告诉他？

惠斯勒：他刚走进来五……

迈克尔：闭嘴！格雷琴，看着我，这一枪是为了莎拉。

苏　珊：我从没杀死莎拉。

迈克尔：我没指望像你这样的人能堂堂正正地承认。

苏　珊：我对天发誓，她还活着。

迈克尔：别侮辱我，也别侮辱她。

苏　珊：她逃走了。我们知道要是你发现了，我们就没有筹码了，我伪造了这一切。

迈克尔：我哥哥看到了……

苏　珊：盒子里的一颗头！死尸的头，你可以问问林肯他看到的是什么。

知识点拨

1. despite 和 although 都有"尽管"的意思，但 despite 是介词，后接名词或代词；而 although=though 是连词，后接表示让步的状语从句。

2. weigh in 表示"参加；称重量；比赛前量体重；发表评论；施加影响"。例：The President's political advisers also weighed in on the plan. 总统的政治顾问也对这项计划发表了看法。

3. right now 表示"此时；立即；此刻，目前"。例：If you have a problem with that, I want you to tell me right now. 如果你有异议，我要你马上告诉我。

4. take from 可以表示"减少，降低；取自"。偏重表示"从我身边带走"。例：I just wanted to see how much could they take from me! 我就是想看看，他们究竟能骗我多少钱！

5. with dignity 表示"庄严，带有尊严地"。例：If we fail let us go down with dignity. 万一失败，那就"宁为玉碎，不为瓦全"。

6. swear to God 表示"对天发誓"。例：I swear to God I want you in my life. 我对上天发誓我需要你走进我的生命里来。

词汇加油站

weigh [weɪ] *vt.* 具有重要性
swear [swer] *v.* 发誓
escape [ɪ'skeɪp] *v.* 逃脱
fabricate ['fæbrɪkeɪt] *vt.* 捏造

dignity ['dɪgnəti] *n.* 尊严
insult [ɪn'sʌlt] *vt.* 侮辱
leverage ['levərɪdʒ] *n.* 优势
cadaver [kə'dævər] *n.* 尸体

时间： 第 1 集 00:06:27—00:07:16
地点： 小巷口
人物： 马霍，迈克尔，惠斯勒
事件： 迈克尔得知锡拉名单之事，惠斯勒遭暗杀。

精彩亮点

1
马霍跟迈克尔联系说知道莎拉的消息，两个人见面后，马霍想跟迈克尔找个隐秘一些的地方详谈，但迈克尔担心自己会中圈套，就跟马霍在码头人多的地方谈并得知苏珊已死的消息。因为公司头目得知苏珊拿来的是假芯片，于是便开枪杀死了她。

2
马霍跟迈克尔谈到了"锡拉名单"，这里面记录着公司所有特工的名字和他们执行的任务，因此，这个芯片对公司而言至关重要，也是马霍等人搞垮公司的重要渠道。他们现在需要迈克尔的帮助。

3
马霍的确不知道莎拉的消息，但惠斯勒知道，惠斯勒突然现身，希望迈克尔能与他们合作，真正的芯片现在就在惠斯勒手中。

4
惠斯勒表示读取这张芯片里的数据还需要进入一幢戒备森严的建筑，这也就是他们需要迈克尔帮助的原因。惠斯勒还没说完就被公司安排的特工一枪毙命，迈克尔和马霍见状赶紧逃跑，特工从惠斯勒的口袋中拿走了芯片。

Mahone: **Gretchen's dead.**☺₁ She never showed up①. Come and talk to me, please. Whistler and I were at that conference to get a data card②. It's like the company's black book③. And it lists all their agents, all their operations. They refer to it as "Scylla". Whistler's got it.

Michael: Alex, talk to me about Sara. That's all I care about④.

Mahone: I understand that. I want nothing more than⑤ to get home to my wife and my son. **But that does not gonna happen for either of us with the company out there trying to kill us.**☺₂

Michael: You don't know anything about Sara, do you?

Mahone: Whistler does. He tells me he does. And he wants to tell you. But He wants something in return⑥.

Michael: What? What does he want from me?

Mahone: To talk to you.

Whistler: **I'm sorry about all that the other night. If I had more time, I would've explained myself better.**☺₃

Michael: Sure. What are we doing here?

Whistler: Alex told you about Scylla?

Michael: Yes.

Whistler: I have it. There's one last step⑦ involved in order to read the data. **And that step involves breaking into a secure structure.**☺₄

····· 译文 ·····

马　霍：格雷琴死了，她不会出现了，跟我来谈谈吧。惠斯勒和我参加那个会议，取一张数据卡。那张卡就相当于公司的黑账本，里面列举了公司所有特工和任务。他们称之为"锡拉名单"，惠斯勒拿到了芯片。

迈克尔：亚历山大，跟我说说莎拉，我只关心她。

马　霍：我理解，我也只想回到我妻儿身边。但如果我们不阻止公司对我们的追杀，就别想如愿。

迈克尔：你是不是根本不知道莎拉的情况？

马　霍：惠斯勒知道，他告诉我说他知道。他想和你面谈，但他有条件。

迈克尔：什么？他想要从我这里得到什么？

马　霍：要你和他谈谈。

惠斯勒：对于那晚的事我很抱歉，要是我有更多的时间，我就能亲自跟你解释。

迈克尔：当然了，我们来这干什么？

惠斯勒：亚历山大跟你说"锡拉名单"了吧？

迈克尔：是的。

惠斯勒：这张卡在我手里，读取里面的数据还有最后一步，需要闯进一幢戒备森严的建筑里。

知识点拨

1. show up 表示"显而易见；到场，（使）看得见；羞辱"。例：There have been four hundred escapes this year, showing up the lack of security. 今年已发生 400 起越狱事件了，这充分显示了安全措施的不到位。

2. data card 表示"数据卡片，诸元记录卡"。例：I have a USB cell phone data card that I use with my laptop. 我有一个可连接我笔记本电脑 USB 接口的移动电话数据卡。

3. black book 表示"黑名册，可疑人物册"。例：The sheriff wants to put you in the black book. 警长已将你放入黑名单了。

4. care about sb./sth. 表示"关心，在乎，关怀；担忧"。例：You don't care about anything but yourself and your precious face. 你什么都不关心，除了你自己和你那张娇贵的脸。

5. nothing more than 表示"仅仅，只不过"。例：Locking up men does nothing more than keep them off the streets. 把这些人关起来只是做到了不让他们上街而已。

6. in return 表示"作为报答；反过来"。例：The deal offers an increase in policy value in return for giving up guarantees. 作为放弃担保的交换，这笔交易将提高保单价值。

7. one last step 表示"最后一步"。例：If migrants are to come, and stay, the government must take one last step. 如果移民潮涌入并安定下来，政府必须采取最后的行动。

 词汇加油站

conference [ˈkɑːnfərəns] *n.* 会议

operation [ˌɑːpəˈreɪʃn] *n.* 经营

explain [ɪkˈspleɪn] *vt.* 说明……的原因

secure [səˈkjʊr] *adj.* 安全的

list [lɪst] *vt.* 列出

refer [rɪˈfɜːr] *vt.* 提到

step [step] *n.* 步骤

structure [ˈstrʌktʃər] *n.* 建筑物

时间： 第 2 集 00:00:50—00:02:10
地点： 机场，基地
人物： 唐·塞尔夫，林肯，罗兰·格林
事件： 众人齐聚共同对抗公司，新成员格林加入。

精彩亮点

起初，迈克尔而并不愿意和塞尔夫合作，他只想找到莎拉后与她幸福地生活，但就在迈克尔和莎拉重逢后，怀亚特持枪冲入了他们的房间。随后迈克尔给塞尔夫打电话说他们同意做这单生意。

1

现在，为了拿到"锡拉名单"而召集的人马已经集合完毕：迈克尔、林肯、马霍、苏克雷、贝里克、莎拉等人再次踏上了逃生之旅。塞尔夫给每个人准备的 GPS 导航器是为了随时了解他们的去向，因为毕竟他们都是曾两次成功越狱的人。

2

迈克尔等人聚集在洛杉矶的一个基地中，政府为了掩饰这项任务，对外宣布他们被关押在国内一座最高戒备级别的监狱里，公司是否能发现这个秘密呢？

3

迈克尔等人进入基地后，却发现了一名新成员。他的到来令众人十分不满，那么这个叫格林的人到底有何来头呢？

4

Don Self: **Welcome to Los Angeles.** ☺1 It turns out, men who have escaped not one, but two penitentiaries, are considered a bit of a flight risk. So we need to know where you are and what you're doing <u>at all times</u>①. **These are GPS ankle monitors.** ☺2 Now <u>step up</u>②, take one and put it on.

Lincoln: I ain't wearing that.

Don Self: Let's <u>make this clear</u>③: I'm your <u>ally</u>, but more importantly, I'm your boss. Which means if this fails — it's my <u>ass on the line</u>④ as much, if not more, than yours? So from this point on, if I ask you to do something, you do it. If I ask you to say something, you say it. And if I ask you to put on a monitor — you put on a monitor. As far as the general public is concerned, you're being contained in a supermax facility somewhere in the United States. **So to avoid any messy explanations and stay off**⑤ **the company's radar — you need to keep your heads down and your ears open.** ☺3 We've provided cell phones, clothing, and toiletries — all the basic necessities to get you up and running.

Roland Glenn: **Hey, uh, you-you patted these guys down**⑥ **before you let them in, right?** ☺4 'Cause I can't be getting shanked or shivved.

译文

唐·塞尔夫： 欢迎各位来到洛杉矶！事实证明，各位都已经不只越狱过一次，而是两次了。为防止你们不安分我们要时刻了解你们身在何处，正在干什么。这些是GPS定位器，现在，每个人都过来拿一个，戴上。

林　　肯： 我是不会戴的。

唐·塞尔夫： 让我们把话说清楚：我是与你们一伙的，但更重要的是，我是你们的老板。这就表明如果搞砸了，得我兜着，我的麻烦比你们大。因此，从现在起，我让你们干什么，你们就乖乖照做！我让你们说什么，就乖乖地说！如果我让你们把定位器戴上，就都给我戴上！现在公众仍然以为你们都被关在一座全美戒备级别最高的监狱里。所以我不做过多解释，要避开公司的眼线耳目。你们得保持低调，提高警惕，我们为你们提供了手机、衣服、洗漱用品以及你们行动的必需品。

罗兰·格林： 喂，你让这些家伙进来之前都搜过身了吧？因为我可不想被暗算。

词汇加油站

penitehtiary [ˌpenɪˈtenʃəri] *n.* 监狱
monitor [ˈmɑːnɪtər] *n.* 监测仪
facility [fəˈsɪləti] *n.* 设备
radar [ˈreɪdɑːr] *n.* 雷达

ankle [ˈæŋkl] *n.* 踝
ally [ˈælaɪ] *n.* 联盟
messy [ˈmesi] *adj.* 麻烦的
toiletry [ˈtɔɪlətri] *n.* 洗漱用品

知识点拨

1. at all times 表示"随时，每时每刻；总是，一直"。例：The chalet was kept ready and waiting for them at all times. 小屋已收拾好随时迎接他们的到来。

2. step up 表示"走上前；（使）增加；（使）加快速度"。例：He urged donors to step up their efforts to send aid to Somalia. 他敦促各捐赠方加快速度将援助物资送往索马里。

3. make sth. clear 表示"说清楚，弄清楚，讲清楚，澄清"。例：I want to make it clear, however, that no one is untouchable in this investigation. 但我想说明白一点，这次调查谁都逃不了。

4. ass on the line 表示"两肋插刀"。例：I put my ass on the line for you. I know you'll do the same for me someday. 我为你两肋插刀，我知道有朝一日你也会为我这么做。

5. stay off 表示"不要上（路），远离（某地）"。例：You stay off their lawn, you little monkeys. 从草坪上下来，你这个小猴子。

6. pat down 表示"轻轻地拍平"。例：He walked out to pat down some bumps in the pitch. 他走出来拍平了沥青路上的一些疙瘩。

237

时间： 第2集 00:09:10—00:10:08

地点： 基地

人物： 林肯，罗兰，马霍，莎拉，苏克雷，贝里克

事件： 众人商议作战方法，罗兰作用凸显。

片段四

 精彩亮点

1 虽然迈克尔众人找到了公司的总部，然而那里防卫森严，他们根本没办法接近"锡拉名单"的持有者斯图尔特·塔克斯霍恩。众人陷入一片迷茫中。

2 就在大家愁眉不展的时候，罗兰的一句话吸引了他们的注意：不用偷这张卡，复制就行了。因为迈克尔等人起初不知道他的来历，所以执行任务时也完全不将其考虑在内，但罗兰有什么好办法吗？

3 一般人认为复制卡里的信息就必须先将卡偷出来，而且还要再把卡还回去，这无疑会更加困难。但罗兰也以讽刺的口吻告诉苏克雷：那是因为你们没有我的帮忙。

4 原来，罗兰是个电脑高手，他发明了一个无线装置，可吞噬任何离它十英尺内的电子数据。甚至可以在十分钟内拿到十个人的身份证和财务决算。这就意味着只要接近持卡人，无需偷卡就可以复制他所持卡片的信息。

Lincoln: What if we don't have to be in the house? If the card — this Scylla — is so important, maybe the guy is carrying it on him. ☺1

Sara: Well, according to public records①, the owner of the estate's name is Stuart Tuxhorn, and he's a CEO of a company called Spectroleum.

Mahone: Heavy hitter② like that's gonna have security 24-7.

Sara: And we gotta get this thing without anyone knowing it's gone, right? So even if he's got it on him, how do we get it off him?

Roland: You don't steal the card. You copy it. Oh, now you're interested in③ what I gotta say, right? ☺2

Sucre: Copying it will make it harder. Not only④ do you have to steal it, you have to return it, genius.

Roland: Only if⑤ you don't got me, hombre. ☺3

Lincoln: What's that?

Roland: This is the reason I got busted.

Bellick: Oh, you stole the cell phone?

Roland: Oh, yeah, yeah, no, I'm lookin' at federal time 'cause I stole a cell phone — seriously? I invented this so that I don't have to steal. It looks like a cell phone but it's really like a digital black hole⑥. ☺4

238

译文

林　肯：要是我们不必在房间里待着呢？如果这卡，这个"锡拉名单"，是如此重要，这个家伙有可能会随身带着它。

莎　拉：根据公共记录，这个房产的户名叫斯图尔特·塔克斯霍恩。他是一个名叫斯皮克托里姆公司的总裁。

马　霍：像他这种重量级人物，肯定有 24 小时全天候的贴身保安。

莎　拉：我们要在不让其他人发现它不见的情况下得到这东西，对吗？所以万一他随身携带，我们怎么能拿到手？

罗　兰：你们不用偷这张卡，复制就行了。哦，现在你们对我说的话感兴趣了对吧？

苏克雷：复制会更困难，你不仅要偷到手，还要还回去，天才。

罗　兰：那是在你们没有我的帮助下，你这个家伙。

林　肯：什么意思？

罗　兰：我就是因此被捕的。

贝里克：哦，你偷了这部手机？

罗　兰：哦，是啊，是啊，我要被判长期监禁，就因为偷了部手机，没开玩笑吧？我发明了这个，所以我不必去偷。它看起来像手机，但实际上它是一个数码黑洞。

 词汇加油站

estate [ɪ'steɪt] n. 房地产
steal [sti:l] vt. 偷
genius ['dʒi:nɪəs] n. 天才
bust [bʌst] vt. 突击搜查

 知识点拨

1. public record 表示"公共记录；政府机构；备案材料"。例：Those photos were culled out of the public record. 那些照片在公共记录中被抹去了。

2. heavy hitter 一般都用来指"既能干又成功的人才"。例：In this prison he is a heavy hitter. 在这个监狱里，他可是个举足轻重的人物。

3. be interested in sth. 表示"对……感兴趣，关心"。例：They haven't seen each other for five years; he might not be interested in her any more. 他们已经5年没有见面了，他或许对她不再感兴趣了。

4. not only…（but also…）前后连接两个句子时，not only 后的句子要用部分倒装，但 but also 后的分句不用倒装。例：Not only did he come, but he saw her. 他不仅来了，而且还见到了她。

5. only if 表示"除非，只要……就，只有当……"。例：I'll do that, but only if we set a few rules. 我可以干，但我们得定几条规矩。

6. black hole 表示"黑洞"，是现代广义相对论中，宇宙空间内存在的一种密度无限大体积无限小的天体。黑洞的引力很大，使得视界内的逃逸速度大于光速。

hitter ['hɪtər] n. 要员；大亨
copy ['kɑ:pi] vt. 复制
hombre ['ɑ:mbreɪ] n. 男人
digital ['dɪdʒɪtl] adj. 数字的

Scene 2 寻卡前路漫漫

时间： 第3集 00:08:11—00:09:09
地点： 基地
人物： 苏克雷，马霍，迈克尔，莎拉，罗兰，林肯
事件： 众人成功破译部分邮件，前往阿纳海姆寻找剩余邮件。

精彩亮点

1 莎拉提醒迈克尔锡拉这个词来源于《奥德赛》中的一种海妖，书中的主角奥德修斯必须牺牲他的六个同伴才能达到目标。这也就意味着锡拉并不只有一张卡，而是有六张卡，这就大大加大了任务的难度。

2 好不容易复制到了第一个持卡人卡中的信息，但罗兰在解码的时候出了差错，结果导致存储卡自动加密，最终他们只弄到了一些邮件和一点儿有用的信息。曾经在联邦调查局工作的马霍敏锐地感知邮件中可能隐含着某个密码。

3 根据马霍的这一提示，迈克尔等人破译了这些邮件隐含的密码，掌握了一个重要的信息：4点钟时，下一个持卡人将会出现并且和第一个持卡人德克斯霍恩接头。但是重要的是，他们会在哪里接头呢？马霍再一次提醒他们：作为秘密会面，肯定会将时间和地点分开发送。

4 在罗兰用计算机专业知识解释了一番后，得出的结论就是：迈克尔等人需要到阿纳海姆的邮件服务器主机去寻找这些邮件。

Sucre: Now, why would he get an e-mail about an arrival in London when he has no business scheduled there?☺1

Mahone: Probably because the e-mail is a code.☺2

Michael: Alex, I'm so glad you joined us. S-C-Y-L-L-A. Scylla, the meeting today at 4:00 is about Scylla. I think we can assume that Tuxhorn did not schedule a meeting① with himself, so that is where we're going to find our next cardholder.

Sara: Okay, so 4:00 p.m. is our when, we need a where.

Mahone: If you were having a secret meeting, you wouldn't send all the information together. You'd send the where and the when② separately as a precaution.☺3

Michael: Were any other e-mails sent to Tuxhorn, at the same time③ as the London e-mail?

Roland: Within a few seconds of the London mail, two more e-mails followed from the same IP④ path, but that's when my device ran out of⑤ hard drive⑥ space. It picked up the IP address, but not the content.

Lincoln: Trace the IP address and find out who sent these e-mails.

Roland: Oh, look, e-mails get bounced to routers all over the world before they end in your inbox. Wherever the mail's been, it leaves a shadow file⑦. Based on the geography, I'm guessing these e-mails probably squatted at the Anaheim server cluster a nanosecond before reaching Tuxhorn.☺4 So that's where you're going to find your shadow file.

240

译文

苏克雷： 那么如果他在伦敦没有商务安排，为何他会收到一封关于抵达伦敦的邮件呢？

马　霍： 或许是因为这封邮件本身就是个暗号。

迈克尔： 亚历克斯，我很高兴你能加入，S-C-Y-L-L-A。"Scylla"，今天4点的会议是与"Scylla"相关的。我想德克斯霍恩肯定不会和自己开会，所以这就是我们要找的下一个"持卡人"的地方。

莎　拉： 好，那我们知道时间是下午4点，地点呢？

马　霍： 如果你要开一个秘密会议，你不会把信息都放在一起发送。你会把时间和地点分开以防万一。

迈克尔： 还有没有其他有关伦敦的邮件是同时发给德克斯霍恩的？

罗　兰： 在第一封有关伦敦的邮件之后的几秒钟，又有两封邮件发自同一个IP路径，但那时我的设备正好没有空间了，只记录下IP地址，没有内容。

林　肯： 跟踪IP地址，看看是谁发的这些邮件。

罗　兰： 哦，看哪，电子邮件在世界各地的路由器上传送，然后才进到个人邮箱。不管邮件到过哪儿都会留下一个影子文件。从地理上看，我猜测这些邮件可能是在阿纳海姆的服务器上驻留过十亿分之一秒，然后再被德克斯霍恩收到的，那就是你们要去找影子文件的地方。

知识点拨

1. schedule a meeting 表示"安排会议"。例：I will call you early next week to schedule a meeting at your convenience. 下周早些时候我将打电话给您，约定一个在您方便的时候会面的时间。

2. where and when 表示"何时何地"。例：Before they left, they got the exactly news about where and when would the helicopter would land on. 在他们离开之前，他们获得了那架直升机将要降落的准确时间和地点。

3. at the same time 可以表示1）"同时，一齐"。表示两者以上的动作同时开始或进行，主要强调某一片刻时间；2）"但是，然而"。主要用于意义的转折，对刚才提到的情况从某一方面加以说明。

4. 网络之间互连的协议（IP）是 Internet Protocol 的缩写，中文简称"网协"。网络之间互连的协议也就是为计算机网络相互连接进行通信而设计的协议。

5. run out of 表示"用完，耗尽；从……跑出"。例：Fears that the world was about to run out of fuel proved groundless. 事实证明对于世界燃料即将耗尽的担忧毫无根据。

6. hard drive 表示"硬盘驱动器"。例：If the problem still occurs, your hard drive may be broken. 如果问题仍然出现，可能是你的硬盘驱动器坏了。

7. shadow file 表示"影子文件，影像文件"。例：The database, shadow file (where UNIX or LINUX systems keep their user passwords), or I/O stream needs to be read. 需要读取数据库、影子文件（UNIX 或 LINUX 系统保存用户密码的地方），或 I/O 流。

词汇加油站

code [koʊd] *n.* 密码

cardholder ['kɑːrdhoʊldər] *n.* 持有信用卡的人

device [dɪ'vaɪs] *n.* 设备

router ['raʊtər] *n.* 路由器

assume [ə'suːm] *v.* 认为

precaution [prɪ'kɔːʃn] *n.* 预防措施

bounce [baʊns] *vt.* 弹跳

inbox ['ɪnbɑːks] *n.* 收件箱

时间： 第3集 00:16:51—00:18:34
地点： 阿纳海姆机房
人物： 迈克尔，林肯，罗兰
事件： 迈克尔罗兰被困机房，林肯及时施救。

片段二

精彩亮点

众人前往阿纳海姆以破译其他邮件，找出持卡人的会面地点。莎拉冒充求职者，趁着前台人员不备偷走了他的工作卡，并把它交给了迈克尔。迈克尔和罗兰成功进入机房，但没想到工作人员发现其工作卡丢失，莎拉遇上了麻烦，迈克尔情急之下拉响了警报。

1

罗兰终于成功复制了邮件信息，但没想到他和迈克尔此时被困在机房里。因为拉响警报后，机房会自动启动保护装置，更糟糕的是，它会抽空机房内的空气。

2

罗兰作为一个宅男，很少运动，没过多长时间，他就因缺氧支撑不住而昏厥，迈克尔拨通了林肯的电话，等待林肯的支援。

3

拉响警报后，大楼内的人们都纷纷向室外跑去，林肯顺势从消防车里拿了一把锤子，径直走向机房，打破了机房的玻璃，迈克尔和罗兰终于获救。

4

Roland: Why won't the door open? What the hell [1] is that?☺1

Michael: It's a fail-safe [2] device, activated when the alarm gets pulled, to protect the server from fire damage [3].

Roland: Then why the hell did you pull it?☺2

Michael: This is an old building. It shouldn't have such an advanced system.

Roland: Oh, yeah? Well, clearly it does. Wha-Wha-What's it do?

Michael: To kill the fire. It sucks all the oxygen out of the room.

Lincoln: Michael, where the hell are you? It's getting crowded out here.

Michael: Linc, Linc, we're trapped.

Lincoln: What?

Michael: We're in the server room [4]. It's sealed. They're sucking all the oxygen out [5]. We've got… two, maybe three minutes of air left. Linc? Linc?

Roland: I can't breathe. I can't breathe.☺3

Michael: Calm down [6].You panic, it gets worse.

Lincoln: Come on. Let's go.☺4

译文

罗　兰：为什么门打不开？那是什么？

迈克尔：这是一个自动保护装置，警报拉响时会自动被激活，可以保护服务器不被火烧毁。

罗　兰：那你为什么拉警报？

迈克尔：这是一幢老建筑了。不应该有这么先进的系统啊！

罗　兰：是吗？很显然，这里就有。它有什么功能？

迈克尔：为了灭火，它会抽空房间里的氧气。

林　肯：迈克尔，你到底在哪里？外面的人越来越多了。

迈克尔：林肯，林肯，我们被困住了。

林　肯：什么？

迈克尔：我们在服务器机房，被封住了。氧气正在被吸走，我们只剩下……大约2到3分钟的空气。林肯？林肯？

罗　兰：我不能呼吸了，我不能呼吸了。

迈克尔：冷静，你要是恐慌的话，消耗的空气就越多。

林　肯：加把劲，我们走吧。

知识点拨

1. what the hell 表示"（用以加强语气或咒骂）究竟，到底"。例："What the hell's eating you？" he demanded. "到底什么事让你心烦啊？"他问道。

2. fail-safe 可做形容词，也可做名词，片中做形容词表示："自动防故障装置的"。例：A fail-safe backup system ensures reliable operation, even if a fault develops in the main circuit. 一个自动防故障装置的后备系统确保运转稳定，即使主要电路产生了故障。

3. fire damage 表示"火灾损失，火损"。例：The engineer's bullets deal additional fire damage and have a chance of setting their targets on fire. 工程师射出的子弹有额外的火焰伤害，并有可能将目标点燃。

4. server room 表示"服务器机房，服务器室"。例：They will, obviously, take care of hardware and server room needs. 显然，这些服务将负责满足硬件和服务器机房的需求。

5. suck out 表示"吸出"。例：They land on you, bite you, suck out some blood and leave behind an itchy welt. 它们飞到你的身上，咬你、吸你的血，然后给你留下痒痕。

6. calm down 表示"（使）平静，镇静，安静"。例：Calm down for a minute and listen to me. 你安静一会儿，听我说。

 词汇加油站

activate ['æktɪveɪt] *vt.* 触发

pull [pʊl] *vt.* 拉

suck [sʌk] *vt.* 吸入

seal [si:l] *v.* 密封

alarm [ə'lɑːrm] *n.* 警报

server ['sɜːrvər] *n.* 服务器

trap [træp] *vt.* 困住

panic ['pænɪk] *v.* （使）惊慌

时间： 第 4 集 00:05:24—00:07:30

地点： 仓库，车里

片段三

人物： 林肯，迈克尔，罗兰，贝里克，马霍，莎拉，塞尔夫，苏克雷

事件： 持卡人跟丢，莎拉得知布鲁斯死讯。

精彩亮点

苏克雷带着一名锡拉存储卡拥有者的车牌号照片找到了迈克尔。罗兰查出这个人名叫埃罗·塔巴克，于是，众人开始了新一轮的"夺卡"行动。

1

他们找到持卡人后，罗兰却告诉他们信号丢失了。先前，他们以为锡拉存储卡一定在埃罗身上，可没想到，这张卡其实在埃罗的妻子手里。

2

当众人得知他们要集齐六张卡时，贝里克深感绝望，他告诉苏克雷成功的机会不大，想让他和自己现在先离开道奇，等过了边境后再想办法解决脚踝上的监控器。苏克雷当然不会同意，但监听他们的罗兰却对贝里克的提议十分感兴趣。

3

公司派怀亚特寻找迈克尔和林肯的下落。怀亚特得知是布鲁斯保释了迈克尔众人后，潜入布鲁斯家，给他注射了一只又一只致迷幻的药物，布鲁斯一直坚持到了最后，终因神志不清而说出了莎拉现在身处洛杉矶的事实。最终，布鲁斯被怀亚特残忍杀害。

4

Lincoln: That's the wife? Sign me up ①. ☺1

Roland: You lost it.

Michael: How?

Roland: Dude ②, I don't know what to tell you other than ③ you lost it. It's gone, man.

Michael: We lost it.

Sucre: What?

Lincoln: How did we lose him? We're right next to him. ☺2

Michael: He's not the cardholder. She is.

Mahone: We gotta get out of here now before we get made. Come on, go! Go!

Roland: You know what we've got in common ④, right?

Bellick: What?

Roland: We both live in the real world as opposed to ⑤ these other knuckleheads. So that whole prior planning thing you were talking about, if you got something on your mind and no one else is interested, you just run it by me, okay? ☺3 And we'll just leave it at that. All right.

Sara: Hello?

Self: Sara? Hey, it's Don Self. Listen, um, I have some bad news. Bruce Bennett was found dead ⑥ in his apartment this morning. I'm sorry. ☺4

译文

林　肯：那是他的妻子？算我一个。

罗　兰：信号没了。

迈克尔：怎么会？

罗　兰：哥们儿，我不知道该跟你们说什么，但信号就是没了。

迈克尔：信号没了。

苏克雷：什么？

林　肯：怎么会跟丢呢？我们就在他旁边啊。

迈克尔：他并不是"持卡人"，她才是。

马　霍：我们得离开这儿，不然就要被逮住了。快点儿，走！走！

罗　兰：你们知道我们的共同之处是什么吗？

贝里克：什么？

罗　兰：我们都生活在现实世界中，和其他那些傻瓜们完全不同。你刚才说到的先前计划什么的，如果你有什么主意但却没人感兴趣，记得找我，好吗？我们先这么说好，怎么样？

莎　拉：喂？

塞尔夫：莎拉吗？嘿，是我，唐·塞尔夫。听着，呃，我有些坏消息要告诉你。布鲁斯·班尼特今早被发现死于他的寓所内。我很抱歉。

知识点拨

1. sign up 表示"报名；跟……签订合同"。例：He saw the song's potential, and persuaded the company to sign her up. 他看到了这首歌的潜力，就说服公司和她签约。

2. dude 于 1883 年首次在英国使用，指的是"衣着过于光鲜亮丽的人物。这也就是为何在辞典里面经常译作"花花公子"的原因。不过目前，dude 一词是美国乃至世界最常用的称呼词之一，可以广泛地指代任何人。

3. other than 表示"除了；不同于；绝不是"。例：There are similar charges if you want to cash a cheque at a branch other than your own. 如果你想在开户行以外的网点兑现支票，也要收取类似的费用。

4. in common 表示"共有，共同"。例：We happened to discover we had a friend in common. 我们凑巧发现我们有一个共同的朋友。

5. as opposed to 表示"和……相反；而不是；与……相对"。例：The market for a cash commodity or actual, as opposed to its futures contract. 现货商品市场，与期货合约市场相反。

6. be found dead 表示"被发现死亡"。例：A seven-year-old boy was found dead after a landslide engulfed a block of flats. 山体滑坡掩埋了一栋公寓楼，造成一名 7 岁男孩丧生。

 词汇加油站

wife [waɪf] *n.* 妻子

cardholder ['kɑ:rdhoʊldər] *n.*（持卡可获得某种权利的）持卡人

common ['kɑ:mən] *adj.* 共有的

knucklehead ['nʌklhed] *n.* 傻瓜

apartment [ə'pɑ:rtmənt] *n.* 寓所

sign [saɪn] *vt.* 打手势

opposed [ə'poʊzd] *adj.* 相反的

prior ['praɪər] *adj.* 先前的

片段四

时间： 第 4 集 00:10:02—00:10:47
地点： 大街上
人物： 迈克尔，林肯，帝博格
事件： 迈克尔兄弟遇见帝博格，向帝博格索要鸟类指南。

精彩亮点

当迈克尔，林肯等人等候埃罗的老婆时，他们在街对面发现了帝博格，并随即追赶他。狡猾的帝博格这次能否逃脱兄弟二人的夹击呢？

1

迈克尔深知惠斯勒的那本鸟类指南在帝博格手里，所以，他们不能杀了他。当初，惠斯勒和迈克尔等人在索纳监狱成功越狱时不慎遗落了他的这本指南，恰巧被眼尖的帝博格拾起。

2

帝博格一直对迈克尔怀恨在心，迈克尔多次将帝博格逼至绝境，对关在索纳监狱的他更是不予施救。最终，帝博格一把火烧了索纳监狱后，成功与贝里克和苏克雷逃脱。

3

令林肯兄弟没想到的是，就在林肯逮到帝博格之后，警察也盯上了他们。于是，兄弟俩人只能放弃继续逼问帝博格鸟类指南的线索，四散而去。

4

T-Bag: Well, if it ain't the Brothers Grim. ☺1

Michael: Easy, Linc. Remember, we need him. ☺2 What are you doing in Los Angeles?

T-Bag: I was thinking about① maybe getting me a career in pictures. Hey! If anyone's got a right to② be pissed, it's me. **You put me out③ to pasture back in Panama. Left me for dead.** ☺3 Which makes it the third time, I believe. So, congratulations, you got yourself a turkey.

Lincoln: Where's the bird book?

T-Bag: Bird book?

Lincoln: Where's the book?

T-Bag: Ooh, look who's looking, pretty. Look who's looking. I don't think the two of you are supposed to be carousing around Angel City any more than I am.

Michael: You don't know what you've gotten yourself into④, Teddy. But if you don't want to find out, you're gonna tell us where that bird book is.

T-Bag: You're gonna let me go right now or all of us are going down⑤ together. Your choice.

Michael: Linc, come on. Let's go, Linc! ☺4

译文

帝博格：要不是因为你们有两个人。

迈克尔：冷静，林肯。记住，我们需要他。你在洛杉矶干什么？

帝博格：我想我或许能在电影业给自己谋个职。嘿！要是说谁最有权发怒的话，那应该是我！你把我扔在巴拿马监狱的草地上，让我在那儿等死，我想那已经是第三次了。所以，恭喜你们，你们可把我惹毛了！

林　肯：那本鸟类指南在哪儿？

帝博格：鸟类指南？

林　肯：那本书在哪儿？

帝博格：噢，看看谁在往这儿看呢，帅哥。看看谁在看我们。我想你们两个人此刻在天使之城并不比我自由。

迈克尔：你都不知道自己被卷进了怎样的麻烦里，泰迪。但如果你不想找麻烦的话，就告诉我们那本鸟类指南的书在哪儿。

帝博格：你们现在就得让我走，否则大家一起玩儿完，你自己选。

迈克尔：林肯，快走！我们走，林肯！

知识点拨

1. think about 表示"考虑……；捉摸……；对……有（某种观点）；回想起……"。例：I told him I'd have to think about that one. 我告诉他那个问题我必须考虑一下。

2. get / have a right to do sth. 表示"有权做某事"。例：The Baltic people get a right to determine their own future. 波罗的海各国人民有权决定自己的未来。

3. put sb. out 表示"因某事给某人带来麻烦；某人感到紧张；使某人昏迷不醒"。例：I shall stop till such time as I think fit to go, unless you send for assistance to put me out. 反正我来到了这里，什么时候想走我才走，除非你找人把我赶出去。

4. get into 表示"进入；陷入；养成"。例：What has got into you today? Why are you behaving like this? 你今天疯了吗？为什么要这样做呢？

5. go down 表示"停止；被接受；沉下；被打败"。例：They went down 2-1 to Australia. 他们以 1 比 2 输给了澳大利亚队。

词汇加油站

grim [grɪm] *adj.* 冷酷的

pasture ['pæstʃər] *n.* 牧场

turkey ['tɜːrki] *n.* 蠢货

angel ['eɪndʒl] *n.* 天使

career [kə'rɪr] *n.* 生涯；职业

congratulation [kən,grætʃu'leɪʃn] *n.* 祝贺

carouse [kə'raʊz] *vi.* 痛饮

choice [tʃɔɪs] *n.* 选择

Scene 3 收集锡拉芯片

片段一

时间： 第 5 集 00:09:43—00:10:27

地点： 仓库，大街上

人物： 迈克尔，塞尔夫，林肯，莎拉

事件： 读取奥伦锡拉卡信息失败，莎拉被怀亚特跟踪。

精彩亮点

1 迈克尔等人通过放大图像识别剩余的持卡人。塞尔夫看到其中一个名叫奥伦的人与他在同一幢大楼里工作，他是财政部洛杉矶办公室的头儿。迈克尔打算想办法打开奥伦的保险柜，复制数据。

2 先前迈克尔计划让塞尔夫以不记名债券被盗为由接近奥伦，塞尔夫硬着头皮找到奥伦，但奥伦也狡猾得很，称自己要马上离开去亚洲开会，让塞尔夫直接找他的助理，所以，此次行动失败了。

3 迈克尔许久没有见到莎拉，不由得有些担心。他打电话给莎拉，莎拉告诉迈克尔自己被跟踪了。那么，跟踪莎拉的人到底是谁呢？

4 根据莎拉的描述——高个子，黑人，大胡子，马霍马上明白是谁在跟踪莎拉了，他就是那个残忍地杀死马霍儿子的杀手——怀亚特。

Michael: We had it for two seconds and then it disappeared. ☺1

Self: It's in the safe. He has this crazy safe in his office. That must have been blocking the transmission. I'll bet you that's where he keeps the card.

Michael: So we need to get into that safe.

Self: Trust me, there's no way ① to crack that thing. ☺2 Look, I'll have the enhanced images ② of the other cardholders in a couple of hours — we'll go from there.

Michael: You can access the building's blueprints, right?

Self: I can't go back up there.

Michael: No one's asking you. We'll take care of ③ that.

Self: Come on, you'll never get past ④ the front door, okay? Even if they don't recognize you, you need a security card that matches…

Michael: Get the blueprints and get back here, all right?

Self: Yeah…

Michael: Sara, what happened?

Sara: I'm fine, but someone was following me. ☺3 I lost him about a mile back. I don't think there's any way he could have followed me here. I made sure of ⑤ that.

Lincoln: What'd he look like ⑥?

Sara: Uh, tall, black. He had a beard. ☺4

译文

迈克尔：我们刚复制了两秒，信号就没了。

塞尔夫：卡在保险柜里，他的办公室里有个保险柜，保险柜一定阻隔了信号传输，我可以肯定卡就在保险柜里。

迈克尔：那我们就得去打开保险柜。

塞尔夫：相信我，这比登天都难。听着，我几个小时内就可以拿到另外几个持卡人的放大影像——我们从那里下手吧。

迈克尔：你可以拿到大楼的设计图，对吧？

塞尔夫：我不能再上楼去了。

迈克尔：没人让你去，我们会负责的。

塞尔夫：得了吧，你连正门都进不去，好吗？即使他们没有认出你，你还需要安保卡……

迈克尔：拿设计图回来，好吗？

塞尔夫：好……

迈克尔：莎拉，发生什么事了？

莎 拉：我很好，不过，我被人跟踪了。我把他甩了有一英里远，我保证他肯定不会找到咱们。

林 肯：他长什么样？

莎 拉：啊，高个头，黑人，大胡子。

知识点拨

1. there's no way 表示"做某事肯定没戏"。例：There's no way we can afford to buy a house at the moment. 眼下我们无论如何也买不起房子。

2. enhanced image 表示"增强图像"。例：In the embedded video image processing system, there are two key issues, quality of the enhanced image and speed of the image-processing, which decide the efficiency of the algorithm. 在嵌入式视频图像处理系统中，图像增强后的效果和图像增强的实时性是决定算法优劣的两个关键问题。

3. take care of 表示"照顾；杀掉；对付；抵消"。例：They leave it to the system to try and take care of the problem. 他们让系统去设法解决这个问题。

4. get past 表示"越过，（使）通过；（时间）超过；超出（某人）的能力"。例：He was never able to get past the border guards. 他从未能够通过边防哨兵的检查。

5. make sure of 表示"确定，确保"。例：He had stopped to catch his breath and make sure of his directions. 他曾停下来歇口气，同时确定一下方向。

6. look like 表示"看起来与（某人或某物）相像/相似；很可能出现/引起（某事、做某事）"。例：You look like a nice upstanding young man. 你看起来像是一个正直的好青年。

 词汇加油站

disappear [ˌdɪsəˈpɪr] vt. 消失

crazy [ˈkreɪzi] adj. 疯狂的；不理智的；离奇的

transmission [trænsˈmɪʃn] n. 传送

enhanced [ɪnˈhænst] adj. 放大的

safe [seɪf] n. 保险箱

block [blɑːk] vt. 阻止

crack [kræk] vt. （使……）开裂

blueprint [ˈbluːprɪnt] n. 设计图

时间： 第 5 集 00:26:00—00:27:36

地点： 山姆办公室，仓库

人物： 迈克尔，林肯，莎拉，罗兰

事件： 迈克尔流鼻血引林肯担心。

精彩亮点

复制奥伦锡拉卡信息失败后，迈克尔等人重新思考对策：山姆的办公室与奥伦的相邻，塞尔夫借与他谈话的机会，邀他共进午餐。迈克尔和林肯进入山姆办公室执行计划，留贝里克和苏克雷在外看守。

1

迈克尔再一次流鼻血了，这不由得让林肯担心。虽然迈克尔嘴上说着这只是炎热气候导致，但他内心也很担心，因为他的母亲就是在他这个年龄去世的。

2

莎拉在团队中表现出卓越的细节观察能力，她发现丽萨·塔巴克要前往老挝，而且奥伦也要前往亚洲，这难道是巧合吗？当然不是，因为奥伦的目的地也是老挝。

3

迈克尔和林肯打穿了山姆办公室的墙壁，看到了墙壁另一侧奥伦保险柜中的锡拉芯片。但他们没有想到的是，将军此时也来到了奥伦的办公室，要亲自查看奥伦是否妥善保管了锡拉芯片。

4

Michael: The safe should be somewhere behind this wall. ☺1 As soon as① you're through the steel, I'll have the thermite ready. What is it②?

Lincoln: How long has it been happening? ☺2

Michael: It's not a big deal.③

Lincoln: It was a big deal when you were 13.

Michael: Just promise me you won't tell Sara.

Lincoln: Sara's a doctor. She can help.

Michael: Look, I acclimating to④ the warmer climate, all right? Come on. We've got work to do. Let's go.

Roland: I don't know what this company is up to⑤, but it sure sounds like there's a whole lot of⑥ money involved.

Sara: I don't know. Lisa Tabak just hopped a flight to Laos, didn't she? ☺3

Roland: Yeah, I guess.

Sara: And now Griffin Oren just said he was going somewhere in Asia.

Lincoln: Down to the cobalt. ☺4

Michael: Right.

译文

迈克尔：保险箱应该就在墙后面，等你弄穿了钢板，我就准备好铝热剂。怎么了？

林　肯：你流鼻血多久了？

迈克尔：没什么大不了的。

林　肯：你从 13 岁开始就很严重了。

迈克尔：你只要答应我不会告诉莎拉就行。

林　肯：莎拉是医生，她能帮上忙。

迈克尔：听着，我只是在适应炎热的气候，好吗？快点儿，我们还有活要干，走吧。

罗　兰：我不知道公司到底有什么目的，但可以肯定的是好像有一大笔钱要进来。

莎　拉：我不知道。丽萨·塔巴克刚上了去老挝的飞机？

罗　兰：我想是这样的。

莎　拉：格里芬·奥伦刚说过他要去亚洲。

林　肯：到层了。

迈克尔：好的。

知识点拨

1. as soon as 表示"一……就……"。例：As soon as I had made the final decision, I felt a lot more relaxed. 我一作出最后的决定就感到轻松多了。

2. What is it? 表示"怎么回事？出什么事了？"例：What is it then? Something's up, isn't it? 那是怎么回事呢？出问题了，是吗？

3. a big deal 表示"要人；重要人物；重要的事"。例：I felt the pressure on me, winning was such a big deal for the whole family. 我感觉到了压力，赢得胜对全家来说是如此重要。

4. acclimate to 表示"适应"。例：She was fine once she had acclimated herself to the cold. 她习惯了寒冷以后身体立即就好了。

5. be up to 表示"胜任；从事于"。例：The exercises in this chapter can guide you, but it will be up to you to do the actual work. 这一章的练习能给你指导，但实际的工作还得靠你自己完成。

6. a whole lot of 表示"一大堆，许多的"。例：Pour a whole lot of cold water over the rice, and bung it in the oven. 往米中倒入大量凉水，然后放在炉子上。

词汇加油站

steel [stiːl] *n.* 钢

deal [diːl] *n.* （一笔）交易

acclimate ['æklɪmeɪt] *v.* 使服水土

hop [hɑːp] *vt.* 登上（飞机）

thermite ['θɜːrmɪt] *n.* 铝热剂

promise ['prɑːmɪs] *vt.* 允诺

climate ['klaɪmət] *n.* 气候

cobalt ['koʊbɔːlt] *n.* 钴类颜料

时间： 第 6 集 00:07:25—00:08:35

地点： 赛马场

片段三

人物： 罗兰，迈克尔，马霍，莎拉，保镖

事件： 第三张锡拉芯片复制成功，莎拉设计拖延。

 精彩亮点

现在，迈克尔他们准备对第四位持卡人艾迪森下手，艾迪森对赛马十分感兴趣，把注押在了神奇小子身上，但林肯已经在 8 号门处做了手脚，神奇小子的马被卡在了那里，愤怒的艾迪森前去找经理谈话，而马霍和迈克尔也在之前潜入经理办公室做好了接收数据的准备。**1**

因为刚才神奇小子出来的时候门被卡住而使许多人输掉了赌注，大厅混乱不堪，警察也随之而至，马霍为迈克尔垫后，伺机趁乱而逃。**2**

莎拉漂亮地打扮一番后试图接近艾迪森的保镖，让他放松戒备，从而可以帮助马霍从他背后的门进入到经理的办公室，因为他要把收集的数据芯片回收。**3**

保镖显然对莎拉的话表现出不耐烦，莎拉见到马霍已成功潜入，于是便离开了。但马霍还需要从经理办公室出来，他能否安全脱身呢？**4**

Roland: 100%. We're all there. ☺₁ Card's all there. You've never jerked a loser before. It's all your fault! We're gonna need some backup.

Michael: Here come the cops. **You'd better go**① **before you get recognized.** ☺₂

Mahone: Someone has to be lookout. I'll take care of it. Go! Go! All right, break it up, guys. Let's go! That's enough.

Sara: Hi, there.② ☺₃ Um, excuse me. I was wondering if you could help me. I placed a bet③ on SparkleKid for my boss. Do you know what happened?

Bodyguard: Not right now, sweetheart.

Sara: Okay. My boss had me put more money on him than I make in a week. Um, he's gonna flip out④ when I tell him about this.

Bodyguard: I'm really not the right person to ask.

Sara: Okay, but, here, I put $500 here for Orca's Revenge. Maybe I could…

Bodyguard: You're gonna have to talk to one of the window clerks.

Sara: But maybe I could add it to that?

Bodyguard: Look, I…I can't help you, all right? Now, move it along⑤, honey.

Sara: Okay, um, listen. I'm just trying to ask you a couple⑥ questions.

Bodyguard: Yeah, well, you asked one too many. ☺₄

译文

罗 兰： 100% 搞定了，卡已到手。没见过你这么笨的，这都是你的错！我们需要些支援。

迈克尔： 警察过来了，你最好在被认出前赶快离开。

马 霍： 必须留人在这盯着，我会搞定的。走！快走！好了，别打了，同志们。我们走吧！行了。

莎 拉： 嗨！那边的。呃，不好意思。不知道你是否能帮我个忙，我帮老板在神奇小子上下注。你知道刚才发生了什么事吗？

保 镖： 小姐，现在不大方便。

莎 拉： 好吧，我老板让我在他身上下的钱比我一周赚的还多。呃，如果我告诉他这事估计他会疯掉。

保 镖： 你真不该问我。

莎 拉： 好吧，但我在这里下了 500 美元在复仇虎鲸上，或许我可以……

保 镖： 你必须要去和窗口的工作人员说。

莎 拉： 或许我可以再在那上面加注？

保 镖： 听着，我……我无法帮你，好吗？现在，走开点儿吧，小姐。

莎 拉： 好吧，呃，听着，我只是想问你一些问题而已。

保 镖： 是啊，你的问题太多了。

知识点拨

1. You'd better do sth. 意为"你最好做什么事"。例：You had better clean your room. 你最好打扫一下你的房间。

2. Hi, there. 是用来打招呼的，基本可以与"How are you doing？"等同，只是更简洁，更加口语化。不适用于正式场合，并且严格讲不适用于晚辈对长辈、下级对上级打招呼。

3. place a bet 表示"下赌注"。例：He went down to the bookmaker's in Chesterton road to place a bet on the race. 他到切斯特顿路上的赛马会对比赛下了赌注。

4. flip out 表示"精神失常，发疯"。例：Because I know he's going to flip out and I hate it when he gets angry. 因为我知道他一定会为此而抓狂，我不想他发怒。

5. move along 表示"（使）往前走，（使）走开"。例：Our officers are moving them along and not allowing them to gather in large groups. 我们的警察正让他们离开，不允许他们大批集结。

6. a couple 可以表示"一对；一双"，也可以表示"几个"。例：I almost lasted the two weeks. I only had a couple of days to do. 我几乎撑过了这两个星期，我只有几天时间去做。

词汇加油站

jerk [dʒɜːrk] *vt.* 猛拉

lookout ['lʊkaʊt] *n.* 警戒

flip [flɪp] *vi.* 蹦蹦跳跳

honey ['hʌni] *n.* 可爱的人

backup ['bækʌp] *n.* 支持

sweetheart ['swiːthɑːrt] *n.* 情人

clerk [klɜːrk] *n.* 办事员

couple ['kʌpl] *n.* 几个人；几件事物

时间： 第6集 00:13:16—00:14:10

地点： 走廊

片段四

人物： 塞尔夫，林肯，布雷恩，迈克尔

事件： 马霍被捕，塞尔夫办公室遭审查。

精彩亮点

马霍正欲离开经理办公室却看到了警察，他向警察解释自己押注失败要经理给自己一个说法，没想到警察对着对讲机说请求支援，马霍被警察围困被捕。

1

马霍手中拿着拷贝了第四位持卡人艾迪森锡拉芯片信息的手机设备，如果他被捕，很有可能这部设备也会被没收，到时，他们的一切努力都将付诸东流。

2

将军的助理先前告知他有人在国安局对他进行了大范围调查，那个人名叫塞尔夫。于是，塞尔夫引起了将军的注意，他随即命令手下调查塞尔夫调查他到底有何目的。

3

林肯给塞尔夫打过电话后，告诉他马霍被捕的消息，塞尔夫并没有给他明确回复。但大家认为既然塞尔夫能把他们这些犯有重罪的人弄出来，就肯定有办法将马霍也弄出来。于是，迈克尔等人开始着手寻找下一位持卡人。

4

Self: What do you mean he got arrested? W… What happened? ☺₁

Lincoln: It's a long story①, but we need you to get Mahone and the device out. ☺₂ Can you do that?

Self: What, what do you think, that every time you guys screw up②, I can just magically make things disappear?

Lincoln: We ain't interested in your excuses. Can you do it or not?

Self: Lincoln, y-you know what? I'll call you back. Excuse me. Who are you? What is this?

Brian: I'm Brian. I work in the IT department. We were getting some registry inconsistencies on the server, so… I'm just running a few routine spot checks③. ☺₃

Self: So you just barge in④ here without asking?

Brain: I have level two clearance. See? It's what I do. I go into people's offices, I fix their computers. I just figured it was better to do it when you weren't here.

Self: Well, you know what? You got to go. Don't come back in here.

Brain: Sure thing⑤. You're all set⑥.

Michael: So what's the word⑦?

Lincoln: Self's on it. ☺₄

译文

塞尔夫： 什么叫他被逮了？发……发生什么事了？

林　肯： 说来话长，但我们需要你把马霍和设备都带出来。你可以做到吗？

塞尔夫： 什么？你以为每次你们这些人把事情搞砸后，我都能奇迹般地把烂摊子收拾掉吗？

林　肯： 我们不想听借口，你到底能不能办到？

塞尔夫： 林肯，你……你知道吗？我等会再给你打回来。不好意思，你是哪位？你这是在做什么？

布雷恩： 我是布雷恩，在信息技术部门工作。我们发现服务器数据库有些问题，所以……我只是来例行公事抽样检查。

塞尔夫： 那你就可以未经询问私自闯入？

布雷恩： 我有二级出入准许证，看见了吗？这就是我的工作。我进入别人的办公室，帮他们修理电脑。我只是想你不在这儿的话会更方便。

塞尔夫： 呃，你知道吗？你得离开。别再来这儿了。

布雷恩： 当然。我全搞定了。

迈克尔： 那么他说什么？

林　肯： 塞尔夫正在想办法。

知识点拨

1. a long story 表示"一个漫长的故事，说来话长"。例：To cut a long story short, I ended up as managing director. 长话短说，我最终当上了总经理。

2. screw up 表示"拧紧；扭歪（脸）；把……搞糟"。例：Somebody had screwed up; they weren't there. 有人把事情搞砸了；他们没在那里。

3. spot check 表示"抽样调查，抽查"。例：I'd like to conduct a spot check of your cash and your transactions for today. 我想对您的现金和您今天的业务情况进行一次现场检查。

4. barge in 表示"闯入，干涉"。例：I'm sorry to barge in like this, but I have a problem I hope you can solve. 很抱歉这样打扰您，但是我有个问题希望您能解决。

5. sure thing 表示"是的，当然"。例：Sure thing, boss. I have them right here. 老板，没问题。就在我这儿，都弄好了。

6. all set 表示"一切准备就绪"。例：Our plans for the new company are all set. 我们开设新公司的计划已准备好了。

7. What's the word? 通常用于某人询问对方另一方给自己带了什么话。

词汇加油站

arrest [əˈrest] *vt.* 逮捕

screw [skruː] *vt.* 扭曲

excuse [ɪkˈskjuːz] *n.* 借口

inconsistency [ˌɪnkənˈsɪstənsi] *n.* 不一致

device [dɪˈvaɪs] *n.* 设备

magically [ˈmædʒɪkli] *adv.* 如魔法般地

registry [ˈredʒɪstri] *n.* 登记

routine [ruːˈtiːn] *n.* 例行程序

Scene 4 苏珊再次登场

时间： 第 7 集 00:01:55—00:03:21
地点： 原惠斯勒公寓
人物： 帝博格，苏珊
事件： 苏珊遇见帝博格，逼其交代锡拉事宜。

精彩亮点

1 眼看帝博格在 GATE 公司假冒科尔·费福尔的事就要被揭穿，他慌忙收拾东西跑回公寓，不想被等候在那里的苏珊一拳击倒在地。

2 帝博格还在编造谎言试图瞒过苏珊，但他没想到的是苏珊以前和惠斯勒共事，怎会不知他说的是谎话？反而帝博格说出锡拉一词时立即引起了苏珊的注意，毕竟锡拉是公司的机密，但他一个外人又怎会知晓？

3 帝博格手中的筹码就是惠斯勒的鸟类指南，他根据这本指南，找到了惠斯勒的公寓，借用了他的化名，混进 GATE 公司，也是根据这本指南，他得知了锡拉的存在，并察觉到这本书背后潜藏的巨大利益。

4 苏珊单刀直入地告诉帝博格她要得到锡拉，并开始在帝博格的手臂上划了一刀，逼迫他选择与自己合作，否则就只有死路一条。

Susan: You have 30 seconds to tell me something that I don't already know. ☺₁

T-Bag: I followed that book from Panama city, where James Whistler and I were co-incarcerated, to a bus locker in San Diego. Inside was information pertaining to ① this apartment. Scylla. How about that? ☺₂ That ring a bell ②, huh?

Susan: What do you know about Scylla?

T-Bag: I know I'm holding the keys, because without me, that bird book's about as meaningful as a fart in a wind storm. ☺₃ I commandeered Whistler's alias ③. I infiltrated his place of business because it's the gateway to the whole damn thing.

Susan: Where's the location?

T-Bag: What do you bring to the jamboree, darling, huh?

Susan: Aside from ④ those baby blues and a knife? This is me. This is Scylla. This is you. ☺₄ I am gonna get Scylla. And it can either be with you or ⑤ through you. So why don't you give me that informed decision right now, before I spill your hillbilly guts all over ⑥ the carpet?

译文

苏 珊：你现在有三十秒的时间告诉我一些我还不知道的事。

帝博格：我在巴拿马城时就开始追踪那本书，我和詹姆斯•惠斯勒在圣地亚哥都被关在一辆巴士上。书里面讲的是关于这个公寓的一些信息……锡拉。这个信息怎么样？这个总有些用吧，啊？

苏 珊：关于锡拉你都知道什么？

帝博格：我知道我握着钥匙，因为没有我的话，那本鸟类指南就像在风中放了个屁一样毫无意义。我借用了惠斯勒的化名，潜入了他做生意的地方，因为那是搞定这件破事的途径。

苏 珊：地点在哪儿？

帝博格：亲爱的，你带了些什么来参加这次狂欢？啊？

苏 珊：除了你的蓝衬衫和一把刀？这是我，这是锡拉，而你在中间。我要拿到锡拉，要么和你一起拿到……要么直接用匕首穿过你拿到。所以，你为什么不直接告诉我你现在的决定呢？趁我还没把你那恶心的内脏都挖出来扔得满地都是？

知识点拨

1. pertain to 表示"属于；关于"。例：I would much rather that you asked Mrs Zuckerman any questions pertaining to herself. 我宁愿你问楚克尔曼夫人的是与她本人相关的问题。

2. ring a bell 表示"听起来熟悉，（心里）有印象"。例：Justin told me I've met his sister before, but her name doesn't ring a bell. 贾斯汀告诉我，我之前曾见过他的姐妹，但是我对她的名字没有印象。

3. alias 表示"别名，化名"。例：Using an alias, he had rented a house in Fleet, Hampshire. 他用化名在汉普郡的舰队街租了间房子。

4. aside from 表示"除……之外；既……又……；暂置不论"。例：Your talk is a little aside from the subject of our discussion. 你的发言稍微偏离了我们讨论会的主题。

5. either... or... 意为"或者……或者……；不是……就是……"，表示两者之一，连接句子中两个并列的成分。either... or... 连接两个主语时，其谓语动词应与最近的一个主语在人称和数上保持一致。

6. all over 表示"到处，周遍，浑身"。例：She has created a style of music that has delighted audiences all over the world. 她创造出了一种能令全世界的听众都感到快乐的音乐风格。

词汇加油站

incarcerate [ɪnˈkɑːrsəreɪt] *vt.* 监禁

pertain [pərˈteɪn] *vi.* 从属

commandeer [ˌkɑːmənˈdɪr] *vt.* 征用

gateway [ˈɡeɪtweɪ] *n.* 入口

hillbilly [ˈhɪlbɪli] *n.* 乡巴佬

locker [ˈlɑːkər] *n.* 寄物柜

meaningful [ˈmiːnɪŋfl] *adj.* 有意义的

infiltrate [ˈɪnfɪltreɪt] *vt.* （使）悄悄进入

jamboree [ˌdʒæmbəˈriː] *n.* 狂欢活动

时间： 第7集 00:09:21—00:11:23
地点： 公寓
片段二
人物： 帝博格，迈克尔
事件： 帝博格抓住迈克尔，要求其破译鸟类指南。

精彩亮点

众人得知下一张卡的持卡者斯库得利现在正搭乘飞机前往拉斯维加斯。迈克尔决定让林肯带着莎拉、苏克雷和罗兰一起去拉斯维加斯，剩下的人则留下来对付帝博格。 **1**

帝博格拿枪指着迈克尔和马霍，让他们跟自己上车，但帝博格现在毕竟只有一只手，行动不便，而且他一心只关注迈克尔。完全将马霍抛在脑后。马霍趁其不备，成功溜走。 **2**

帝博格对迈克尔恨之入骨，迈克尔曾多次对他见死不救，甚至还总想着把他送回监狱。但他也知道，要得到锡拉少不了要利用迈克尔的聪明才智，他将手中的鸟类指南交给迈克尔，让他进行破解。聪明的迈克尔特意撕下其中一页，为赶来的马霍留下了关键信息。 **3**

帝博格只看到了锡拉的背后可能是一笔巨大的财富，但他根本不清楚锡拉是什么，也不知道找寻锡拉的过程充满艰险。 **4**

Michael: **Why don't we skip the theatrics and you just tell us what you want.** ☺1

T-Bag: I'd love to put a hole right in your head. Time's up[①]. Him, too. Let's all get in the van. Let's all get in the van now. **You, too, Mahone. Mahone!** ☺2 I remember the day we met, pretty. You were a scared little college boy sittin' up[②] on those benches, tryin' to keep your ass out of the game. Now look at you. Cold. Hard. Like a dried up[③] flower wanting to get watered.

Michael: Just tell me what you want.

T-Bag: I want to make you bleed. I want to release the sinner inside of me that got me incarcerated so many years ago. But it seems you caught yourself a break, pretty. I need you. Now. You gonna cooperate right quick or so[④] help me I'm gonna stomp you till you can't stand. **The pages-look at them.** ☺3 Looks like some kind of map, right?

Michael: I don't know.

T-Bag: You know enough to chase me down[⑤] looking for this. Now don't lie to me[⑥], pretty.

Michael: Whatever's in that book — it is bigger than you and me.

T-Bag: What, like Scylla big?

Michael: **This is not a game.** ☺4

译文

迈克尔： 我们干脆废话少说吧，不如你告诉我们你想要什么。

帝博格： 我想要一枪毙了你，时间到了，他也是。都给我上车，都给我上车，快点儿！你也是，马霍，马霍！帅哥，我还记得我们见面的那天。你就是一个坐在长椅上的被吓坏了的大学生，不想要蹚我们的浑水。现在，看看你，冷酷又严厉，就像一朵枯萎的花儿在等待着浇灌。

迈克尔： 你就告诉我到底想要什么吧。

帝博格： 我想要你的鲜血。我想要释放内心的罪恶，这个多年前曾被我囚禁的恶人，但看来你得到了喘息的机会，帅哥。现在，我需要你……你必须得马上跟我合作或者我把你打到站不起来。这些记录……看，看起来像一张地图，对吧？

迈克尔： 我不知道。

帝博格： 你知道怎么找到我，看这个。现在别欺骗我，帅哥。

迈克尔： 不管那本书里有什么……都不是你我能弄明白的。

帝博格： 什么？像锡拉那么复杂？

迈克尔： 这可不是游戏。

知识点拨

1. time's up 表示"时间到了"。例：I'm a pirate, and I don't care of my time's up! 我可是个海盗，我才不管什么时间到没到的！

2. sit up 表示"熬夜；（使）端坐；晚睡；引起注意"。例：Her head spins dizzily as soon as she sits up. 她一坐起身来就感到天旋地转。

3. dry up 表示"干巴；枯窘；枯竭"。例：The pool had dried up and was full of bracken and reeds. 水塘已经干涸，里面都是欧洲蕨和芦苇。

4. or so 表示"左右，大约"。例：It was only an hour or so later that I discovered that my gun was missing. 仅仅约一个小时之后，我发现我的枪不见了。

5. chase sb. down 表示"努力寻找"。例：Ness chased the thief down and held him until police arrived. 内斯追上小偷，按住他，一直等到警察赶到。

6. lie to sb. 表示"对某人撒谎，对某人说谎"。例：I forgive you this time, but you can't lie to me again. 这次我原谅你，但你不能再对我撒谎了。

词汇加油站

skip [skɪp] *vt.* 跳过

hole [hoʊl] *n.* 洞

bleed [bli:d] *vt.* 使出血

incarcerate [ɪnˈkɑːrsəreɪt] *vt.* 监禁

theatrics [θɪˈætrɪkz] *n.* 戏剧演出

van [væn] *n.* 厢式货车

sinner [ˈsɪnər] *n.* 罪人

stomp [stɑːmp] *v.* 践踏

时间： 第8集 00:03:52—00:04:44

地点： 教堂

片段三

人物： 迈克尔，苏珊，塞尔夫

事件： 迈克尔、塞尔夫与苏珊会面，双方正式结盟。

精彩亮点

　　迈克尔和马霍联手将帝博格锁在地下，没想到，等到他们出来时接到了苏珊的电话，迈克尔手上只有第77页鸟类指南，苏珊表示如果迈克尔他们不放了帝博格，就不要想着得到剩余的页数。于是。他们约定好在教堂见面。

1

　　苏珊首先对迈克尔示好，表示在索纳监狱只是奉公司之命行事，希望迈克尔能摒弃前嫌，与自己展开合作。

2

　　苏珊也想得到锡拉，虽然她并不清楚锡拉到底是什么，但有了锡拉就能牵制公司，牵制将军。自己作为公司曾经的一员，因巴拿马任务失败险些被将军杀死，在暗室饱受折磨，她发誓要报仇。

3

　　塞尔夫认为如果可以从苏珊那里得到有关锡拉的信息，就可以与她展开合作。这样一来，摧毁公司这一共同目标将迈克尔等人和苏珊联系在了一起，双方正式"结盟"。

4

Michael: **Just relax.** ☺₁

Susan: First off ①, Panama was a job.

Michael: Some other time ②. What do you want with Scylla?

Susan: **That's my business.** ☺₂

Michael: We're not in Panama anymore, and I'm not behind a fence, so, again, what do you want with Scylla?

Susan: The same thing you want, bring down ③ the Company.

Michael: Great. Then why don't you give me those missing pages and disappear?

Susan: I'd love to. You remember that day at the Roosevelt when Whistler made off ④ with Lief's card? Who do you think took the fall ⑤ for that? **Our names are at the top of the same hit list.** ☺₃ Now, I don't know what arrangement you two have, but I need some traveling money.

Self: Let's talk about that later.

Michael: Why don't we talk about the kind of scum you're willing to put on the payroll?

Self: Give me a way to do it without her, and we'll do it. We need the pages.

Susan: It's a package deal ⑥. Are we partners? ☺₄

Michael: Partners.

译文

迈克尔：放松一点儿。

苏　珊：首先，在巴拿马我只是奉命行事。

迈克尔：回来再说吧，你想从锡拉那里得到什么？

苏　珊：那是我的事。

迈克尔：我们已经不在巴拿马了，而且我也不在监狱里，因此，我再问一遍，你想从锡拉那里得到什么？

苏　珊：和你一样，扳倒公司。

迈克尔：太棒了，那你为什么不把那些缺页给我，然后消失呢？

苏　珊：我很乐意给你。你还记得那天在罗斯福酒店惠斯勒带着那张卡逃走的时候吗？你觉得那是谁干的？我们的名字都在首要的暗杀名单上。现在，我不知道你们有什么安排，但我需要一些旅行费。

塞尔夫：这个晚点儿再说。

迈克尔：为什么我们不谈谈你愿意如何支付这笔旅费呢？

塞尔夫：给我一个不需要她帮忙的办法，那我们就去做，可我们需要那几页纸。

苏　珊：这是一揽子交易，现在我们是伙伴了？

迈克尔：伙伴。

知识点拨

1. first off 表示"马上，立刻"。例：First off, huge apologies for last month's confusing report. 首先，要对上个月那篇交代不清的报道表示深深的歉意。

2. some other time 表示"改天吧"。例：I must first talk to our director, and discuss it with you some other time. 我得先和我们主管商量一下，然后和您找个时间再谈。

3. bring down 表示"降（价）；把（某物，某人）抬下（楼、山）；使（某物或某人）掉下（倒下）；击败……"。例：They were threatening to bring down the government by withdrawing from the ruling coalition. 他们威胁要退出执政联盟，让政府垮台。

4. make off 表示"匆匆逃掉"。例：They broke free and made off in a stolen car. 他们挣脱后开着一辆偷来的车逃之夭夭。

5. take the fall 表示"代人受过，做替罪羊"。例：See, now you gonna have to take the fall for this bullshit. 看，你现在得收拾这些烂摊子了。

6. package deal 表示"一揽子交易；一揽子交易中的条款"。例：We are offering a package deal which include the whole office computer system, staff training and hardware maintenance. 我们提供一整套服务，其中包括提供整个办公的计算机系统、人员培训和硬件维修。

 **词汇加油站**

fence [fens] *n.* 围墙
disappear [ˌdɪsəˈpɪr] *vi.* 消失
arrangement [əˈreɪndʒmənt] *n.* 安排
package [ˈpækɪdʒ] *n.* 一组建议

page [peɪdʒ] *n.* 页
hit [hɪt] *n.* 打击
payroll [ˈpeɪroʊl] *n.* 工资总支出
partner [ˈpɑːrtnər] *n.* 同伙

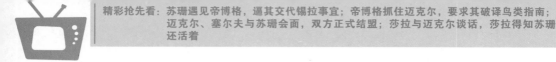

时间： 第 8 集 00:19:27—00:20:10

地点： 仓库

片段四

人物： 莎拉，迈克尔

事件： 莎拉与迈克尔谈话，莎拉得知苏珊还活着。

精彩亮点

莎拉从林肯那里得知了迈克尔及其母亲的情况。迈克尔从小就时常流鼻血，而他的母亲在 31 岁时因患脑癌而去世，迈克尔今年正好 31 岁，莎拉十分关心他的身体状况。**1**

迈克尔责怪林肯多事，他之前已经告诉林肯这件事要对莎拉保密，他不想让她担心，但迈克尔也知道，林肯也是担心自己。他只能安慰莎拉说林肯是因为小时候亲眼看着母亲死去而变得过分保护家人。**2**

不久前，迈克尔接到了一通电话，那熟悉的声音让迈克尔大为震惊：那就是曾被宣告已死亡的格雷琴。**3**

莎拉听到格雷琴还活着这个消息不禁不寒而栗，之前格雷琴对自己施与酷刑的一幕幕呈现在她的脑海。格雷琴还当着莎拉的面枪杀了曾经试图救莎拉逃走的一位女医生。**4**

Sara: I need to talk to you. So your brother told me about ① your nosebleeds. And he told me about your mom. ☺1

Michael: That wasn't his place.

Sara: To be worried about ② you?

Michael: When Mom got sick, Linc was at the hospital every day, holding her hand, watching her die, and he was 13. It changed him. ☺2 It made him overprotective. And now he's jumping to all the wrong conclusions ③ for all the wrong reasons, and it's... it's over nothing because I'm fine.

Sara: You don't look fine.

Michael: Well, maybe that's because there's something I have to tell you. Gretchen's alive. ☺3 She's working with T-Bag, and they have several pages from Whistler's bird book, and they want in on Scylla. Self is cutting them a deal ④ as we speak. Self knows that they have their own agenda, but so do we and as soon as we get those pages back, Gretchen and T-Bag are going to pay for ⑤ everything. They're going to get exactly what's coming to ⑥ them.

Sara: Okay. This isn't about Gretchen. It's not about any one person. And we... we have to finish it. I need a minute. Please. ☺4

译文

莎　拉：我需要和你谈谈，你哥哥告诉了我你流鼻血的事，他还跟我说了你妈妈的事。

迈克尔：那不是他应该管的。

莎　拉：他关心你有错吗？

迈克尔：当妈妈生病的时候，林肯每天都在医院，握着她的手，看着她死去，那时他才 13 岁。这件事改变了他，让他变得过分保护他的家人。现在，他因为一些错误的原因，得到的都是错误的结论，不过已经……结束了，因为我很好。

莎　拉：但你看起来并不好。

迈克尔：好吧，或许是因为我必须告诉你一些事。格雷琴还活着。她在与帝博格合作，他们手中持有惠斯勒那本鸟类指南里的几页，他们想参与找到锡拉。塞尔夫正打算和他们合作，他知道他们有自己的计划，但我们也有，我们一拿回那些书页，格雷琴和帝博格就要为这一切付出代价。他们会承受一切报应。

莎　拉：好吧。这不关格雷琴的事，与任何人也无关，我们……我们必须要结束这一切。让我单独待会，拜托了。

 知识点拨

1. tell sb. about sth. 表示"告诉某人某事"。例：Making a formal presentation can be very challenging. Tell me about a formal presentation that you were most satisfied. 做一个正式的报告会很有挑战性，请告诉我你最满意的一个正式报告。

2. be worried about 表示"为某事 / 某人忧虑，烦恼的"。例：I knew you'd be worried about that point. 我知道你会在这一点上担心的。

3. jump to conclusion 表示"妄自断定，过早下结论"。例：I didn't want her to jump to the conclusion that the divorce was in any way her fault. 我不想让她草率地断定离婚完全是她的错。

4. cut sb. a deal 表示"与某人签协议"。例：Two years ago he caught me and cut a deal. 他两年前抓住了我，和我签了个协议。

5. pay for 表示"赔偿；为……付钱；因……受罚 / 痛苦；替某人付款；为某事付出代价"。例：She feels it's a small price to pay for the pleasure of living in this delightful house. 她觉得，和住在这套令人愉快的房子里的那种快乐相比，这点代价不算大。

6. come to 表示"苏醒；到达；共计；突然想起"。例：As I write, a very interesting case has come to my notice. 在我写作过程中，一个非常有趣的案例引起了我的注意。

 词汇加油站

nosebleed ['noʊzbliːd] *n.* 鼻出血

conclusion [kən'kluːʒn] *n.* 结论

several ['sevrəl] *adj.* 几个的

exactly [ɪg'zæktli] *adv.* 确切地

overprotective [,oʊvərprə'tektɪv] *adj.* 过分保护的

alive [ə'laɪv] *adj.* 活着的

agenda [ə'dʒendə] *n.* 议事日程

263

Scene 5 英雄贝里克

时间： 第9集 00:00:59—00:02:01
地点： 仓库
片段一 **人物：** 林肯，迈克尔，莎拉，贝里克，怀亚特，马霍
事件： 众人活捉怀亚特，马霍残忍折磨怀亚特。

精彩亮点

> 林肯等人活捉了怀亚特。怀亚特一副天不怕地不怕的样子，林肯想到如此多的人都因他而丧命难忍心中怒火，但无论林肯怎么打他，怀亚特都无动于衷。
>
> **1**

> 莎拉尝试感化怀亚特，但怀亚特却告诉她他认识政府的一些人，可以帮助她和迈克尔，并试图以此为条件，让莎拉放过他。莎拉意识到感化他的方法根本行不通。
>
> **2**

> 迈克尔认为对于一个训练有素的军人，很容易就能听出他人语气中的恐惧。即使把怀亚特打到求饶，也不会使将军信服。因此，他们想到让莎拉和他谈话，塞尔夫想出将怀亚特的声音进行合成，并播放给将军听这一方法。
>
> **3**

> 位于墙角的马霍早已等得不耐烦了，等到合成完怀亚特的声音后，塞尔夫便将他交由马霍处置。怀亚特曾开枪打死了马霍心爱的儿子，马霍誓要使用最残忍的方法将怀亚特折磨致死。
>
> **4**

Lincoln: Now, tell the General you killed us. Otherwise, my hand, it ain't going to get tired.☺₁

Wyatt: I just hope your mouth gets tired.

Lincoln: That's funny.

Bellick: Come on ①, buddy, come on. Enough already, come on, Linc.

Sara: Believe me now? Beating him isn't going to work, Lincoln.☺₂

Lincoln: You tried your way. We want General Krantz to think Wyatt took us out ②.

Michael: Even if ③ you do break him, and he does call the General, you don't think a trained military veteran is going to hear the fear in his voice? They're going to know he was coerced.☺₃

Lincoln: Yeah, it will. We'll take more time with him ④.

Michael: I hear you, Linc, but he can't make the call ⑤ if he's unconscious.

Bellick: However we do it, we better get what we need from Wyatt soon, because Mahone ain't going to wait.

Mahone: I'm trying to find the son of a bitch ⑥ who killed my kid!☺₄

译文

林　肯： 现在你告诉将军，你已经把我们杀了。否则，我不介意多打你一会儿。

怀亚特： 我倒希望你的嘴巴累了，而不是拳头。

林　肯： 真有意思。

贝里克： 好了，老兄，好了。已经够了，别打了，林肯。

莎　拉： 现在相信我了？拷打他是不会奏效的，林肯。

林　肯： 你的方法也没奏效，我们想让克兰茨将军以为怀亚特已经把我们处理掉了。

迈克尔： 就算你打到他求饶，他也同意打电话给将军，但你以为一个训练有素的军人会听不出他语气中的恐惧吗？他们会听出来他遭到了胁迫。

林　肯： 是啊，看来我们得在他身上多花点儿工夫。

迈克尔： 我知道，林肯，但要是他失去意识了，还怎么打电话。

贝里克： 不管我们怎么做最好动作快点儿，马霍是不会等的。

马　霍： 我要找到杀死我儿子的混蛋！

知识点拨

1. 让我们一起来看一看 come on 的意思：1）表示请求、鼓励、劝说等，意为"来吧；行了"。2）用来催促别人快走（做），意为"快点儿"。3）表示责备或不耐烦等，意为"得了；行了；够了"。4）用于挑战或激怒对方，意为"来吧；好吧；试试吧"。5）用于体育竞赛等场合鼓励队员，意为"加油"。

2. take out 表示"取出；除去；拔掉；把……带出去；邀请（某人）外出"。例：In my neighbourhood, the local crack dealers would have taken him out a long time ago. 我们这片的本地毒贩早就想废了他了。

3. even if 表示"哪怕，虽然，即使，纵然"。例：Even if you are right, that's not the way to put it. 就算你对了，也不该那么说呀！

4. take more time with sb. / sth. 表示"在某人、某物身上花费更长时间"。例：You could take a little more time with your face, you know. 你应该在脸上多花点儿时间，你知道的。

5. make the call 表示"打电话"。例：Give me the phone; we need to make the call. 把电话给我，我们要打个电话。

6. son of a bitch 表示"坏家伙；讨厌的工作；浑蛋"。例：And you're the son of a bitch that got my partner shot. 你这个坏家伙，你射杀了我的伙伴。

 词汇加油站

general ['dʒenrl] *n.* 上将
buddy ['bʌdi] *n.* 密友
veteran ['vetərən] *n.* 老兵
coerce [koʊˈɜːrs] *vt.* 逼迫

tired ['taɪərd] *adj.* 疲倦的
beat [biːt] *vt.* 接连地击打
voice [vɔɪs] *n.* 声音
unconscious [ʌnˈkɑːnʃəs] *adj.* 无意识的

片段二

时间： 第9集 00:22:57—00:24:39

地点： 主管道控制中心，GATE 公司地下室

人物： 贝里克，林肯，迈克尔，苏克雷

事件： 众人分别行动，水管暂时停止供水。

精彩亮点

根据塞尔夫提供的地图，迈克尔看到惠斯勒做了一个"X"的记号，他猜测是一堵墙，但没想到墙的那边竟然是水管。要想抵达公司总部，只有穿过水管，因此，必须让水管的水暂时停流一段时间。迈克尔的方法就是让林肯和贝里克两人烧掉控制主管道的线路。**1**

在这一季中，贝里克给观众的印象不再是自私自利的形象，例如面对罗兰的死，林肯表示这种背叛了他们的人死有余辜，但贝里克却表现出对他的怜悯。在谈到他的父亲时，贝里克眼神中透露出对父亲的爱与思念更是打动了每位观众的心。**2**

苏克雷和迈克尔这边的任务也不轻松，他们要直接穿过大水管是不可能的，因此，要将一根小水管插入大水管中，从小水管进入公司内部。苏克雷正费力地抬着这根小水管，这时，迈克尔发现已经听不到水流声了，这说明林肯已经成功地烧掉了线路。**3**

烧掉主水管线路后，上千户人家会停水，市政府很快就会收到消息，并着力修补线路，恢复供水，因此，留给迈克尔他们的时间很有限——仅有一小时。**4**

Bellick: So, how are you holding up①, you know, not being with L.J. and all? ☺1

Lincoln: Good, he's a smart kid. He can look after② himself.

Bellick: I can see it, how much you love him. My dad died when I was a little kid. **But he was a good father.** ☺2

Lincoln: Let's just focus and get this thing done, all right?

Bellick: Michael said the manual override should be somewhere near the main conduit. This look like the main conduit to you?

Lincoln: One way to find out③. That look like it to you?

Bellick: Looks like it.

Lincoln: Fire it up④. All right, let's get out of here.

Sucre: **Hurry up, bro!** ☺3

Michael: Almost done, buddy. All right, ease it back⑤. It worked.

Sucre: How long we got?

Michael: I don't know. **Water cut off⑥ to thousands of people.** ☺4 The city will probably have that taken care of in about an hour, which means we've got… 60 minutes to do 90 minutes worth of work. Or we don't get to Scylla.

译文

贝里克： 那么，没有 L.J. 在身边，你是怎么撑过来的？

林　肯： 还好，他是个聪明的孩子，他能照顾好自己。

贝里克： 我能看得出来你有多爱他，我还是个孩子时我爸爸就死了，但他是个好父亲。

林　肯： 我们只管集中精力把这件事做好，好吧？

贝里克： 迈克尔说手动控制……应该就在主管道附近。你看这个像主管道吗？

林　肯： 有个办法能看得出来，你看像吗？

贝里克： 我看像。

林　肯： 烧了它，好了，我们快离开这儿。

苏克雷： 快点儿，哥们！

迈克尔： 就快好了，哥们。好了，现在慢慢往后抬，奏效了。

苏克雷： 我们有多长时间？

迈克尔： 我不知道，上千户人家停水了。估计市政府会在一个小时内解决问题，这就意味着，我们要在六十分钟的时间内……做九十分钟的活。否则，我们是拿不到锡拉的。

知识点拨

1. hold up 表示"举起，支撑；耽搁；持械抢劫"。例：Mills have iron pillars all over the place holding up the roof. 工厂里四处都立有支撑着房顶的铁柱。

2. look after 表示"照顾，照料，料理，打理"，片中表示"照顾"。例：I sent word to her to go and look after you. 我给她送个信儿，让她去照料你。

3. find out 表示"发现；使发作；使受惩罚"。例：You can find out whether they are prepared to share the cost of the flowers with you. 你可以弄清楚他们是否愿意和你一起分担买花的费用。

4. fire up 表示"点燃，点火；发动（机器）；（使）突然生气"。例：Put on a helmet, fire up your engine and head out on the open road. 戴上头盔，发动引擎，开上乡村干道。

5. ease back 表示"回软；轻轻拉回"。例：Some poses, such as the Warrior poses, can also help to ease back pain and sciatica. 一些体式，如战士式可以减少背痛和坐骨神经痛。

6. cut off 表示"切除，切 / 隔断，剪 / 切，砍下；迅速离开；（疾病等）使（人）死亡"。例：They were almost completely cut off from the outside world. 他们几乎完全与外界绝缘了。

 词汇加油站

smart [smɑːrt] *adj.* 聪明的
manual ['mænjuəl] *adj.* 用手的
main [meɪn] *adj.* 主要的
fire [faɪər] *vt.* 燃烧

focus ['foʊkəs] *vt.* 集中注意力
override [ˌoʊvərˈraɪd] *n.* 超驰控制装置
conduit ['kɑːnduɪt] *n.* 水道
ease [iːz] *vt.* 小心缓缓地移动

片段三

时间： 第10集 00:01:18—00:02:30
地点： 仓库
人物： 苏克雷，塞尔夫，林肯，马霍
事件： 贝里克牺牲，众人要求将其遗体转交给他的母亲。

精彩亮点

1 眼看大水就要冲进来了，迈克尔在外面高声呼喊着让林肯和贝里克放弃任务，赶快撤回，但贝里克害怕有意外，他怕万一水的冲击力太大会把沉重的水管再次压塌，所以选择守在里面，因此壮烈牺牲。

2 塞尔夫说出这句话时即冷静又冷漠，他丝毫不将一个罪犯的生命看在眼里，他认为执行任务的过程中难免会有危险与死亡。足见他为达目的不择手段、冷酷无情。

3 当初，塞尔夫召集他们几个人去寻找锡拉时，曾经向他们保证，如果在执行任务的过程中牺牲，塞尔夫会将他们的遗体交给家属。但是，此时的塞尔夫却否认这一协议，不得不让人怀疑他的初衷。

4 塞尔夫的话惹恼了苏克雷，塞尔夫只关注他的个人利益，根本没有把贝里克的牺牲当回事。苏克雷提到了贝里克的母亲，母亲一直都是贝里克的依靠，他希望母亲能为他感到骄傲。

Sucre: Where's Brad's body now? ☺₁

Self: We got it on its way to the morgue, and it's in the cooler at Homeland Security where nobody can find it. ☺₂

Lincoln: That ain't part of the deal. ☺₃

Mahone: You said if anything happened to us, that we'd be returned to next of kin① .

Self: No. That's not exactly what I said.

Mahone: No, that is exactly what you said.

Self: No, it isn't exactly what I said, okay? And he needs to stay a John Doe② until I say otherwise. Okay? I'm dealing with enough stuff already, and I've had my ass chewed out③ …

Sucre: He's got… He's got a mother, you know. ☺₄

Mahone: If you want Scylla, and I assume you still do, Brad Bellick's body goes home to his mother.

Self: All right, all right. All right, I'm gonna take care of the body. But you guys need to get out of mourning. Okay, we need to get back to work. You need to pack Brad's stuff up④ , and we need to get back to work⑤ . And Fernando, my friend, let me tell you something. If you ever put your hands on me again, I promise you, okay, there's gonna be two bodies in the fridge.

译文

苏克雷： 布拉德的遗体现在在哪儿？

塞尔夫： 我们在尸体移至停尸房之前拦截到了，现在在国土安全部冷藏箱里，没人会发现。

林　肯： 这可和你之前约定的不一样啊。

马　霍： 你说如果我们发生了意外，就会把遗体转交给亲属。

塞尔夫： 不是，我没这么说。

马　霍： 不，你就是这么说的。

塞尔夫： 不，我不是这么说的，听到了吗？除非我同意，否则他只能是个无名氏。明白吗？我现在要处理的事已经够多了，还要被上司批得狗血淋头……

苏克雷： 他还有……他还有一位年迈的母亲，你知道吗？

马　霍： 如果你还想得到"锡拉名单"，我劝你还是把布拉德·贝里克的遗体送回他母亲那里比较好。

塞尔夫： 好吧，好吧，好吧，我会妥善安置遗体的，但你们也都节哀顺变吧，行吗？我们要回去工作了，你们把布拉德的东西收拾好，然后就去干活吧。还有费尔南多，我的朋友，我要告诉你件事。如果你再敢对我动手我向你保证，待在冷冻箱里的就会有两具尸体了。

知识点拨

1. next of kin 表示"近亲"。例：He is my next of kin. 他是我的近亲。

2. John Doe 多用来指代不知名的男性。如果是不知名的女性，则多用 Jane Doe 来指代。如果是小孩子、婴儿的话，还有 Baby Doe。

3. chew out 表示"严厉责备"。例：He chewed out the player, who apologized the next time I saw him. 他训斥了那个球员，我再次看见那个球员时，他道了歉。

4. pack up 表示"收拾，打包；停止工作，停止运转"。例：They had worked hard all day, so at six o'clock they decided to pack up. 他们努力工作了一整天，因此在 6 点钟他们决定收工了。

5. get back to work 表示"回去工作"。例：Now that the misunderstanding is cleared up, we can get back to work. 现在误会已经消除，我们可以回去工作了。

词汇加油站

morgue [mɔːrg] *n.* 停尸房

kin [kɪn] *n.* 亲戚

chew [tʃuː] *vt.* 深思

promise ['prɑːmɪs] *vt.* 允诺

cooler ['kuːlər] *n.* 冷却器

stuff [stʌf] *n.* 资料

assume [ə'suːm] *v.* 认为

fridge [frɪdʒ] *n.* 电冰箱

片段四

时间：	第 10 集 00:04:14—00:06:04
地点：	仓库
人物：	迈克尔，马霍，苏克雷，塞尔夫，莎拉
事件：	迈克尔和马霍破解公司地下室地图玄机。

精彩亮点

1

马霍在收拾贝里克的遗物时发现了他的警徽。即使被送进监狱，处境再不堪，贝里克也一直没有舍得丢弃自己的警徽。成为一名警官是他的理想，他希望让母亲看到自己身穿警服的样子，让母亲为自己感到自豪。

2

格雷琴按照约定与迈克尔和塞尔夫会面，将剩下的几页鸟类指南交给了迈克尔。同时，她告诉迈克尔和塞尔夫将军决定明天就将锡拉转移到宾州的一个地堡，因此，迈克尔他们的时间非常紧迫。

3

迈克尔拼凑出完整的公司地下室地图后发现上面只有几个简单的符号，这些符号代表的事物之间没有任何意义，而当把这些字母拼在一起时，就组成了 see me（看我）。

4

大卫·贝克就是曾经为公司设计地下室的建筑师，马霍找到了他，想让他告诉自己地下室里有什么机关，不料公司的人也随后而至，贝克的妻子在马霍逃跑时递给他一张纸，上面记载了破解重重机关的方法。

Mahone: Look at this. He kept a badge from the police benefit. ☺1

Sucre: When he was a CO in Fox River, he-he failed the test to get into the academy five times. ☺2

Self: These are right, right? This is a map of the Company's basement, right?

Michael: I don't know. It looks too simple. I assumed it would be a lot more complicated than this. These symbols… they're… They don't make any sense ①, and the letters, uh... There's just something wrong. This letter C… it usually designates some kind of ② heating vent ③. The M designates a meter. This is some sort of condensing unit ④. This is a plumbing part. It's called a P-trap. They're all completely dissimilar items. Logical design dictates they'd never be installed that randomly. It just, um… It doesn't make sense. C, M, E. C… M… E. That's "See me". ☺3

Sara: These letters don't make any sense if you think of them as symbols, but they do if you think of them literally.

Mahone: Do you see me? He's asking if you see him.

Sucre: Where?

Michael: Here. David Baker? ☺4

Sucre: Yeah, but who besides you two, would come up with ⑤ something like that, huh? I mean, what's the point? ⑥

270

译文

马　霍：看这个，他还保留着一个警徽。

苏克雷：当他还在福克斯河监狱做狱警时，考了五次都没能考进警官学校。

塞尔夫：这些完全吻合，对吧？这是公司地下室的地图，对吗？

迈克尔：我不知道，这看上去太简单了，我本以为应该比这更复杂些。这些标志，它们……它们根本没任何意义。而这些字母……呃……肯定哪里有问题。字母 C 通常代表供热器通风口，字母 M 代表仪表测量仪，这应该是某种制冷器，这里是配管系统，这叫作 P 形管结构，这几样东西根本毫不相关。从逻辑结构上说，这几样东西根本不能随意组装，这……根本说不通。C, M, E. 就是 "See me"（看我）。

莎　拉：如果你仅把它们看作是标志，这些字母一定没有意义，但如果以字面意义来分析，就说得通了。

马　霍：你看到我了吗？他是在问你有没有看到他。

苏克雷：在哪儿？

迈克尔：这儿。大卫·贝克？

苏克雷：是啊，但除了你俩以外，还有谁能分析出这种鬼东西？我是说，这到底什么意思？

知识点拨

1. don't make any sense 表示"说不通；没意思，没意义"。例：We couldn't make any sense of his sudden outburst. 我们被他这没头没脑的话给弄愣了。

2. some kind of 表示"某种"。例：There has to be some kind of way out. 一定会有某种解决办法的。

3. heating vent 表示"通风管道"。例：He ran into that heating vent right there. 他跑进了那边的通风管道。

4. condensing unit 表示"冷凝机组，冷凝装置"。例：With cooling water flowing through the internal pipes, much of the heat in the condensing unit is carried away. 当冷却水流经内部管道时，冷凝器中的许多热量就会被带走了。

5. come up with 表示"想出，提出；追赶上；设法拿出"。例：Several of the members have come up with suggestions of their own. 有几位成员提出了自己的建议。

6. What's the point? 表示"某事物的重点/意思/意义/目的……是什么"。例：What's the point in writing in when you only print half the letter anyway? 只打印出一半就把信寄出去到底有什么用呢？

词汇加油站

badge [bædʒ] *n.* 徽章

academy [əˈkædəmi] *n.* 专科学院

designate [ˈdezɪgneɪt] *vt.* 表明

condense [kənˈdens] *v.* 冷凝

install [ɪnˈstɔːl] *vt.* 安装

police [pəˈliːs] *n.* 警察

basement [ˈbeɪsmənt] *n.* 地下室

vent [vent] *n.* 排气孔

plumbing [ˈplʌmɪŋ] *n.* 管路系统

Scene 6 迈克尔病倒

时间： 第 11 集 00:03:14—00:05:40
地点： 公司总部，仓库门外
人物： 莎拉，迈克尔，马霍，苏克雷，林肯
事件： 苏克雷、马霍执行计划，迈克尔拒绝去医院。

精彩亮点

迈克尔在仓库中因身体不支而倒下，莎拉等人送他来到医院，但迈克尔十分谨慎，生怕会暴露自己的身份。而他的主治医生也确实知道迈克尔的身份，但他出于对迈克尔的健康考虑，向他保证不会揭穿他的身份，但迈克尔还是拉着莎拉离开了医院。莎拉表示等检查结果出来让医生与她联系。 **1**

这边苏克雷和马霍继续执行着计划，苏克雷怀念当初和迈克尔为越狱挖墙洞的日子，他是迈克尔的好兄弟，十分担心迈克尔的身体状况。 **2**

马霍也很担心迈克尔，但他知道，如果此时连他们也败下阵来，等待迈克尔的就是牢狱之灾，那远比现在的境况糟糕得多。 **3**

莎拉和林肯更是担心迈克尔，但现在迈克尔坚决不去医院，莎拉本希望林肯能劝一劝弟弟，但林肯太了解迈克尔了，在完成计划前，迈克尔是不会去医院的。 **4**

Sara: Michael, Dr. Malden can see you today.☺₁ He's given us his word he won't alert the authorities. If you put this off① and you, you collapse, you're going to be treated by another doctor. Do you want to roll the dice② that they're not going to call the cops?

Michael: There's still so much to do. All right③.

Sara: Three o'clock?

Sucre: Last time I drilled a hole④ in the wall⑤, it was with an eggbeater back in Fox River with Michael.☺₂ I just can't believe it's all coming to an end⑥, and he's not here.

Mahone: He'll be all right.

Sucre: How do you know?

Mahone: I don't. I'm just trying to keep us focused.☺₃ He's sick, but I guarantee you one thing that'll make him worse—going back to jail. If we don't get in there… That's where we're all going.

Sara: He's going to be okay. I'm scared, too, but a hospital's the best place for him right now.

Lincoln: He won't go without a plan to complete the job.☺₄

Sara: Well, Alex and Fernando should be back soon with the video, right?

Lincoln: Should be, yeah.

译文

莎　拉：迈克尔，莫尔登医生今天可以给你看病，他向我们保证不会报警的。如果你推迟去看病，你再倒下的话，给你看病的可能就不是他了。你想掷骰子来赌他们会不会报警吗？

迈克尔：我还有好多事情要做，好吧。

莎　拉：3 点钟如何？

苏克雷：上次我在墙上钻洞时还是在福克斯河监狱里和迈克尔两个人用搅蛋器做的。我只是不能相信等这一切都要结束了，而他不却在这儿。

马　霍：他会没事的。

苏克雷：你怎么知道？

马　霍：我不知道，我只是试着让我们集中注意力。他病了，但我向你保证，有件事将会让他的情况更糟，那就是重回监狱。如果我们进不了那里，监狱就是我们的归宿。

莎　拉：他会好起来的。我也很害怕，但现在医院是对他而言最好的地方。

林　肯：没想出完成任务的计划之前，他是不会去医院的。

莎　拉：呃，亚历克斯和菲尔南多很快就会带着录像回来了，对吧？

林　肯：应该是的。

知识点拨

1. put off 表示"延期；敷衍；使分心；脱去（衣、帽等）"。例：The old priest tried to put them off, saying that the hour was late. 老牧师搪塞他们说时间太晚了。

2. roll the dice 表示"掷骰子"，引申为"孤注一掷"。例：You wanna investigate me, roll the dice and take your chances. 你想调查我，尽管看看你有多大的机会好了。

3. all right 表示"尚可；（确保对方同意或理解）如何；可允许（的）；正确的"。例：Things have thankfully worked out all right. 谢天谢地，事情终于圆满解决了。

4. drill a hole 表示"钻了一个孔"。例：The small metal shaft will be removed, and I'll drill a hole to accept the radar shafts. 小金属轴将被删除，我会钻一个孔，接受雷达轴。

5. 我们一起来看一下 on the wall 与 in the wall 的区别：图画、黑板、风筝等"在墙上"，是在墙的表面，故用 on the wall。门窗、钉子、洞、孔等"在墙上"，是在墙的里面，故用 in the wall。

6. come to an end 表示"结束，终止，完事；期满；平息"。例：It has not come to an end even after three years. 三年了，事情还没个结局。

词汇加油站

authority [ə'θɔ:rəti] *n.* 当权者
treat [tri:t] *v.* 对待
dice [daɪs] *n.* 骰子
eggbeater ['eg,bi:tər] *n.* 打蛋机

collapse [kə'læps] *vt.* 使瓦解
roll [roʊl] *vt.* 滚动
drill [drɪl] *vt.* 钻（孔）
jail [dʒeɪl] *n.* 监狱

时间： 第 11 集 00:07:10—00:08:11
地点： 仓库
人物： 迈克尔，莎拉，林肯，塞尔夫
事件： 莎拉向迈克尔讲述手术事宜，众人准备拿走锡拉。

精彩亮点

1　迈克尔的主治医生给莎拉打来了电话，迈克尔见莎拉的表情就知道肯定是医生告诉了莎拉自己的诊断结果。勇敢的迈克尔走向莎拉，向她询问自己的病情。

2　听到莎拉说的话，林肯有些受不了，他并不希望让弟弟承受这种痛苦，也担心如此一来会给迈克尔带来压力，但迈克尔却表示自己想听，足见迈克尔的勇敢与坚强。

3　201 个洞，听到这里相信听众们都会为迈克尔不禁潸然泪下，然而迈克尔坚定的眼神再次显示了他的坚强与勇敢。相信他也曾预想过这样的结果，但善良的他将自己的生死置之度外，而将他人的生死与幸福视为第一位。

4　塞尔夫帮助迈克尔准备好了前往将军办公大楼的必备品。迈克尔坚持要与林肯等人一同前往完成任务，因为此次任务最具危险性，如果他没有陪伴在他们身边，万一有人发生不测，即使手术成功，他也会一辈子生活在悔恨之中。

Michael: **What'd you find out?** ☺₁

Sara: You'll <u>be awake</u> ① the whole time. The only anesthetic you're going to need is four minor injections of local… Two in your forehead and two in the back of your head.

Michael: And that's for the brace?

Sara: The frame, yeah, and… attaching that is going to be the most uncomfortable part. They're going to have to secure four pins into your skull. And they're going to need a small drill to do it.

Lincoln: **Do we have to listen to this?** ☺₂

Michael: I want to hear this, Linc. And then what?

Sara: Uh, another <u>CT scans</u> ②. The doctor will use the <u>three-dimensional</u> ③ imagery to pinpoint the exact location of the growth.

Michael: And once you have that?

Sara: Then it's the <u>Gamma Knife</u> ④ unit. They'll <u>fit you with</u> ⑤ a helmet. **They'll calibrate it so that each of the 201 holes are aimed directly for the tumor.** ☺₃ And <u>at that point</u> ⑥ …

Self: I've got two more boxes in the car that you guys got to bring in yourself. All right. You okay? Because the last time I saw you…

Michael: Yeah, I'm fine. I was just a little dehydrated.

Self: All right, good. **This is the stuff you requested.** ☺₄ You sure this is going to get you in?

译文

迈克尔：你发现什么了？

莎 拉：手术全程你都会醒着。你只需要在四个小地方注射麻醉一下……两针在你的前额，两针在你的后脑勺。

迈克尔：那是用来支撑我的吗？

莎 拉：这个架子，是的，还有……装上这个将是最难受的。他们会在你的头骨里固定四根针，并且需要用小钻来进行这个手术。

林 肯：我们必须要听这些吗？

迈克尔：林肯，我想听。然后呢？

莎 拉：呃，再做一次 CT 扫描，医生会用三维图像定位肿瘤。

迈克尔：定位之后呢？

莎 拉：然后就用伽玛刀切除，他们会给你戴上一个头盔，然后将 201 个洞直接对准肿瘤，到那时……

塞尔夫：我车上还有两个箱子，你们自己去提过来。好了，你还好吗？上次我见你的时候……

迈克尔：没事，我挺好，就是有点儿脱水。

塞尔夫：好吧，这是你要的东西。你确定这些能帮你潜进去吗？

知识点拨

1. be awake 表示"醒着的"。例：He seemed to be awake when I went into his room. 我进屋时，他似乎醒了。

2. CT scans 表示"计算机断层扫描"。例：CT scans and MRI showed enlargement of right medial rectus muscle. 计算机断层与核磁共振皆显示右侧内直肌增大。

3. three-dimensional 表示"三维的，立体的，空间的"。例：From this data three-dimensional laser mapping can produce highly detailed and accurate three-dimensional models. 从这个数据的三维激光测绘可以产生非常详细和准确的三维模型。

4. Gamma Knife 是瑞典公司医科达有限公司的注册商标。该商标的中文直译为"伽玛刀"。例：How do we observe clinical effects of a whole-body Gamma Knife treatment? 怎样观察体部伽玛刀的临床效果？

5. fit sb. with 表示"给某人装配"。例：I must ask the dentist to fit me with some new teeth. 我必须请牙医给我镶几颗新牙。

6. at that point 表示"就在那时"。例：If we had been spotted at that point, I don't know what would have happened to us. 如果当时我们被发现了，我不知道会有什么后果。

词汇加油站

anesthetic [ˌænəsˈθetɪk] *adj.* 麻醉的

injection [ɪnˈdʒekʃn] *n.* 注射

skull [skʌl] *n.* 颅骨

pinpoint [ˈpɪnpɔɪnt] *vt.* 精准定位

tumor [ˈtuːmər] *n.* 瘤

minor [ˈmaɪnər] *adj.* 较小的

brace [breɪs] *n.* 支持物

imagery [ˈɪmɪdʒəri] *n.* 图像；照片

calibrate [ˈkælɪbreɪt] *vt.* 校准

片段三

时间： 第12集 00:12:58—00:14:12
地点： 将军办公室
人物： 林肯，乔纳森，林肯父亲
事件： 众人控制了将军，将军警告迈克尔等人不要与公司作对。

精彩亮点

1. 公司的人在监控录像中看到了迈克尔在锡拉的所在处，将军马上带领一队人马赶赴现场，试图活捉迈克尔，没想到早已埋伏在此的苏克雷、林肯和马霍及时控制了将军。

2. 锡拉里面到底包含了什么内容，值得公司如此大费周章地要保护它？难道仅仅是一些黑名单吗？实则不然，依据将军所说，它的价值远不止于此。

3. 林肯的父亲曾为公司卖命，甚至还替公司杀掉了一些阻碍公司的人。后来，他意识到公司的腐败后便离开了公司，还成立了一家旨在搞垮公司的组织。

4. 将军此话一方面是嘲讽林肯父亲不惜一切搞垮公司，最终还是命丧黄泉，另一方面警告迈克尔等人不要白费力气，与公司作对不会有好下场。

Lincoln: **All that design just to hold some names and reports.** ☺1

Jonathan: **Names and reports?** ☺2 Is that information from the government? Or your father?

Lincoln: Careful.

Jonathan: Top right-hand drawer. It's something that should be of interest to① you. I pulled it when your names came up②.

Lincoln: Why did you leave?

Lincoln's father: I took a position with a group of multinationals we call the company. They call every shot③ this country takes.

Jonathan: I knew your father since before you were born. **You do know he worked for the company?** ☺3

Lincoln: Yeah. He was data analyst④.

Jonathan: Is that what he told you? Well, it makes sense⑤. He wants to protect you from the truth.

Lincoln: I'm warning you.

Jonathan: Your father was a brilliant man. **But he could never have defeated the company.** ☺4 You don't have to make the same misguided, fatal mistake that he did. There's so much you don't know about the company… about scylla… about your dad… about your mother.

Lincoln: I swear to God⑥, I'll kill you.

276

译文

林　肯： 所有这些设计只是为了保存一些名单和报表。

乔纳森： 名单和报表？这是你从政府那里得到的信息？还是你父亲说的？

林　肯： 小心点儿。

乔纳森： 右手边最上面那个抽屉，那里面有些东西你应该感兴趣。当你们的名字出现在名单中时，我就把它翻出来了。

林　肯： 你当时为什么要离开？

林肯父亲： 我在一个我们称之为公司的跨国集团就职，他们掌控着整个国家的命脉。

乔纳森： 在你出生之前我就认识你父亲了，你知道他为公司工作吧？

林　肯： 是的，他是一名数据分析员。

乔纳森： 他就是这么告诉你的吗？好吧，这样也说得通。他希望保护你们，不让你们知道真相。

林　肯： 我可警告你。

乔纳森： 你父亲很聪明，但他永远也无法打倒公司，你无须走他的老路，不必再犯他所犯过的致命错误。关于公司你还有很多东西未曾了解……关于锡拉……关于你父亲……关于你母亲。

林　肯： 我发誓，我要杀了你。

知识点拨

1. be of interest to sb. 表示"某人会感兴趣的"。例：The report will be of interest to teachers and others in the education field. 老师们和其他教育界人士会对这个报告感兴趣。

2. come up 表示"上来；发生；提到；开庭"。例：Someone came up the subject during a pre-dinner drink with our guests. 在与客人喝餐前酒的时候，有人提到了这个话题。

3. call the shots 作为习惯用语就是"掌管、做主并发号施令"的意思。有时我们也说 call the shot，这时它的意思是"做出一个决定，或者在某一件事情上做主"。

4. data analyst 表示"数据分析师，数据分析员"。例：I'm going to hazard a guess that you didn't put data analyst on your list of meaningful jobs, but this worker sees how tasks are more than their simple mechanical description. 我会冒险揣测你并没有将数据分析员列在你认为有意义的工作的条目里，但是这个工作者看到了比简单机器描述得更多的工作内容。

5. make sense 表示"有意义；理解；讲得通；……是明智的"。例：This is to help her to come to terms with her early upbringing and make sense of past experiences. 这旨在帮助她认可自己早先所受的教育，并让她了解自己过去的经历。

6. swear to God 表示"对天发誓"。例：I swear to God, I'll kill you right there. 我发誓，我就在那儿杀了你。

 词汇加油站

drawer [drɔːr] *n.* 抽屉

multinational [ˌmʌltiˈnæʃnəl] *adj.* 跨国的

analyst [ˈænəlɪst] *n.* 分析家

misguide [ˌmɪsˈɡaɪdɪd] *adj.* 被误导的

pull [pʊl] *vt.* 拉

shot [ʃɑːt] *n.* 企图

brilliant [ˈbrɪliənt] *adj.* 才华横溢的

fatal [ˈfeɪtl] *adj.* 致命的

精彩抢先看：苏克雷和马霍执行计划，迈克尔拒绝去医院；莎拉向迈克尔讲述手术事宜，众人准备拿走锡拉；众人控制将军，将军警告迈克尔等人不要与公司作对；将军欲劝众人放过他，迈克尔等人安全走出大楼

时间：	第 12 集 00:15:50—00:16:46
地点：	将军办公室
人物：	马霍，乔纳森，迈克尔
事件：	将军欲劝众人放过他，迈克尔等人安全走出大楼。

 精彩亮点

1 迈克尔等人历经周折终于拿到了锡拉。将军嘲笑他们整座大楼都置于自己的掌控之下，迈克尔等人怎能逃离出去？林肯用枪抵住将军的背，众人乘电梯来到将军办公室。

2 将军想以马霍前妻帕姆的性命威胁马霍妥协，但在这紧要关头，马霍又怎会轻易被他的条件利诱？将军见说服马霍未果，又去说服迈克尔。

3 此时的迈克尔的身体状况十分糟糕，但他想要摧毁公司，将将军送入监狱的强烈愿望一直支撑着他。迈克尔似乎十分有把握他们能从这座大楼走出去，他到底有什么计划呢？

4 原来，小组成员莎拉早已盯住了在外赴宴的将军的女儿丽莎，她买通了服务生，故意将食物打翻，弄脏了丽莎的衣服，丽莎去卫生间时，莎拉则拿枪对准她，逼迫她拨通了将军的电话。将军担心女儿的性命，无奈只得放迈克尔等人出去。

Mahone: You think you can just throw some cash at us, huh? We'll forget everything, call it a day① ? ☺₁

Jonathan: Pam needs you, Alex. Now more than ever② . You're both still hurting. But given time, it'll pass. And maybe some day you'll be ready to③ be parents again, and if money is no object④ …

Mahone: You should hear yourself right now. ☺₂ The desperation in your voice. You hear it?

Jonathan: But listen to what it is I'm saying.

Mahone: Get away from⑤ me.

Jonathan: Whatever you want…

Mahone: Get away from me.

Jonathan: Whatever you want, I can provide. Airline tickets for you and Sara anywhere in the world.

Michael: What I want is to see the company burn to the ground⑥ . And you in prison. ☺₃ It's what we all want.

Jonathan: That'll never happen. ☺₄

278

译文

马　霍： 你以为你只要用一点儿钱就能收买我们，哈？然后我们会忘记一切，就此收手了？

乔纳森： 亚历克斯，帕姆需要你，比任何时候都需要你。你们俩人仍在互相伤害；但只要给你们一点儿时间，一切都会过去的。或许有一天你们准备好可以再次为人父母，如果你认为金钱没有用的话……

马　霍： 你现在应该听听你自己的声音，你声音里的绝望。你听到了吗？

乔纳森： 但听一听我说的是什么。

马　霍： 离我远点儿。

乔纳森： 不管你想要什么……

马　霍： 离我远点儿。

乔纳森： 不管你想要什么，我都能提供给你。为你和莎拉准备到世界上任何地方的机票。

迈克尔： 我想要的就是看着公司被夷为平地，看着你进监狱，这是我们所有人都想要的。

乔纳森： 看来是不太可能了

知识点拨

1. call it a day 表示"收工；到此为止"。例：Faced with mounting debts, the decision to call it a day was inevitable. 面对着不断增加的债务，最终难免做出将其结束的决定。

2. more than ever 表示"超出任何时候"。例：More than ever before, the food industry is paying attention to young consumers. 食品工业比以往任何时候都更加关注年轻消费者。

3. be ready to 表示"预备，即将；甘于。肯，乐意"。例：He may now be ready to sanction the use of force. 他现在可能打算批准使用武力。

4. no object 表示"没有限制；不成问题"。例：Although he was based in Wales, distance was no object. 虽然他主要住在威尔士，但是距离不成问题。

5. get away from... 表示"远离……，摒弃……"。例：She'd gladly have gone anywhere to get away from the cottage. 只要能离开那个小屋，去哪儿她都乐意。

6. burn to the ground 表示"全部焚毁，付之一炬"。例：Before I lose it, I will burn it to the ground. 在我失去它之前，我定将其付之一炬。

 词汇加油站

cash [kæʃ] *n.* 现金
hurt [hɜːrt] *vt.* 使受伤
desperation [ˌdespəˈreɪʃn] *n.* 绝望
burn [bɜːrn] *vt.* 烧毁

forget [fərˈget] *vt.* 忘掉
object [ˈɑːbdʒekt] *n.* 对象
airline [ˈerlaɪn] *n.* 航线

Scene 7 塞尔夫的真面目

时间： 第 13 集 00:09:34—00:10:10
地点： 仓库
人物： 林肯，迈克尔，苏克雷，莎拉
事件： 塞尔夫露出真面目，众人一起思考策略。

精彩亮点

塞尔夫终于露出了他的真正面目，他并不是要拿到锡拉搞垮将军，而是要拿着锡拉去找买家，他也不是诚心想帮迈克尔，他给迈克尔的赦免文件竟是一叠白纸。同时，狡猾的塞尔夫主动打电话给国土安全部的赫尔伯，告诉他米里亚姆已经被迈克尔等人杀死了，还声称自己也中弹了，一边说一边向空中开了一枪，试图将两起谋杀案的罪名同时扣在迈克尔等人身上。**1**

国土安全局的赫尔伯派人来到仓库，他和迈克尔通了电话，表示希望与他们坐下来谈一谈。眼看他们就要抵达仓库，老大哥林肯只是一心想着干脆跟他们拼了，殊不知这样做只会让他们几个人全部丧命。**2**

在拿到锡拉后，林肯告诉儿子自己马上就会回家与他和索菲娅团聚，但没想到竟然遭到塞尔夫的算计，林肯宁可与国土安全部对抗到底也不愿回到监狱。**3**

迈克尔并不赞同逃跑这个策略，他不想再回到住汽车旅馆，每日担惊受怕的日子了，他表示他们要继续执行计划，将公司搞垮。**4**

Lincoln: We did what they said. I ain't going down on some trumped-up[①] murder charge. **Self pinned two murders on[②] us.** ☺1

Michael: What are you doing, Linc?

Lincoln: If Homeland Security comes… ☺2

Michael: Then we'll handle it.

Lincoln: You know what? There's gotta be a point where you draw the line[③]. Now's the time to draw that line.

Sara: Don't be stupid. You can't fight off[④] all of Homeland.

Lincoln: **Stupid is listening to the government. I ain't going back to death row[⑤].** ☺3

Michael: We can still hold onto our deals. All we have to do is flush Self out[⑥], prove he has Scylla.

Sucre: How are we gonna do that, huh?

Michael: **We have to devise another strategy.** ☺4

Sucre: We should start devising a plan that can get us a hundred miles across the Mexican border. That's what we should do. My cousin Petey can hook us up[⑦].

译文

林　肯：我们按他们所说的去做了，我可不想再搅入什么捏造的谋杀指控里去了。塞尔夫把两项谋杀的罪名都栽赃给了我们。

迈克尔：林肯，你在干什么？

林　肯：要是国土安全部的人来了……

迈克尔：那么我们会处理好的。

林　肯：你知道吗？万事都有个底线，现在到了划那条底线的时候了。

莎　拉：别做傻事，你是斗不过整个国土安全部的。

林　肯：听政府的话才傻呢，我是不会回死牢的。

迈克尔：我们还能依靠那个交易。我们要做的就是找出塞尔夫，证明是他拿走了锡拉。

苏克雷：我们到底该怎么做呢？

迈克尔：我们必须要制定另一个策略。

苏克雷：我们应该制定个计划，能够让我们顺利经过几百英里穿越墨西哥边境，那才是我们应该做的，我堂兄珀泰能给我们搭上线。

知识点拨

1. trumped-up 表示"捏造的，伪造的"。例：He was brought to trial on a trumped-up charge of aiding and abetting. 他被一个捏造的教唆别人犯罪的罪名，推上了审判台。

2. pin on 表示"钉上，别上；把（某事）归咎于（某人），把（责任等）强加于（某人）"。例：The only rationale for punishing buyers of CDs protection is the blame policymakers unjustifiably try to pin on them for the crisis. 惩罚 CD 买方的唯一合理解释就是，政策制定者毫无道理地试图把造成危机的责任推到了他们头上。

3. draw the line 表示"划一界线，划定最后界限"。例：You have to know what's what and when to draw the line. 你必须搞清状况以及自己的底线。

4. fight off 表示"在战斗（自卫）中击败（某人）；竭力摆脱（驱走，阻止，回避……）"。例：The government had to fight off charges that its economic policy was in tatters. 政府不得不对指责其经济政策一团糟的言论加以驳斥。

5. death row 表示"死囚室"。例：Most death row inmates avoid execution for many years by filing several appeals. 大多数死囚通过进行数次上诉将行刑时间拖延许多年。

6. flush out 表示"驱赶，逼出；把大量液体灌入……冲洗"。例：The police fired tear gas to flush out the terrorists. 警察放催泪弹赶出了恐怖分子。

7. hook up 表示"连接；联播；联机；结婚"。例：Anthrax have hooked up with Public Enemy for a metal / rap version of *Bring On The Noise*. 炭疽乐队和公敌乐队联手合作了重金属加说唱版的歌曲《带来噪音》。

 词汇加油站

trump [trʌmp] *vt.* 捏造

pin [pɪn] *vt.* 钉住

stupid ['stuːpɪd] *adj.* 愚蠢的

devise [dɪ'vaɪz] *v.* 策划

murder ['mɜːrdər] *n.* 谋杀

handle ['hændl] *vt.* 处理

flush [flʌʃ] *vt.* 冲刷

hook [hʊk] *vt.* 用钩挂

片段二

时间： 第 13 集 00:13:06—00:14:24
地点： 临时旅馆
人物： 莎拉，迈克尔，马霍，林肯
事件： 莎拉担心迈克尔身体，众人乱作一团。

精彩亮点

1 电视里报道了警方在抓捕帝博格和格雷琴的消息，他们枪杀了 GATE 公司的总裁和一位新雇员。

2 莎拉十分担心迈克尔的身体状况，当几个人召开会议讨论时，她也是坚决反对现在逃亡，因为迈克尔需要马上做手术，否则就会有性命之忧。

3 迈克尔是个极有责任心的人，他认为现在大家沦落至此自己要负主要责任，所以，在搞垮公司前，自己是不会坦然活着的。事实上，莎拉十分清楚迈克尔的性格，她能做的只有陪伴在迈克尔身边支持他。

4 林肯十分焦急，他实在咽不下这口恶气，誓要马上抓住塞尔夫，而现在，塞尔夫正带着帝博格潜伏在苏珊家里，那里有她的妹妹和女儿，他想要以此威胁苏珊。

Sara: How long does it take to find a pay phone① in this city? ☺₁

Michael: They'll be back.

Sara: Okay. Same deal as before.

Michael: Yeah. No physical duress for the next eight hours.

Sara: Here's the thing. **You need help.** ☺₂ And running around② trying to track down③ Self isn't… safe. We could be in Mexico in a few hours. There are doctors there that I trust. And you've been taking care of all of us. I think it's really okay if we take care of you.

Michael: Surgery or no surgery… **I'm never gonna be able to live with myself unless I find a way to take these people down.** ☺₃ It's that simple, and, uh… I get it. I'm not gonna demand that you feel the same way.

Mahone: I'm telling you, we can't trust anyone — government, law enforcement… Which is all the more reason④ we should consider getting out of here.

Lincoln: No. We deal with⑤ this now.

Mahone: I want this guy as much as you do, but we're scrambling here. **I mean, I don't know how long Self has been planning this thing and from the looks of it, it's pretty air-tight⑥.** ☺₄

译文

莎　拉：在这座城市找部付费电话要多久？

迈克尔：他们会回来的。

莎　拉：好了，和以前一样。

迈克尔：是的，未来八小时不能强迫自己做事。

莎　拉：现在情况是这样的：你需要帮助。为了找塞尔夫到处跑，你的身体……会撑不住的。我们可以在几小时内到达墨西哥，那里有我信任的医生，你一直都照顾我们所有人，我们也想照顾你。

迈克尔：不管做不做手术……我都无法坦然地活着，除非我把公司搞垮了。就这么简单，对，呃，我也明白。我不会要求你认同我。

马　霍：我跟你说，我们现在无法信任任何人——政府，法官……所以更要想办法离开这里。

林　肯：不，我们现在得抓到塞尔夫。

马　霍：我和你一样也想抓住塞尔夫，但我们已经乱了阵脚。我的意思是，塞尔夫不知道花了多长时间策划了这件事，我们找不到他的。

知识点拨

1. pay phone 表示"投币式公用电话"。例：I dropped a quarter into the slot of the pay phone. 我向付费电话的投币孔里投了一枚25 分硬币。

2. run around 表示"东奔西跑，奔忙，（尤指孩子）到处玩耍游逛"。例：No one noticed we had been running around emptying bins and cleaning up. 没有人注意到我们一直都在东奔西跑地倒垃圾，打扫卫生。

3. track down 表示"追寻，查获，追捕到，追查出"。例：She had spent years trying to track down her parents. 她已经花了好多年时间试图追寻父母的下落。

4. all the more reason 表示"更加正当的理由"。例：That is all the more reason to confront this new illness as aggressively and rapidly as we can. 这就更有理由尽可能积极主动和行动迅速地对抗这种新疾病。

5. deal with 表示"应付，对待，惠顾，与……交易"。例：In dealing with suicidal youngsters, our aims should be clear. 在对待有自杀倾向的青少年时，我们的目标应当很明确。

6. air-tight 表示"不漏气，气密的，密封的；天衣无缝的"。

 词汇加油站

pay [peɪ] **v** 付费
track [træk] **vi** 沿着轨道前进
surgery ['sɜːrdʒəri] **n** 外科手术
scramble ['skræmbl] **v** 快速爬行

duress [du'res] **n** 威胁
Mexico ['meksɪkoʊ] **n** 墨西哥
enforcement [in'fɔːrsmənt] **n** 执行
tight [taɪt] **adj** 紧的

时间： 第 14 集 00:02:28—00:03:56

地点： 仓库，房顶

人物： 塞尔夫，苏克雷，迈克尔，莎拉，林肯

事件： 塞尔夫索要锡拉剩余部件，众人机智应对。

精彩亮点

谨慎的迈克尔先前将锡拉的一个小部件拆卸下来后交给了塞尔夫。塞尔夫兴奋地带着锡拉和苏珊一起会见买家时，买家告诉他少了一个部件，气急败坏的塞尔夫打电话给迈克尔索要这个部件。

1

迈克尔做好了准备等待塞尔夫，没料到塞尔夫竟然使用催泪弹，迈克尔等人想要逃出仓库不想塞尔夫直接朝他们开枪。他们只得躲回仓库，难道迈克尔等人要被困于此了吗？

2

此时，塞尔夫在不停地向他们投射催泪弹，用不了多久所有人就会窒息，在这关键时刻，老大哥林肯又身在何处呢？

3

原来，迈克尔兄弟早就策划好，让林肯在外面做好埋伏，就在塞尔夫想要继续投射催泪弹时，林肯用枪顶住了他的后脑勺。

4

Self: You're surrounded. Come out[①] with your piece of Scylla, Michael. ☺1

Michael: You first.

Self: Come out, or I'm going to gas you out. If it's the latter, I have a full magazine with 30 rounds. Want to bet at least one of them could outrun you?

Michael: What makes you think I'd even keep the piece on me? ☺2

Self: I know you, Michael. You're not letting that thing out of your sight[②].

Michael: I stand by[③] my original offer. Come and get it.

Self: OK...

Michael: Stay low. Let the gas rise to the ceiling.

Sara: This is a big space, but it won't take many more of those before we start to asphyxiate.

Sucre: Where's Lincoln?! ☺3

Self: Here we go[④], Michael.

Michael: All right, now we take a ride[⑤] and we pick up Scylla.

Lincoln: Or I put a bullet in your head.

Self: It ain't gonna happen.

Lincoln: Try me[⑥]. ☺4

译文

塞尔夫： 你们被包围了。迈克尔，拿着你的锡拉芯片出来。

迈克尔： 你先。

塞尔夫： 出来！否则我拿烟把你们熏出来。如果你选择后者，我有足够的弹药，奉陪到底。想不想打个赌看看这些子弹如何能打到你？

迈克尔： 你为什么确定我手上有芯片？

塞尔夫： 我了解你，迈克尔。你是不会让那东西离开你的视线的。

迈克尔： 我坚持最初的条件，你过来自己来拿。

塞尔夫： 好吧。

迈克尔： 低下，让毒气从屋顶散出去。

莎　拉： 这地方很大，但用不了多久我们就窒息了。

苏克雷： 林肯在哪儿？

塞尔夫： 我来了，迈克尔。

迈克尔： 好了，现在上车，我们去拿锡拉芯片。

林　肯： 不然我一枪崩了你。

塞尔夫： 你不会的。

林　肯： 你试试看。

知识点拨

1. come out 可以表示"出来，出现；出版；出狱"。片中表示"出来"。例：Oh, look. The sun's come out. 喂，瞧，太阳出来了。

2. out of sight 表示"看不见，在视野之外"。例：We dodged behind a pillar out of sight of the tourists. 我们躲到柱子后面，避开了观光者的视线。

3. stand by 表示"支持；准备行动；信守诺言；站在旁边"。例：I wouldn't break the law for a friend, but I would stand by her if she did. 我不会为朋友去犯法，但如果她犯了法的话我会陪在她身边。

4. here we go 表示"我们来了；我们开始吧"。例：Okay, here we go. Edwards, get her to first aid! 好了，我们来了，爱德华兹，把她送到急救室！

5. take / have a ride 表示"兜风；搭便车，搭顺风车"。例：She will take a ride to the city. 她将搭便车去市里。

6. try me 用于表示自己可能会做出使人意想不到或不大可能的事情来，可以翻译为"你来试试看吧"！例：So how about you try me? 那你为什么不试试对我说呢？

 词汇加油站

surround [sə'raʊnd] *vt.* 包围
gas [gæs] *vt.* 使吸入毒气
outrun [ˌaʊt'rʌn] *vt.* 逃脱
asphyxiate [əs'fɪksɪeɪt] *vt.* 使窒息

piece [pi:s] *n.* 部分
magazine ['mægəzi:n] *n.* 弹药库
original [ə'rɪdʒənl] *adj.* 最初的
bullet ['bʊlɪt] *n.* 子弹

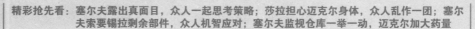

时间： 第 14 集 00:01:43—00:02:49

地点： 仓库，苏珊家

片段四

人物： 迈克尔，林肯，莎拉，苏珊，塞尔夫

事件： 塞尔夫监视仓库一举一动，迈克尔加大药量。

精彩亮点

1
林肯抓住塞尔夫后，将他带到迈克尔等人面前，让他交代了自己的身份。塞尔夫的确是一名国土安全部的工作人员，但他为公司兢兢业业做了 17 年却什么也没有得到。于是，他打算将锡拉卖掉，来换取上亿美元。

2
林肯为这一桩生意能换来这么多钱而心动了，但迈克尔知道即使他们不将锡拉给将军，拥有锡拉的人也会成为下一个将军。因此，他们不能做这笔买卖。

3
苏克雷成功潜入塞尔夫的后备厢，得知他们的去处。就在苏克雷从车中下来时，他发现后备箱中塞尔夫向仓库投放的催泪弹竟含有摄像头。

4
塞尔夫将他的计划告诉了苏珊，果然，他们能够洞察仓库里所有人的一举一动。而通过录像，塞尔夫和苏珊获悉了迈克尔将锡拉的部件藏在了卫生间的房顶上。

Lincoln: **The Company gets destroyed and we get paid. It's a great deal.** ☺₁

Michael: This guy is just another General Krantz waiting to happen. Let's say① we do sell it to him and the Company burns. **You know what happens then?** ☺₂ Another company is built right on top of that one. We're not selling. **Sucre pulled it off**②. ☺₃

Lincoln: Great.

Susan: **Is this going to work?** ☺₄

Self: It's like an ultrasound. It can see through③ everything.

Sara: You're building up④ a tolerance.

Michael: Then we'll up the dosage.

Sara: Yeah, I have, and at this point, a higher dosage would have more side effects⑤ than the tumor itself.

Michael: I'll manage without it.

Lincoln: Sit this one out⑥. Let me and Sucre handle it.

Michael: I'm going. Why can't he understand I need to finish this? Everything that happened, it all started with the Company.

Sara: Maybe not for Lincoln. Maybe for him, this all started with his little brother breaking him out of prison. Michael, you saved his life. If anything happens to you, he spends the rest of his life feeling guilty for that.

译文

林　肯：毁了公司，我们拿钱。这生意划得来。

迈克尔：这家伙只是另一个克兰茨将军，想要坐收渔利。就算我们把锡拉卖给他，公司也倒台了，你知道会发生什么吗？另一个公司会重新崛起，我们不能卖。苏克雷成功了。

林　肯：太棒了。

苏　珊：这个有用吗？

塞尔夫：这就像超声波一样，你能看穿一切。

莎　拉：你的身体状况已经到极限了。

迈克尔：那就给我增大剂量。

莎　拉：是的，我已经加大剂量了，但现在，再增大剂量，会造成比肿瘤还严重的伤害。

迈克尔：没有药我也能应付的。

林　肯：你这次别去了，让我和苏克雷去处理吧。

迈克尔：我要去，为什么他不能理解呢？我必须完成这件事。发生的一切，都源于公司。

莎　拉：或许对林肯而言不是这样。也许对他来说，这都源于他弟弟要帮他越狱。迈克尔，你救了他的命。如果你出了什么事，他会愧疚一生。

知识点拨

1. let's say 表示"比方说"。例：Let's say I choose the one that goes in that direction. 比如我选择了那个方向的。

2. pull off 表示"脱去；胜利完成；捣鬼"。片中表示"胜利完成"。例：The National League for Democracy pulled off a landslide victory. 全国民主联盟获得了压倒性的胜利。

3. see through 表示"做到底，帮助渡过难关；看穿，拆穿"。例：I saw through your little ruse from the start. 从一开始我就看穿了你的小计谋。

4. build up 表示"逐步建立，增进；（在某个地方）盖满了建筑物；宣扬"。例：The regime built up the largest army in Africa. 该政权逐渐建立起一支非洲规模最大的军队。

5. side effects 表示"边际效应；反作用，副作用"。例：The drug is extremely potent, but causes unpleasant side effects. 这种药药效极强，但会产生不良的副作用。

6. sit out 表示"在户外坐；出席直至完全结束；不参加某种活动"。例：The only thing I can do is keep quiet and sit this one out. 我唯一能做的就是保持沉默，等待这件事结束。

词汇加油站

destroy [dɪ'strɔɪ] *vt.* 摧毁
ultrasound ['ʌltrəsaʊnd] *n.* 超声
dosage ['doʊsɪdʒ] *n.* （药物等的）剂量
manage ['mænɪdʒ] *vt.* 设法对付

pull [pʊl] *vt.* 赢得
tolerance ['tɑ:lərəns] *n.* 宽容
tumor ['tu:mər] *n.* 瘤
guilty ['gɪlti] *adj.* 内疚的

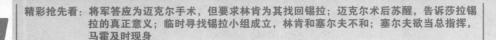
Scene 8 迈克尔进行手术

时间： 第 15 集 00:01:54—00:03:13
地点： 手术室门外
人物： 迈克尔，林肯，莎拉，将军，医生
事件： 将军答应为迈克尔手术，但要求林肯为其找回锡拉。

精彩亮点

就在迈克尔已经拿到锡拉但因身体超负荷流血而倒下时，他被公司的人带上了车。莎拉以为迈克尔此次定是凶多吉少，但没想到林肯找到将军，将军竟答应为迈克尔做手术。将军如果想杀掉迈克尔肯定早就杀掉他了，因此，林肯确信将军会救迈克尔，但将军的真正意图何在呢？ **1**

医生为迈克尔做了急救后，向迈克尔阐述了手术的流程。莎拉从没有看过这种手术方法，怀疑将军是想拿迈克尔做实验，而将军声称这种方法曾成功救助过一个人，而那个人现在活得很健康。 **2**

原来将军开出的为迈克尔做手术的条件是让林肯帮助他找回锡拉，并让他与自己签订协议，否则，将军就不会让医生为迈克尔做手术。 **3**

林肯希望得到关于塞尔夫和格雷琴的所有信息，但将军表示答应给他找个同伙，而这个同伙正是格雷琴、塞尔夫和帝博格。 **4**

Lincoln: It's going to be all right, Sara. Trust me. ☺₁

Doctor: Mr. Scofield, although you're going to be anesthetized and should feel no significant pain ①, we will need to keep you awake for the duration of the procedure. As a safety precaution, we'll need to continually monitor your speech and sensory activity to insure the tissue being removed will not leave you impaired in any way ②.

Michael: What hospital is this? ☺₂

Sara: Don't worry about ③ it. You've got some good doctors who are going to take great care of you.

Michael: I have to get Scylla.

Sara: No, no, no, no. Not now.

Michael: Where's Linc?

Sara: He's here. He's just fine.

Lincoln: I'm not leaving until Michael has his surgery.

General: And I'm not starting surgery until you prove you can hold up your end of the deal. ☺₃ Scylla's slipping through our fingers ④ as we speak. Time is not on our side ⑤, nor on your brother's. Now, you'll get full cooperation from my office. If you need anything, just call this number.

Lincoln: I'm gonna need everything you've got on Self and Gretchen. Aliases ⑥, whatever you got.

General: How about an accomplice? ☺₄

译文

林　肯：莎拉，迈克尔会没事的，相信我。

医　生：斯科菲尔德先生，虽然您将被麻醉，不会有明显的疼痛感，但我们需要您在手术期间保持清醒。安全起见，我们要持续监控您的语言能力与感知能力，以保证我们移除病体的同时不会给您带来任何后遗症。

迈克尔：这是什么医院？

莎　拉：别担心。这里有最好的医生会给你治疗。

迈克尔：我必须要拿回锡拉。

莎　拉：不，不，不，不，现在不行。

迈克尔：林肯在哪儿？

莎　拉：他就在旁边，他很好。

林　肯：直到迈克尔手术完成前，我是不会离开的。

将　军：如果你不履行我们之间的承诺，我是不会让他们开始手术的。在你我谈话之时，锡拉离我们越来越远了，我们和你弟弟都没有时间了。现在，你会得到我手下的全力支持。如果你需要帮助，就打这个号码。

林　肯：我要所有关于塞尔夫和格雷琴的信息。化名什么的，所有信息。

将　军：给你个同伙，怎么样？

知识点拨

1. significant pain 表示"明显的疼痛"。例：Practically, it's unlikely that this will result in significant pain relief for pain in areas other than the hands, and the ongoing duration of the relief is not known. 实际上，这不会减少除了手的其他部位的明显疼痛感，而且疼痛缓解的持续时间也不明确。

2. in any way 表示"以任何方式"。例：Her study was not in any way intended to prejudice the future development of the college. 她的研究绝对无意损害这所大学未来的发展。

3. worry about sth. / sb. 表示"担忧，烦恼，惦念，挂虑"。例：I'll not worry about it. I'll let nature take its course. 我不再为此事发愁了，顺其自然吧。

4. slip through one's fingers 表示"从某人指缝中溜掉；错过（机会）"。例：He was sorry to have let the chance slip through his fingers. 他很遗憾，白白把这个机会丢掉了。

5. on one's side 表示"侧身；支持某人"。例：A decent dressing at first meeting will get on one's good side. 第一次见面时得体的衣着会给人留下好印象。

6. aliases 表示"别名，化名（alias 的名词复数）"。例：Notice that for both the Cloud group and the IP group, we provided aliases. 注意，对于云组和IP组，我们都提供了别名。

 词汇加油站

anesthetize [əˈniːsθətaɪz] *vt.* 使麻醉

precaution [prɪˈkɔːʃn] *n.* 预防措施

tissue [ˈtɪʃuː] *n.* 组织

surgery [ˈsɜːrdʒəri] *n.* 外科手术

duration [duˈreɪʃn] *n.* 期间

sensory [ˈsensəri] *adj.* 感官的

impair [ɪmˈper] *vt.* 损害

accomplice [əˈkɑːmplɪs] *n.* 共犯

时间： 第 15 集 00:36:37—00:38:03
地点： 手术台
人物： 迈克尔，莎拉，将军，查尔斯
事件： 迈克尔术后苏醒，告诉莎拉锡拉的真正意义。

精彩亮点

1
迈克尔手术后醒来，见到了他心爱的女友莎拉。在迈克尔进行手术期间，他的脑电波极为活跃，他梦见了已去世的查尔斯。

2
梦境中的查尔斯告诉迈克尔他已经有了答案，但迈克尔并不清楚问题是什么。查尔斯告诉他"事情不能只看表面"，这一句话点醒了迈克尔。

3
聪明的迈克尔在梦境中将bargain 一词拆开来看，他得到了一些元素符号，这些元素代表着能源，从而他明白了锡拉并不是公司的什么黑名单，而是能源，是世界的未来。

4
听了迈克尔的话，莎拉又联想到公司提供给迈克尔的医疗设备和药物在市场上都无迹可寻。而那些想得到锡拉的人也不是要摧毁公司，而是要成为公司的主宰，控制一切。

Michael: **You're gonna laugh, but I had a dream about Scylla.** ☺₁ The only thing we really know about it is what Self told us.

Sara: You need to rest.

Michael: I'm serious. What if ① it's not just the Company's little black book ②? What if it's…

Charles: **Not everything is as it seems.** ☺₂

Michael: …Something more ③?

Sara: Like what?

Michael: **Something good.** ☺₃ Why go to so much trouble ④ to protect information about the past? Information the Company could just delete any time they wanted to? The General said…

General: As long as we have Scylla, we have power.

Michael: I don't think he was talking about power like control or influence. I think he was talking about energy. Boron. Argon. Gallium. Indium. Bargain. There's a theory that if you can find a way to combine these elements into the design of a solar cell ⑤, you can harness 100% of the sun's energy. With that kind of power, possibilities are limitless.

Sara: It would certainly explain all the security around Scylla. They're not protecting the past. They're protecting the future. **Wonder what else ⑥ is on it.** ☺₄

290

译文

迈克尔：你肯定会笑我，但我跟你说我做了一个关于锡拉的梦，我们只知道塞尔夫的片面之词。

莎　拉：你需要休息。

迈克尔：我是认真的，如果它指的不仅是公司的黑名单呢？如果是……

查尔斯：事情不能只看表面。

迈克尔：别的什么？

莎　拉：比如呢？

迈克尔：一些好的东西。为什么要费这么大劲保护一些公司可以随时删除的过去的信息？将军说过……

将　军：只要我们有锡拉，我们就有力量。

迈克尔：我认为他说的力量，不是指控制力或影响力，我认为他说的是能源。硼（B），氩（Ar），镓（Ga），铟（In）。合起来就组成，BARGAIN。有个理论是：如果你有办法把这些元素组合进太阳能蓄电池的设计中，就能100%地控制利用太阳能。一旦拥有这样的能量，没有什么是不可能的。

莎　拉：这当然就能解释为什么要如此保护锡拉。他们不是在保护过去，而是为了保护未来，真不知道还有什么。

知识点拨

1. what if 表示"要是……又怎样？"例：What if relations between you and your neighbor have reached deadlock, and their behavior is still unacceptable? 如果你和你的邻居已闹僵了，而他们的行为还是令人难以接受，那怎么办？

2. black book 表示"黑名册，可疑人物册"。

3. something more 表示"别的东西，更多的东西"。例：Instead of rushing at life, I wanted something more meaningful. 我不想混日子，我想做点儿更有意义的事情。

4. go to so much trouble to do sth. 表示"费尽周折做某事，花费工夫做某事"。例：Please don't go to so much trouble. I don't want to put you out. 请不要费那么多工夫，我不想给你添麻烦。

5. solar cell 表示"太阳能电池"。例：Many important experiment results were gained in researching dye-sensitized solar cell by the test system. 本系统已在染料敏化太阳电池研究中获得了多项重要实验结果。

6. what else 表示"别的什么，其他的"。例：What else have you had for your birthday? 你还收到了别的什么生日礼物？

 词汇加油站

delete [dɪ'liːt] *vt.* 删除
Argon ['ɑːrgɑːn] *n.* <化> 氩
Indium ['ɪndɪrm] *n.* <化> 铟
harness ['hɑːrnɪs] *vt.* 利用

Boron ['bɔːrɑːn] *n.* <化> 硼
Gallium ['gælɪəm] *n.* <化> 镓
element ['elɪmənt] *n.* 元素
limitless ['lɪmɪtləs] *adj.* 无限制的

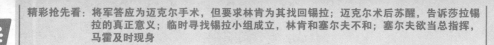

时间： 第16集 00:02:21—00:03:10
地点： 将军办公室
人物： 林肯，莎拉，苏珊，帝博格，塞尔夫
事件： 临时寻找锡拉小组成立，林肯、塞尔夫不和。

片段三

精彩亮点

林肯接通了莎拉的电话，想要询问迈克尔的情况，但没想到莎拉现在被公司囚禁到了一个宾馆，也不知道迈克尔的情况。林肯当初与将军约定，只要为迈克尔做手术，他就帮助将军找回锡拉。

1

林肯希望将军为他提供所有的关键信息，但将军表示要为他寻找几个帮手。这些帮手不是别人，正是林肯恨之入骨的苏珊、帝博格和塞尔夫。

2

塞尔夫面对林肯仿佛什么事也没有发生过一样，当初塞尔夫以找到锡拉为条件，答应事成之后会赦免迈克尔和林肯等人，没想到关键时刻，他背信弃义，拿着到手的锡拉去做交易。

3

眼看林肯和塞尔夫就要打起来了，苏珊连忙劝阻，毕竟现在的关键是要找到锡拉，否则他们所有人都要玩完。

4

Lincoln: You know what, Sara, I'm doing my best[1]. Just, just call me if you hear anything about Michael, please.☺[1]

Susan: Linc, the Company's data tech finally got a hit on our guy's cell phone.☺[2] It's a number, and it goes to this address—The Grafton; it's a club.

Lincoln: How many calls?

Susan: Three. All outgoing.

T-Bag: How do we know this guy's still in Miami, that he hasn't sold it already, huh? Not that I'm complaining. I've had some filthy, filthy times in this state.

Self: Don't screw this up[2], all right? Because that's our only lead on this guy.

Lincoln: Be thankful I haven't killed you.☺[3]

Self: Oh yeah? Wh-What are you, Eliot Ness now? What, are you upset because I screwed you over[3], Linc? Because don't act like you haven't done that to ten times as many people. All right? We're just crooks that got caught, Lincoln. This…this guy, this isn't gonna work.

Susan: Why don't we all just focus on[4] who's got Scylla? What do you say[5]?☺[4]

292

译文

林　肯：你知道吗，莎拉？我已经竭尽所能了。如果听到迈克尔的消息，就给我打电话。

苏　珊：林肯，公司终于追踪到那个家伙的手机了。那个号码在这个地址，格拉夫顿，这是个俱乐部。

林　肯：有多少通电话？

苏　珊：三通，全是打出去的。

帝博格：为什么我们就确定他还在迈阿密，说不定东西已经被转手了呀？我不是在抱怨，这里实在是太乱了。

塞尔夫：别把事情搞砸了，好吗？毕竟这个人是我们唯一的线索。

林　肯：我没杀你你应该感到庆幸。

塞尔夫：哦，是吗？你以为你是谁？艾略特·奈斯？怎么，被我整很不爽吗，林肯？你自己也不是什么好人，不是吗？我们不过是一根绳子上的蚂蚱，林肯。这个……这个人，会把事情搞砸的。

苏　珊：我们为什么不关心一下锡拉在谁手上呢？你们觉得呢？

知识点拨

1. do one's best 表示"尽全力，尽心竭力"。例：Don't try to mimic anybody. You have to be yourself if you are going to do your best. 不要试图仿效任何人，要是你想做到最好，就得做你自己。

2. screw up 表示"拧紧；扭歪（脸）"，片中"表示把……搞糟"。例：You can't open the window because it screws up the air conditioning. 你不能打开窗户，那样空调就不起作用了。

3. screw someone over 表示"毁掉某人，压榨某人，欺负某人"。例：I had such an opportunity to screw over another guy, I'm ashamed to say, but I took it. 我有过这样一个机会毁掉另外一个家伙，说起来有点儿惭愧，但我还是做了。

4. focus on 表示"致力于，使聚焦于，对（某事或做某事）予以注意，把……作为兴趣中心"。例：The talks will focus on economic development of the region. 会谈将着重讨论该地区的经济发展。

5. what do you say 表示"你说什么，你说呢，你有何意见"。例：I think we should tell him, what do you say? 我想我们应该告诉他，你说呢？

词汇加油站

tech [tek] *n.* 技术
address ['ædres] *n.* 地址
complain [kəm'pleɪn] *vt.* 抱怨
screw [skruː] *vt.* 扭曲

hit [hit] *n.* 击中，命中
outgoing ['aʊtɡəʊɪŋ] *adj.* 外出的
filthy ['filθi] *adj.* 下流的
crook [krʊk] *n.* 钩

时间： 第16集 00:18:29—00:19:43
地点： 将军办公室
人物： 迈克尔，林肯，苏珊，塞尔夫，诺尔顿医生，马霍
事件： 塞尔夫欲当总指挥，马霍及时现身。

片段四

精彩亮点

1. 塞尔夫不甘由林肯带领这个临时小分队。林肯在追捕拿走锡拉的斯科特时被他的女友欺骗，塞尔夫借此为由说服帝博格今后听从他指挥。

2. 将军组建的寻找锡拉这个四人小分队，成员分别为：林肯、苏珊、帝博格和塞尔夫。而此时，塞尔夫赢得了帝博格的支持，苏珊也表示干脆让塞尔夫当头算了，林肯并不介意谁来带领这个小组，只要能找到锡拉，并且他要求塞尔夫保证不会把它卖给他人。毕竟将军控制了塞尔夫的女友，估计他也不会轻举妄动。

3. 惠勒在押送马霍的途中，马霍逃逸。之前，马霍出于对朗的信任，本以为惠勒会让自己接触到司法部长，但不想惠勒还是不信任他，最终，马霍成功从朗手下脱逃，逃逸后的马霍立即来与林肯等人会合。

4. 此时的迈克尔刚刚接受完脑部手术，公司的人将他带到了树林里一座与世隔绝的房子，迈克尔试图逃离这里，但没有发现可用的武器。诺尔顿医生奉命要为迈克尔注射一种药物，帮他洗脑。

Self: And if you notice, even Gretchen hasn't leapt to your defense[①]. ☺1

Susan: Linc, just let him wear his crown.

Lincoln: I would if I thought he wasn't gonna sell this thing. ☺2

Self: Oh, what, am I the only one who's thought about that? Look, here's the deal, Linc. At some point, you'll have a vote. But until then, you're done, all right? We're shutting' you down, okay? You're no longer in charge[②].

Susan: Uh-oh, looks like there's been a recount. ☺3

Mahone: Bad time?

Lincoln: No, perfect. The second you stop doing what I tell you to do, I'm gonna blow your brains out[③].

Michael: Bring her back[④]. ☺4

Lincoln: It's not gonna be the same.

Dr. Knowlton: Stir any memories?

Michael: I was ten. We were on a camping trip[⑤] in Jackson Hole.

Dr. Knowlton: Fishing, hiking. Family huddled under a blanket in front of the bonfire.

Michael: You can stop now.

译文

塞 尔 夫：不知你有没有注意到，就算是格雷琴也没帮你说话。

苏 珊：林肯，就让他当头吧。

林 肯：我会的，前提是他不会卖掉这个东西。

塞 尔 夫：哦，什么？我是唯一一个想要卖掉它的人吗？听着，林肯，这是规矩。从某种角度讲，你也有一票。但是从现在起，你完蛋了好吗？我们把你搞下台了，好吗？我们不再听你指挥了。

苏 珊：哦，看起来要重新计票了。

马 霍：我来的不是时候？

林 肯：不，来得太巧了。下次你再拒绝我让你做的事，我就让你脑袋开花。

迈 克 尔：把她带回来。

林 肯：不是那么回事。

诺尔顿医生：想起什么了吗？

迈 克 尔：我 10 岁时我们在杰克逊小镇露营。

诺尔顿医生：钓鱼，徒行。你们一家挤在一起，坐在篝火前。

迈 克 尔：你说到这儿就可以了。

知识点拨

1. come / rush / leap / spring to sb's defense 表示"挺身为某人辩护"。例：Yet rationalists such as Gary Becker or Robert Barro might leap to your defense. 不过，加里·贝克或罗伯特·巴罗等极端理性主义者可能会站出来为你辩护。

2. be in charge of sth. 表示"负责，主管，管理"。例：He will be in charge of all hiring and firing at PHA. 他将负责公共房产管理局所有人员的雇用和解聘事务。

3. blow one's brains out 表示"把某人的脑浆打出来，让某人脑袋开花"。例：The only way to change me is maybe blow my brains out. 唯一能改变我的方法，大概是把我的头打爆。

4. bring back 表示"带回（某人或某物），还回（某物）；回忆（回顾，回想起）往事；使（某人）恢复（某状态）"。例：It's very thoughtful of you to bring me back a souvenir. 你带纪念品给我，真是太周到了。

5. camping trip 表示"露营，野营旅行"。例：The troops will be passing through our village on their camping trip. 野营部队要从咱们村过。

词汇加油站

leap [li:p] *vi.* 跳

crown [kraʊn] *n.* 王冠

stir [stɜ:r] *vt.* 唤起

blanket ['blæŋkɪt] *n.* 毯子

defense [dɪ'fens] *n.* 辩解，辩白

recount [rɪ'kaʊnt] *n.* 重新计算

huddle ['hʌdl] *vi.* （因寒冷或害怕）蜷缩

bonfire ['bɑ:nfaɪər] *n.* 篝火